Chinese Politics

"Westerners tend to interpret any discontent in authoritarian polities as evidence that the critics want democracy. But this book shows that, in China, they usually want better deals and lawful administration instead. Chinese citizens now participate in politics more than before, and their normal aim is to get justice from local officials in an era of pluralized groups and greed for money. Creating the book, a truly talented team of senior and young researchers presents a vision of China's political future that is sensitive to this big country's geographic, functional, and demographic diversity. These essays become required reading on contemporary China."

Lynn T. White III, *Princeton University, USA.*

Written by a team of leading China scholars, this text interrogates the dynamics of state power and legitimation in twenty-first century China.

Despite the continuing economic successes and rising international prestige of China there have been increasing social protests over corruption, land seizures, environmental concerns, and homeowner movements. Such political contestation presents an opportunity to explore the changes occurring in China today – what are the goals of political contestation, how are Chinese Communist Party leaders legitimizing their rule, who are the specific actors involved in contesting state legitimacy today, and what are the implications of changing state–society relations for the future viability of the People's Republic?

Key subjects covered include:

- the legitimacy of the Communist Party
- internet censorship
- ethnic resistance
- rural and urban contention
- nationalism
- youth culture
- labour relations

Chinese Politics is an essential read for all students and scholars of contemporary China as well as those interested in the dynamics of political and social change.

Peter Hays Gries is the Harold J. & Ruth Newman Chair and Director of the Institute for U.S.-China Issues at the University of Oklahoma, USA. His many publications include *China's New Nationalism: Pride, Politics, and Diplomacy* and *State and Society in 21st Century China: Crisis, Contention, and Legitimation.*

Stanley Rosen is the director of the East Asian Studies Center and a professor of political science at the University of Southern California, USA.

Asia's Transformations
Edited by Mark Selden,
Cornell University, USA

The books in this series explore the political, social, economic, and cultural consequences of Asia's transformations in the twentieth and twenty-first centuries. The series emphasizes the tumultuous interplay of local, national, regional, and global forces as Asia bids to become the hub of the world economy. While focusing on the contemporary, it also looks back to analyze the antecedents of Asia's contested rise.

This series comprises several strands:

Asia's Transformations
Titles include:

Debating Human Rights*
Critical essays from the United States and Asia
Edited by Peter Van Ness

Hong Kong's History*
State and society under colonial rule
Edited by Tak-Wing Ngo

Japan's Comfort Women*
Sexual slavery and prostitution during World War II and the US occupation
Yuki Tanaka

Opium, Empire and the Global Political Economy*
Carl A. Trocki

Chinese Society*
Change, conflict and resistance
Edited by Elizabeth J. Perry and Mark Selden

Mao's Children in the New China*
Voices from the Red Guard generation
Yarong Jiang and David Ashley

Remaking the Chinese State*
Strategies, society and security
Edited by Chien-min Chao and Bruce J. Dickson

Korean Society*
Civil society, democracy and the state
Edited by Charles K. Armstrong

The Making of Modern Korea*
Adrian Buzo

The Resurgence of East Asia*
500, 150 and 50 year perspectives
Edited by Giovanni Arrighi, Takeshi Hamashita, and Mark Selden

Chinese Society, second edition*
Change, conflict and resistance
Edited by Elizabeth J. Perry and Mark Selden

Ethnicity in Asia*
Edited by Colin Mackerras

The Battle for Asia*
From decolonization to globalization
Mark T. Berger

State and Society in 21st Century China*
Edited by Peter Hays Gries and Stanley Rosen

Japan's Quiet Transformation*
Social change and civil society in the 21st century
Jeff Kingston

Confronting the Bush Doctrine*
Critical views from the Asia-Pacific
Edited by Mel Gurtov and Peter Van Ness

China in War and Revolution, 1895–1949*
Peter Zarrow

The Future of US–Korean Relations*
The imbalance of power
Edited by John Feffer

Working in China*
Ethnographies of labor and workplace transformations
Edited by Ching Kwan Lee

Korean Society, second edition*
Civil society, democracy and the state
Edited by Charles K. Armstrong

Singapore*
The state and the culture of excess
Souchou Yao

Pan-Asianism in Modern Japanese History*
Colonialism, regionalism and borders
Edited by Sven Saaler and J. Victor Koschmann

The Making of Modern Korea, second edition*
Adrian Buzo

Re-writing Culture in Taiwan
Edited by Fang-long Shih, Stuart Thompson, and Paul-François Tremlett

Reclaiming Chinese Society*
The new social activism
Edited by You-tien Hsing and Ching Kwan Lee

Girl Reading Girl in Japan
Edited by Tomoko Aoyama and Barbara Hartley

Chinese Politics*
State, society and the market
Edited by Peter Hays Gries and Stanley Rosen

Asia's Great Cities
Each volume aims to capture the heartbeat of the contemporary city
from multiple perspectives emblematic of the authors' own deep familiarity
with the distinctive faces of the city, its history, society, culture, politics,
and economics, and its evolving position in national, regional, and global
frameworks. While most volumes emphasize urban developments since the
Second World War, some pay close attention to the legacy of the *longue durée*
in shaping the contemporary. Thematic and comparative volumes address
such themes as urbanization, economic and financial linkages, architecture
and space, wealth and power, gendered relationships, planning and anarchy,
and ethnographies in national and regional perspective. Titles include:

Bangkok*
Place, practice and representation
Marc Askew

Representing Calcutta*
Modernity, nationalism and the colonial uncanny
Swati Chattopadhyay

Singapore*
Wealth, power and the culture of control
Carl A. Trocki

The City in South Asia
James Heitzman

Global Shanghai, 1850–2010*
A history in fragments
Jeffrey N. Wasserstrom

Hong Kong*
Becoming a global city
Stephen Chiu and Tai-Lok Lui

Asia.com
Asia.com is a series which focuses on the ways in which new information and communication technologies are influencing politics, society, and culture in Asia. Titles include:

Japanese Cybercultures*
Edited by Mark McLelland and Nanette Gottlieb

Asia.com*
Asia encounters the Internet
Edited by K. C. Ho, Randolph Kluver and Kenneth C. C. Yang

The internet in Indonesia's new democracy*
David T. Hill and Krishna Sen

Chinese Cyberspaces*
Technological changes and political effects
Edited by Jens Damm and Simona Thomas

Mobile media in the Asia-Pacific
Gender and the art of being mobile
Larissa Hjorth

Literature and Society
Literature and Society is a series that seeks to demonstrate the ways in which Asian literature is influenced by the politics, society and culture in which it is produced. Titles include:

The body in postwar Japanese fiction
Douglas N. Slaymaker

Chinese Women Writers and the Feminist Imagination, 1905–48*
Haiping Yan

Routledge Studies in Asia's Transformations
Routledge Studies in Asia's Transformations is a forum for innovative new research intended for a high-level specialist readership. Titles include:

The American Occupation of Japan and Okinawa*
Literature and memory
Michael Molasky

Koreans in Japan*
Critical voices from the margin
Edited by Sonia Ryang

Internationalizing the Pacific
The United States, Japan and the Institute of Pacific Relations in war and peace, 1919–1945
Tomoko Akami

Imperialism in South East Asia*
'A fleeting, passing phase'
Nicholas Tarling

Chinese Media, Global Contexts*
Edited by Chin-Chuan Lee

Remaking Citizenship in Hong Kong*
Community, nation and the global city
Edited by Agnes S. Ku and Ngai Pun

Japanese Industrial Governance
Protectionism and the licensing state
Yul Sohn

Developmental Dilemmas*
Land reform and institutional change in China
Edited by Peter Ho

Genders, Transgenders and Sexualities in Japan*
Edited by Mark McLelland and Romit Dasgupta

Fertility, Family Planning and Population Policy in China*
Edited by Dudley L. Poston, Che-Fu Lee, Chiung-Fang Chang, Sherry L. McKibben, and Carol S. Walther

Japanese Diasporas*
Unsung pasts, conflicting presents and uncertain futures
Edited by Nobuko Adachi

How China Works*
Perspectives on the twentieth-century industrial workplace
Edited by Jacob Eyferth

Remolding and Resistance among Writers of the Chinese Prison Camp
Disciplined and published
Edited by Philip F. Williams and Yenna Wu

Popular Culture, Globalization and Japan*
Edited by Matthew Allen and Rumi Sakamoto

medi@sia*
Global media/tion in and out of context
Edited by Todd Joseph Miles Holden and Timothy J. Scrase

Vientiane
Transformations of a Lao landscape
Marc Askew, William S. Logan and Colin Long

State Formation and Radical Democracy in India
Manali Desai

Democracy in Occupied Japan
The U.S. occupation and Japanese politics and society
Edited by Mark E. Caprio and Yoneyuki Sugita

Globalization, Culture and Society in Laos
Boike Rehbein

Transcultural Japan*
At the borderlands of race, gender, and identity
Edited by David Blake Willis and Stephen Murphy-Shigematsu

Post-Conflict Heritage, Post-Colonial Tourism
Culture, politics and development at Angkor
Tim Winter

Education and Reform in China*
Emily Hannum and Albert Park

Writing Okinawa: Narrative Acts of Identity and Resistance
Davinder L. Bhowmik

Maid in China
Media, mobility, and a new semiotic of power
Wanning Sun

Northern Territories, Asia-Pacific Regional Conflicts and the Åland Experience
Untying the Kurillian knot
Edited by Kimie Hara and Geoffrey Jukes

Reconciling Indonesia
Grassroots agency for peace
Birgit Bräuchler

Singapore in the Malay World
Building and breaching regional bridges
Lily Zubaidah Rahim

Pirate Modernity
Delhi's media urbanism
Ravi Sundaram

The World Bank and the Post-Washington Consensus in Vietnam and Indonesia
Inheritance of loss
Susan Engel

Critical Asian Scholarship
Critical Asian Scholarship is a series intended to showcase the most important individual contributions to scholarship in Asian Studies. Each of the volumes presents a leading Asian scholar addressing themes that are central to his or her most significant and lasting contribution to Asian studies. The series is committed to the rich variety of research and writing on Asia, and is not restricted to any particular discipline, theoretical approach or geographical expertise. Titles include:

Southeast Asia*
A testament
George McT. Kahin

Women and the Family in Chinese History*
Patricia Buckley Ebrey

China Unbound*
Evolving perspectives on the Chinese past
Paul A. Cohen

China's Past, China's Future*
Energy, food, environment
Vaclav Smil

The Chinese State in Ming Society*
Timothy Brook

China, East Asia and the Global Economy*
Regional and historical perspectives
Takeshi Hamashita
Edited by Mark Selden and Linda Grove

The Global and Regional in China's Nation-Formation*
Prasenjit Duara

* Available in paperback

Chinese Politics

State, society and the market

**Edited by Peter Hays Gries
and Stanley Rosen**

Routledge
Taylor & Francis Group

LONDON AND NEW YORK

First published 2010
by Routledge
2 Park Square, Milton Park, Abingdon, Oxon OX14 4RN

Simultaneously published in the USA and Canada
by Routledge
711 Third Avenue, New York, NY 10017

Routledge is an imprint of the Taylor & Francis Group,
an informa business

Typeset in 10/12pt Times New Roman by
Graphicraft Limited, Hong Kong
Printed and bound in Great Britain by
CPI Antony Rowe, Chippenham, Wiltshire

British Library Cataloguing in Publication Data
A catalogue record for this book is available
from the British Library

Library of Congress Cataloging-in-Publication Data
Chinese politics : state, society and the market / edited by Peter Hays Gries and Stanley
Rosen.
    p. cm.
    1. China – Politics and government – 2002–   2. China – Economic conditions –
2000–2003. China – Social conditions – 2000–   I. Gries, Peter Hays, 1967–   II. Rosen,
Stanley, 1942–
DT779.46.C45 2009
951.06 – dc22

2009035978

ISBN10: 0-415-56402-6 (hbk)
ISBN10: 0-415-56403-4 (pbk)
ISBN10: 0-203-85642-2 (ebk)

ISBN13: 978-0-415-56402-1 (hbk)
ISBN13: 978-0-415-56403-8 (pbk)
ISBN13: 978-0-203-85642-0 (ebk)

For Mônica, Julia, and Zeus
For Sheila, Dorothy, Debbie, and Melanie

Contents

Illustrations

Figures

Tables

Contributors

Bruce J. Dickson, Professor of Political Science and International Affairs, George Washington University.

Mark W. Frazier, Conoco Phillips Professor of Chinese Politics and Associate Professor, School of International and Area Studies, University of Oklahoma.

Peter Hays Gries, Harold J. and Ruth Newman Chair, Institute for U.S.–China Issues, and Associate Professor, University of Oklahoma.

Richard Kraus, Professor Emeritus of Political Science, University of Oregon.

Lianjiang Li, Professor of Government and Public Administration, Chinese University of Hong Kong.

Colin Mackerras, Professor Emeritus, Department of International Business and Asian Studies, Griffith University, Brisbane.

Andrew Mertha, Associate Professor of Government, Cornell University.

Kevin J. O'Brien, Alann P. Bedford Professor of Asian Studies and Professor of Political Science, University of California, Berkeley.

Stanley Rosen, Director of the East Asian Studies Center and Professor of Political Science, University of Southern California.

Vivienne Shue, Leverhulme Professor and Director, Contemporary China Studies Programme, Oxford University.

Dorothy J. Solinger, Professor of Political Science, University of California, Irvine.

Jessica C. Teets, Assistant Professor of Political Science, Middlebury College.

Patricia M. Thornton, Department of Politics and International Relations and Merton College, University of Oxford.

Martin King Whyte, Professor of Sociology, Harvard University.

Teresa Wright, Professor of Political Science, California State University, Long Beach.

Acknowledgments

This volume grew from ground prepared by our 2004 co-edited volume *State and Society in 21st-century China: Crisis, Contention, and Legitimation*. The four chapters by Dickson, Shue, Kraus, and Mackerras here are updates of their chapters in that volume. The remaining nine chapters are new to this volume, although the Li and O'Brien chapter was previously published in the *China Quarterly*. We would like to thank Cambridge University Press for their permission to reprint it here. We would also like to welcome five new contributors to this volume, Jessica C. Teets, Andrew Mertha, Lianjiang Li, Martin King Whyte, and Mark W. Frazier.

Peter Gries would like to acknowledge financial support provided by the University of Oklahoma, the intellectual camaraderie of many colleagues at OU, and the support for China studies provided by OU President David Boren and many other university leaders. He would also like to thank the fifteen contributors to this volume. Four generations of China scholars lie between the covers of this book. Vivienne Shue taught Kevin J. O'Brien at Yale, O'Brien taught Peter Gries at Berkeley, and Gries taught Jessica C. Teets at Colorado. And now Teets is teaching a new generation of China scholars at Middlebury College.

Stanley Rosen would like to acknowledge the support of the College of Letters, Arts and Sciences, the US–China Institute and the Residential Life program at the University of Southern California for financial support to travel to "Greater China" (Beijing, Shanghai, Hong Kong, and Taiwan) to conduct research and gather materials for this book. He would also like to thank the staff of the Universities Service Centre for China Studies at the Chinese University of Hong Kong for their help on his frequent visits to that wonderful library for contemporary materials on China, as well as his staff at USC's East Asian Studies Center for being so efficient that he could spare the time to work on this project.

Finally, Gries and Rosen would like to jointly thank the many people at Routledge who have greatly improved the final manuscript. Thanks in particular go to acquisitions editor Stephanie Rogers, editorial assistant Leanne Hinves, series editor Mark Selden, production editor Stewart Pether, and copy editor Lisa Williams. They would also like to thank Zhang Cong, who designed the cover graphic for the paperback.

Introduction

Political change, contestation, and pluralization in China today

Jessica C. Teets, Stanley Rosen, and Peter Hays Gries

In 2008 and 2009, Chinese leaders celebrated a number of important events – the thirtieth anniversary of "reform and opening" (*gaige kaifang* 改革开放), the twentieth anniversary of Tiananmen, and hosting the Olympics for the first time. Despite the continuing economic successes and rising international prestige of China, these events occurred in the context of increasing social protests over corruption, land seizures, environmental concerns, and home-owner NIMBY (not in my backyard) movements. Such political contestation presents an opportunity to investigate the changes occurring in China today – what are the goals of political contestation, how are Chinese Communist Party (CCP) leaders legitimizing their rule, and what are the dynamics of changing state–society relations?

Thirty years of economic reform and transition to a "socialist-market economy" have led to huge economic gains, with China averaging a 10 percent GDP growth rate and raising more people out of poverty than any other country. While these gains are impressive, the neoliberal growth policies of Deng Xiaoping and Jiang Zemin generated a number of social consequences that Hu Jintao's administration must address, such as growing income inequality, persistent bureaucratic corruption, a bankrupt local-state welfare model, and illegal land seizures. As a result of a development policy skewed toward the coastal versus the central and western regions and toward urban versus rural areas, income inequality increased steadily. This imbalance was even more pronounced inside of rural areas between cities and the agricultural countryside, due in part to rising government investment in cities of interior provinces.[1] Responding to this inequality, economic migrants move to urban areas in search of work. Most, however, are unable to access public services without city registration papers (*hukou* 户口). China's economic migrants, or "floating population" (*liudong renkou* 流动人口), increased from approximately 70 million in 1993 to 140 million in 2003, exceeding 10 percent of the total population and accounting for about 30 percent of the rural labor force. According to the results of China's Fifth Population Census, 65 percent of migrants are floating within a province and 35 percent across provinces, with 80 percent of migrants between the ages of 15 and 35.[2] With the increasing development of interior cities and the stagnating export market in the coastal cities due to the global economic crisis, migration is shifting from the 1980s and 1990s model of economic migration from the interior to the coast to a more regional model, as well as forcing a new conception of citizenship in China not tied to geography.[3] While rural protest linked to income inequality is relatively unheard of due to migrant remittances dampening the effects of income inequality, rising unemployment caused by the slowdown in exports will increase pressure on the local governments for welfare provision as well as pressure on the central government to raise investment in the interior provinces.[4]

The other three significant problems of persistent bureaucratic corruption, a bankrupt local-state welfare model, and illegal land seizures mostly occur at the local-state level. Opportunities for corruption by local government officials grew dramatically beginning with economic reform, when local government cadres were encouraged to "jump into the sea" (*xiahai* 下海) of capitalism.[5] Corruption stems from poor institutional design as well as economic and cultural reasons. Some corruption, however, takes the form of levies and fines used by local governments to fill gaps in official budgets.[6] Although such explanations do not address personal or individual corruption by local cadres, they focus on one of the structural causes of local corruption and illegal land sales which fuel the majority of protest in China – the decentralization of fiscal responsibility to the local state.[7] Fiscal decentralization from the central government to local governments during the reform era caused the responsibility for public-goods provision to shift to local governments. While some scholars viewed decentralization as an opportunity for a more representative local government, the majority of scholars find that this shift created expensive responsibilities for local governments in the form of pension, unemployment, education, and health expenditures.[8] Currently most provinces are in debt, and spend more each year than they officially have access to through taxes and central transfers. As official tax rates decline and welfare burdens increase, local governments search for new ways to meet these unfunded mandates. Subsequently, extra-budgetary revenue is increasingly used to meet these mandates, and is generated through fees, fines, and land sales.[9] As the guardians of land, local officials have the ability to sell land at higher rates than they compensate the dispossessed family and keep the remainder for local expenses or for themselves. Given the property boom in China over the last decade, this has become a profitable way for local governments to cover budget shortfalls. Both the imposition of illicit fees and land seizures incite increasing protests and petitions at the local level, as does the insufficient provision of public goods, leading to local governments being the targets for most protests in China.

In addition to these areas of political contestation, development and globalization have stimulated increasing social complexity in China.[10] Growing social complexity means that scholars must disaggregate both the Chinese state and society in ever smaller ways to fully understand state–society dynamics. As we discuss below and the authors address later in this volume, the "state"

is comprised of a multitude of different and often competing actors, including the CCP, government ministries and agencies at the central level, and
local party cadres, government officials, and bureaus at the local (provincial,
prefectural, county, and township) level. "Society" is comprised of an even
larger array of actors, including intellectuals, private enterprises, non-profit
organizations (NPOs), homeowners' associations, journalists, and trade and
professional associations, to name a few. Both state and social actors possess
varying interests, resources, and strategies to achieve their disparate goals.

Political contestation and legitimacy in China today

One of the most eagerly anticipated events of 2008 was the Beijing
Olympics. For many, this event illustrated China's rising international
status and economic achievements, invalidating references to "the sick man
of Asia" and the "century of humiliation."[11] However, as the *Economist*
noted, "nationalism is both an asset to the party (it helps to bolster its sense
of legitimacy) and a complication in its efforts to convince the world that
China's rise poses no threat to Western interests."[12] While the official performances during and prior to the Olympics highlighted the gains made by
China under CCP rule, protests in Tibet and abroad during the Olympic torch
relay focused attention on human rights deficiencies. For many Chinese, the
Western media's focus on human rights during the Olympic torch and Tibet
protests was an expression of Western cultural imperialism, manifested in
biased media coverage. Young nationalists used the Internet to combat this
perceived bias, establishing an anti-CNN website in spring 2008 to mobilize
anti-Western protests by ethnic Chinese around the world.

What does the lack of domestic protest at the Beijing Olympics tell us
about the state–society relationship in China and CCP legitimacy? There
are two competing interpretations of the lack of domestic protest during the
Beijing Olympics: first, that the security forces severely repressed all dissent
prior to the event and, second, that most citizens believe that they have other
channels to express their grievances and that they did not want to embarrass China in international eyes.[13] These interpretations refer to different state
and societal actors. Increasing social complexity in China, and in Tibet as
discussed on pp. 15–17, renders both explanations at least partially valid.
For example, the Tibetan protests in March 2008 consisted of two different
groups of protesters with diverging goals.[14] One group, consisting mostly of
monks, engaged in non-violent protest to draw attention to the anniversary
of the Dalai Lama's exile so as to provoke dialogue on religious rights and
autonomy in Tibet. However, these protests were closely followed, and in
many ways overshadowed, by violent protests led by young, unemployed
Tibetans directed at Han businesses in the Tibetan old town. Accelerated by
the completion of the new Lhasa railway, Han migrants have been arriving
in ever increasing numbers in Lhasa to open businesses and work in the tourism
industry as taxi drivers, waitresses, and in similar service roles. As Colin

Mackerras notes in Chapter 10, these Han migrants disproportionately receive the economic benefits of increased tourism and industry, which engender alienation and anger among young, unemployed Tibetans toward the Han migrants.[15] The goal of this wave of protests was different from the monks' protests, in that these young Tibetans desired a larger share of further economic gains.[16] These were not separatist demands, but economic ones.

As Chinese leaders were still addressing the issues of international Olympic protests and continuing Tibetan protests, a massive earthquake struck Sichuan Province (*Wenchuan dadizhen* 汶川大地震) on May 12, 2008. According to the State Council Information Office, the death toll from the earthquake was approximately 70,000; 7,000 classrooms collapsed, and approximately 10,000 of the confirmed deaths were schoolchildren.[17] The collapse of many "tofu dregs schoolhouses" (*doufuzha xiaoshe* 豆腐渣校舍) focused attention on local corruption as the culprit for shoddy construction, but also the inability of the central government to regulate local governments' adherence to central standards and policies.[18]

Although many citizens expressed outrage over the school construction scandal, the Chinese government, led by "Grandpa Wen" (Premier Wen Jiabao 温家宝), also received both domestic and international praise for its quick, effective, and open response, especially in comparison to Myanmar's blockade of humanitarian aid during Cyclone Nargis.[19] The CCP allowed unprecedented access to relief efforts for journalists, relief organizations, and civil society groups, and was seen as dealing with the crisis in a very open and effective manner.[20] However, in the aftermath of the relief efforts, the state increasingly turned to coercion as some parents refused payoffs and continued to protest the role of local corruption in the collapse of their children's schools. Some parents filed a class-action lawsuit against the local government.[21] These disparate state responses to different social actors illustrate the dynamic social complexity of state legitimation in China. Groups that seek a role – albeit clearly subordinate to the CCP leadership – in policy making and implementation are welcomed, while groups that appear to challenge the legitimacy claims of the CCP are repressed. Although these divide and conquer strategies to address social unrest are not new, the variation in the number and types of strategies utilized by the party-state is novel and indicates changing state–society relations. For example, local government officials appeared genuinely impressed with civil society relief efforts and began to build a more sustainable and cooperative relationship with these groups.[22]

The Grass-Mud Horse (*Cao Ni Ma* 草泥马) video and the Green Dam (*Luba · Huaji Huhang* 绿坝·花季护航) software further illustrate the dynamic nature of state–society relations, and the growing pluralism of public policy formation. Since appearing on a Chinese Web page and then on YouTube in January 2009, the Grass-Mud Horse children's song has drawn over 1.4 million viewers. The story, which appears at first to be a children's fable about a grass-mud horse's struggle against the evil "river crab" (*hexie* 河蟹) but is actually a play on different Chinese characters with a similar pronunciation to denounce censorship or "harmonization" (*hexie* 和谐) on the Internet in China, has spread across the Chinese online community. Wang Xiaofeng, a journalist and blogger based in Beijing, contends that the animal neatly illustrates the futility of censorship. "When people have emotions or feelings they want to express, they need a space or channel," he said. "It is like a water flow – if you block one direction, it flows to other directions, or overflows. There's got to be an outlet."[23] Chinese netizens observed an increase in censorship online after a group of highly regarded intellectuals released an online petition, entitled Charter 08, calling for an end to the Communist Party's monopoly on power.[24] In response, the ease with which this video was published online and shared with other netizens in China and abroad showed the slow and limited nature of the censors' response.

In May 2009, the Ministry of Industry and Information Technology stated that, as of July 1, 2009, manufacturers must ship computers to be sold in mainland China with Green Dam Youth Escort filtering software preloaded. This software restricts viewing and downloading of online pornography by automatically downloading the latest updates of a list of prohibited sites from an online database. To test the capabilities of this software, hackers in China accessed the keyword library and administrative codes, revealing only 2,700 keywords relating to pornography but over 6,500 politically sensitive keywords, which included "4 June," "Tibet," and "Falun Gong," and also found that the software injects a DLL file into Internet Explorer that prohibits the use of programs commonly used to bypass the Golden Shield Project, a surveillance and censorship program (*jindun gongcheng* 金盾工程).[25] This announcement unleashed complaints from Chinese software and computer manufacturers, trade associations, international companies, and netizen protest.[26] In response, the Ministry announced that it would delay the compulsory implementation date of Green Dam software for an unspecified period, which suggests, at the least, a more pluralistic approach to policy formation and implementation: "They do watch public opinion very carefully," former Deputy Assistant Secretary of State Susan Shirk said of China's Communist Party leaders. "There's a very dynamic interaction between the Party authorities and the Internet public."[27] This outcome reflects the dynamic state–netizen relationship that Patricia Thornton explores in her chapter on censorship and surveillance in Chinese cyberspace, particularly in her discussion of the use of "human flesh engines" (*renrou sousuo* 人肉搜索) by netizens seeking to compel the authorities to discipline local officials who are guilty of moral or economic corruption.

Competing views of political contestation in China

These events engender two different responses from Western scholars, as seen in the chapters in this volume. One interpretation is to view society as contesting the legitimacy of CCP rule.[28] For example, one could point to

Tibetans protesting for human (religious) rights and autonomy, or the grass-mud horse authors fighting the propaganda agencies of the CCP for freedom of speech. A differing response would suggest that these events illustrate the growing pluralism in China's public policy process, and that citizens are contesting policy, not the regime itself.[29] As Lianjiang Li and Kevin O'Brien, and Teresa Wright point out in Chapters 4 and 5, both aims may be present either in the form of different actors, or when one goal turns into the other in response to official repression. In light of growing social complexity, it is important to analyze incidents of protest from the perspective and goals of participants themselves rather than from a Western-based perspective in which every act of protest is an act of contesting the legitimacy of the regime out of a desire for democracy. Interviews with Chinese protestors suggest that they profess a high level of trust in the central government, desire policy change and not regime change, and express a cultural/historical desire for stability and unity currently met by the CCP. We briefly address each of these three findings on pp. 13–16.

In Chapter 4, Lianjiang Li and Kevin O'Brien interview rural protest leaders who shape collective claims, recruit activists and mobilize the public, devise and orchestrate contention, and organize cross-community efforts. They find that framing is important to protest success, and most leaders usually attribute villagers' woes to local violations of a central policy, thus placing the blame squarely on rural officials and identifying a powerful potential ally in the central government (i.e. rightful resistance). Most leaders begin by organizing collective petitions, but when they meet with repression they either stop their activities or are radicalized: "In rural China, instead of deactivating them, repression at times transforms occasional and opportunistic petitioners' representatives into dedicated and committed protest leaders."[30] When repression continues or intensifies, protest leaders may become completely disillusioned with the regime and begin to act like movement entrepreneurs.

In Chapter 5, Teresa Wright similarly finds that many rural protest leaders attempt to work within the system to address a problem with a policy or its implementation, but if these efforts are met with repression, these same leaders might then move on to contest the legitimacy of the regime itself. Wright documents increasing rural protest over corruption in local land sales. Between 1990 and 2002, an estimated 66.3 million farmers had their land confiscated, and in many cases peasants received little compensation. For example, a 1999 study of a township in Yunnan province found that county and township governments took 60–70 percent of all income from land sales, village governments received 25–30 percent, and peasants were given only 5–10 percent. In response, peasant protesters have increased from nearly 900,000 participating in incidents in 1997 to nearly 2 million in 2003, and in the first half of 2004 alone, government sources reported nearly 47,000 cases of land protests nationwide. The number of petitions filed by peasants has also increased, with 60–80 percent of the annual petitions initiated by peasants related to land disputes (out of 10 million in 2003 and 13 million in

2005). However, despite increasing rural protests over land disputes, farmers continue to trust and support the central government while distrusting and confronting the local government. Thus, while rural protest creates a challenge for the legitimacy of local government, it does not appear to challenge the legitimacy of the central government. As survey evidence shows, peasants believe the central government enacts policies that are beneficial (or benevolent, as Vivienne Shue contends in Chapter 2) to peasants, such as reducing tax burdens and demanding higher amounts be paid to peasants for land sales. However, many peasants believe that these policies are not implemented by local officials so that they may enrich themselves. Moreover, just as peasants disaggregate the state into local and central entities when expressing grievances, Wright disaggregates "peasants" into those who still depend on agriculture for their livelihood and those who do not, and finds that the mobility and socioeconomic status of non-agricultural peasants have steadily increased and led to more contentment with the political system than for those who depend on agriculture.

In Chapter 6, Martin King Whyte argues that although many analysts and Chinese officials claim that rising income inequality presents a challenge to the regime's legitimacy, the majority of Chinese are not angry about current inequalities and do not harbor strong resentments against China's rich. Although the polled Chinese believe the state should help the poor, they do not want the state intervening to adjust income equality. In fact, other than education, most polled citizens believe that public-goods provision should be shared between society and the government. In a similar manner to Wright's findings, rural discontent appears to be more about local corruption than income gaps caused by the central government's development policies.

Furthermore, in Chapter 11, Dorothy J. Solinger argues that the Minimum Livelihood Guarantee program (*zuidi shenghuo baozhang* 最低生活保障) helps the regime maintain "benevolence," which Vivienne Shue contends in Chapter 2 is one of the main criteria for regime legitimacy in China. However, Solinger argues that while the 40–50 million recipients (13 percent of the population) are not satisfied with the payment program, they are grateful to the state for any help, even if it is not sufficient. Local governments, on the other hand, treat recipients with distrust and make the program difficult to which to enroll and easy from which to be removed. Solinger suggests that, owing to decades of state propaganda, the poor still trust the government or are simply too vulnerable to stand up to it: "These varied forms of dependency, vulnerability, and incompetence uniformly incline these subjects, at a loss as to where else to look, toward the state as, they trust, the ultimate provisioner."[31] Rural and urban protesters, in short, seek mostly to draw attention to a local problem so that the central government will intervene. They maintain high levels of trust in the central government's benevolence as long as their protest efforts are not repressed.

Andrew Mertha also argues that the goal of contestation is for policy change and not regime change. In Chapter 3, he argues that Western scholarship emphasizing the prospects for future democratization in China has contributed to a blind spot in the literature which obscures the current evolution of a more pluralistic policy process. Marginalized or disgruntled officials, nongovernmental organizations (NGOs), and activists are not simply resisting policies but are seeking to change the substance of broader policies. These policy entrepreneurs focus on entering into and working within the policy process to meet their principal policy-related goals. Mertha contends that they have succeeded in part because they follow the rules of policy making under the "fragmented authoritarianism" framework.[32] The point of entry for policy entrepreneurs is the fragmentation and agency slack that result from institutions that are unable to adapt sufficiently to rapid socioeconomic change, aggressive lobbying of interest groups, or the changing expectations of the citizenry. Changing levels and norms of political participation have occurred under the same political structure of "fragmented authoritarianism," where policy made at the center becomes increasingly malleable to the parochial organizational and political goals of various vertical agencies and spatial regions charged with enforcing that policy. Outcomes are shaped by the incorporation of interests of the implementation agencies into the policy itself. In short, the policy process consists of incremental change via bureaucratic bargaining. What has changed in the new "fragmented authoritarianism 2.0," as Mertha calls it, is the number and types of new entrants participating in the policy process, and the fact that these groups are influencing policy itself rather than merely responding at the stage of implementation. Thus, scholars need to study political liberalization and pluralization as opposed to democratization as the more likely explanation for the explosion of interest articulation within the People's Republic of China's (PRC) continuing authoritarian governance system.

Patricia M. Thornton, in Chapter 8, agrees that empirical evidence linking democracy, political liberalization, and Internet adoption is tenuous at best. While the term "the Great Firewall" conjures images of an ill-fated xenophobic regime struggling to erect and maintain technologically advanced barriers of censorship to limit access to information by its perpetually restive subject population, Thornton argues that Chinese citizens are easily able to avoid most of these barriers and therefore utilize the Internet to push for political change and accountability. Thornton uses numerous examples of self-organized publics of Chinese netizens collectively mobilizing their power on the Internet to investigate issues or incidents of interest to them. Some "human flesh engines" (*renrou sousuo yinqing* 人肉搜索引擎) involve netizens confronting officials over corruption, but others illustrate the ways netizens intimidate people with differing opinions (such as Duke student Grace Wang during the Olympic torch relay protests).[33]

Mark W. Frazier examines labor protests in Chapter 12, arguing that the new pension law reflects public preferences for a national, unified pension system in which the state provides the majority of financing, and eligibility based on citizenship rather than residency. The law would create a social security system similar to the US where workers (perhaps as many as 770 million) contribute to social insurance funds managed by local governments. This is a change from existing social insurance because workers would be conceived of as "contributors" to various funds and therefore possessing rights to the money: "Workers who a generation ago were expected to be loyal subjects who received welfare benefits from a benevolent state are becoming 'contributors' or 'taxpayers' . . . who will demand social services and accountability for the operation of pension and other social insurance funds." Again, this is a new state–society relationship similar to Andrew Mertha's description (in Chapter 3) of policy entrepreneurs who are beginning to shift from policy subjects to policy participants. Co-production of welfare benefits might also lead to a different state–society relationship than Dorothy J. Solinger argues exists with current unemployment insurance. Co-production creates a new social contract between citizens and the CCP as an exchange of support for its legitimacy in return for social security, welfare, and services. However, the central government spends very little on pensions, about 50–100 billion yuan in annual subsidies to provincial governments; whereas in 2005, local governments paid 404 billion yuan in pension benefits and 106 billion yuan for civil servant pensions. As welfare benefits increase, this fiscal burden is shifted to local governments, creating problems of unfunded mandates. As these authors find, activists' and protesters' relationship with the state, at both central and local levels, is changing, but the state led by the CCP appears to retain legitimacy in spite of such protest. All of these authors find that the vast majority of activists and protesters desire policy change and not regime change.

The authors examining the question of CCP legitimacy find a historical and/or cultural desire for stability and unity currently being met by the CCP. For example, in Chapter 7, Stanley Rosen argues that after Tiananmen, Chinese leaders realized they had to find a solution to the legitimacy crisis among the youth and moved to more of a performance-based legitimacy. Reflecting the increasing pluralization of Chinese society after thirty years of reform, Chinese youth today are far from unified in their belief systems or behaviors, with competing and often contradictory influences shaping their attitudes and values, particularly in the wealthy coastal areas. The post-Tiananmen "coming out party" has provided opportunities that did not exist twenty years ago. Thus, Chinese youth, now knowing far more about the West – both the positive and the negative – have replaced the unabashed, uncritical internationalism of the late 1980s with a dual emphasis on materialism and patriotism. Information emanating from Western media sources is viewed skeptically by well-educated, well-informed young Chinese, who assume that such reporting furthers a pro-Western agenda (i.e. CNN's reporting on the Tibetan protests). During "normal" times, materialism and the pursuit of individual success will overwhelm other values. However, patriotic and nationalistic surges will arise during "abnormal" times, when there is a perceived outside threat or insult to China. Although the government continues to promote political education, it does so in a manner intended to appeal to tech-savvy youth, as in politically correct video games. Given current youth values, these games have been far less popular than such online political commentary as spoofing (*egao* 恶搞), as the fable of the grass-mud horse discussed on p. 171 indicates. Where political participation does take place, it tends to be private participation, through friends, family, and in anonymous Internet activities. In like manner, party membership is pursued because of the practical advantages such membership brings. In the end, Rosen does not currently see the youth as a major force for political change as long as the party remains unified, furthers the expansion of middle-class opportunities for youth now entering the workforce, and continues the expected rise of China to world-power status. The CCP faces a new set of performance challenges, brought on in part by the worldwide economic crisis and the resulting demands to ensure necessary employment levels, and in part by the familiar issue of maintaining social stability. In 2009, 6 million college graduates joined their classmates from 2008 who were still hunting for jobs. Thus far the CCP has successfully advocated a performance-based legitimacy, but growing nationalism and economic insecurity among the youth could pose legitimacy questions.

In Chapter 10, Colin Mackerras disaggregates minority groups in China to examine whether the notion of ethnicity poses a challenge to the legitimacy of the Chinese state, and finds that there is considerable diversity in the ways members of ethnic groups, even those from the same ethnic group, view the CCP's legitimacy. While he notes that many Tibetans and Uyghurs make ethnic claims for greater autonomy, Mackerras does not see separatism as a large challenge to China's legitimacy, as the state has won over enough of the economic and political elite in these areas, and maintains a strong military presence there. Additionally, market forces and modernization have both exerted a profound impact on China's ethnic groups, by altering the interests of young minorities toward cooperating with the Chinese state rather than opposing it, and by weakening traditional cultures. Similar to the performance difficulties the CCP faces with the youth, the challenge facing the CCP in its minority regions is the feeling of increasing marginalization in both education and work opportunities by Tibetans and Uyghurs. As recent events in both Tibet and Xinjiang have shown, they must encourage local governments to find ways to defuse ethnic tensions by integrating minority groups into the economic modernization in which many would like to participate.

As Richard Kraus contends in Chapter 9, political legitimacy is often a cultural concept, like Cultural Revolutionary struggles over a bureaucratic seal believed to be the talisman of office. When political legitimacy is imagined to derive from art objects which reside outside the nation, domestically the objects are associated with nationalist policies and internationally associated with the elite political world of fine arts and diplomacy. Kraus examines how the zodiac statues from the 1860 plundering of Yuanming Yuan (the Garden of Perfect Brightness) have come to represent nationalist politics in China. The politics of art repatriation, he argues, contributes to nationalist legitimacy for the CCP as the party that stands up to the West and reverses "the shame of a Qing dynasty army which lost the art to foreign troops."[34] The CCP seeks the return of imperialist plunder, estimated at over a million high-quality cultural artifacts in the collections of 200 museums in 47 countries, as part of overcoming the shame of the "Century of Humiliation." Domestically the return of imperialist plunder affirms the CCP's legitimacy as the guardian of national unity and stability; however, China's demand for repatriation of art objects can contribute to international anxieties about China's rise.

Bruce J. Dickson and Vivienne Shue examine questions of CCP legitimacy in a broader sense than the preceding three authors, but still find the CCP meeting popular demands for stability and unity. In Chapter 1, Bruce J. Dickson argues that despite the expectation from liberal reformers in China and many outside observers that economic liberalization, integration in the global economy, and rising living standards will inevitably lead to democratization, the CCP has proven to be more resilient and adaptable than most observers ever imagined. In fact, CCP leaders believe that these economic changes will bolster its popularity and legitimate its claim to be China's ruling party, rather than trigger its demise. In recent years, new problems caused by economic privatization, such as massive layoffs, unpaid wages, excessive taxation and fees, and rampant corruption, have triggered recurrent and widespread protests, raising questions about the stability of the country and the CCP's ability to maintain control. While many in the party argue in favor of the necessity of adapting to these new challenges, a small but stubborn faction insists that such changes, especially the loss of ideological consistency, are weakening the party and undermining its claim to legitimate rule. Currently dominated by the "adaptionist faction," the CCP has been tolerant of social demands that are economic in nature, has created corporatist-style organizations to integrate new economic actors and mediate concerns, and has pursued a cooptive strategy of recruiting new members into the party. At the same time, the CCP continues to suppress other demands for political reform and liberalization, such as the formation of new political parties and independent labor unions that it perceives as threats to its ruling party status. Thus, the party has abandoned its attempt to control all aspects of economic and social life, and with the liberalization of the post-Mao era has also relinquished the tools that would allow it to do so. In its place, it has adopted a more flexible approach, permissive in some respects but still repressive in others. However, the party does not survive simply because of coercion, but also due to its claims of legitimacy from economic modernization, historic origins, patronage machine, and as a safeguard against national disunity and political instability. The diversification of classes and fluidity of China's social structure are leading the party to change who it recruits and who it claims to represent. The CCP still retains its political monopoly, but tries to be more inclusive and therefore more representative.

In Chapter 2, Vivienne Shue finds that the further dismantling of the old socialist system, the deepening marketization of economic relations, and the redistribution of property rights are all contributing to social change and providing a cause for popular protest. Most of these actions have remained local as the police, the military, and the civil official hierarchies all worked hard to contain such incidents, "defusing crises when necessary with some measured concessions, and decapitating in embryo as many groups or units as they deemed might develop into the organizational skeletons for larger-scale collective actions."[35] Thus, in China since Tiananmen, there have been many popular protests but no major sustained movement of popular opposition until the emergence of Falun Gong, a group of qigong meditation practitioners. This group challenged CCP legitimacy by invoking historical images of religious sects opposing dynastic rulers, such as the Taiping Heavenly Kingdom and the Boxers, and by going overtly "national," making a bid for broader public sympathy and staging demonstrations in symbolic spaces such as Zhongnanhai and Tiananmen. Shue does not expect the Falun Gong challenge to the CCP to succeed since the governing apparatus in China has far greater organizational capacity and control over domestic affairs than that commanded by the overextended late-Qing civil and military hierarchies. In addition to increased government capacity, discontented state-sector workers and peasants have been prone to frame their protests in localized and limited ways, taking as their protest targets not the architects of central policy but local "bad" officials and "incompetent" firm managers. The combined effects of decentralization and marketization have worked to the advantage of the central state, then, making it somewhat easier for the center to contain and quell those protests that have arisen while simultaneously sustaining its own appearance of legitimacy.

Shue argues against overly simplistic assumptions that the CCP's main claims to legitimacy rest in its economic achievements, in an improving standard of living, and in "growth" or "development." While recognizing that steady economic growth or the lack of it may well act as an important factor influencing support for the government, it is also clear that economic success alone is neither a necessary nor a sufficient condition for political legitimacy. As is discussed in more detail on pp. 14–16, ongoing reforms promoting greater accountability, transparency, and popular participation at the local level in China are making important contributions to building and maintaining the party-state's legitimacy.[36] However, Shue argues that accountability, transparency, and broadening participation are not first-order, but only second-order principles. They are to be pursued, not for themselves, but as tools and techniques, organizational and behavioral habits that are helpful in the attainment of yet another, quite different, grand normative ideal of governance – that of rule in accord with the expressed "will of the people."[37] Instead, Shue posits that the core of CCP legitimacy claims is stability – the conditions of social peace and order. The present regime stakes its legitimacy not on its technical capacity to steer and to grow the economy, but on its political capacity to preserve a peaceful and stable social order under which, among other good things, the economy can be expected to grow. She finds this claim to legitimacy to be based in historical and cultural ideas of good governance:

> The best rulers and officials, those who governed in accord with universal truths and manifested the proper benevolence toward their subjects, might hope and expect to preside over a stable and harmonious order, and the very florescence of economy, the arts, and of philosophy that would emanate from such an enviable order would, in turn, engender awe on the part of all those who beheld it, and would thereby further glorify the Sinic civilization and all the lands and peoples under the sway of the empire.[38]

The findings of the authors in this volume lead to the conclusion that most protest and contestation in China is not driven by the desire for regime change but instead for better access to the government policy-making and implementation process. A great deal of recent research on political contestation in China finds that the primary goal of non-profits and other social organizations is to influence policy. For example, Scott Kennedy and Kellee Tsai's work on private business associations, Lily Tsai's research on rural kinship groups, Andrew Mertha's work on environmental groups, and Ben Read's research on private housing associations all find that these social actors intend to effect policy change, not regime change.[39] As both Stanley Rosen (Chapter 7) and Vivienne Shue (Chapter 2) discuss in this volume, many Chinese citizens feel that the CCP has performed well on most legitimacy criteria, such as economic development, social stability, and China's international profile. In the instances where citizens feel that legitimacy criteria have not been met, protesters contend that this is because of problems of policy development or implementation rather than because the purpose or intention of the policy is detrimental toward the common people (*laobaixing* 老百姓). Under this logic, protesters first try to bring the attention of higher levels of government to these policy problems, often through letters and visits to offices (*xinfang* 信访).[40] Only when this channel is not effective do protestors take to the streets to force the government to address their concerns. Therefore, government response to citizen attempts to enter into a previously closed policy process in large part determines whether contestation is a challenge to regime legitimacy. In recognition of this dynamic of protest in China, the government follows a divide and conquer policy where leaders of protests are fined or jailed as criminal elements while participants are often given at least some of what they are demanding (e.g. pension payments, removal of corrupt officials, and land restitutions).[41]

In response to the increasing social complexity and political contestation that has accompanied economic reform and opening, the Hu Jintao
administration has pursued a number of governance reforms broadly grouped
under the rubric of "Harmonious Society" (*hexie shehui* 和谐社会). This
policy platform includes reducing peasant burdens through the reduction of
taxes and fees, investing in economic development projects in the western
and interior provinces to even out income inequality, and governance
reforms to promote transparency, accountability, and competition at the local
level.[42] The goal of these reforms is to reduce the causes of political contestation and build new monitoring mechanisms, such as village elections and
civil society, to ensure that local governments implement both the letter and
spirit of central policies. This platform differs from Jiang Zemin's "Three
Represents" in that the focus is on reducing social and political friction created by the fast growth of the previous two decades rather than simply achieving economic growth. These reforms taken as a whole serve to change the
role of the government in both state and society. The central state under Deng
and Jiang began to withdraw the state from society (and the market) under
the philosophy of "small state, big society" (*xiaozhengfu dashehui* 小政府大
社会), where the state's relationship with society was one of regulator rather
than active agent. However, under Hu Jintao, the role of the state is to continue to withdraw from society where "social intermediaries" exist, but at
the same time to serve as an active agent in guiding economic development
and building a welfare system. This vision of the appropriate role of the state
informs the current "China model" of a mixture of state intervention
and private initiative in the market.[43] More so than the other aspects of
"Harmonious Society," governance reforms designed to increase transparency, accountability, and competition at the local level have influenced
changing state–society relations in China. The introduction of village elections,
laws on local transparency, use of the courts to battle corruption, and plans
to increase the number of candidates competing for election all seek to address
the problems of policy implementation and governance at the local level.[44]
However, what these reforms also create are additional channels and space
for societal actors to begin to participate in policy making and governance.[45]

In short, we contend that in response to increasing social complexity
and political contestation, limited governance reforms pursued by the CCP
create more space and channels for political participation. This has changed
the definition of policy making in China – who is a policy maker, how this
process is conducted, and the linkage between policy and regime. This is
not to say that Chinese leaders fully embrace new policy entrepreneurs or
political contestation. While both the local and central state accept policy
contestation, if the mobilization becomes too great or protests begin to challenge legitimacy instead of policy, Chinese officials, especially at the local
level, continue with divide and conquer strategies of punishing leaders while
coopting masses. Interaction between state and social actors is driving the
authoritarian state to be more responsive and inclusive, but not leading

inexorably to democratization. The emphasis from the majority of actors in both the state and society is to improve governance in China, which is the basis of legitimacy for any government, rather than fundamentally challenging the existing single-party system. According to most surveys, CCP members and citizens consistently argue that the CCP is effective as a government at improving economic development and citizen welfare, maintaining a robust international image, and securing territorial integrity and social stability.[46] In fact, in the light of the ongoing global economic crisis, many Western analysts and governments are touting the strength of the "China model."

Disaggregating the socialist market: increasing social complexity and policy pluralization

Economic reform and opening under Deng Xiaoping and especially Jiang Zemin created unprecedented access for market actors to influence policy decisions. The creation of private enterprise generated interests for market policies, leading to greater economic success, which aligned with central and local government interests and served to create informal access to policy making. In recognition of these similar interests, Jiang Zemin extended party membership to private entrepreneurs, allowing direct access to policy making in 2001. Under Jiang's leadership, the central state began a slow withdrawal from the economy primarily by reforming the state-owned enterprise (SOE) sector and moving the state role to being more of a regulator than an active agent in the economy. Under Hu's leadership, the central government has slowed down SOE reform out of concern for unemployment, and has championed the idea of the appropriate role of the state as a regulator for private business and leader for SOEs and other pillar industries (e.g. software development, biotechnology, automobiles, medical devices, and super-computers). The "socialist-market economy" in China is comprised of three different models of state–market relationship operating concurrently: the state-owned sector, the directed sector, and the private sector. The state-owned and directed sectors consist of three different types of firms: central and local SOEs, township and village enterprises (TVEs), and private firms categorized as pillar industries. Representing the legacy of the communist past, the party-state directly controls SOEs, which are funded through state-owned banks. The SOE sector is currently comprised of 159 enterprises under central government control in such key areas as utilities, heavy industry, and energy resources.[47] These SOEs own and control tens of thousands of subsidiary firms. The remaining SOE sector and a policy of strong state intervention in the economy are the key identifying characteristics of the "socialist-market economy."[48] The resulting hybrid market is the result of an incremental process of reform and bureaucratic bargaining, not a coherent "China model."[49]

In this part of the economy, the state's relationship with these firms is similar to the previous command economy. However, the party-state requires that these firms earn profits if possible, introducing market mechanisms that did not exist under the command economy. The state-owned and directed sectors operate under two distinct logics – one political and the other economic. When these two logics conflict, firms must decide how to balance between the two, with some firms choosing to find ways around political constraints and others choosing to bargain with the government to reconcile the two logics. For example, state-owned newspapers depend heavily on advertising revenue, which sensitizes them to an economic logic of reporting on sensational issues.[50] However, the Central Propaganda Department routinely issues warnings to newspaper outlets not to publish on "sudden incidents" to avoid inciting social unrest. Given this conflict between economic and political logics, newspaper outlets employ a number of creative solutions, including waiting until someone posts a story online or a foreign newspaper publishes a story.[51] Then the Chinese newspaper publishes a story the next day based on that account, which is reporting on someone else's reporting on the sudden incident. Often the journalist herself is the one posting the story online or giving the details to a foreign correspondent.[52] In the aftermath of the Sichuan earthquake, many news outlets got around injunctions against reporting on the earthquake by immediately sending correspondents to Sichuan to begin reporting *before* the Propaganda Department could issue an injunction.[53] Another strategy employed, especially by large SOEs, is to bargain with the government to create a compromise between political and economic logics. For example, throughout the 1990s, during the reform of the SOE sector, the government divided SOEs into large and small firms ("grasping the big and letting go of the small"), with the small firms allowed to merge with larger firms or go bankrupt. As a large and profitable SOE, Qingdao's Haier was ordered by the local government to merge with smaller unprofitable firms. However, as this exerted a drain on Haier's ability to invest in research and development and remain successful, Haier's leadership negotiated a compromise with the local government that the government would pay Haier for the cost of integrating the unprofitable firm.[54] In this case, the two conflicting logics were reconciled through negotiation. In certain instances, such as the newspaper example, the existence of these two conflicting logics might present a challenge to CCP legitimacy; however, as the Haier case illustrates, increasing policy pluralization creates space for negotiated compromises between conflicting logics.

Increasing social complexity has led to a proliferation of interests in the Chinese economy. To take one example, a former unified category such as "workers" now divides into SOE employees versus private employees, large versus small/medium-sized enterprise (SME) employees, service versus industrial employees, and domestic-market versus export-oriented sector employees. These different types of "workers" have varying and often competing interests, which they attempt to articulate inside of an authoritarian system where lobbying is still an illegal activity. In response to the diversification of market interests and economic reforms, there has been a proliferation of market-based groups, such as private business associations, and trade and professional associations, that seek to influence policy. These groups use both informal and formal channels to access policy making and advocate for favorable policies.[55] A good example of their growing policy influence is the July 2009 decision to delay the enforced implementation of Green Dam filtering software on all computers sold on the mainland. The Ministry of Industry and Information Technology (MIIT) delayed implementing this policy only after a barrage of criticism from business groups, foreign officials, and Chinese computer users. An announcement issued by the MIIT said that they had determined that computer manufacturers needed more time to comply with the rule.[56] In Chapter 3, Andrew Mertha offers another example of an entrepreneur from Wenzhou participating in setting China's World Trade Organization (WTO) policy. Interaction between state and market actors creates a more pluralistic and responsive governing process, with high levels of support for the state from middle-class entrepreneurs.[57] Although they do not conceive of themselves as a coherent group outside of their associations, these entrepreneurs believe that they have avenues for protest and influence without challenging the regime.[58]

All of these major events in 2008–9 illustrate how thirty years of economic reform and opening have created growing social complexity in China, which is altering state–society relationships to include more pluralism in the policy process. Additionally, aided by telecommunications and governance reforms, there are more voices in the Chinese policy process and public sphere than ever before. In conclusion, we find that despite increasing contestation in China, these protests are less often challenges to CCP legitimacy than they are attempts to play a policy role – challenging old ideas of by whom and how policy is made in China today. As we contended in an earlier work, "Legitimacy, in Mao's China and today, is never a state *possession*; instead, state and social actors continuously contest it."[59] The importance of this change is not just that there is more space for political participation than we might expect in an authoritarian system, but rather, following Andrew Mertha's "new fragmented authoritarianism," that we are seeing a fundamental shift in the nature of policy making in China around the understanding of who is a policy maker and how policy is made. This change in governance beliefs and systems is partly due to the CCP's adaptability to social complexity and political contestation, but is also due to global interactions and ideational exchanges with corporations, NGOs, and other governments. However, despite the current state–society agreement on good governance lending legitimacy, this is only one factor in a complex cocktail of legitimacy – both ideological and performance based. Governance quality and response to political contestation vary widely among different state actors, making state–society relations in China a dynamic space. In the past decade, governance reforms have focused on increasing accountability, transparency, and competition, but they are subject to reversal. In fact, at the 2009 session of the National People's Congress (NPC), government leaders indicated that they would roll back or freeze governance reforms after the start of the global economic crisis owing to fears that social stability might be threatened as a consequence of rising unemployment.[60] Additionally, as both Lianjiang Li and Kevin O'Brien, and Teresa Wright find, when attempts at policy influence and political contestation are met with repression, the danger is that efforts to change policies transform into efforts to change the regime. These obstacles to continued policy participation must be carefully observed, because, while this trend will not lead to democracy in the short term, it may lead to better governance and continued political pluralization in China. As Robert Dahl contends, pluralism exists when political life is a competition for group influence, and this state of affairs is a positive development for both state and society.[61] In China today, political life is marked by an increasing competition among group interests, which is a fundamental shift in the policy process and in state-society relations.

Notes

1 Ximing Wu and Jeffrey M. Perloff, "China's Income Distribution, 1985–2001," *Review of Economics and Statistics*, 2005.
2 "China's Floating Population Tops 140 Million," *People's Daily*, July 27, 2005.
3 Dorothy J. Solinger, "China's Floating Population: Implications for State and Society," Roderick MacFarquhar and Merle Goldman, eds., *The Paradox of China's Post-Mao Reforms* (Cambridge: Harvard University Press, l999), pp. 220–40.
4 "China Avoids Major Social Unrest," *BBC News*, June 18, 2009, *news.bbc.co.uk/2/hi/asia-pacific/8102233.stm.*
5 Bruce Dickson, *Red Capitalists in China: The Party, Private Entrepreneurs, and Prospects for Political Change* (Cambridge: Cambridge University Press, 2003).
6 Melanie Manion, *Corruption by Design: Building Clean Government in Mainland China and Hong Kong* (Cambridge: Harvard University Press, 2004); Yufan Hao and Michael Johnston, "Reform at the Crossroads: An Analysis of Chinese Corruption," *Asian Perspective* (1995); and Christine Wong, "Central–Local Relations in an Era of Fiscal Decline: The Paradox of Fiscal Decentralization in Post-Mao China," *China Quarterly* (1991).
7 Christine Wong, "Central–Local Relations Revisited: The 1994 Tax-Sharing Reform and Public Expenditure Management in China," *China Perspectives* (2000).
8 Hehui Jin, Yingyi Qian, and Barry Weingast, "Regional Decentralization and Fiscal Incentives: Federalism, Chinese Style," *Journal of Public Economics* (2005); and Albert Park, Scott Rozelle, Christine Wong, and Changqing Ren, "Distributional Consequences of Reforming Local Public Finance in China," *China Quarterly* (1996).
9 Ran Tao and Dali Yang, "The Revenue Imperative and the Role of Local Government in China's Transition and Growth," presented at the *Coase Conference on China's Economic Transformation*, Chicago, July 2008.
10 Jude Howell, "Prospects for NGOs in China," *Development in Practice* 5 (February 1995); Wenfang Tang and William Parish, *Chinese Urban Life Under Reform: The Changing Social Contract* (Cambridge: Cambridge University Press, 2000).
11 Michael Collins, "China's Olympics," *Contemporary Review* (2002), pp. 135–41; see also Peter Hays Gries, *China's New Nationalism: Pride, Politics, and Diplomacy* (Berkeley: University of California Press, 2004).
12 "China Before the Olympics: Welcome to a (Rather Dour) Party," *Economist*, July 31, 2008.

13 Austin Ramzy, "Beijing's Complaint-Free Protest Zones," *Time Magazine*, July 25, 2008; Edward Wong, "Would-Be Olympic Protester Sentenced to 3 Years in Prison," *New York Times*, January 15, 2009.

14 David Barboza, "Pressed Over Tibet, China Berates Foreign Media," *New York Times*, March 25, 2008; Elizabeth C. Economy and Adam Segal, "China's Olympic Nightmare: What the Games Mean for Beijing's Future," *Foreign Affairs* (July/August 2008).

15 This argument also applies to the Uyghurs in Xinjiang: Edward Wong, "Ethnic Clashes in Western China Are Said to Kill Scores," *New York Times*, July 7, 2009.

16 "Monks on the March," *Economist*, March 13, 2008.

17 Edward Wong, "Grieving Chinese Parents Protest School Collapse, *New York Times*, July 17, 2008.

18 "School Quake Scandal: Bereaved Parents Accuse China Government of Allowing Shoddy Construction," *Toronto Sun*, June 5, 2008.

19 "Days of Disaster," *Economist*, May 15, 2008.

20 Andrew Jacobs, "A Rescue in China, Uncensored," *New York Times*, May 14, 2008.

21 Jill Drew, "Tangled Blame in Quake Deaths: Chinese Parents Facing Uphill Battle for Redress Over Collapsed Schools," *Washington Post*, June 2, 2008; Edward Wong, "China Presses Hush Money on Grieving Parents," *New York Times*, July 24, 2008.

22 Jessica C. Teets, "Post-Earthquake Relief and Reconstruction Efforts: The Emergence of Civil Society in China?" *China Quarterly* 198 (June 2009), pp. 330–47.

23 Michael Wines, "A Dirty Pun Tweaks China's Online Censors," *New York Times*, March 11, 2009.

24 Vivian Wu, "Censors Strike at Internet Content after Parody Hit," *South China Morning Post*, April 3, 2009.

25 "Chinese Regime's 'Anti-Pornography' Software Targets Falun Gong," *Epoch Times*, June 13, 2009, accessed at http://www.theepochtimes.com/n2/content/view/18096/.

26 Richard Koman, "China's not Backing Down but Green Dam Girl Fights Back," *ZDNet*, June 18, 2009, accessed at http://government.zdnet.com/?p=4988.

27 Chris Buckley and David Stanway, "China Backs Away from Internet Filter," *Reuters*, June 30, 2009.

28 Jeffrey Wasserstrom, *Student Protests in Twentieth-Century China: The View from Shanghai* (Stanford: Stanford University Press, 1991); Elizabeth J. Perry, *Challenging the Mandate of Heaven: Social Protest and State Power in China* (Armonk, NY: M.E. Sharpe, 2002).

29 Scott Kennedy, *The Business of Lobbying in China* (Cambridge: Harvard University Press, 2005); Kellee Tsai, *Capitalism without Democracy: the Private Sector in Contemporary China* (Ithaca: Cornell University Press, 2007).

30 See p. 97.

31 See p. 252.

32 Kenneth Lieberthal and Michel Oksenberg, *Policy Making in China: Leaders, Structures, and Processes* (Princeton: Princeton University Press, 1988).

33 Grace Wang, "Caught in the Middle, Called a Traitor," *Washington Post*, April 20, 2008, p. B01.

34 See p. 205.

35 See p. 42.

36 David Shambaugh, *China's Communist Party: Atrophy and Adaptation* (Berkeley: University of California Press, 2009); Thomas Heberer and Gunter Schubert, "Political Reform and Regime Legitimacy in Contemporary China," *Asien* 99 (April 2006), pp. 9–28.

37 See p. 59.

38 See p. 47.
39 Scott Kennedy, *The Business of Lobbying in China* (Cambridge: Harvard University Press, 2005); Kellee Tsai, *Capitalism without Democracy: the Private Sector in Contemporary China* (Ithaca: Cornell University Press, 2007); Lily Tsai, *Accountability without Democracy: How Solidary Groups Provide Public Goods in Rural China* (Cambridge: Cambridge University Press, 2007); Andrew Mertha, *China's Water Warriors: Citizen Action and Policy Change* (Ithaca: Cornell University Press, 2008); Ben Read, "Democratizing the Neighbourhood? New Private Housing and Home-Owner Self-Organization in Urban China," *China Journal* (2003).
40 Xi Chen, "Collective Petitioning and Institutional Conversion," Kevin O'Brien, ed., *Rightful Resistance in Rural China* (Cambridge: Harvard University Press, 2008).
41 Timothy B. Weston, "'Learn from Daqing': More Dark Clouds for Workers in State-Owned Enterprises," *Journal of Contemporary China* 11 (2002), pp. 721–34.
42 C. Cindy Fan, "China's Eleventh Five-Year Plan (2006–10): From 'Getting Rich First' to 'Common Prosperity'," *Eurasian Geography and Economics* 47 (2006), pp. 708–23.
43 Orion A. Lewis and Jessica C. Teets, "A China Model? – Understanding the Evolution of a 'Socialist Market Economy'," *Glasshouse Forum* (August 2009); Randall Peerenboom, *China Modernizes: Threat to the West or Model for the Rest?* (Oxford: Oxford University Press, 2007).
44 Yang Cao and Victor Nee, "Controversies and Evidence in the Market Transition Debate," *American Journal of Sociology* 105 (January 2000), pp. 1175–89, based on debates in the 1996 *AJS* market transition symposium; Edward Cody, "Pioneering Chinese City Offers a Peek at Political Ferment," *Washington Post*, June 30, 2008, p. A01; "China Issues Landmark Decree to Encourage Government Transparency," *People's Daily Online*, April 24, 2007, accessed at http://english.people.com.cn/200704/24/eng20070424_369114.html.
45 Andrew Mertha, *China's Water Warriors: Citizen Action and Policy Change* (Ithaca: Cornell University Press, 2008).
46 Andrew Nathan, "Political Culture and Diffuse Regime Support in Asia," *Asian Barometer*, working paper 43 (2007): Nathan finds that diffuse support, synonymous with political legitimacy and not performance legitimacy, is very high in China.
47 Becky Chiu and Mervyn K. Lewis, *Reforming China's State Owned Industries and Banks* (Edward Elgar Publishing, 2006), pp. 10–11.
48 Wang Mengkui, ed., *China's Economic Transformation over 20 Years* (Beijing: Foreign Languages Press, 2000).
49 Sebastian Heilmann, "From Local Experiments to National Policy: The Origins of China's Distinctive Policy Process," *China Journal* 59 (January 2008).
50 Yuezhi Zhao, *Communication in China: Political Economy, Power, and Conflict* (Lanham, MD: Rowman & Littlefield, 2008).
51 Judy Polumbaum, Lei Xiong, and Margaret Kearney, *China Ink: The Changing Face of Chinese Journalism* (Lanham, MD: Rowman & Littlefield, 2008).
52 Guobin Yang, "The Co-Evolution of the Internet and Civil Society in China," *Asian Survey* (2003).
53 Orion Lewis, "The Evolution of the News Media in China," unpublished dissertation manuscript, 2009.
54 Liu Xiangfeng, "Response of SOEs to Economic Liberalization in China," *Institute of Developing Economies* (2006).
55 Scott Kennedy, "Transnational Political Alliances: An Exploration with Evidence From China," *Business & Society* 46 (2007), pp. 174–200.

56 David Pierson, "China to Delay Requiring Green Dam Youth Escort Filtering Software," *Los Angeles Times*, July 1, 2009.

57 Scott Kennedy (2005).

58 Kellee Tsai (2007); Margaret Pearson, *China's New Business Elite: the Political Consequences of Economic Reform* (Berkeley: University of California Press, 1997).

59 Peter Hays Gries and Stanley Rosen, "Introduction: Popular Protest and State Legitimation in 21st-Century China," Peter Hays Gries and Stanley Rosen, eds., *State and Society in 21st-century China: Crisis, Contention, and Legitimation* (New York: RoutledgeCurzon, 2004), p. 6.

60 See NPC Chairman Wu Bangguo's speech: "Top Legislator Stresses Differences between Chinese, Western Political Systems," *Xinhua News Agency*, March 9. 2009.

61 Robert Dahl, *Pluralist Democracy in the United States: Conflict and Consent* (Chicago: Rand McNally, 1967).

1 Dilemmas of party adaptation

The CCP's strategies for survival[1]

Bruce J. Dickson

The Chinese Communist Party (CCP) faces a daunting dilemma: how to preserve the Leninist nature of the political system while presiding over the privatization of the economy. It seeks to maintain its monopoly on political organization – a hallmark of Leninism – even while it promotes increased competition in the market. Most observers, by contrast, believe that current conditions in China's political and economic systems are incompatible, and expect political change of some kind will be necessary. Liberal reformers in China, and many outside observers, anticipate that economic liberalization, integration in the global economy, and rising living standards will inevitably lead to China's democratization. The few remaining leftists within the CCP similarly warn that the party's "reform and opening" (*gaige kaifang* 改革开放) policies have created economic and social changes that will eventually lead to the party's collapse. So far, the CCP has stymied these predictions of its demise. It has proven to be more resilient and more adaptable than most observers ever imagined.[2] In fact, the CCP hopes that these kinds of economic changes will bolster its popularity and legitimit its claim to be China's ruling party, rather than trigger its demise.

The CCP's reform policies have nonetheless exposed severe problems. Some have been generic features of the post-1949 People's Republic, others are unique to the post-Mao era. From the early 1950s to the present, the CCP has debated the question of whom to rely upon for popular support and political and technical skills. Throughout the post-Mao period, the party has wrestled with the need to open up the economic system without also losing political control. Labor unrest, cadre corruption, and the center's inability to monitor and enforce the local implementation of policy have also been recurrent problems, with varying degrees of intensity, long before the 21st century. In recent years, new problems caused by economic privatization, such as massive lay-offs, unpaid wages, excessive taxation and fees, and rampant corruption, have triggered recurrent and widespread protests, raising questions about the stability of the country and the CCP's ability to maintain control. But as this chapter will show, the CCP has a variety of political and practical advantages that have allowed it to survive, despite these challenges.

On the list of dilemmas facing the CCP, most people would not include ideological consistency as a cause of concern, especially at a time when pragmatism guides the party's approach to policy, and technocracy defines its style of leadership. But the CCP, or at least some of its leaders, continues to believe that the party requires an ideological rationale for its continued rule and the economic, political, and organizational reforms it has undertaken. During the Maoist era, when ideological issues helped determine political survival and even personal well-being, Chinese citizens and outside observers paid careful attention to ideological debates and propaganda formulations. After economic modernization replaced class struggle as the party's top objective, and communist goals were abandoned in all but name, interest in ideology waned, and rightfully so. Nevertheless, the party expends a great deal of effort to publicize ideological innovations, emphasizing how its reform agenda is consistent with its traditional goals and in the national interest, despite appearances to the contrary. In addition, attention to ideological debates still offers a window on basic conflicts within the party. As will be shown on pp. 30–34, while most in the party insist that adaptation is necessary for its survival, a small but stubborn fraction insist that such changes are weakening the party and undermining its legitimate claim to rule.

The CCP finds itself confronted by competing political and economic demands. Its response varies, depending on the nature of the claims. On the one hand, the party has been tolerant of demands that are economic in nature. It has created corporatist-style organizations for various professions, particularly industry and commerce, as a way to integrate itself with individuals and groups who contribute to the economic modernization of the country. In addition to these institutional ties, it has also pursued a cooptive strategy of recruiting new members into the party. No longer simply a vanguard party of the "three revolutionary classes," that is, peasants, workers, and soldiers, the party now claims to represent advanced productive forces, advanced culture, and the interests of the majority of the Chinese people, the so-called "three represents" (*san ge daibiao* 三个代表). While this effort to relegitimate itself is often derided as window dressing at best and hypocritical at worst, it reflects the party's efforts to adapt itself to the changed economic and social environment in China. At the same time, the CCP continues to suppress other demands for political reform and liberalization, such as the formation of new political parties and independent labor unions, that it perceives as threats to its ruling party status. For the vast majority of Chinese, the political atmosphere is more relaxed and less obtrusive than in the Maoist period, but for political activists who resist the party's authoritarian rule and challenge restrictions on personal and political freedoms, the CCP's hand can still be quite heavy.[3]

In short, the party's strategy of accommodation reflects what Kenneth Jowitt described as the phase of "inclusion" for Leninist regimes.[4] Without surrendering its monopoly on legitimate political organization, the party has attempted to be more inclusive, drawing in a wider range of social groups, reducing its emphasis on its traditional bases of support, and embracing the modernist paradigm while continuing to pay lip-service to the goals of socialism. But it is not open to all groups and goals within Chinese society. It continues to exclude and repress those that pose a challenge to its authority and contest its claims to "benevolence, truth, and national glory," as noted in Vivienne Shue's contribution to this volume (Chapter 2). As Alfred Stepan has argued, a state can pursue a combination of inclusive and exclusive policies at the same time, and that certainly has been the case for the CCP.[5]

This multifaceted nature of the CCP's relationship with Chinese society merits better understanding and appreciation. While coercion and repression remain a part of the political reality in contemporary China, it is only part of the reality. The party has abandoned its attempt to control all aspects of economic and social life, and with the liberalization of the post-Mao era has also relinquished the tools that would allow it to do so.[6] In its place, it has adopted a more flexible approach, permissive in some respects but still repressive in others. The irony is that its efforts at adaptation may in fact be counter-productive. This is the dilemma that political parties and other organizations face when they contemplate reform: will the changes lead to rejuvenation or further decline?

This chapter begins with a discussion of the factors that have allowed the CCP to endure as the ruling party of China. It will then describe the evolution of the party's relationship with society. It will look at changes in party recruitment, which reflect this evolving relationship with society, and its efforts to create new institutional links with certain sectors of society. Following from this, it will then look more closely at the "three represents" slogan, both as a reflection of the party's strategy and as a guide to its policies. Finally, it will briefly discuss areas where the party retains its traditional approach to other sectors, excluding them from the party and repressing their attempts at organized political activity.

Enduring features of party rule

The CCP's continued status as the ruling party of China is based first and foremost on its monopoly on legitimate political organization. Leninist organizational principles prohibit the formation of competing organizations that could challenge the CCP, and the party strictly enforces this prohibition. This was seen most vividly in the refusal to recognize autonomous associations for students and workers in 1989, and has been repeated in its suppression of efforts to form autonomous labor unions, the Chinese Democracy Party, and spiritual and religious groups like the Falun Gong and house churches (see Chapter 2). It also restricts the types of social organizations that are allowed to exist, controls the media to limit the dissemination of unflattering stories of corruption and governance failure, and actively monitors the

Internet for politically suspect content. The inability to organize in opposition to the state and to obtain accurate and timely information significantly raises the cost of collective action and reduces the likelihood of a successful challenge.[7]

The party's survival is not just a result of coercion, however. It has other assets which allow it to remain in power. First of all, the dramatic economic growth rates of the post-Mao era have raised living standards for many Chinese and created new economic opportunities that did not exist in the past. In addition, the goals of the "Reform and Opening" policies also resonate with China's historical pursuit of wealth and power. As China's economic and political status in the international community has risen, so have nationalist sentiments within China. Economic development is clearly one of the sources of the CCP's popular support, but is not the only factor that legitimizes its rule.

A second factor concerns the CCP's historic origins. Although any legitimacy derived from its victory in the 1949 revolution has largely dissipated by now,[8] the CCP still has advantages that many other Leninist parties lacked. Whereas ruling communist parties in Eastern Europe were mostly imposed by the Soviet Union, and therefore lacked legitimacy in the eyes of many of the people they governed, the CCP came to power via an indigenous revolution that ousted a discredited and unpopular government. The CCP was not tainted with the image of an outside occupying force, as was the case for Eastern European parties and even the Kuomintang (KMT) on Taiwan.[9] The result is that it does not have to "sink roots" into society, although it is increasingly concerned about the health and viability of its social roots. While some of the party's policies and practices may not be popular today, it came to power with demonstrable popular support, and is currently able to draw upon different strands of historical traditions to help sustain its rule.

A third factor legitimizing CCP rule is the apparently widespread belief that it is the best and only safeguard against national disunity and political instability. These are prominent and deeply felt fears among both the state and society. Political protest and regime change inevitably entail disruption and uncertainty. The CCP can utilize the cultural preference for stability to discredit those who would challenge its monopoly on power. This is one reason why the CCP has stoked nationalistic feelings throughout society. As Stanley Rosen and Richard Kraus note in Chapters 7 and 9, at a time when it no longer promotes class struggle or other communist goals it can claim to promote nationalistic aspirations, beginning with maintaining national unity and order.

The CCP also enjoys material resources that can engender support. For instance, it is an effective patronage machine. It still controls many key jobs, not just in government but also in the financial and academic worlds. With the privatization of the economy, the CCP may not control as many managerial positions in enterprises as it did before, but its influence is still considerable. Party membership can also smooth access to important resources, such as business and investment opportunities and permission to travel abroad. This is a double-edged sword: while it encourages some people to join to get their slice of the pie, it also contributes to the party's image as a corrupt and self-serving machine with little regard for collective well-being.

Recognizing that the party is the only game in town, and that party membership is beneficial to many career goals, growing numbers of young intellectuals and private entrepreneurs are applying for party membership. This may seem surprising, because they enjoy the educational and entre- preneurial credentials to succeed on their own. While some are unwilling to join the CCP out of principle or a concern that party membership would constrain their options, others are willing to join for practical reasons because membership still provides important privileges, especially for administrative careers.[10] In recent years, the combination of higher learning or entrepreneurial acumen with a party card has tangible benefits for many in professional and business careers. These kinds of people are not the tra- ditional sources of support for the party, but the party recognizes they are necessary partners in its pursuit of economic modernization. The CCP uses the growing number of applications to join the party and the profiles of those who seek admission as evidence of the party's continued popularity. While this may be a self-serving misreading of the data, there is no question that the party continues to grow, from almost 40 million in 1982 to almost 75 million in 2007.

In short, the CCP has remained in power because it enjoys a political monopoly, has been able to achieve remarkable economic development, can draw upon Chinese traditions and foster nationalism, can provide tangible benefits to its members, and successfully attracts new members from the modernizing sectors of Chinese society. These are not static factors, and the CCP has not been passive. As will be seen in the sections below, the CCP has been transforming its organization and its relations with society to adapt itself to the economic and social environment its reforms are bringing about. Its future prospects largely depend on the success of this transformation.

Corporatism and cooptation: the CCP's policies of inclusion

As the CCP entered the post-Mao period, it abandoned the class struggle policies and campaigns that characterized the Maoist era, particularly the Cultural Revolution, in favor of promoting economic modernization. With that shift in the basic work of the party came commensurate changes in the party's organization and its relationship with society. Whereas party recruit- ment and job assignments in the Maoist era had emphasized mobilization skills and political reliability, the new focus on economic modernization put a premium on practical skills and technical know-how for party members and especially for cadres. Beneficiaries of the Cultural Revolution were removed from their posts, and even the victims of the Cultural Revolution were quickly eased into retirement to make way for younger technocrats.[11]

This shift in the party's priorities for its members and key personnel had a dramatic impact. The proportion of party members with high school or higher levels of education rose from 12.8 percent in 1978 to 52.5 percent in 2002. This rise is the result of the CCP's implicit quota in party recruitment: throughout the post-Mao era, roughly two-thirds of new members have at least a high school education. The trend is even more apparent among party elites. In 1982, none of the Politburo members had a university degree; among the 25 Politburo members selected at the 17th Party Congress in 2007, 23 (92 percent) have a university degree. In the CCP's central committee, the percentage of those with college degrees rose from 23.8 in 1969 to 55.5 in 1982 and most recently to 97 in 2007. As the level of education among top party leaders has increased, it has also become more diverse. China's leaders were once thought of as largely "technocrats," with education and professional experience in the hard sciences, engineering, or management. Among the Politburo members selected in 1997, 14 were technocrats and the number rose to 18 in 2002. In the Politburo selected in 2007, however, only 13 were technocrats. Technocrats on the central committee rose from only 2 percent in 1982 to 51 percent in 1997, but then declined to 36 percent in 2007. Instead, backgrounds in social sciences and humanities have become more common: 10 of the Politburo members with university degrees majored in economics, political science, or the humanities.[12]

The most tangible symbol of the party's transformation is the reduction of peasant and worker members. Formerly the mainstay of the party and the basis of its popular support, they now comprise a minority of party members. Their numbers dropped from 83 percent of party members in 1956 to 63 percent in 1994 and to only 42 percent in 2007. This was a drop not only in relative terms, but in absolute numbers as well, from approximately 34 million to 31 million in the years between 1994 and 2007.[13] New recruitment among peasants and workers is not keeping pace with retirements and deaths among existing members. The CCP no longer gives priority to the subordinate classes for whom it fought the revolution – as Dorothy J. Solinger forcefully argues in Chapter 11 on the plight of the urban poor – but instead reaches out to the technological, professional, and entrepreneurial elites that have emerged in the wake of the party's reform and opening policies. As a consequence, the CCP has redefined its relationship with society to reflect its current priorities.

By declaring the end of class struggle at the outset of the post-Mao era, the CCP implied that its relationship with society would be more harmonious. Rather than relying on the familiar Maoist instruments of ideological mobilization and coercion, the party adopted a two-pronged strategy of adaptation: creating new institutions to link state and society, and coopting new elites into the party.[14] The party no longer views society as rife with class enemies determined to overthrow the CCP, but as the source of the talent and ambition needed to modernize the economy. While it continues to suppress those it deems to be threats to the regime, the CCP seeks to cooperate with others who share its economic goals.

The first element of the CCP's new policy of inclusion was the creation of new institutional links with society. Beginning in the 1980s, and accelerating in the 1990s, China experienced the formation of myriad types of social organization, including chambers of commerce, professional associations, sports and hobby clubs, etc.[15] The growing numbers of these organizations have led some observers to speculate about the potential for civil society emerging in China. However, these organizations for the most part do not enjoy the type of autonomy expected of a civil society. Instead, their relationship to the state is more akin to a corporatist perspective: they are sanctioned by the state, are granted a monopoly on the interest they represent, at least in their locality, and many even have party or government officials in their leadership. This corporatist strategy was designed not to abandon party control but to accentuate it with more flexible instruments. As the party reduced its penetration into the daily life of most of its citizens, these organizations replaced the direct and coercive control over society that characterized the Maoist era with more indirect links.

The second element of the CCP's strategy of adaptation was coopting newly emerging social elites, in particular professional and technical elites and private entrepreneurs. Given the party's focus on economic modernization, this was an appropriate strategy. It let the party be connected directly to the kinds of people who were primarily responsible for the growth and modernization of the Chinese economy. The success at recruiting better educated members was noted above. Although the party banned recruiting private entrepreneurs in August 1989, local officials found ways of getting around the ban. In some cases, they claimed the entrepreneurs were managers of individual, collective, or joint stock enterprises and therefore were not, technically speaking, private entrepreneurs. In other cases, local officials simply ignored the ban, arguing that it was unfair to exclude people who were succeeding due to the party's own policies. Because promoting economic growth was a key criterion for evaluating the work performance of local officials, many were eager to cooperate with the entrepreneurs who could provide that growth. As the private sector grew in importance, the percentage of entrepreneurs who belonged to the party grew, from 13 percent in 1993 to 38 percent in 2007. Most of these "red capitalists," however, were already in the party before going into the private sector. Many of the most prominent capitalists are former party and government officials and state-owned enterprise managers. In other words, many of the people in this supposedly new social stratum had their origins in the party and state apparatus.

After the CCP's ban on recruiting entrepreneurs was lifted at the 16th Party Congress in November 2002, the rate of recruitment among entrepreneurs was expected to grow. That did not happen immediately, however. There was no groundswell of entrepreneurs joining the party. Many entrepreneurs were no longer interested in joining the party, due to its corrupt image and doubts about the advantages of party membership. Moreover, the CCP's support for the private sector had become so strong that party membership was less necessary for success in business. In addition, after the party congress, the new leadership of the CCP, especially Hu Jintao and Wen Jiabao, subtly yet significantly shifted the party's focus away from the new elites that Jiang courted in favor of the traditional base of the party. They put less of a priority on courting capitalists, but nevertheless continued the CCP's commitment to the private sector, which now provides the lion's share of economic growth, new jobs, and tax revenue.

This strategy of corporatism and cooptation served to weaken the party's traditional emphasis on party building. It experienced declining recruitment from the "three revolutionary classes" (peasants, workers, and soldiers) and its party organizations in the cities and countryside atrophied. In the mid-1990s, the party declared that half its rural organizations were inactive. An estimated 2.5 million party members joined the "floating population" of migrant workers, further weakening the party's presence in the countryside. Even though the party was recruiting the owners of private enterprises, it was less active in recruiting and organizing workers in the private sector. Of the estimated 1.2 million private enterprises in 1998, less than 1 percent had party organizations and only 14 percent had party members among their workers.[16] Over time, however, party building efforts in the private sector began to grow. By 2007, roughly 30 percent of private firms had party cells and 40 percent had workers who had joined the party in recent years.[17] In short, the party's presence was shrinking in the countryside, where roughly 70 percent of the population still live and work, and gradually increasing in the private sector, the most dynamic part of the Chinese economy. As the party shifted its attention toward new professional, technical, and entrepreneurial elites, its ties to the rest of society were allowed to weaken.

As will be seen on pp. 30–34, however, this shift in the party's work and especially in its recruitment priorities was contested by those in the party who opposed the abandonment of party traditions. While some in the party felt adaptation was necessary for the party's survival and popular legitimacy, others feared that the inclusion of such diverse – and non-proletarian – interests in the party would destroy the party's unity and ultimately lead to its dissolution.

Who does the party represent?

As China's economic reforms have transformed its social structure, leading to the emergence of new elites and potential rivals, the CCP has altered its relationship to society. In the past, the CCP claimed to be the vanguard of the proletariat, but this claim seems quaint in the midst of the rapid marketization of China's economy and the accompanying transformation of its social structure. To remain relevant, the CCP has redefined its relationship with society with the so-called "three represents" slogan: the CCP now represents the advanced productive forces (primarily the growing urban middle class of businessmen, professionals, and high technology specialists), the promotion of advanced culture (as opposed to both "feudalism" and modern materialism), and the interests of the majority of the Chinese people. This concept was first introduced by Jiang Zemin in spring 2000, and then propagated through an extensive media campaign. Its purpose was to offer a new rationale for the CCP's legitimacy. But it was a contentious claim, met with opposition from some in the party and with indifference from much of society.

Jiang unveiled the slogan during his spring 2000 inspection tour of several key economic cities in south China. He visited joint ventures, private enterprises, township and village enterprises, as well as state-owned enterprises, and investigated party building efforts in these different types of firms. In Zhejiang, he met several private entrepreneurs, all of whom reportedly expressed an interest in joining the party but were prohibited from doing so by the party's ban. This experience reportedly helped inspire the "three represents" slogan, because Jiang recognized the party could not represent the estimated 130 million workers in the private sector if private firms did not have party organizations in them.[18]

Jiang Zemin did not change the definition of the proletariat, as Deng Xiaoping had done in 1978 by adding intellectuals to the working class. Instead, he broadened the definition of the party's mass character by incorporating new social strata whose interests were equivalent to those of the working class. The CCP replaced its claim to be the vanguard of the proletariat with a "two vanguards" thesis: it represented the interests of both the working classes (comprising workers, farmers, intellectuals, party and government officials, and those in the military) and the vast majority of the people, especially entrepreneurs, professionals, and high-tech specialists. While this sleight of hand kept the party's propaganda writers busy for years, the careful parsing of the "three represents" slogan and its implications also served to highlight the discrepancy between the ideological needs of the party and China's dynamic society.

Jiang's efforts to popularize his "three represents" slogan were hampered by the party's ban on recruiting entrepreneurs into the party. This ban was enacted in August 1989 out of concern that some entrepreneurs had supported the Tiananmen demonstrators (particularly Wan Runnan, founder of the Stone Corporation) and that the presence of entrepreneurs in the party was compromising its class character. It was not hard to find an ideological rationale to support the ban. Lin Yanzhi, a member of Jilin's provincial party committee, made a succinct argument against coopting entrepreneurs:

> If we allow private entrepreneurs [to join the party], it would create serious conceptual chaos within the party, and destroy the unified foundation

of the political thought of the party that is now united, and destroy the baseline of what the party is able to accommodate in terms of its advanced class nature . . . A pluralistic political party would certainly fragment . . . The party name, the party constitution, and the party platform all would have to be changed . . . Therefore, we not only cannot permit private entrepreneurs to join the party, we must encourage those members of the Communist Party who have already become private entrepreneurs to leave.[19]

While the ban on recruiting entrepreneurs made good ideological sense, it was increasingly out of step with the party's goal of promoting economic development and also with the growing complexity of China's society. If the party was basing its legitimacy largely on economic growth, it made little sense to exclude the people whose success was the result of following the party's policies. Traditional class divisions were also being broken down by economic reform, as workers moved between jobs in the state-owned, collective, and private sectors, and as former farmers, intellectuals, and party and government officials took the chance to "plunge into the sea" (*xiahai* 下海) by opening their own business. As *People's Daily* noted, the new social strata "were originally farmers, intellectuals, managerial personnel of state-owned enterprises, cadres of party and government institutions, scientific and technical personnel, and students who had returned from their studies abroad."[20] As a result, they were said to be different from the capitalists and exploiters of the pre-communist era.[21] Because they were contributing to China's development by following the party's own policies, excluding such people was clearly not in the party's long-term interests.

The coopting of entrepreneurs and other new social strata into the party was not only designed to benefit the party by tapping new sources of support, it was also intended to preempt a potential source of opposition. Jiang Zemin reportedly acknowledged in January 2001 that the party was considering lifting the ban on entrepreneurs, perhaps to prevent them from aligning themselves with the pro-democracy political activists.[22] Along these same lines, Wang Changjiang of the Central Party School argued that if the party did not embrace the vast majority of the Chinese people, they would seek to organize themselves outside the political system. Inclusion was intended, at least in part, to prevent organized opposition to the party, and to maintain political stability and party leadership.

Finally, Jiang Zemin publicly recommended lifting the ban on entrepreneurs in his July 1, 2001 speech marking the eightieth anniversary of the founding of the CCP. In reviewing the consequences of reform and opening policies, he noted that private entrepreneurs, freelance professionals, scientific and technical personnel employed by Chinese and foreign firms, and other new social groups had emerged. "Most of these people in the new social strata have contributed to the development of productive forces and . . . are working to build socialism with Chinese characteristics." While claiming that the workers, farmers, intellectuals, servicemen, and cadres would remain the "basic components and backbone of the party," Jiang claimed the party also needed "to accept those outstanding elements from other sectors of society."[23]

The party's propaganda machine actively promoted Jiang's "three represents" slogan and his recommendation to incorporate China's new social strata into the party. Several themes were prominent in this campaign to square "three represents" with the party's traditions. First, the party claimed its class nature was not determined solely by the economic class of its members. "The practical experience of our party shows that the structure of party membership is related to and to a certain degree influences the party's character. However, it is not the decisive factor affecting the party's character."[24] Historically, workers were never the majority of party members; peasants, intellectuals, soldiers, and students were. Yet they were all said to represent proletarian interests.

Second, the party claimed there was no necessary conflict between its claim to represent both the proletariat and the vast majority of the people. According to this syllogism, because the majority of Chinese are workers and farmers, if the party represents the interests of the majority of the people they thereby represent the interests of workers and farmers. One conclusion from this was that the party could maintain its proletarian class nature even if it recruited from other social strata. Even non-proletarians could allegedly have a proletarian outlook. But what if the other classes wanted to represent their own interests, or those of their professions? Membership in the party would supposedly change those interests:

> Like a big furnace, the party can melt out all sorts of non-proletarian ideas and unify its whole thinking on Marxist theory and the party's program and line. Today, in admitting the outstanding elements from other social strata into the party, so long as we uphold the principle of building the party ideologically and require all party members to join the party ideologically, we will surely be able to preserve the ideological purity of the party members and the advanced nature of the party organizations.[25]

The "three represents" slogan recognized that diverse interests now exist in China, but the rationale used to justify the slogan only legitimated proletarian interests.

A third theme of the "three represents" propaganda campaign was that the party's claim to represent the interests of the majority of the Chinese people was allegedly nothing new. Numerous commentators pointed out that the party passed a resolution asserting that it was the vanguard of both the proletariat and the whole nation at the Wayabao conference in 1935. This is a very weak precedent, however, because it ignores the next sixty-five years of the party's history, and also ignores the historical context of that resolution: the party's appeal to nationalism in the face of Japanese invasion. And despite the claims that the CCP always represented the interests of most

Chinese, the media also emphasized the need to conduct extensive education and training of incumbent cadres and the selection of new cadres on the basis of these claims. Apparently, this party tradition was not clear to all.[26]

Commentators were also careful to distinguish Jiang's call to recruit "the outstanding elements from all social strata into the party" from the reviled concept of a party of the whole people (*quanmindang* 全民党) first advanced by Nikita Khrushchev. The distinction is that not all people in each stratum deserve to join the party, just the truly outstanding ones who also meet the other criteria of party membership. Wang Changjiang of the Central Party School made this point most clearly:

> When the party expands its social foundation to various social strata and groups, it doesn't mean that all the people in these strata and groups can join the party . . . What we want to absorb are the outstanding elements of these strata and groups. Possessing the political consciousness of the working class and willingness to fight for the party's program constitutes the common characteristics of these outstanding elements and also the qualifications they must meet in order to join the party . . . There is no connection between this kind of party and the so-called "a party of all the people."[27]

In a journal for party cadres, he argued that "since the elements [i.e., party members] influence the nature of the party *to some extent*, we cannot just throw open the doors of the party and welcome everyone . . . Allowing entrepreneurs into the party is not the same as saying that any entrepreneur can join the party."[28] Other party media repeated this warning. According to *People's Daily*, "We allow the worthy people in the new social strata to join the party. However, this does not mean that we keep our doors wide open in an unprincipled manner. Still less should we drag into the party all those who do not meet our requirements for party membership."[29] The CCP journal *Qiushi* (求是) advised against "using erroneous methods to measure the new criteria for party membership, such as admission based on economic strength, on the amount of donation to society, and on personal reputation."[30] These easily determined criteria – as opposed to the more abstract considerations of supporting the party's program and "standing the test of time" – were undoubtedly the ones used by many local committees in recruiting from the new social strata.

The 16th Party Congress adopted the "three represents" slogan as a basic doctrine and revised the party constitution accordingly, adding it to the ideological pantheon along with Marxism–Leninism–Mao Zedong Thought and Deng Xiaoping Theory. This symbolized the party's embrace of the new social strata and the party's pro-business orientation. After the fourth generation of leaders, led by Hu Jintao and Wen Jiabao, replaced Jiang Zemin and the other third generation leaders, the themes of the Jiang era were quietly but quickly abandoned. Whereas Jiang placed priority on achieving a "relatively prosperous society" by courting the advanced productive forces, Hu and Wen promoted the need for a "harmonious society" that would promote the interests of the vast majority of the people. Their concern was less for the economic elites that Jiang courted and more for the people and regions of the country that had not yet benefited from the rapid growth of the 1990s. Jiang's focus on urban and coastal China had succeeded in achieving rapid growth, but also contributed to the growing individual and regional inequality and resentment among those who felt they were being left behind. The cozy relationship between local officials and capitalists also led to corrupt deals and illegal land-grabs that further antagonized the people who were forced out of their homes and fields for the sake of new commercial and industrial developments. These tensions led to increased political instability: between 1999 and 2005, the number of protests throughout the country grew from 39,000 to 87,000. To address these popular concerns, the CCP began a new program to raise living standards in the less developed areas. It began sending income subsidies directly to rural residents and increased public investment in inland and western provinces to promote their development. In short, Hu and Wen abandoned the elitist strategy of the Jiang era for a more populist orientation.[31] Nevertheless, they remained committed to the continued expansion of the private sector. They preferred a more balanced pattern of growth, but above all they favored rapid growth, and the private sector was the engine of that growth. They did not attempt to slow the pace of development, but to adopt policies that would ameliorate some of the imbalances that were the direct if unintended consequences of growth.

The continued exclusion of unsanctioned claims

As noted on pp. 24–26, the CCP makes several claims to legitimate its continued status as China's ruling party. Its ability to promote prosperity, raise living standards, guard against instability, and champion nationalistic aspirations is the basis of its claim to represent the common interests of most Chinese and define "truth, benevolence, and glory." But legitimacy alone cannot preserve the CCP's hold on power. In particular, basing its legitimacy on economic performance is risky; the inevitable economic downturn, as began in late 2008, would threaten to de-legitimate it, and its claim to rule would be jeopardized. In addition, as Adam Przeworski has noted, it is not legitimacy that keeps an authoritarian regime in power, but the absence of a preferable (and, we should add, viable) alternative.[32] Following that rationale, the CCP also strives to prevent the emergence of a viable alternative, whether that be autonomous unions, an opposition party, or an organized dissident movement. The CCP's implicit strategy is to increase the cost of collective action by arresting political and labor activists and keeping most social organizations dependent on the state for their survival and success. In the process, it aims to prevent the emergence of a "critical realm" of civil society and prevent it from making claims on the state.[33]

The success of this strategy is seen in the nature of protest in China today. Rural protests are typically parochial in nature, directed against immediate grievances without demands for political change or attempts at coordination with neighboring communities.[34] As the research of Kevin J. O'Brien and Lianjiang Li in this volume (Chapter 4) and elsewhere has shown, rural protests can be successful if they are limited to "rightful resistance," that is, challenging the local implementation of policy, but not the propriety of the policy itself.[35] Complaints against excessive taxes and fees, unpaid IOU's for grain purchases by the state, uncompensated land seizures, improper implementation of local elections, and cadre corruption can often be successful if they are framed as violations of central policy, not simply unjust, and if they can get the attention of higher level officials or the media. But even as it addresses specific complaints, the CCP is reluctant to let its concessions in one incident become a precedent for others. It limits media coverage of local protests and their resolution, and punishes activists who spread news about successful protest tactics from one community to the next, advise protestors on their legal rights, and help them pursue their claims. The CCP will accommodate isolated protests, especially those with material as opposed to political demands, but will not tolerate organized collective action.

Those engaged in labor protests are normally careful not to be well organized, lest their leaders be identified and arrested. In most cases, protests are limited to bread and butter issues: unpaid wages, stolen pensions, harsh working conditions, and so forth. Rarely do they venture into political issues, such as demanding a change of leaders or the creation of new unions. To do so would doom them to immediate repression.[36] Large scale labor unrest in spring 2002 in several industrial cities was an exception to this rule, and those who broke the rule paid a heavy price. In Liaoyang, workers called for the ouster of the city's leader. In both Daqing and Liaoyang, workers chosen as leaders of the protest were quickly identified, isolated, and arrested. Local leaders resolved the conflicts with a combination of carrot and stick, recognizing the legitimate nature of the economic demands but ignoring the political issues and punishing the workers who played a leadership role. While in custody, some of the labor leaders reportedly betrayed their fellow prisoners to protect themselves or their families. After their release, the solidarity that led tens of thousands of workers to protest in the streets turned to suspicion.[37] As the economy began to slow in 2008, many private factories closed and their owners fled, leaving behind vast numbers of workers who were owed back wages and inclined to protest to get what they were owed. Even though the closed firms were privately owned, local governments stepped in to pay at least a portion of what workers were owed to maintain the peace.[38] From the state's perspective, the resolution of these protests was generally positive. The protests ended with minimal violence, the costs of the settlement would likely be compensated by the central government, and, as in the 2002 protests, the atmosphere of mistrust among the workers would make future collective action less likely. These episodes demonstrate the elements that make sustained social movements, as opposed to sporadic local protests, so difficult in China: the coercive power of the state, the absence of autonomous organizations, the difficulty of protestors communicating and coordinating effectively, and low levels of interpersonal trust, especially as the stakes begin to rise.

Similarly, even activists on non-political issues are reluctant to organize themselves to engage in collective action lest they arouse the insecurities of the state and risk repression. A case in point is the environmental movement. Most people recognize that pollution of all types – air, water, land, noise, light – is a severe and growing problem in China, and yet non-governmental environmental organizations are largely limited to public education on the importance of a clean environment rather than advocacy of tighter regulations and improved implementation.[39] A movement on college campuses to ban the use of disposable chopsticks faced the dilemma of how to succeed in this collective action without suffering retaliation for being too well organized. As a consequence, its actions on various campuses were largely informal and uncoordinated.[40]

Conclusion

Although economic modernization has not yet changed China's political system, it may be changing the party. The diversification of classes and the fluidity of China's social structure is leading the party to change who it recruits and who it claims to represent. This is not quite equivalent to pluralism, because the party does not allow fully autonomous interest groups or opposition parties. The CCP still retains its political monopoly, but tries to be more inclusive and therefore more representative. But the idea that the party can represent the vast majority of the people may expose it to even greater criticism and cynicism. The notion that a single party can properly represent the diverse social forces in China is odd, especially from a Western perspective of a society made up of diverse interests. These interests need not be incompatible, but they normally desire, even demand, their own organization to represent their interests toward the state and not grant that responsibility to a vanguard party.

One key to the party's survival is its Leninist foundation. The CCP is monolithic neither in its relationship with society nor in its attitude toward adaptation. Instead, it has forged multi-dimensional relationships, depending on the sector of the society, how it fits into the party's modernization strategy, and the nature of its claims. Even though the party has abandoned its efforts to monitor and control all of society, it still protects its monopoly on legitimate political organization. Not all interests are able to organize themselves, and some groups, such as farmers, are not allowed any organizations at all, not even officially sponsored mass organizations like the All-China Women's Federation or the All-China Federation of Trade Unions.

The merits and logic of this multi-dimensional relationship have also been contested within the party. Some argue it is necessary to preserve the party's right to rule and promote its economic program. Others argue it is a betrayal of the party's traditions and raison d'être. Rather than bolstering the party's legitimacy, critics allege the party's policies of inclusion will undermine the party's authority, both by abandoning its traditional bases of support and by admitting new members who are likely to further divert the party from its original mission and dilute its organizational coherence.

Nevertheless, the CCP is confronted with numerous challenges from an increasingly restive society. Its reform and opening policies have achieved dramatic and sustained growth rates, but for many the benefits of growth have been offset by a host of problems. The seemingly unstoppable spread of corruption de-legitimates the party. In some areas, local party and government officials are seen as in cahoots with organized crime, or indistinguishable from it. Throughout the post-Mao era, but especially in the 1990s and into the early twenty-first century, rapid growth has been accompanied by rising inequality. Privatization of the economy has created vast numbers of newly unemployed workers, many too old and lacking the requisite skills to find new jobs in the private sector. Laid off from their old jobs and without the benefits of a welfare system, they rightly feel betrayed by a system that formerly promised them lifetime security. Decollectivization of agriculture and the decline of incomes in the countryside have compelled tens of millions of rural workers to migrate to the cities in search of work. The spread of modern values, international influences, and the logic of the marketplace undermine the party's ability to define the policy agenda and control the flow of information for the nation at large. The party's limited policies of corporatism and cooptation are unlikely to meet these challenges successfully, and the "three represents" and "Harmonius Society" slogans are equally unlikely to provide a suitable response.

Under the leadership of Hu Jintao and Wen Jiabao, the CCP has moved in a more populist direction. Rather than simply promoting rapid growth, it has attempted to distribute the benefits of growth more evenly. But even with this change in orientation, the CCP remains committed to defending its monopoly on political power. It does not tolerate organized opposition and works to limit access to the coordination goods that would make collective action more feasible. To fully understand the survivability of the CCP, its organizational adaptability, sources of popular support, and coercive powers must all be part of the equation.

Notes

1 This is a revised and updated version of an essay that was first published in the *American Asian Review* 21(1) (Spring 2003), pp. 1–24. I would like to thank the journal's editors for granting permission to use material in the original essay for this chapter.

2 Andrew J. Nathan, "Authoritarian Resilience," *Journal of Democracy* 14(1) (January 2003), pp. 6–17; David Shambaugh, *China's Communist Party: Atrophy and Adaptation* (Berkeley and Washington, DC: University of California Press and Woodrow Wilson Center Press, 2008).

3 This distinction between economic and political demands is derived from Yanqi Tong and Gordon White, Jude Howell, and Shang Xiaoyuan, who make similar distinctions about the different dynamics and sectors of civil society. See Tong, "State, Society, and Political Change in China and Hungary," *Comparative Politics* 26(3) (April 1994), pp. 333–53, and White *et al.*, *In Search of Civil Society: Market Reform and Social Change in Contemporary China* (Oxford: Oxford University Press, 1996).

4 Jowitt, "Inclusion," in *New World Disorder: The Leninist Extinction* (Berkeley: University of California Press, 1992), pp. 88–120.

5 Alfred C. Stepan, *The State and Society: Peru in Comparative Perspective* (Princeton: Princeton University Press, 1978).

6 Andrew G. Walder, "The Decline of Communist Power: Elements of a Theory of Institutional Change," *Theory and Society* 23(2) (April 1994), pp. 297–323.

7 Sidney Tarrow, *Power in Movement: Social Movements and Contentious Politics*, 2nd edn. (New York: Cambridge University Press, 1998); Bruce Bueno de Mesquita and George W. Downs, "Development and Democracy," *Foreign Affairs* 84(5) (September/October 2005), pp. 77–86.

8 Wang Zhengxu, "Political Trust in China: Forms and Causes," in Lynn T. White, ed., *Legitimacy: Ambiguities of Political Success or Failure in East and Southeast Asia* (Singapore: World Scientific, 2005); Bruce Gilley, "Legitimacy and Institutional Change: The Case of China," *Comparative Political Studies* 41(3) (March 2008), pp. 259–84.

9 Tun-jen Cheng, "Democratizing the Quasi-Leninist Regime on Taiwan," *World Politics* 41(4) (July 1989), pp. 471–99; Bruce J. Dickson, *Democratization in China and Taiwan: The Adaptability of Leninist Parties* (Oxford and New York: Oxford University Press, 1997).

10 Andrew G. Walder, "Career Mobility and the Communist Political Order," *American Sociological Review* 60(3) (June 1995), pp. 309–28; Bruce J. Dickson and Maria Rost Rublee, "Membership Has Its Privileges: The Socioeconomic Characteristics of Communist Party Members in Urban China," *Comparative Political Studies* 33(1) (February 2000), pp. 87–112; Walder, Bobai Li, and Donald J. Treiman, "Politics and Life Chances in a State Socialist Regime: Dual Career Paths into the Urban Chinese Elite, 1949 to 1996," *American Sociological Review* 65(2) (April 2000), pp. 191–209.

11 Hong Yung Lee, *From Revolutionary Cadres to Party Technocrats in Socialist China* (Berkeley: University of California Press, 1991); Melanie Manion, *Retirement of Revolutionaries in China: Public Policies, Social Norms, Private Interests* (Princeton: Princeton University Press, 1993).

12 The changing characteristics of party elites are drawn from Dickson, *Democratization in China and Taiwan*, pp. 135 and 147; Cheng Li, *China's Leaders: The New Generation* (Lanham, MD: Rowman and Littlefield, 2001), p. 41; and biographical data taken from *China Vitae* (www.chinavitae.com).

13 Lee, *From Revolutionary Cadres to Party Technocrats*, p. 56; Dickson, *Democratization in China and Taiwan*, p. 152; "Number of CPC Members Rises to 73 Million," 17th National Congress of the Communist Party of China Press Center, accessed athttp://english.cpcnews.cn/92247/6279373.html.

14 The following analysis is based on my *Wealth into Power: The Communist Party's Embrace of China's Private Sector* (New York: Cambridge University Press, 2008).

15 Minxin Pei, "Chinese Civic Associations: An Empirical Analysis," *Modern China* 24(3) (July 1998), pp. 285–318; Tony Saich, "Negotiating the State: The Development of Social Organizations in China," *China Quarterly*, no. 161 (March 2000), pp. 124–41.
16 *Renmin ribao*, September 12, 2000, p. 11.
17 Jie Chen and Bruce J. Dickson, *Allies of the State: The Political Beliefs of China's Private Entrepreneurs* (Cambridge: Harvard University Press, 2010).
18 You Dehai, "The Background of the Launch of the 'Three Represents,'" *Xuexi yu shijian* (Wuhan), September 2000, pp. 18–20, 45; the author was president of the party school in Wuhan. See also Xinhua, February 25, 2000, in FBIS (Foreign Broadcast Information Service), February 29, 2000.
19 Lin Yanzhi, "How the Communist Party Should 'Lead' the Capitalist Class," *Shehui Kexue Zhanxian* (Social Science Battlefront), June 20, 2001, translated in FBIS, July 14, 2001. This article, written by a deputy party secretary of the Jilin Provincial Party Committee, was originally published in the May issue of *Zhenli de zhuiqiu*.
20 *Renmin ribao*, September 17, 2001, in FBIS, September 17, 2001.
21 "Reviewing the 'Three Points' of Deng Xiaoping," *Liaowang*, November 12, 2001, in FBIS, November 20, 2001.
22 Kyodo News International, January 15, 2001.
23 Jiang's speech was carried by Xinhua, July 1, 2001, in FBIS, July 1, 2001. See also John Pomfret, "China Allows Its Capitalists to Join Party: Communists Recognize Rise of Private Business," *Washington Post*, July 2, 2001; Craig S. Smith, "China's Leader Urges Opening Communist Party to Capitalists," *New York Times*, July 2, 2001.
24 *Qiushi*, November 16, 2001, in FBIS, November 29, 2001.
25 *Jiefangjun bao*, August 15, 2001, in FBIS, August 15, 2001.
26 See for example *Qiushi*, June 1, 2001; *Renmin ribao*, December 2, 2001, p. 1, in FBIS, December 3, 2001.
27 *Liaowang*, August 13, 2001, in FBIS, August 22, 2001.
28 *Zhongguo Dangzheng Ganbu Luntan* (Beijing), January 6, 2002, in FBIS, February 4, 2002; emphasis added.
29 *Renmin ribao*, September 17, 2001, in FBIS, September 17, 2001.
30 *Qiushi*, November 16, 2001, in FBIS, November 29, 2001.
31 Bruce J. Dickson, "Beijing's Ambivalent Reformers," *Current History* 103(674) (September 2004), pp. 249–55; Cheng Li, "The New Bipartisanship within the Chinese Communist Party," *Orbis* 49(3) (summer 2005), pp. 387–400; Barry Naughton, "China's Left Tilt: Pendulum Swing or Midcourse Correction?" in Cheng Li, ed., *China's Changing Political Landscape: Prospects for Democracy* (Washington, DC: Brookings, 2008).
32 Adam Przeworski, "Some Problems in the Transition to Democracy," in Guillermo O'Donnell, Philippe C. Schmitter, and Laurence Whitehead, eds., *Transitions from Authoritarian Rule, vol. 3: Comparative Perspectives* (Baltimore: Johns Hopkins University Press, 1986).
33 "Critical realm" is Yanqi Tong's term to describe the political or dissident portion of civil society which poses a threat to the state, in contrast to the "non-critical realm," which refers to economic and professional activities that do not necessarily threaten the state and may even be welcomed and encouraged by it. White, Howell, and Shang make a similar distinction between the "political dynamic" and "market dynamic" of civil society. See Tong, "State, Society, and Political Change in China and Hungary," and White *et al.*, *In Search of Civil Society*.
34 Thomas P. Bernstein and Xiaobo Lu, *Taxation without Representation in Contemporary Rural China* (New York: Cambridge University Press, 2003).

35 Lianjiang Li and Kevin J. O'Brien, *Rightful Resistance in Rural China* (New York: Cambridge University Press, 2006).
36 See Ching Kwan Lee, "Pathways of Labor Insurgency," in Elizabeth J. Perry and Mark Selden, eds., *Chinese Society: Change, Conflict, and Resistance* (London and New York: Routledge, 2001), pp. 41–61, and "Is Labor a Political Force in China?" in Elizabeth J. Perry and Merle Goldman, eds., *Grassroots Political Reform in Contemporary China* (Cambridge: Harvard University Press, 2007), pp. 228–52.
37 Philip P. Pan, *Out of Mao's Shadow: The Struggle for the Soul of a New China* (New York: Simon and Schuster, 2008), pp. 113–46.
38 Ariana Eunjung Cha, "As China's Jobless Numbers Mount, Protests Grow Bolder: Economic Woes Shining a Light On Social Issues," *Washington Post*, January 13, 2009, p. A07.
39 Elizabeth Economy, *The Rivers Runs Black: The Environmental Challenge to China's Future* (Cornell University Press, 2005).
40 Philip P. Pan, "China's Chopsticks Crusade," *Washington Post*, February 6, 2001.

2 Legitimacy crisis in China?[1]

Vivienne Shue

Stability, no less than revolution, may have its own kind of Terror.

(E.P. Thompson)[2]

At the turn of the twenty-first century, the strenuous conditions of social existence in China offered up plenty of cause for popular protest. The further dismantling of the old socialist system, the deepening marketization of economic relations, and the startling redistributions of property rights were all contributing to social change and disruptions on a grand scale. Tens of thousands of state-sector workers were being laid off from their jobs without adequate benefits and without much prospect of re-employment. Tens of millions of poor migrant laborers, many of them still children, were streaming into the cities from rural areas to compete for jobs, but were left more or less entirely to fend for themselves, and could survive, often, only by enduring appalling living and working conditions. Those who opted to stay on the land, and they amounted still to a majority of the total population, were frequently denied a fair price for their crops even as they were too often subject to brutally inequitable tax assessments and other arbitrary levies by local officials. The poverty became so desperate in some rural areas that medical investigators sent back reports about whole villages full of people, many dying of AIDS, who had become infected with HIV when they had resorted to selling their own blood to survive. Women of childbearing age all over the country lived under relentless, sometimes vicious, official insistence that they limit their pregnancies even as they had to endure, for all that, painful family pressures to produce more sons. Artists and intellectuals, becoming ever more enmeshed in corrosively commodified relations of creative work and production, were at the same time still denied full freedom of expression, and remained subject to the rigors of a system of state censorship which, though it was clearly eroding, could nonetheless exert itself in ways that ranged from risibly obtuse to odiously oppressive. Ethnic minority groups with grievances against the Party and the state were subject to wary official surveillance and were still denied meaningful opportunities to express their views in public. Thus, nearly voiceless, minority peoples in the western regions of the country looked on in mounting anger and frustration as incoming waves of Han migrant settlers threatened to engulf them in their own homelands. Meanwhile, massive damage to China's natural environment – to the air, to the water, to the forests, and to the land – the effects of pesticide mismanagement and of over-rapid and under-regulated processes of industrialization and urbanization, literally sickened the brains and bodies of many unwitting victims and threatened the health and safety of millions more.

There is abundant evidence that, throughout the decade of the 1990s, numerous episodes of popular protest against such conditions of life did in fact take place in China – protests often directly aimed against state policies, state practices, and state officials.[3] Work stoppages, sit-ins, tax refusals, complaint petitions, public demonstrations, suicides meant to shame officials into action, riots, terror bombings, and an even richer repertoire, licit and illicit, of more covert measures of resistance and evasion have all been reported over recent years and on up to the present. Most of these actions have remained local or otherwise limited in scope, however. The police, the secret police, the military, and the civil official hierarchies, ever watchful, have all worked hard to contain such incidents, defusing crises when necessary with some measured concessions, and decapitating in embryo as many groups or units as they deemed might develop into the organizational skeletons for larger-scale collective actions. Thus, in China since that paroxysm of state violence on June 4, 1989, we have seen many popular protests, some limited protest "waves" perhaps, but no major social movements – no sustained movement of popular opposition from workers, migrants, poor farmers, women, students, intellectuals, ethnic minorities, or environmentalists. No opposition movement, that is, until (of all things) Falun Gong.

Falun Gong: history and heresy

In the spring of 1999, near Zhongnanhai,[4] a throng (estimated at something over 10,000 – not a tremendously large number in the Chinese context) of *qigong* meditation practitioners staged a mostly silent and composed, cross-legged, one-day sit-in. They were protesting having been slandered and harassed for their beliefs by a few secular-science activist intellectuals and publicists and some municipal government officials in Tianjin who were apparently trying to dissuade young people from the practice of *qigong*.[5] This dramatically resolute, peaceful "appeal" to the government for a redress of grievances apparently so shocked and surprised state leaders that they hurriedly launched an intensive investigation of the Falun Gong group and its leader, Li Hongzhi. Less than two months later, after the investigation was completed, top officials declared Falun Gong to be an "heretical sect," and its believers and their activities to constitute nothing less than a fearful and profound threat to China's social peace and stability. They banned the group, then ordered and relentlessly carried out a nationwide campaign to dissolve its network of teachers and disciples and to discredit Li Hongzhi and his followers. The official assertion that this previously nearly unheard-of group of non-violent, mystic, popular religionists, who liked to gather in public parks to practice their meditation exercises, posed a threat of the gravest kind to social order, peace, and political stability in the country seemed incongruous to many.[6] Yet precisely that claim formed the ultimate basis and the justification for the reign of terror that ensued. And the state's campaign of suppression – which still goes on – has been so intense, so embittered, and so harsh as to have shocked and surprised, in its turn, numerous observers in the West.[7] With so many other structural reform crises and plausibly pressing causes for protest on the social agenda in China these days, few of us working in the field would have been likely to predict ahead of time that the first serious social protest movement to challenge the authority of the state since Tiananmen would crystallize around issues of spirituality, *qigong* meditation, and mystic syncretism.[8] But should we all have been taken quite so much by surprise?

As the Falun Gong events unfolded, students of modern Chinese history naturally pointed to some of the more obvious past parallels. Syncretic popular religious sects and secret societies have been implicated more than once before in challenging state power and provoking political crises in China. White Lotus rebels shook the last dynasty at the end of the eighteenth century; the armies of the Taiping Heavenly Kingdom nearly brought the sagging dynasty down in the middle of the nineteenth; and the bloody violence of the Boxers contributed both directly and indirectly to the final collapse of the Qing at the beginning of the twentieth.[9] The implication that was meant to be drawn by those who reacted to the Falun Gong phenomenon first of all by pointing out the historical parallels was plain enough. Contemporary Chinese leaders, it can be presumed, know their own history; or at least they have been taught some version of it. When, to their horrified astonishment, in the closing hours of the twentieth century, they discover budding in their very midst what appears to them to be a cult-like sect of popular religionists who practice curious healing exercises, who meditate with the aim of acquiring certain supernormal powers, and who use millennial-sounding language, a sect complete with a charismatic teacher for a leader, whose actual organizational base may be rudimentary but who claims to have millions of followers – well, the historical resonances in all of that are just too rich to be ignored. Such a group, however much it may insist that its motives are benignly apolitical, must, by these facts alone, be counted as a political threat, because groups like it have effectively threatened sitting states in China before and have brought chaos and instability in their wake.[10] Everyone who has been taught even a little bit about China's modern history knows what such groups have been capable of in the past. Thus, the chilling warning to people in power contained in that single Falun Gong demonstration, the insinuation of the possibility of potentially devastating social insubordination, was palpably and directly intelligible to any Chinese, however meekly it may have been delivered by middle-aged ladies milling around in padded jackets.

Still, pointing in this fashion to historical parallels, however correctly drawn and symbolically potent they may be, can take us only part of the way toward understanding. History does not, as we know, simply repeat itself. An association with what was powerful once in the past need not prove powerful today. The governing apparatus in China has changed profoundly since late-imperial times, for one thing. It has far greater organizational capacity and control over domestic affairs than could possibly have been commanded by the precariously overextended late-Qing civil and military hierarchies that were so badly rocked by sectarian rebellion in earlier times. And Chinese society has changed profoundly as well. People in China who are attracted, for their health and general well-being, to *qigong* meditation regimens and the like nowadays get their lessons from cassette tapes and videos or from the Internet, and they schedule their meetings with one another via cell phones. Though in some ways their beliefs and actions may be plainly reminiscent of past social protest movements, the mental and the material worlds that today's Falun Gong practitioners inhabit are not by any means the same as those of the Boxers or the White Lotus rebels. Comprehending the symbolic politics of the present in light of what is known and remembered about the past, thinking as Charles Tilly has taught us, in terms of an only-very-slowly evolving repertoire of protest,[11] can indeed help us to understand why certain distinctive political modes and tactics keep seeming to reappear within a society, even as they are also updated to meet the needs of changing times. Yet there would seem to be, even beyond this important insight, a still more fundamental issue waiting to be considered. Why was it that China was prone to produce precisely this form of popular protest in the first place? And why is it that rather than appearing merely as a quaint anachronism, this form of protest can be made so salient in the present moment? What is it about popular transcendental spiritual sects that makes them such a good mode for the expression of oppositionist sentiment in Chinese politics? Or, to turn the question around, what has it been about the systems of authority and domination that have arisen in China that has provoked opposition in the form of mystic religious sects and movements?

The logic of legitimation (and opposition)

As Max Weber observed, different systems of domination deploy different logics for the legitimation of their rule. And the specific logics of legitimation that are advanced have consequences for the concrete forms of compliance that are required of citizens and subjects, as well as for the forms of political contention that arise in different societies. As Weber succinctly summarized this basic insight:

> every . . . system [of domination] attempts to establish and to cultivate the belief in its legitimacy. But according to the kind of legitimacy which is claimed, the type of obedience, the kind of administrative staff developed to guarantee it, and the mode of exercising authority, will all differ fundamentally.[12]

And as more contemporary students of political authority and contention, such as E.P. Thompson and Jim Scott, have further made clear, the very bases on which claims to legitimacy are advanced provide "the raw material for contradictions and conflict" in a society.[13] Scott, for example, has argued that

> the very process of attempting to legitimate a social order by idealizing it . . . provides its subjects with the means, the symbolic tools, the very ideas for a critique . . . For most purposes, then, it is not at all necessary for subordinate classes to set foot outside the confines of the ruling ideals in order to formulate a critique of power.[14]

Or, to put it another way, embedded in the very logic of legitimation advanced by a system of domination we can find the grammar that may be used most effectively by citizens and subjects in making statements in opposition and in resistance to that system.[15] The legitimacy of most systems of domination is subject to continuous contestation. This is a point to which we will return. For the moment, I wish to argue only that by examining closely the specific grounds on which the legitimacy of a system is alleged, we will better appreciate why it is that certain kinds of counter-allegations – particular forms of opposition and protest – are the ones that can be used most potently against that system. Let us consider, then, what have been the main claims made in Chinese logics of legitimation.

Looking at the present regime, many analysts would surely be tempted to offer the opinion that the Chinese state's main claims to legitimacy rest in its economic achievements, in an improving standard of living, in "growth," or in "development." Some such working assumption about state legitimation is frequently made in both journalistic and scholarly writing on China these days. The pressing question that starting from just such an assumption inevitably leads analysts to pose then becomes: "What if the Chinese economy cannot keep on growing at its recent unprecedented rates? What legitimacy would the government in power then have left?" But this approach to the matter, in my view, is seriously flawed. For while recognizing that steady economic growth or the lack of it may well act as an important conditioning factor influencing the popularity of a government, we also know beyond doubt that economic success alone is neither a necessary nor a sufficient condition for political legitimacy.

In China, furthermore, it is important to note that now, more than ever in recent memory, central state authorities are ill positioned to claim direct credit for whatever economic advances are in fact taking place. The heart of the post-Mao reform project, after all, has been to pry away what is figured as the "dead hand" of central state planning from its stranglehold on the economy. Since the reforms first got underway in earnest in 1978, much of the responsibility for economic development has been reallocated away from central power-holders. It has settled in two quite different quarters. First, economic responsibility now resides much more in communities, localities, and at lower levels of the governing apparatus, since these units have been given far greater resources and broader discretion with which to craft and pursue localized strategies of growth and development, or not.[16] And second, of course, under the post-Mao reforms, much more power has been granted to (or is now exerted through) the workings of markets. The vaunted magic and the notorious vagaries of markets now account for much more of the actual economic growth and change that take place in China than was the case before. And this new reality serves even further to obscure the question of who might rightly take the credit for growth – or take the blame for economic failure. As legitimate responsibility for the economy has been dispersed and, to some extent, obfuscated in this way, so we have seen that popular protests arising out of the economic and social pain of the transition in China have likewise been dispersed. Suffering state-sector workers and peasants have been prone to frame their protests in localized and limited ways, taking as their protest targets not the architects of central reform policy but local "bad" officials, "incompetent" firm managers, and "heartless" employers. The combined effects of decentralization and marketization have worked to the advantage of the central state, then, making it somewhat easier for the center to contain and quell those protests that have arisen while simultaneously sustaining its own appearance of legitimacy.[17]

This is not to say that central authorities either can or would even want to wash their hands entirely of responsibility for economic performance. Official trumpeting of glowing statistics remains a part of the trappings of rule in China now, as it was under Mao. But central state responsibility for the economy has now become once-removed from what used to be called "the production front." Beijing authorities claim a kind of credit only for their excellent and enlightened general policies (*zhengce* 政策) today – policies that permit and encourage the economy to flourish. *The maintenance of the conditions in which the economy does develop and the people do enjoy more prosperity* – this, I believe, comes much closer to capturing the actual core of the contemporary Chinese state's claims to rule legitimately. What, then, are held to be the general conditions the maintenance of which will most likely produce such happy effects? Those conditions are, in a word, the conditions of *stability* – the conditions of social peace and order. The present regime stakes its legitimacy, as I read it, not on its technical capacity to steer and to grow the economy, but on its political capacity to preserve a peaceful and stable social order under which, among other good things, the economy can be expected to grow.

Deconstructing stability: the ideals of Truth, Benevolence, and Glory

The idea that good government is about taking responsibility for maintaining harmony with the natural cosmos and peace in the social order has an ancient genealogy in China – a genealogy far too long and too subtle to be traced to its earliest sources here.[18] Fortunately, however, the work of H. Lyman Miller, on the later imperial era, can provide us with a more manageable historical starting point for considering the role that ideas about order and stability had, by that time, come to play in Chinese political thought:

> China in the late imperial period was governed by a bureaucratic monarchy. The seat of political authority resided in the person of the emperor. The emperor's purview was in principle comprehensive, and so his pronouncements were authoritative in every arena of human thought and action . . . His authority was legitimated by a Confucian cosmology that placed him at the pivot between the cosmic natural order and the human social order – the "Son of Heaven" . . . [T]he emperor's character and behavior – particularly his observance of proper rituals and ceremonies – and by extension the ethical conduct of the officials of his regime ensured harmony between and within the natural and social orders. If the emperor's character was upright, if he performed the proper rites, and if his administration was just, then peace and order would prevail . . . By the same token, deficiencies of the emperor and his government in any of these respects could be expected to bring disorder in the natural and social worlds: floods, droughts, earthquakes . . . in the former, and social disorder and rebellion in the latter. In hindsight, the collapse of a dynastic house and its replacement by another could be understood and so legitimated in terms of this moralistic cosmology.[19]

In the long tradition of Chinese statecraft that endured into the early part of the twentieth century, the legitimacy of a sitting government was linked to the preservation of social order and this, in turn, was linked to the emperor's and his bureaucrats' true knowledge of and participation in a moralistic cosmology, an ethical science of the universe encompassing both its human and its natural elements. Rule was legitimated first and foremost by the ruler's claim to possess this true knowledge, as this knowledge was revealed through study and learning, through divination, and through the perfection of certain arts and sciences such as music and astronomy. Governance that was legitimate was also conceived as suffused with ethical goodness which expressed itself in the magnanimity of the emperor and his officials. Good government was characterized by benevolence – by taking responsibility for the welfare of the people and showing a degree of compassionate care for them. Good government – legitimate rule that was based on true knowledge of the universe and characterized by humane benevolence – was, furthermore, itself taken to be the embodiment and the exemplification of the very superiority and glory of the Sinic culture. The best rulers and officials, those who governed in accord with universal truths and manifested the proper benevolence toward their subjects, might hope and expect to preside over a stable and harmonious order, and the very florescence of economy, the arts, and of philosophy that would emanate from such an enviable order would, in turn, engender awe on the part of all those who beheld it, and would thereby further glorify the Sinic civilization and all the lands and peoples under the sway of the empire.

Thus, three of the key components in the logic of legitimation and the pursuit of harmony and stability were Truth, Benevolence, and Glory. These three do not constitute an "exhaustive list" of all the possible elements of state legitimation in imperial times. They were, I think it safe to say, however, certainly among the most important constitutive concepts in the complex constellation of Chinese thought relating to state power and to legitimacy.[20] China's imperial rulers diligently made great display of their own and their court's earnest pursuit of these very high ideals. Emperors maintained whole academies of learned scholars and scientists, for example, dedicated to searching out the natural and the ethical truths embedded in the way of the cosmos. Armed with the moral truths discovered through study and self-cultivation, the entire apparatus of the Chinese state went on to take "moral instruction as a basic aspect of rule," and "aimed to shape the education of both elites and common people."[21] The goal of the imperial state was not merely to discover and to act itself in accord with the truth, but to spread the truth throughout society, to "shape popular beliefs and reduce the appeal of heterodox thought."[22]

In pursuit of the ideal of benevolence in its rule, also, the late imperial state made enormous commitments of effort and wealth. On the premise that good government required "supporting the people and regulating their livelihoods,"[23] state officials intervened extensively in what R. Bin Wong refers to as "ecological and economic matters." As he recounts,

> The search for social order led to state policies designed to stabilize the supply of various goods, especially food . . . During the Qing dynasty, a sophisticated system of food-supply management was created in which the central government gathered information on grain prices, weather, and rainfall from local officials in order to predict when and where in the empire serious food shortages might occur and to react to difficulties when they did appear. The centerpiece of state efforts at intervening in food-supply conditions in both routine and extraordinary ways was a granary system which stored several million tons of grain. Located mainly in county seats and small market towns, granaries represented official commitments to material welfare beyond anything imaginable, let alone achieved, in Europe.[24]

Grain shortages and famines could not always be averted, of course. The state's efforts to ensure and promote the popular welfare often failed, however much more precociously this value appeared as part of the logic of legitimate rule in China than it did in the West. Still, legitimation for local officials and members of the elite may have depended more, at times, on the display of benevolent concern itself, rather than on the actual saving of lives.[25] Through the granary system and through a whole array of formally and informally state- and local-elite-supported orphanages, widow homes, and public relief projects, the late imperial system of domination made a point of displaying the virtue of charitability.[26]

As for the goal of enhancing the glory of Sinic culture and civilization, Qing emperors pursued a policy of territorial expansion, subduing militarily a number of regions and peoples in Inner Asia. They vigorously sought to expand and reproduce their conception of civilization and their vision of social order through space whenever possible. And when their military forces were inadequate for further conquest, which was the case a good deal of the time, they relied instead on the tribute system as a means to assert their cultural superiority and to project the glory of China outward into the world beyond. According to Wong again,

> Despite [military] weaknesses, or perhaps in part as a response to them, the Chinese state succeeded in creating a framework for its international relations that placed other countries in a tributary status, a ritual position confirmed by the presentation of tribute, the presentation of gifts by the Chinese to the emissaries, and various agreements on a set schedule of visits every several years . . . From the Chinese point of view, the tribute system met the challenge of ordering the Chinese world with the Chinese state at the center . . . Foreign governments generally allowed the Chinese to promote this view without necessarily accepting it themselves.[27]

In the imperial logic of legitimation, securing the domestic order and stability came first. From a stable order at home might follow the necessary revenues and the other means for making further territorial conquests. But if not by conquest, then by cultural splendor and the projection of a confident superiority itself, the empire could still manage to command the respect of those powers on its periphery and beyond that might otherwise pose a threat, and literally awe them into cautious symbolic subordination.

By the mid- to late nineteenth century, however, China's military and technological weaknesses made this older vision of a world order centered on Sinic civilization very difficult to sustain. China's cultural superiority became harder and harder simply to assume, and her national glory came to be measured not in its radiant splendor, but in painful comparisons with other rising empires and competitor states. By the end of the century, the legitimating ideal of national "glory" had been redefined by Chinese philosophers and statesmen. Glory came to be understood no longer primarily in terms of civilized behavior and cultural florescence, but in the more vulgarly material terms of "wealth and power." Tributes and other polite forms of ritualized respect from foreign powers would remain sensitive issues, extremely important to twentieth- and twenty-first-century Chinese rulers. But by the time

the last dynasty fell, the ideal entailed in projecting the glory of Sinic civilization out into the rest of the world had been infused with more modern
meanings – military might, advanced technology, industrialization, and (to
return to an earlier point) more modern-day conceptions of economic
"growth" and "development." The old values of Truth, Benevolence, and
Glory were never conceded. They were, rather, stretched by modernity to
encompass some new contents and meanings – new knowledges, new social
projects, and new measures of grandeur.

Possession of a special knowledge of transcendent truth, benevolent care
for the common people, and the conscious glorification of the Chinese
nation were each to exhibit remarkable endurance as ideals of good government, however, despite the nineteenth century's deep shocks to the last
dynasty and even long after the final ruin of the imperial system. Most of
the key realities of government and politics in China were to be radically
altered, as we know, during the turbulent course of the twentieth century.
Yet these three basic themes in the rhetoric of state legitimation were not,
by any means, to vanish from the scene. Far from becoming simply outmoded
or being erased by newer ideas, in fact, these three legitimating norms have
been revived again and again, in new and different guises. The specific content of their meanings has been continually adjusted and altered to suit the
needs of changing times. But the ideals of Truth, Benevolence, and Glory
have been constantly renewed in Chinese discussions around the subject of
good governance and in China's modern politics of state legitimation and
opposition. These three were plainly visible as governmental claims to
authority under Mao.[28] And it is one of the chief contentions of this essay
that they remain central themes in the state legitimation project of the post-
Mao era.

The doctrines of Truth nowadays professed by Chinese leaders are no longer
those of Confucian learning and Daoist cosmology, of course. The official
standards for judging what knowledge is "true" knowledge now are those
of modern scientific rationalism and pragmatic empiricism. "Seek truth
from facts," as Deng Xiaoping so memorably put it. Scientific knowledge
and technological know-how are presented by the state not only as exhibiting and belonging to a universal set of established, non-falsifiable truths; they
are figured also as morally sound and good because, through science and
technology, modernization will be achieved. The transcendently positive
ethical value attached to the teleology of attaining modernity suffuses the
scientific empiricism accepted and promoted as the only allowable epistemology
by the Chinese state today.[29]

The state today also continues to base its legitimacy in part on its claim
to practice humane Benevolence toward its subjects. The requisite governmental care and concern for the poor and for those at risk are no longer
expressed in what were some of the more paternalist policies associated with
the Maoist past. But they now take many other new and interesting forms,
ranging from numerous small acts of patronage undertaken individually by

sitting officials, to massive government-led efforts at mobilizing charitable relief through nationwide foundations and emergency funds.[30] It remains imperative in the contemporary logic of governmental legitimacy that both national-level officials and local office-holders be seen to take the lead in mobilizing the charitable provision of social support for those in dire need. Helping to underwrite orphanages and old-age homes has once again become a prominent vehicle for the expression of official benevolence. But the repertoire of magnanimous gestures has been updated, too, to include such modern "good causes" as providing scholarships for needy students and organ donations for the sick, and for the sake of science.[31]

As for the enhancement of the nation's Glory, the present government, as we have all had occasion to note, associates itself most vigorously with the vision of a newly "rising China," a China that will no longer tolerate the bullying or the disdain of other nations, a China that will one day definitely outstrip the accomplishments of all other competitors.[32] Assertively nationalistic official posturing about the glories of Han culture have been so pronounced since the 1989 debacle, in fact, that some observers have been tempted into believing (incorrectly, in my view) that patriotic sentiment has become the only popular value on which the contemporary state now bases its appeals for legitimacy. As with promoting the nation's economic growth and development, protecting and enhancing China's international prestige and military prowess should not be supposed to be an independently or comprehensively legitimating value in itself. The alternating expressions of pride and anxiety we find in China concerning these two grand ambitions are better understood, rather, as continuing sub-themes within a larger saga – the saga of upholding the Glory of the Sinic civilization. It is important to appreciate that the state's logic of legitimation today is not a reductionist or a singular one; it remains, much as it was in imperial times, multifaceted and composed of intricately interlaced assertions about cosmological truth, humane benevolence, and the glories of China's past and China's future.

Reading the logic of legitimation backwards

To return to our earlier analytic hypothesis, then, in any system of domination's own logic of legitimation we should be able to find encoded the basic grammar for protest, the "raw material" that is available to be used most powerfully in opposition to that system. If legitimate authority is claimed on the basis of bloodlines and royal descent, opposition politics can be expected to revolve heavily around family genealogies, cloak-and-dagger plots and counter-plots inside the court, and the real or imagined *bona fides* of pretenders to the throne. If a state's legitimate authority is claimed on the basis of holy writ, opposition political movements will likely coalesce around alternative versions of the sacred texts and canons, and differing interpretations of the heavenly will be revealed in them. If a state's legitimate authority is claimed on the basis of democratic elections, charges of vote tampering, election fraud, and illegal or unwholesome campaign finance practices will be likely to figure prominently in the politics of opposition. If, as argued in the preceding section, in China some of the most central claims to legitimacy have rested on the combined ideals and values of Truth, Benevolence, and Glory, then what sorts of counterclaims would serve most powerfully to contest that legitimacy and galvanize political opposition?

The assertion that state actions are enhancing the national glory may be countered in several powerful ways. Charges of traitorousness at top levels, of selling out the nation and the people can be made, as indeed they were so devastatingly against the "alien" Manchus during the closing decades of the Qing, and against the warlord government that signed the Versailles Treaty in 1919. Popular movements and demonstrations arising out of incensed national pride have been a common and highly effective form for the expression of political opposition in China for well over a century. The 1980s and 1990s witnessed many national-cultural patriotic outbursts in Chinese cities, and the politics of national pride remains a highly sensitive area for state legitimation and de-legitimation today, as the essays by Rosen (Chapter 9) and Kraus (Chapter 7) in this volume both show very well. Chinese leaders can never afford to be outflanked by social forces that manage to portray themselves as more ardently patriotic than the government. Yet the government's own intense official nationalism, projected through the media and other forms of propaganda, often only serves to raise the ante where the passionate defense of national glory is concerned. This is a potentially dangerous political syndrome, a somewhat volatile dimension along which we can expect to continue to see the legitimacy of the contemporary Chinese state called into question by opponents of the system.

The assertion that the state behaves benevolently toward the people is also open to challenge on several grounds. Most prominent among these perhaps, rampaging popular discourses on the subject of official corruption in China have served, time and again, to galvanize political opposition and give the lie to the officially cultivated mystique of benevolent governance. Official claims to be carrying out the business of the state in the spirit of humane and magnanimous charity have almost always been contested in the Chinese people's critiques of their rulers, where cynical reference is so readily made to the corruption, the venality, and the self-serving behavior of sitting officials. That officialdom can and must be expected to be shot through with nepotism and corruption is, in fact, an axiom of Chinese popular political culture. But when ordinary people in China allege, as they so frequently do, that corruption is rampant, they are not merely pointing the finger at some particular guilty officials; they are challenging the authority of the entire state system that stakes a claim to legitimacy on the basis of official selflessness and benevolence. Popular disgust and protest over corrupt practices were factors leading to the collapse of many a former dynasty and regime, not least visibly in the dramatic withdrawal of public support that led to the expulsion of the Guomindang government and the victory of the Communist Party on the mainland. In the vigor and the unrelenting din of popular discourse on corruption in China today, then, we hear again the ruled speaking back to the rulers on the subject of benevolence. The critique of power being leveled at the contemporary Chinese state along this dimension undeniably constitutes another one of the most salient and powerful challenges to its legitimacy and to its capacity to rule authoritatively.[33]

If in the angry and bitter popular discourses on official corruption we find oppositionist challenges to the legitimacy of the state's claims to be governing humanely and benevolently, and if in the melodramatic indignation of popular discourses on national strength and national humiliation we find oppositionist challenges to the legitimacy of the state's claims to be upholding and advancing the glory of China, where then do we find popular challenges to the state's claims to be acting in accord with the highest of moral truths to be found in the way of the cosmos? We find these most powerfully, I would suggest, in the discourses and practices of popular religion. Contemporary popular religious sects, with their syncretic systems of thought and action, posit an even higher, more all-encompassing, and more potent ethical and epistemological order than the one embraced by the state. They insist on a mystical moral order that transcends the modern-rational scientific mode of knowing what is true. Chinese popular religious beliefs and practices invoke a universe of ghosts and deities, of animal spirits and immortals, whose positive power to affect the human condition cannot be explained by modern science, and whose ethically based motives for action and inaction do not fit comfortably with the norms and values intended to guide human choices that are put forward for the edification of the people by the Chinese state. In this lies the special potency of sectarian religion as a vehicle for denying the authority of the state and for mobilizing protest against it.

The state's claim to "truth" and the challenge of popular religion

In imperial China, unlike medieval and early modern Europe, there was no autonomous system of church schools taking care of the basic education and the moral training of the social and political elite. There was no separate organization of the guardian faith to conduct inquisitions and suppress heterodox popular religious beliefs and practices. Moral training for the elite and the suppression of popular religious heresies were the affair of the state in China. As James Watson has argued,[34] the imperial state maintained its own approved pantheon of recognized deities, and it attempted to "standardize the gods" throughout the realm by encouraging the worship only of those spirits admitted to the official pantheon. It promoted its own preferred deities, encouraging their worship by ever-wider circles of the populace. But the state also at times co-opted into its official pantheon pre-existing popular deities who had acquired important followings, taking advantage for itself of their prestige and presumed potency while, at the same time, avoiding a stand-off between official and non-official religion, and blurring the lines between the two.[35] The state maintained the final word on what did and did not constitute true belief. But, in practice, any given deity might come to symbolize different (and sometimes competing) values to different groups in society, and the state exercised only a loose control over the actual content of belief. It exerted its authority in social life through what Prasenjit Duara has conceived of as a broad "cultural nexus," an interlacing of official and non-official roles in local society which included the participation of state bureaucrats in the life of religious temples and shrines.[36] In this complexly multi-stranded cultural nexus linking state and society, much productive ambiguity about the bases of temporal and supernatural "power" was deliberately sustained. The state, on the one hand, authorized the worship of certain deities. And yet, the mystical power these local gods and spirits were already believed by the people to possess also adhered, in a way, to the state's own officials as they acted out their leading roles in the rituals and ceremonies of village and small-town life. State officials had the power to validate popular deities, and popular deities had the power to validate the state.

As Duara has argued, the productive ambiguities of ruling through the cultural nexus were relentlessly broken down in China by the processes of modern state-making that took place after the Qing collapse. Facing up to the challenges posed by imperialism – the confusing and terrifying jolts delivered by foreign military and technological superiority, alien religious and secular philosophies, and Western conceptions of modernity and power – the educated classes of Chinese gradually turned their backs on the resources for rule that were embedded in popular religious god and ghost worship. Both the Guomindang and the Communist Party-states launched repeated campaigns to try to get people to give up popular religious beliefs and ritual practices. These came to be labeled as mere "superstition," something shameful to be eradicated and not eligible to be incorporated in the modes of modern governance. If peasants and petty urbanites continued, well into the twentieth century, to venerate gods and ghosts, to propitiate spirits with offerings, to make pilgrimages to holy mountains, and to consult geomancers and shamans, these practices could be comprehended by state officials and by members of the Chinese intelligentsia alike only as the lamentable markers of continuing Chinese backwardness. And as Duara has further pointed out, contrasting some of the choices made by twentieth-century Indian intellectuals with those made by their Chinese counterparts,

> the consuming commitment of Chinese intellectuals to the narrative of modernity . . . has obscured the vitality of popular culture, religion, and their associational life and delegitimated the critique of modern ideologies originating outside of modern discourses. Despite the repeated persecution of the intelligentsia by the Chinese state, it is this shared narrative [of modernity] which has thrown so many of them repeatedly into the arms of the state and at the same time alienated both from the living

cultures of the "masses" and of "tradition." While the state has made effective use of the narrative of modernity to expand its own powers, the Chinese intelligentsia has robbed itself of alternative sources of moral authority which it might have found in history and popular culture.[37]

After 1949, secular-scientific Marxism and Mao Thought ascended to become the new official cosmological "truths" upheld and purveyed by the state. Marx's universalist teleology of progress, leavened by the moral sensibilities of proletarian class struggle and the Maoist ideals of revolutionary virtue, was relentlessly pressed upon the people. Alternative popular histories, cosmologies, virtues, and beliefs were denounced and driven underground. Shrines and temples were destroyed. Shamans were put through forced re-education. State suppression of popular heterodoxies was, for a generation or so, extremely intense. In recent years, a state-orchestrated public re-evaluation of Mao Thought and of the Marxian theory of history has taken place in China. Some of the older interpretations given to Marxist verities have had to be dropped or, anyway, very sharply bent in order to accommodate the present government's new guiding theory of "socialism with Chinese characteristics." But the post-Mao period has seen no official backing down from the secular-rational empiricist-modernist values embedded in Marxism. Popular religious belief and practice remain, according to the state's truth, mere superstition. Insofar as people still believe in gods and immortals, make offerings to appease the ghosts of the departed, or think about their moral choices in terms of karma and the transmigration of souls, the state has failed in its pedagogic project of building "spiritual civilization" and in its modernizing effort to civilize the subaltern.[38] In the state's view, and in the view of most of China's intelligentsia, widespread popular religious practice can be evidence only that the "quality" (*suzhi* 素质) of a large proportion of the population still remains deplorably "low."[39]

Yet, in the various social spaces opened up by the post-Mao reforms, there has emerged nothing short of a vigorous popular religious revival in China, one that embraces Buddhism, Daoism, and a host of syncretic sects. Kenneth Dean has characterized this revival as "an extraordinary renaissance of reinvented traditional forms of ritual activity":

> Hundreds of thousands of temples have been restored, rebuilt, and reconsecrated. Millions of people have taken part in ritual events which have become more frequent each year as well as more complex and multifaceted. This activity has been most intense in southeast China, particularly in Fujian, Guangdong, and Zhejiang, but there is increasing evidence that local religious practices are spreading all across China.[40]

Some of these reinvented traditions, including the ones that Dean has studied, are tied closely to localities. They are spiritual expressions, often of community-based collaborations and competitions.[41] In sects of this type, popular religion can be "the pivot for a complex network of forms of local social organization that counterbalance state interventions from above: family, lineages, village, regional alliances of villages." Their ritual practices may work to "interrupt the downward flow of state signification aimed at reforming the individual."[42] They can, as Dean argues, be regarded as a somewhat contained form of resistance or opposition to state domination and an expression of the ongoing human effort to "achieve autonomy and self-definition."[43] Even so, state officials, and especially local state officials, may find it expedient to tolerate and even encourage their activities. Their performances and gatherings, their shrines and processions, can be good for local business. They can even attract tourists from Taiwan, Southeast Asia, and Hong Kong, bringing in with them foreign currency, donations, and investments.[44] These local religious activities can have "picturesque" and "exotic" qualities that fold well into the commodification of certain Chinese cultural performances and artifacts that also form part of the contemporary state's agenda for dealing with social diversity.[45] For reasons such as these, some localized popular religious sects may be able to find official shelter and support in the ambiguities of the local "cultural nexus" of state and society now being reconstructed in some parts of the country.

The Falun Gong phenomenon, however, does not fit this more tolerable type of religious sect. Not localized at all, it has proven to be eminently transportable, spreading throughout China and, via the Internet, around the world.[46] Falun Gong's leader, Li Hongzhi, has cultivated a charismatic image and, in the wake of the state's campaign against him, has adopted a combative demeanor toward the government in Beijing and toward China's high officials. Falun Gong websites have referred to those who arrest and suppress believers inside China as "monsters" and "demons," and have carried cartoons lampooning top party-state leaders. Nor does Li's ethical philosophy fit well with the consumerist values of the commodity culture that the Beijing government broadcasts. Master Li teaches his followers to try to let go of all earthly attachments, and he castigates as demonically evil the corrosive values of the marketplace.[47] Li not only rejects the ideals of the socialist market economy which the Chinese state now seeks to foster; he also rejects the claims to cosmological truth that are accorded by the state to the demystified rationality of modern science. Li claims knowledge of a higher science, one that is not yet comprehended on earth. He utilizes the language of modern science and medicine in his teachings at times, speaking of tumors, of time–space dimensions, and the like. But this, as he explains, is simply because these terms and categories are the only ones that will be widely understood by people on earth at this time. Li's cosmology is, his disciples are given to understand, much greater than the scientistic official cosmology. It features a host of paranormal possibilities, from predatory fox spirits that can inhabit human bodies, to contacts with extraterrestrials. Li's standards of morality are also far more demanding than the official ones. His followers must cultivate goodness for its own sake. They must turn away from all desires for fame and fortune, or they will not be saved.

The challenge posed by popular religious beliefs and practices like those of Falun Gong cuts right to the heart of the Chinese state's own logic of legitimation. Falun Gong teaches people to disdain, as rigid but patently imperfect, the whole modernist, secular-scientific understanding of the cosmos in which the state roots its governing authority. And Falun Gong teaches people to regard as pitiably misguided the poor conception of morality and goodness that has come to characterize Chinese society under the state's own program of market socialist reform. The teachings of Li Hongzhi thus stand in the profoundest possible opposition to the present political order. They assail the ethical truths on which the entire political construct is meant to rest. However peacefully they practice their meditation exercises and however much they may regard "politics" as being beneath them, those swept up in the Falun Gong phenomenon never had a chance of remaining "apolitical" in China.[48] With its slogan *"Zhen, Shan, Ren"* (真，善，忍) – "Truth, Goodness, and Forbearance" – Falun Gong makes almost a perfect counter-hegemony. Truth! – but not the state's narrow empiricist truths. Goodness! – but not the state's dubious versions of benevolence. Forbearance! – but not the state's vulgarly assertive "wealth and power" concept of what it means to attain transcendent glory.

Precisely because Falun Gong does represent such an absolute challenge – a challenge to the very foundations of the state's authority and legitimacy – government officials insist on complete extermination of the threat. It is one thing to demonstrate for lower taxes or better benefits. These are goods the state can, if it will, (benevolently) confer upon those who can show they have righteous claims to consideration. The people's demand itself implies the power and the authority of the state to satisfy the need. It is quite another thing, however, to demonstrate for Truth, Goodness, and Forbearance. The demand itself implies the lack. An assault like Falun Gong's, on the legitimating foundations of state authority, is thus perceived as a threat to the entire existing system of domination – a threat to order and stability. And the enormity of the threat itself is, in turn, used to justify the draconian severity of the repression. Intimidations, arrests, tortures – the crackdown has been a hard one, carried out by "a hard lot of men."[49] This is the apt phrase used by E.P. Thompson (in the passage from which the quotation that begins this essay is drawn; see p. 41) to characterize Walpole and the Hanoverian Whigs of the 1720s and 1730s, as they pushed through the cruel punishments of the "Black Act" to crack down on hunters, whom a nervous state, fearing armed sedition, wished now to classify as "poachers." As Thompson strives to remind us, it has been in the name of safeguarding "stability" that some of history's nastiest political terrors have been excused.

The logic of state legitimation in China makes popular religious practice and belief a challenge to authority – because it celebrates a higher truth. It is the state's own logic of rule that endows popular religious movements with their political salience and makes them potent vehicles for the expression of opposition and protest. When such popular religious sects and movements are content to operate furtively and on the margins, or when they remain explicitly locally bounded in their activities and scope, or when they seek and secure protections from local officials who hope to gain something from their existence, the heresies and the other dangers entailed in their beliefs are often, somehow, found to be tolerable. But when, as in the case of Falun Gong, such a sect goes overtly "national," making a bid for broader public sympathy and staging its rituals and demonstrations in nationally/symbolically sacred spaces such as Zhongnanhai and Tiananmen, then syncretism will be officially equated with sabotage. The legitimacy of the entire system, which rests on the preservation of a stable public order, will then be seen to depend utterly on the obliteration of heretical beliefs among the people.[50]

Until and unless the Chinese state moves on to a newer repertoire of legitimation claims – one that does not include official knowledge of ultimate ethical truths – we can expect popular religious belief and practice to continue to be perceived *always as a potential*, and *sometimes as an active*, counter-hegemonic danger to stability and order. And we can expect the high value accorded to stability, by the great majority of the rulers and the ruled alike, to contribute to the sanctioning of Inquisition-like trials and terrors to suppress China's new-style old believers.

But, the question can be plausibly asked: "Is the Chinese state not now at last, perhaps, actually moving on to just such a new repertoire of legitimation claims?" Since this essay was first published (in this volume's 2004 edition), its central message – underscoring the various complexes of inter-related concepts and moral values that have been and still are involved in striving to create and maintain political legitimacy in the Chinese context – has not been very widely embraced. Most commentators on the subject have continued, as they had done before, to argue more simply that the party-state has rested its claims to legitimacy throughout the reform era not on any such complexes of historically resonant noble ideals or values as those posited here, but primarily on its good performance in the here and now in delivering welcome growth and relative economic prosperity to millions of still-poor and struggling people. Still, there have been at least a few observers who have not been content so to reduce the party-state's arguments for its legitimacy and its fitness to rule to matters of economic performance alone. David Shambaugh, for example, has lately given us an extended discussion of what he sees as the complex "ideological work" that has had to be done within the party in recent years, in the effort to "win the hearts and minds of its members and the public."[51] And others, like Thomas Heberer and Gunter Schubert,[52] have suggested further that the party-state's rather strenuous efforts to reform and reinvent itself (both normatively and institutionally) have in fact been having important positive effects on its "regime legitimacy." They propose that some serious study of these ongoing reforms in Chinese political thought and practice may contribute substantially to our understanding of the apparent continued resiliency of one-party rule in China. Heberer and Schubert, responding in part to this essay, argue in particular that ongoing reforms promoting greater "accountability," "transparency," and popular "participation" at the local level in China are making important contributions to building and maintaining the party-state's legitimacy. "Benevolence, glory, stability and accountability," they therefore conclude, "might . . . be the formula for ensuring continuous one-party rule in China."[53]

Interesting and welcome as this positive intervention by Heberer and Schubert is, however, it may be worthwhile, in reply, to record here my own view that the values of accountability, transparency, and of broadening popular participation cannot in fact logically be put on a par with those of benevolence, truth, and glory. Although expressed here – no doubt quite inadequately, in mere short-hand terms like humane "benevolence," moral "truth," and civilizational "glory," such grand complexes of ideals as lie behind these condensed concepts need to be understood as first-order philosophical principles: they are meant to signify, that is, values and virtues regarded as self-evidently good, ones to be pursued for their own sake. Accountability, transparency, and broadening participation are not first-order, but only second-order principles. They are to be pursued, not for themselves, but as tools and techniques, organizational and behavioral habits, that are very helpful in the attainment of yet *another,* quite different, grand normative ideal of governance – that of rule in accord with the expressed "will of the people." I offer this distinction – which I trust will not appear to be merely a petty one – between first- and second-order philosophical principles as a way to raise the further question of whether, in adopting now some of the language and some of the practices of accountability, transparency, and participation, the Chinese party-state is (or is not) aiming to reinvent itself in line with the inspiration provided by that other grand ideal of legitimate government as "government conducted in accord with the expressed will of the people."

If, as suggested by the work of Heberer and Schubert, accountability, transparency, and regularized popular participation are ideals now being promoted and pursued within the Chinese polity almost entirely at the local and lower-middle levels of the system, then I would want to suggest that the "will of the people" has not in fact been admitted at the top as one among the most fundamental first-order philosophical principles of regime legitimation. If popular elections, and citizens' suits filed under the administrative litigation law, and press monitoring and exposure of official corruption and malfeasance remain almost entirely confined to local offices and low-level officials – if there are few regularized and effective institutions of participation or accountability, in other words, that can be brought to bear at central or national levels – then the case could not be well argued, I believe, that the party-state now rests its legitimacy on achieving or on heeding the popular will. If this new governance rhetoric, these interesting emerging legal-bureaucratic practices and apparently rising good-discipline regimes of accountability, transparency, and popular participation are, instead, primarily deployed by the center in a tutelary spirit – as part of a cadre-restraining project or part of a popular-pedagogical project of mimicking modernity –

then we will need to be careful in assessing what the probable long-term effects of such reforms may actually be where the legitimacy of the self-reinvented party-state is concerned.

In short, if grand inspirational first-order principles of legitimation like "benevolence," "truth," "glory," "stability," or "harmony" remain the province of central authority, while only mid- and lower-level party-state officials are expected to heed the expressed "will of the people" by demonstrating their accountability, transparency, and openness to popular political participation, then the actual perceived legitimacy produced in the eye of the citizen-beholder may end by being quite unevenly (and perhaps quite ironically) distributed across different levels of the political system. By underscoring the gulf that is posited to exist between the center's transcendently grand moral governance ideals and its own lower-order officials' pusillanimous need to be kept constantly accountable to society and the people, central power-holders may well now be attempting to make a very deft move to retain for themselves the popular support they require to command loyalty, and even sacrifice, from the people. But if, as they wave the banner of more democratic accountability, these central power-holders perpetually resort to calling into question the dependable legitimacy of their own agents in local offices around the realm, to the point eventually of hollowing out the perceived political legitimacy of those agents, they may ultimately rob themselves of the capacity they require to govern China's modern society in the orderly manner they so desire.

A crisis of legitimacy or two cheers for ambivalence?

I have argued here against giving in to reductionist conceptions of what is entailed in having, and in holding onto, political legitimacy in contemporary China. In China, as in other modern political systems which have grown gradually out of older and prior forms of polity, the legitimacy claims of the state are layered deep historically, multi-stranded, and complex. I have also suggested that, in the patterns of contentious politics that surround state legitimation and de-legitimation in the Chinese context, it is the government's capacity to sustain stability and social order that is generally held up as the touchstone value. The very goodness that is imagined to be attendant on social order is, further, closely related to certain very particular high ideals – ideals of seeking and promoting the epistemological and moral Truth, of governing with a degree of humane Benevolence, and of protecting and enhancing the national Glory. The state's antagonists in society, those who doubt or deny its legitimacy, I have further argued, "speak back" to power with charges and counterclaims that tend to be constructed along these very same dimensions of value. State claims to be advancing the national Glory are met by popular counterclaims of leadership weakness, vacillation, or betrayal. State claims to be governing with Benevolence are met by popular counterclaims of callousness, corruption, and venality. And state claims to be promoting the demonstrable empirical and moral Truth are met by powerful alternative epistemologies, popular counter-truths, and counter-moralities such as those of Falun Gong.

Each one of these three hallmark patterns of contentious politics – so clearly related to the processes of state legitimation and de-legitimation in China – is broadly and prominently in evidence today. And this has no doubt contributed to the penchant of many observers these days to speculate, somewhat loosely, about an ongoing "crisis of legitimacy" in China. The arguments that have typically been advanced along these lines, often simplistic ones, are surely already familiar, so they may be summarized very briefly. Belief in Maoism and Marxism is said to be "dead" in China today, killed off by the market reforms and the transparently self-serving behavior of power-holders at all levels of the system. The resultant sudden crisis of faith is so severe among the people of China, who are supposed previously to have lived in thrall to the official ideology, that the state has had to scurry to find some other doctrine to fill the void. By most such accounts, official nationalism is that chosen new doctrine, and patriotism has thus been pumped up by the state to take the place of the old ideological commitment in the minds of China's hapless masses.[54] On this view of things, one whole coherent set of relatively uncomplicated beliefs about the state's legitimacy is imagined to have been pulled out of people's heads, while another whole set of even more uncomplicated principles has been plugged in to fill the empty slot. Functionalist analyses like these, in my view, grossly misread the complexity of the lived world of belief most human beings encounter. Such approaches to questions of legitimacy downplay human agency and creativity and ignore the multiplicity of the worlds of value we all inhabit.

Citizens and subjects, as students of popular resistance and protest have taught us, almost never swallow whole the legitimacy claims of their rulers. Even at the most totalizing of authoritarian political moments, popular dissent and disbelief are commonly expressed as people negotiate the precise terms on which they will give their obedience to the state. As Karen Petrone has concluded in her noteworthy study of official holidays and mass celebrations during the high-Stalinist era, "While citizens within reach of Soviet discourse were bombarded with carefully censored messages, they interpreted these messages in a wide variety of ways and used the discourse of the state to create alternative visions of their worlds."[55] Likewise, during the most radical of radical moments in China, the Cultural Revolution, we clearly witnessed people calculatedly and creatively deploying the state's own rhetoric of "class struggle" to pursue interests, values, and identities of their own. On closer inspection, then, ordinary people rarely turn out to be the gullible true believers that states (and some social scientists) may imagine. Or, to quote E.P. Thompson once again, this time making reference to the sartorial habits of the British court system, "people are not as stupid as some structuralist philosophers suppose them to be. They will not be mystified by the first man who puts on a wig."[56] They will, much more commonly, take the raw material that state logics of legitimation offer them and do their best to bend these to ends and visions of their own.

Yet I submit that while citizens and subjects may, most often, not be mystified by the prevailing legitimacy claims of states, neither are they always consciously and systematically engaged in countering the state's hegemony – as some of the literature on "everyday forms of resistance" might lead us to expect. Most people, most of the time, I would suggest, are quite appropriately ambivalent about the legitimacy of the system in which they find themselves. They know – through their own experiences, through the trusty testimony of others, through rumor, and through humor – of plenty of good reasons to accept and plenty of good reasons not to accept their state's authority. Their multi-stranded knowledge and experience of living in society teach them that some officials are, after all, honest, well-meaning, or efficient; that some claims made by governments do, in the end, prove out. They know these things to be true even as they also know that numerous other officials are venally abusing their trust and that governments frequently lie. The inhabitants of complex societies sustain correspondingly complex and highly inflected understandings of their own social reality and of social possibility. This is true even of those who are scarcely literate and who live in remote regions.[57] The very experience of domination most often marries objection with acceptance. It is bivalent, and so people are ambivalent.

The state in China today strives continuously, agonistically, as all states must strive, more or less perpetually, against antagonists, to validate and revalidate their authority. In China, no doubt due to the very breadth and magnitude of the grand social and economic transformations that are currently underway, the pressures being brought to bear in this contest and the stakes of the game may seem higher than usual. The level of contention over authority is elevated throughout society. And so, not unexpectedly, is the expressed level of popular doubts and ambivalences about power. This palpable heightening in the expression of mixed feelings on the part of the people has contributed, I think, to the view some hold that the state in China now faces "a crisis of legitimacy." But the condition of human ambivalence experienced amid a swirl of claims and counterclaims about the legitimacy of power should not in itself, in my view, be taken as evidence of crisis. Living in a state of acute ambivalence might be considered, rather, quite the most common fate for citizens and subjects everywhere who must confront what Max Weber called "the generally observable need of any power, or even of any advantage of life, to justify itself."[58]

Notes

1 My thanks to four indulgent colleagues, Marc Blecher, Kenneth Foster, Dorothy Solinger, and Sidney Tarrow, for reading and offering challenging comments and criticisms on an earlier draft of this essay. I wish it were possible to respond adequately to each one.

2 E.P. Thompson, *Whigs and Hunters: The Origins of the Black Act* (New York: Pantheon, 1975), p. 258.
3 For some recent scholarly discussions of worker protest, see Ching Kwan Lee, "Pathways of labor insurgency," in Elizabeth Perry and Mark Selden, eds., *Chinese Society: Change, Conflict and Resistance* (London: Routledge, 2000), pp. 41–61, and Ching Kwan Lee, "Lost between histories: labor insurgency and subjectivity in reform China," paper presented at the 53rd Annual Meeting of the Association for Asian Studies, 22–5 March, 2001. See also Wang Zheng, "Gender, employment and women's resistance," in Perry and Selden, *Chinese Society*, pp. 62–82. On migrants, see Dorothy Solinger, *Contesting Citizenship in Urban China* (Berkeley: University of California Press, 1999); Michael Dutton, *Streetlife China* (Cambridge: Cambridge University Press, 1998); Hein Mallee, "Migration, hukou and resistance in reform China," in Perry and Selden, *Chinese Society*, pp. 83–101; and Li Zhang, "Migration and privatization of space and power in late socialist China," *American Ethnologist* 28(1) (2000), pp. 179–205. On peasant protest, see Thomas Bernstein, "Instability in rural China," in David Shambaugh, ed., *Is China Unstable?* (Armonk, NY: M.E. Sharpe, 2000), pp. 95–111, and Thomas Bernstein and Xiaobo Lü, *Taxation without Representation in Contemporary Rural China: State Capacity, Peasant Resistance, and Democratization, 1985–2000* (New York: Cambridge University Press, 2003). See also Lianjiang Li and Kevin O'Brien, "Villagers and popular resistance," *Modern China* 22(1) (1996), pp. 28–61; Kevin O'Brien, "Rightful resistance," *World Politics* 49(1) (1996), pp. 31–55; and Jonathan Unger, "Power, patronage and protest in rural China," in Tyrene White, ed., *China Briefing 2000* (Armonk, NY: M.E. Sharpe 2000), pp. 71–94. On artists and intellectuals, see Merle Goldman, "The potential for instability among alienated intellectuals and students in post-Mao China," in Shambaugh, *Is China Unstable?*, pp. 112–24; Gérémie Barmé, "The revolution of resistance," in Perry and Selden, *Chinese Society*, pp. 198–220; and Robert Efird, "Rock in a hard place: music and the market in nineties Beijing," in Nancy Chen, Constance Clark, Suzanne Gottschang, and Lyn Jeffery, eds., *China Urban* (Durham, NC: Duke University Press, 2001), pp. 67–86. On women's issues, see Zheng, "Gender, employment and women's resistance"; Tyrene White, "Domination, resistance and accommodation in China's one-child campaign," in Perry and Selden, *Chinese Society*, pp. 102–19; and Cecilia Milwertz, "Control as care: interaction between urban women and birth planning workers," in Kjeld Brødsgaard and David Strand, eds., *Reconstructing Twentieth-century China* (Oxford: Clarendon Press, 1998), pp. 92–112. On ethnic minorities, see June Dreyer, "The potential for instability in minority regions," in Shambaugh, *Is China Unstable?*, pp. 125–42, and Uradyn Bulag, "Ethnic resistance with socialist characteristics," in Perry and Selden, *Chinese Society*, pp. 178–97. And finally, on environmental protests, see Jun Jing, "Environmental protests in rural China," in Perry and Selden, *Chinese Society*, pp. 143–60.
4 This is the office and residential compound used by high party-state officials, adjacent to Tiananmen Square, in the heart of Beijing.
5 The general term *qigong* refers to regimens of breath and body exercises that may be studied and practiced, individually and in groups, by those in pursuit of greater physical, mental, and spiritual self-control and well-being. The initial article assailing the Falun Gong group of *qigong* practitioners, which appeared in a teen science and technology journal published in Tianjin, was written by He Zuoxiu, a leading physicist and member of the Chinese Academy of Sciences. See Danny Schechter, *Falun Gong's Challenge to China: Spiritual Practice or "Evil Cult"* (New York: Akashic Books, 2000), ch. 6, for an account of the events leading up to the protest demonstration at Zhongnanhai.

64   *Vivienne Shue*

6 As Elizabeth Perry has noted in *Challenging the Mandate of Heaven: Social Protest and State Power in China* (Armonk, NY: M.E. Sharpe, 2002), p. xix, "The [Falun Gong] gatherings were nonviolent and remarkably disciplined. While the government insisted that these demonstrations were the most serious political threat since the 1989 student uprising, it was hard to see why."

7 As Patsy Rahn points out in "The Falun Gong: beyond the headlines," "Most people in the West see the campaign as unnecessarily exaggerated and harsh, similar to political campaigns waged during the Mao era." And many inside China clearly joined in with this view. As Perry, *Challenging the Mandate of Heaven*, p. xix, reports, "judging from discussions with people in China at the time, this particular campaign was not a resounding success . . . The draconian nature of the campaign was suggestive of a deeply frightened and insecure central leadership. People wondered out loud: Had crimes so serious as to warrant the arrest of thousands really occurred?" See www.let.leidenuniv.nl.bth/FalunRAHN.htm (2000, p. 1), accessed July 9, 2001.

8 Some anthropologists were on to these issues earlier than the rest of us, however. See, e.g., Nancy Chen, "Urban spaces and experiences of *qigong*," in Deborah Davis, Richard Kraus, Barry Naughton, and Elizabeth Perry, eds., *Urban Spaces in Contemporary China* (New York: Cambridge University Press, 1995), pp. 347–61, and Kenneth Dean, *Taoist Ritual and Popular Cults of Southeast China* (Princeton: Princeton University Press, 1993).

9 On the White Lotus, see Susan Naquin, *Shantung Rebellion: The Wang Lun Uprising of 1774* (New Haven: Yale University Press, 1981); on the Taiping, see Franz Michael, *The Taiping Rebellion* (Seattle: University of Washington Press, 1966), and Jonathan Spence, *God's Chinese Son: The Taiping Heavenly Kingdom of Hong Xiuquan* (New York: W.W. Norton, 1996); and on the Boxers, see Joseph Esherick, *The Origins of the Boxer Uprising* (Berkeley: University of California Press, 1987), and Paul Cohen, *History in Three Keys: The Boxers as Event, Experience, and Myth* (New York: Columbia University Press, 1997).

10 For an attempt at a dispassionate summary of some of the content of Master Li's teachings and a consideration of why these particular moral teachings could pose a threat to the state, see Vivienne Shue, "Global imaginings, the state's quest for hegemony, and the pursuit of phantom freedom in China: from Heshang to Falun Gong," in Catarina Kinnvall and Kristina Jönsson, eds., *Globalization and Democratization in Asia: The Construction of Identity* (New York: Routledge, 2002). The best introduction to Falun Gong philosophy can be found in the Master's own writings: Hongzhi Li, *Zhuan Falun*, 2nd edn, English version (New York: Universe Publishing Co., 1998).

11 Charles Tilly, *The Contentious French* (Cambridge, MA: Harvard University Press, 1986).

12 Max Weber, *Economy and Society: An Outline of Interpretive Sociology* (Berkeley: University of California Press, 1978), p. 213.

13 The phrase comes from James Scott, *Weapons of the Weak: Everyday Forms of Peasant Resistance* (New Haven: Yale University Press, 1985), p. 336.

14 *Ibid.*, p. 338.

15 "Read backwards," as John Sidel puts it, "legitimacy claims specify what exactly, in a given setting, is considered dangerously *illegitimate*." Sidel's insightful analysis goes on, in a manner that Weber would no doubt have well approved of, to illustrate how several different grammars, or what he calls "languages of legitimation," may be operative within a single system of domination. See John Sidel, "The Philippines: the languages of legitimation," in Muthiah Alagappa, ed., *Political Legitimacy in Southeast Asia: The Quest for Moral Authority* (Stanford: Stanford University Press, 1995), p. 139.

16 For a discussion of some of the consequences of this new concentration of eco-
nomic power and dynamism at local levels, see Marc Blecher and Vivienne Shue,
"Into leather: state-led development and the private sector in Xinji," *China
Quarterly* 166 (2001).

17 I owe this particular insight to some very thoughtful comments made by Sally
Sargeson at the workshop entitled "Mapping the local state" convened by
Richard Baum and Tony Saich at UCLA, June 2001. For an excellent discussion
of the limitations on the framing of recent workers' protests in China, see also
Lee, "Lost between histories."

18 Its roots are to be found in the major streams of thought, Confucianism and Daoism,
that emerged (after the decline of even more ancient forms of Chinese religion)
during the period known as the Eastern Zhou Dynasty, 771–221 BCE. On the interplay of these and other strands in very early Chinese political thought, interested
readers may consult the magisterial study by Benjamin Schwartz, *The World of
Thought in Ancient China* (Cambridge: Belknap Press, 1985).

19 H. Lyman Miller, "The late imperial Chinese state," in David Shambaugh, ed.,
The Modern Chinese State (Cambridge: Cambridge University Press, 2000), pp.
17–18.

20 For a much deeper consideration of all the issues raised here and more, see the
rigorous comparison of European and Chinese patterns of state-making in R. Bin
Wong, *China Transformed: Historical Change and the Limits of European
Experience* (Ithaca: Cornell University Press, 1997).

21 *Ibid.*, p. 96.

22 *Ibid.* Making the interesting comparison with Europe, Wong here argues that "There
is no early modern European government equivalent to the late imperial Chinese
state's efforts at dictating moral and intellectual orthodoxy, nor were such efforts
particularly important to Europe's state-making agenda, as they were in China.
Early modern European states did not share the Chinese state's view that shaping society's moral sensibilities was basic to the logic of rule" (*ibid.*, p. 97).

23 *Ibid.*, p. 93.

24 *Ibid.*, p. 98. For more on the ideas concerning popular welfare that lay behind
the imperial state granaries, see Pierre-Etienne Will and R. Bin Wong, *Nourish
the People: The State Civilian Granary System in China, 1650–1850* (Ann Arbor:
University of Michigan Center for Chinese Studies, 1991).

25 On this point, see, further, Joanna Handlin Smith, "Chinese philanthropy as seen
through a case of famine relief in the 1640s," in Warren Ilchman, Stanley Katz,
and Edward Queen, eds., *Philanthropy in the World's Traditions* (Bloomington:
Indiana University Press, 1998), pp.133–68.

26 A close and revealing study of these charitable institutions can be found in Angela
Leung (Liang Qizi), *Shishan yu Jiaohua: Ming Qing de Cishan Zuzhi* (*Charity
and Enlightenment: The Charitable Organizations of the Ming and Qing*) (Taipei:
Lianjing, 1997).

27 Wong, *China Transformed*, p. 89.

28 This assertion really requires lengthy supporting elaboration, which I cannot pause
to develop here. In brief, I believe it makes sense to see the Maoist party-state's
claims to legitimacy based on its possession of a transcendent universal ethical
Truth to have been manifested very clearly in the heavy-duty moral instruction
of the masses that accompanied the propagation of Marxist theory and Mao
Thought during that era. The party-state's claim to Benevolence in those days
took such forms as "iron rice bowl" guarantees of livelihood, cradle-to-grave subsistence needs met within the capsulized life of the *danwei* (单位), and repeated
fervent expressions and demonstrations of state solidarity with the proletariat and
the "poor peasantry." The state's claims to be promoting national Glory then

took many interesting forms as well, from the cleansing and militarization of Chinese culture itself, to the obsessions with industrialization, anti-imperialism, and China's pretensions to international leadership within the context of the Third World.

29 On the ethical value accorded by the state to science and to modernity, see Ann Anagnost, *National Past-times: Narrative, Representation, and Power in Modern China* (Durham, NC: Duke University Press, 1997).

30 A discussion and analysis of some of the many contemporary forms of state-led charity can be found in Vivienne Shue, "State power and the philanthropic impulse in China today," in Ilchman *et al., Philanthropy in the World's Traditions*, pp. 332–54. State-led charitable programs and projects such as Project Hope and many others have been ceaselessly, didactically publicized in the Chinese media under Deng and Jiang.

31 On organ donation, see Vivienne Shue, "Donation and the nation: altruism and patriotism in 20th-century China," unpublished paper presented at the Institute for Chinese Studies, Edinburgh University, April 2003.

32 On the official cultural nationalism of the Chinese state, see Gérémie Barmé, *In the Red: On Contemporary Chinese Culture* (New York: Columbia University Press, 1999), ch. 10; see also Søren Clausen, "Party policy and 'national culture': towards a state-directed cultural nationalism in China," in Brødsgaard and Strand, *Reconstructing Twentieth-century China*, pp. 253–79, and Shue, "Global imaginings." Note in particular the interesting linkage made by Barmé between national-culturalist assertiveness and self-loathing in China. For a different perspective on Chinese national assertiveness and the sense of insecurity, see Fei-Ling Wang, "Self-image and strategic intentions: national confidence and political insecurity," in Yong Deng and Fei-Ling Wang, eds., *In the Eyes of the Dragon: China Views the World* (New York: Rowman and Littlefield, 1999), as well as some of the companion essays collected in that volume.

33 For one major study of corruption and communism in China, see Xiaobo Lü, *Cadres and Corruption: The Organizational Involution of the Chinese Communist Party* (Stanford: Stanford University Press, 2000). The pervasiveness of the oppositionist popular discourse on corruption in China today has been widely noted in journalistic and scholarly accounts. In fact, anyone who lives in China, even for a short time, inevitably hears the angry and sometimes threatening complaints made openly by common people against corruption in government.

34 James Watson, "Standardizing the gods: the promotion of T'ien Hou ('Empress of Heaven') along the South China Coast, 960–1960," in David Johnson, Andrew Nathan, and Evelyn Rawski, eds., *Popular Culture in Late Imperial China* (Berkeley: University of California Press, 1985), pp. 292–324.

35 On these issues, see also the excellent introduction in Meir Shahar and Robert Weller, eds., *Unruly Gods: Divinity and Society in China* (Honolulu: University of Hawaii Press, 1996), ch. 1.

36 Prasenjit Duara, *Culture, Power, and the State: Rural North China 1900–1942* (Stanford: Stanford University Press, 1988).

37 Prasenjit Duara, *Rescuing History from the Nation* (Chicago: University of Chicago Press, 1995), pp. 226–7.

38 For sensitive analyses of the pedagogic project of the contemporary Chinese state, see Ann Anagnost, "Politics and magic in contemporary China," *Modern China* 13(1) (1987), pp. 41–61, and Anagnost, *National Past-times*.

39 For an analysis of the state's discourse on raising the "quality" of the people, see Anagnost, *National Past-times*, ch. 5.

40 Kenneth Dean, "Ritual and space: civil society or popular religion?" in Timothy Brook and B. Michael Frolic, eds., *Civil Society in China* (Armonk, NY: M.E. Sharpe, 1998), p. 172.

41 This category of syncretic sect has been most thoroughly explored in *ibid.*, and also in Kenneth Dean, *Lord of the Three in One: The Spread of a Cult in Southeast China* (Princeton: Princeton University Press, 1998).

42 *Ibid.*, p. 289.

43 *Ibid.*, p. 295.

44 For one account of a local government's attempt to turn a shrine into a profit-earning tourist attraction in south China, see Jonathan Unger and Anita Chan, "Inheritors of the boom: private enterprise and the role of local government in a rural south China township," *China Journal* 42 (1999), pp. 45–74.

45 See Anagnost, *National Past-times*, ch. 7. On ethnic tourism and the commodification of minority culture in China, see Louisa Schein, *Minority Rules: The Miao and the Feminine in China's Cultural Politics* (Durham, NC: Duke University Press, 2000), pp. 155–9 and 125–7.

46 For more on the transnational aspect of *qigong* practice and of Falun Gong in particular, see Nancy Chen, *Breathing Spaces: Qigong, Psychiatry, and Healing in China* (New York: Columbia University Press, 2003), esp. ch. 7.

47 For more on the content of Li's teachings, see Shue, "Global imaginings."

48 Li Hongzhi and other Falun Gong spokespersons have steadfastly maintained that their beliefs and practices are entirely apolitical. Most ordinary Falun Gong practitioners doubtless also share this view of their activities, even, one suspects, many of those who have made the decision to confront state prohibitions directly by continuing their demonstrations.

49 Thompson, *Whigs and Hunters*, p. 258.

50 Or, as Perry, *Challenging the Mandate of Heaven*, p. xx, explains: "Fear of the loss of the Mandate of Heaven was generally seen as the driving force behind the campaign [to suppress Falun Gong]." See here also (pp. xv–xvi) Perry's analysis of the factors of "timing, scale, and composition" of the movement as contributors to the Chinese government's determination to launch a "drastic initiative" to wipe it out – "an initiative so out of step with its [more permissive and conciliatory] attitude toward labor disputes, tax riots or even student . . . demonstrations."

51 David Shambaugh, *China's Communist Party: Atrophy and Adaptation* (Berkeley: University of Califiornia Press, 2008), p. 111 and *passim.*

52 Thomas Heberer and Gunter Schubert, "Political Reform and Regime Legitimacy in Contemporary China," *Asien* 99 (2006), pp. 9–28.

53 *Ibid.*, pp. 13–14.

54 By some of these accounts, however, "not even nationalism could replace the yearning for spiritual fulfilment." So popular religious beliefs and practices such as those of Falun Gong are seen as helping to fill the "vacuum" left by the destruction of "the myth and cult-like image of the late Chairman Mao." John Wong and William Liu, *The Mystery of China's Falun Gong: Its Rise and its Sociological Implications* (Singapore: East Asian Institute, Singapore University Press, 1999), pp. 47–9.

55 Karen Petrone, *Life Has Become More Joyous, Comrades: Celebrations in the Time of Stalin* (Bloomington: Indiana University Press, 2000), p. 209. And as Petrone further points out (p. 9), "Although it was published much later, Bakhtin's very influential definition of carnival was written in the Soviet Union in the late 1930s and can itself be read as resistance to the Stalinist order. Bakhtin rejected official Soviet celebrations as the 'official truth' and looked to popular culture for opportunities to overthrow the official discourse, at least temporarily." For more on the recalcitrance of popular culture even during the high-Stalin era, see also Anne Gorsuch, *Youth in Revolutionary Russia: Enthusiasts, Bohemians, Delinquents* (Bloomington: Indiana University Press, 2000).

56 Thompson, *Whigs and Hunters*, p. 262.

57 On this point, see the moving account of the highly intricate and deeply moral understanding of state, society, legitimacy, and responsibility held by the people of a remote community in south-west China, in Erik Mueggler, *The Age of Wild Ghosts: Memory, Violence, and Place in Southwest China* (Berkeley: University of California Press, 2001).

58 Weber, *Economy and Society*, p. 953.

3 Society in the state

China's nondemocratic political pluralization[1]

Andrew Mertha

In the 1990s, a growing number of scholars attempted to graft onto China the civil society framework emerging from the various "soft" revolutions in Eastern Europe. There were a number of good reasons for seeking to do so. First, if we could identify enough significant parallels, we would be able to leverage our understanding of these phenomena and make robust cross-sectional generalizations, and even predictions. Second, from a normative standpoint, it certainly appeared that the political outcomes tended to be better for the societies than had been life under state socialism. Finally, the 1989 crackdown in Beijing, Chengdu, and elsewhere in China caused a number of Sinologists to rethink their assessments of the People's Republic and left them struggling to find an explanation for what had happened.

Although some excellent scholarship emerged at that time,[2] what distinguished it from the majority of less successful attempts was the former's willingness to incur criticism over their "Chinese exceptionalist" approaches because they simply did not see the similarities between the Chinese and the Eastern European cases that so many others had wanted to see. In China during the early half of the 1990s, government and Chinese Communist Party (CCP) intrusion into non-state institutions, associations, and practices continued apace and the lines where state left off and where society began (and vice versa) remained impossibly murky. This was not simply a function of China's coercive infrastructure. It was also because of the basic dynamics of governance in China since the founding of the People's Republic in 1949. Except perhaps between 1973 and 1977, there was never a time in China where János Kádár's famous remark that "those who are not against us are with us" truly fit: the Chinese state was always sufficiently activist to require, and receive, more than passive acceptance from its citizenry.

Nevertheless, even as the Eastern European model fell by the wayside, the desire for political freedom evinced by the students and citizenry in 1989 was difficult to simply discard as an anomaly: there continued to be dynamics in society that were not consistent with the goals of the state. And it was difficult to capture these with the existing political frameworks that focused predominantly on the state. As China entered its third decade of reform, this is truer now than it has ever been.

Contentious politics

Recent literature on democratization in China tends to focus on elite-driven change, either from the top or through grassroots efforts in line with the Organic Law.[3] But this stressing of democratization in China has contributed to a blind spot which obscures the political liberalization taking place right in front of our eyes, in real time, specifically, the evolution of a more pluralistic policy process.

Other recent scholarship focuses on the fact that while state capacity has eroded to the extent that organized protest is increasingly becoming a political reality in China, the state's coercive power remains strong enough to resist the demands of many of these protests, rendering the latter more symbolic than substantive.

The State Security Bureau has released widely cited figures of 58,000 protests in 2003, 74,000 in 2004, and 87,000 in 2005,[4] which represent a dramatic upward trajectory since 1993. There has been debate over the significance of these numbers. Some argue that these figures are relatively small when one looks at China's overall population or that only a few of these are large-scale organized protests as we might imagine them in the West, and that a large percentage of them are small and insignificant.[5] Others argue that urban workers have been similarly ineffective as they are hindered by the fragmentation of the workforce, the poor prospects for workers disenfranchised by reform, the strong deterrent measures for potential protest leaders, and the strategic dismantling of the state-owned enterprise sector to minimize social instability (or, rather, to isolate into smaller groups those laid-off workers who would be most likely to lead a protest).[6]

Certainly, there has been no shortage of discrete events which have captured the attention of the Chinese public and the world.

- In 2007, the story of Chongqing's "nail house" (*dingzi hu* 钉子户) achieved the status of legend. Wu Ping (吴平), a homeowner in Chongqing (重庆), refused to give up rights of return on her property when she was offered what she considered insufficient compensation from developers who wanted to build a luxury apartment complex. Wu and her husband held out for three years until their house, perched on a lone column of land surrounded by the excavation site, was finally demolished in April 2007. Wu's "nail-like" (*xiang dingzi yiyang* 象钉子一样) tenacity transformed her into a folk hero.
- In Wanzhou (万州), also in Chongqing, on October 18, 2004, a full-scale riot involving tens of thousands of citizens erupted when a man named Hu Quanzong beat up porter Yu Jikui for allegedly bumping into him and his wife (and muddying her pant leg) as they were walking down the street. Hu claimed (falsely) that he was a high official (he is, in fact, a fruit vendor) and exhorted the crowd to "knock off" (*da* 打) Yu, adding that he would pay 20,000 RMB to have it done. The protests emerged

less because of the altercation itself – which is a fairly common occurrence in China – but rather because this *faux* cadre's words rang true: officials were largely above and beyond the law.[7]

- In Weng'an (瓮安) County, Guizhou Province, on June 28, 2008, thousands protested what they deemed local authorities' investigation into the alleged rape and murder of a sixteen-year-old girl after she was last seen walking off with two men with ties to the Public Security Bureau.[8]
- The July 5, 2009, riots in the capital city, Urumqi, as well as in the prefecture municipality, Kashgar, of the Xinjiang Uyghur Autonomous Region (*Xinjiang weiwuer zizhiqu* 新疆维吾尔自治区), have laid bare the simmering resentments of the traditionally dominant minority, the Uyghur, against increasing Han in-migration, the growing income inequalities in the region, and the steady erosion of Uyghur culture, all in the name of modernization and economic development. The rioting left approximately 200 people dead and thousands injured.[9]

Still others have focused on the process of the protests themselves and how protesters can come away with something, even if they lose. In their work on "rightful resistance," O'Brien and Li conceptualize it as "a form of popular contention that operates near the boundary of authorized channels, employs the rhetoric and commitments of the powerful to curb the exercise of power, hinges on locating and exploiting divisions within the state, and relies on mobilizing support from the wider public." Specifically, rightful resistance "entails the innovative use of laws, policies, and other officially promoted values to defy disloyal political and economic elites."[10]

Yet, the limitations of these actions are all-too-readily apparent. A 2004 survey by Chinese Academy of Social Sciences (CASS) sociologist Yu Jianrong found that even though petitions to the central government had risen by 46 percent from 2002 to 2003, "only two-hundredths of 1 percent of those who used the system said it worked."[11]

My argument – while perfectly consistent with O'Brien and Li's – focuses rather on different processes, occurring in tandem, but largely independent of the more grassroots processes they document. In the case I present here, opponents to state policy are not simply content with *resisting* policies that affect them directly; they also seek to *change* the substance of broader policies. Second, a related point, their principal targets are not merely those local officials whose corruption and other malfeasance run counter to legal and other norms. Rather, their focus is on entering and working within the policy process to meet their principal policy-related goals.

While certainly lacking the drama of the protests listed above, quieter but more systematic and wider-ranging developments have also been taking shape whereby the Chinese policymaking process has become increasingly pluralized. Under this pluralization, otherwise marginalized officials, non-governmental organizations (NGOs), and activists of all stripes have managed to push their way into the policymaking process and even help shape policy outcomes. They have succeeded in part because they have understood and accepted the general rules of the game of policymaking under the rubric of "fragmented authoritarianism."[12]

"Fragmented authoritarianism 2.0"

There are few well-informed China watchers who would argue with the statement that China has become less authoritarian over the past two decades. There are several reasons for this. First, the institutions that arose during the pre-reform era have adapted to the issues facing China today only imperfectly. The problems these bureaucracies face are arguably more fast-moving and complex than was the case under Mao. The 1998 government downsizing, as well as the proliferation of leadership small groups and the diluting of the concept of *xitong* (系统; clusters of bureaucracies joined by particular policies) all attest to this. The state has responded by delegating responsibilities to economic, social, and other types of actors, whether NGOs, attached units run by government agencies that provide budgetary revenue through profitable commercial activities, or other non-state or quasi-state hybrids under the rubric of "small state, large society" (*xiao zhengfu da shehui* 小政府大社会). Second, there seems to be a gradual recognition by state actors that as information becomes more accessible to China as a whole, there are experts who use such information in a way that is useful to these state actors (who themselves do not possess these same skills) and are thus sought out by the latter. Finally, there is a reinforcing effect whereby success breeds more success: once policy entrepreneurs participate in the policy process and their efforts contribute to a demonstrably successful outcome without drawing prohibitive sanctions the result is more – rather than less – policy entrepreneurship in the future.

Yet the basic political structure has not changed. The "fragmented authoritarianism" (FA) framework, first proposed in 1988, has remained the most durable heuristic through which to study Chinese politics. It asserts that policy made at the center becomes increasingly malleable to the parochial organizational and political goals of various vertical agencies and spatial regions charged with enforcing that policy. Outcomes are shaped by the incorporation of interests of the implementation agencies into the policy itself. In short, FA explains the policy process as being governed by incremental change via bureaucratic bargaining.

What *has* changed is that some key actors previously barred from engaging in political and policy processes are now allowed – sometimes grudgingly tolerated, sometimes enthusiastically welcomed – to participate. This chapter suggests that previously excluded members of the policymaking process in China, officials only peripherally connected to the policy in question, the media, NGOs, and individual activists have successfully entered the political process precisely by adopting the strategies necessary to work within the structural and procedural constraints of the FA framework. The point of entry is the fragmentation and agency slack that result from institutions unable to adapt sufficiently to rapid socioeconomic change, aggressive lobbying of interest groups, or the changing expectations of the citizenry. These spaces are fertile ground for policy change, provided that the right set of elements are in position.

Policy entrepreneurs

The most important of these are "policy entrepreneurs." John Kingdon defines policy entrepreneurs as "advocates for proposals or for the prominence of an idea" and describes their defining characteristic as "their willingness to invest their resources – time, energy, reputation, and sometimes money – in the hope of a future return . . . [including] in the form of policies of which they approve."[13] A fragmented political system allows policy entrepreneurs a key resource necessary to compete in such a way within the policy process, specifically, the existence of the "spaces" necessary for them to exist without being snuffed out by the coercive apparatus of the state. In fragmented political systems, territorial, jurisdictional, and other political cleavages provide comparatively fertile ground for various contending state interests to push their agendas and to arrive at compromises that better reflect their own parochial or institutional goals, which is exactly the method employed by the policy entrepreneurs in China. In other words, the political dynamics captured in the FA framework provide policy entrepreneurs with a road map, a playbook by which they can pursue their policy goals. They adopt the strategies that traditional institutions have used for decades to pursue their agendas and institutional mandates.

There are three new types of policy entrepreneurs in China that figure prominently here: disgruntled or disenfranchised officials, the media, and NGOs.

The first are officials within Chinese government agencies opposed to a given policy, often because of official organizational mandates. These units are able to voice their opposition in part because their policy portfolios give them a degree of political cover. Conversely, by refraining from pursuing their organizational mandates, these units run the risk of being seen as weak or even irrelevant, a potentially deadly label in the current era of administrative downsizing and bureaucratic fat-cutting. Similarly, they may be officials embedded in weak or non-influential offices who seek to enlarge their jurisdictional mandates through extending them to new policy areas.[14]

A second category of policy entrepreneurs is comprised of journalists and editors in a gradually evolving, increasingly liberal media environment. Although it is important to avoid overstating the growing parameters of acceptable discourse in China, newspapers, magazines, and television broadcasts have provided a platform for journalists to pursue stories that match their own increasingly progressive interests and agendas. This, in turn, has been reinforced by a Chinese media increasingly required to generate its own budgetary revenue. As a result, it must rely on advertising, which can be attracted only by increased circulation and readership.[15] Toward this end, there has been a dramatic increase in the proportion of tabloid journalism stories that, in addition to racy sex stories, cover government injustice, civil protest, and the like.

One particularly important node of the media's power is the close relationship it shares with many Chinese NGOs. Indeed, the successes of NGOs in Chinese politics can be explained, at least in part, by the large number of officers and staff members who were trained as journalists or editors, giving them especially close access to the media. NGOs are a critical set of actors that define the contours of policy entrepreneurship in China. There are anywhere from 300,000 to 2 million NGOs in China today. Of course, such NGOs can range from the grassroots good governance advocates deep in the countryside to the lobbying associations identified by Scott Kennedy, as well as local trade associations that emerge largely independent from – indeed, often in contention with – government policy. What characterizes all of these NGOs is that they are different from those helping to bring about regime change in the Soviet Union and Eastern Europe because they must work *within* the Leninist party-state and must avoid even the appearance of threatening the structural status quo if they wish to survive, let alone effect policy change.[16]

Issue frames

Policy entrepreneurs interpret events using existing ideas in a new way, often with the goal of convincing potential supporters. This can be done by "articulating" how an issue is described. Entrepreneurs link up and assemble events in order to establish a natural and persuasive narrative, offering a fresh, alternative perspective on the issue in question.[17] They pick symbols that can be packaged in such a way that they offer an alternative perspective by which to understand and appreciate events, objects, and situations.[18] Policy entrepreneurs also "amplify" the issue by identifying its core components and bundling them into an engaging narrative, which they can sell to potential supporters. Such narratives contain deliberate references to historical antecedents, metaphors and analogies, and images.[19]

Berinsky and Kinder articulate the notion of framing as "complicated event sequences [organized] . . . in a manner that conforms to the structure of a good story." How an issue is framed, they argue, helps explain why some events are better remembered than others.[20] Social movement scholars have taken this one step further and have argued that issue framing not only aids in the recollection of events, but can even act to actually mobilize citizens to engage actively in the political process.[21]

The concept of framing is important because it suggests a number of dimensions not captured in the current literature on policymaking in China. First, it shows a degree of heft within the Chinese media in its ability to report critically on issues that would have been unthinkable a decade or more ago. It also shows a sophistication of the media in providing its consumers with stories on events that are couched in terms that obviate Beijing's monopoly on how to spin them. Third, it further shows the effects of NGOs in China – many of their leaders are current or former journalists or editors – in spearheading this media assault. Fourth, it demonstrates the intimate contact between these media outlets and government leaders in Beijing and in the localities and how this has dramatically affected the policy*making* process, and not simply the *implementation* of policy already agreed upon in Beijing. Finally, it provides the open door necessary to "expand the sphere of political conflict," in Schattschneider's now-classic phrase,[22] by transforming hitherto irrelevant actors not traditionally associated with the policy (but which are now relevant because of the oppositional issue frame cast by the initial policy entrepreneurs) into allies.

In China, "state framing"[23] is somewhat indistinguishable from official propaganda. Some types of framing appear to be quite strong – the shift of Falun Gong from a somewhat suspicious homegrown spiritual society to its current conception as a poisonous cult – and is backed up by the state's coercive apparatus. Similarly, one is likely to find very little deviation from the government "line" (*dixian* 底线) on hot-button issues like Taiwan and Tibet. Others, such as "The Three Represents" (*sange daibiao* 三个代表), have drawn scorn from both citizens and, privately, many officials.

What is far more interesting is the *unofficial* framing that has emerged and how it has shaped the policy processes in the past several years. Of course, there is some scholarship on the role of framing in the political process in China, but it tends to focus almost exclusively on the mass protests of 1989,[24] a set of events that is largely unique and unlikely to be replicated while the current regime remains in power. As such, it is not particularly helpful in allowing us to generalize beyond that single, special case.

The international political economy of cigarette lighters

I have made this argument elsewhere with regard to the issue of China's hydropower policy.[25] In this chapter, I extend this to the policy area of international trade. In doing so, I am making the following claim: this political pluralization is not simply an outcome of the interaction of domestic and international factors; it can also explain China's foreign policy behavior. In other words, these processes cannot be conceptually limited to domestic structures and processes, but apply to international ones as well, as the case that follows makes clear.

Lighters are a fairly recent luxury in China. Until the early 1990s, most smokers used matches. Wenzhou began producing lighters in the late 1980s. Based on the experience in Japan a generation or so earlier, the Wenzhou lighter industry began working on medium-quality lighters, including windproof ones. In the early days, household businesses would emerge in which there was intense specialization in various component parts of the lighters, much like the extensive supply chain we see in Japan.

In 1991, Huang Fajing established the Rifeng Corporation. Far from cornering the market, Huang faced an environment of intense competition. In 1993, there were 2,000 lighter and lighter components manufacturers (assembling from parts made by local companies) in Wenzhou. These companies were largely family operations run out of peoples' homes. The family patriarch was usually the boss, and the employees included brothers, sisters, and cousins. The average size of these operations was between four and five people (the shift from cottage industries to factories began in earnest in 1994, around which time technical expertise also began to take off). Because of the inevitable problems of quality control that arose from such an environment of unbridled competition, the Wenzhou government established an office to test and inspect each factory, and if the factory and its products were not up to threshold quality, they were denied a license. This brought the number of lighter and lighter-parts factories down to around 300.

At the end of 1992, the Wenzhou Lighter Industry Association (WLIA) was established. This association was able to rein in the collective action problem so that quality grew and Wenzhou could begin developing its own designs for lighters. In addition, the WLIA began a program to protect industry from unfair competition in which each industry association member was compelled to sign an affidavit to defer to association rulings when applying for product design rights (i.e. de facto patents). These designs are then evaluated and published in local newspapers for comment. If nobody opposes the new design within a five-day window, the "patent" (*zhuanli* 专利) is granted. As a result, there is an intellectual property right (IPR)/patent mechanism *completely within the industry association*. If there are found to be cases of infringement, the association handles them.[26] The WLIA was one of the first associations to do this, but it is now an increasingly common feature of industry associations.

However, in 1994, international developments stretched the WLIA's abilities to breaking point. The United States was instituting a standard that required lighters valued at US$2 or less to adopt child-resistant properties. This took the Wenzhou lighter industry, which was still in its infancy, completely by surprise. As a result of the passage of this law, export volume in Wenzhou dropped 70 percent *in one month*. Huang resolved that he would not be caught off guard by such exogenous shocks again.[27]

His vigilance was tested in 2001. In April, Huang was advised by ELIAS (European Lighter Importers Association) President Klaus Troeber that the European Union (EU) was planning on establishing a child safety standard. Although this came as a shock to the Chinese manufacturers, these developments had already been going on within the EU for several years. In 1998, four years after the adoption of the regulations in the US, the European Commission issued a mandate (in reality, a request) to the European Standardization Organization (CEN) to develop a European standard for lighters covering child resistance (CR) requirements, which were to take into account the US standards. The Chinese saw no meaningful difference in the language between the two sets of regulations except that the proposed EU standards had substituted a €2 threshold instead of the $2 threshold in the US regulations. On Troeber's advice, Huang put the WLIA's opposition to the proposed CR standards on the record.[28]

These proposed standards were part of the EU–China negotiations over China's World Trade Organization (WTO) accession package.[29] In October, Huang drafted a document for the State Quality Examination Supervision and Quarantine General Bureau, its Wenzhou counterpart, and to other relevant municipal units, outlining the views of WLIA, and sought to provide the context on how Chinese industries would be negatively affected. Everywhere the response was the same: we appreciate your predicament, but lighter manufacturing is simply not a strategically important part of the economy.

Huang was a bit more successful with the media. At the same time as he was appealing for support from the government, Huang sent out press releases for a conference that he was sponsoring at the Wenzhou International Hotel. He personally invited WLIA members, local and national media outlets, and officials (such as Wenzhou Jucheng District Chief Li Zhongsu) in their capacity as private citizens to a conference on December 21, 2001. The meeting was entitled the "Wenzhou Study Meeting of Common Interests to Resist the Proposed EU CR Law." By bankrolling the event himself, he was able to go beyond official government talking points. The media duly reported on it and thus elevated the issue onto the media wires and into cyberspace.

In the months that followed, Huang Fajing wrote a number of reports and op-ed pieces in various Chinese media sources, which found wide distribution. Some of his reports also made their way into the restricted internal government news sources, the *Neibu cankao ziliao* (内部参考资料). Indeed, when asked about this issue during the annual Bo'an Forum, then Premier Zhu Rongji stated that he was already aware of it.[30]

At the same time, a happy coincidence of shared interests was being forged. The Fair Trade Bureau (FTB) (*Jinchukou gongping maoyi ju* 进出口 公平贸易局) of the Ministry of Commerce (MOFCOM) was established in November 2001, immediately after China's accession to the WTO. The charge of the FTB is to remedy trade barriers, including specifically responding to and initiating anti-dumping procedures (there is a "trade barriers division," *Maoyi bilei diaocha chu* (贸易壁垒调查处) [although "trade" has since been dropped from the title to expand its scope to include investment], which handles foreign trade barriers, as distinct from "foreign allegations of Chinese trade barriers"). The latter are handled by various government bureaus, depending on the nature of the actual allegations (most are handled somewhere in MOFCOM).

The CR lighter case arrived at the doorstep of the FTB in January 2002. The FTB had not been fully established. Indeed, between November 2001 and January 2002, the FTB was mostly focusing on administrative issues necessary to actually set up the office. Most of these efforts were centered on informing others that the office actually existed (i.e. propaganda). Since the FTB was fishing around for a case to begin to do its work, it embraced the CR issue.[31]

In addition to direct contact with Huang, this case also came up "through a very strange channel": Vice Premier and former trade negotiator Wu Yi was in Wenzhou on a fact-finding trip that took her to several cities in Zhejiang province. While in Wenzhou, she met with the local lighter association, who informed Wu Yi about their situation.

On February 6, ranking national officials led by FTB Director Wang Jiechun came down to Wenzhou to discuss the CR draft law. By this time, local officials were getting the message from Beijing that they should take this seriously: Huang received support from the Wenzhou Municipal Government and from municipal bureaus that not long before had rebuffed Huang's efforts.[32]

Things on the European side were moving apace. The voluntary standard (EN 13869) was adopted in 2002.[33] But this was regarded as suboptimal by many in the EU. This provided an opportunity for the Chinese side to try to influence the decision to move it closer to Beijing's ideal point. In the spring of 2002, another delegation led by the Deputy Director-General of the FTB (and including Huang Fajing) went to Europe to discuss the issue with the EU authorities.[34]

On March 21, 2003, an official body was established that indicated that, for the first time, the government was officially involved in the discrete EU CR issue. This body eventually became known as the Chinese Government Joint Delegation (*Zhongguo zhengfu lianhe daibiaotuan* 中国政府联合代表团). This group embarked on a tour of six EU countries, including Germany, Italy, Belgium, Spain, France, and Portugal. The group included four people from government (i.e. the FTB) and three from industry, including Huang Fajing. The business people paid for themselves and the government people paid for *them*selves, even though, as Huang Fajing himself noted, "we [the industry people] paid for the banquets and incidentals." The Chinese were able to evince that the Europeans had begun to appreciate the Chinese position and the Chinese points of view. These efforts were reported in the European media, including the local Chinese media in Europe. In China the impact was even greater. "Almost everybody in China" was aware of what was going on, according to Huang, who added, "if the people know, so does the government."[35]

In 2004, 2005, and 2006, Beijing sent an ever-growing set of delegations to the EU, which visited an increasing number of countries. These delegations included representatives from the FTB, Wenzhou and Ningbo lighter businesses, European importers of Chinese lighters, representatives from the Wenzhou government, and, of course, Huang Fajing. Over time, the two sides became increasingly sympathetic to the concerns of the other side. Bringing the situation full circle, in late 2006, the Ministry of Commerce sponsored a panel discussion in Wenzhou on lighter child safety standards, with Huang as one of the organizers.[36]

The European Commission was still trying to ameliorate what it saw as an imperfect situation,[37] ultimately proposing that member states adopt a specific Commission Decision (not a Directive) under article 13 of the GPSD, to ban non-CR lighters as well as novelty lighters.[38] Although the language of the standard includes the €2 threshold, the Decision includes technical parameters to distinguish between lighters in or outside the scope of the Decision because EU member states felt that lighter safety should not be linked to the cost of a product. In essence, the €2 standard was rendered toothless. This was seen as a significant victory by the Chinese side because they saw that their concerns had been incorporated into the Decision.[39]

Traditional foreign trade policy: Sino–EU CR lighter trade policy

Policy entrepreneurship: Huang Fajing

Although a simple Google search easily illustrates Huang Fajing's talent for self-promotion, it is nevertheless extraordinary that China's first dispute – the first battle it chose to fight – as a WTO member was driven by the strategic concerns of a local lighter manufacturer in the backwater of a Wenzhou suburb. Huang Fajing's role as a policy entrepreneur was absolutely critical to shaping this entire process. He began as an "interested party" (*youguan dangshiren* 有关当事人) and coordinated these activities to get key Chinese officials to go to Europe to discuss these issues, particularly from MOFCOM's Fair Trade Bureau. He has interacted with the EU Health and Consumer Protection Directorate, EU member health directorates, and EU manufacturers and producers. Huang himself was honored as one of China Central Television's "Men of the Year" (*niandu renwu* 年度人物) in 2003,[40] and in late 2007 a feature film was released in China documenting Huang's travails, entitled "Brilliance in Europe" (*dianliang Ouzhou* 点亮欧洲).[41] Finally, this has also emboldened other Wenzhou-based industries, particularly eyeglass and leather shoes, to get involved in EU anti-dumping cases.

Issue framing: recasting "child safety" to appeal to Chinese nationalism

In addition to exploiting the chance opportunity of an underworked Fair Trade Bureau, Huang's policy entrepreneurship was best illustrated by the way in which he framed the issue. His December 2001 conference title – the Wenzhou Study Meeting of Common Interests to Resist the Proposed EU CR Law – was a clever device that evoked two long-running political themes. First, the use of the verb "resist" (*dizhi* 抵制) is particularly resonant of the language of the Korean War (or the "Resist America and Aid Korea" (*kangMei yuanChao* 抗美援朝) era. By injecting this phrase, Huang was able

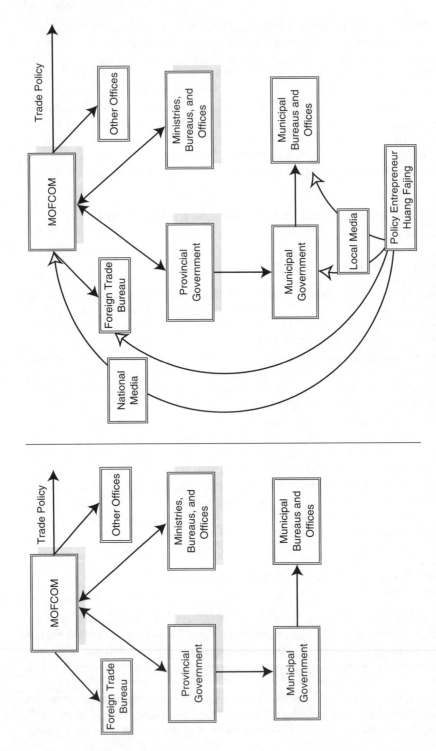

Figure 3.1 Traditional foreign trade policy

Figure 3.2 Sino–EU CR lighter trade policy

to animate this association for his audience. In addition, and perhaps less directly, Huang was able to evoke the national meta-narrative of China's "Century of Humiliation" (*bainian guochi* 百年国耻),[42] inspired by Europe yet again trying to prevent China from benefiting from, and thus being able to take its rightful place within, the global free trading system. In sum, Huang was able to reframe the issue from what was a bone-dry technical dispute to another, contemporary chapter of the long history of China being disadvantaged by the West under the heading of "fair trade under WTO rules" (*shimaozuzhide gongping maoyi guize* 世贸组织的公平贸易规则). At the time, "WTO fever" was running high in China and any story on the WTO seemed to find a media outlet. *This* story, in particular, that is, "the EU is violating its own WTO rules," was irresistible to the media, which made up a large part of the conference participants and dutifully reported on it.

Conclusion

In this chapter, I have argued that in addition to the many other forms of "contentious politics" taking place in China today, there is another, perhaps ultimately more substantively influential process that is unfolding. This idea of political pluralization within the constraints of the fragmented authoritarianism framework is different from other forms of contentious politics along several dimensions. First, it is not simply concerned with "letting off steam" or "standing on principle," but is focused on actual substantive policy change. Although not immune to criticism of "cooptation by the state," such a process is perhaps more akin to the post-1960s social movement conclusion that "to change the system, you have to become part of it," or at the very least to "work with it."

Second, unlike other forms of contentious politics in China today, this political liberalization is far less threatening to the status quo of state power in China. This is due in no small part to the conscious decision on the part of policy entrepreneurs not simply to appear nonthreatening, but to actually provide some sort of benefit to their potential allies within the system.

Finally, this means that such a framework is far more amenable to transportability to other policy areas. Unlike the more contentious dialectical model of "protest, crackdown, possibly improve upon the status quo ante (but really focus on ensuring that anger is nipped in the bud as opposed to resolved)," the framework I identify here has the benefit of securing government cooperation. It is therefore far more generalizable to other policy areas. Although it is important to avoid being Pollyannaish by overextending these findings, we should similarly start looking at political liberalization and pluralization – as opposed to democratization – as the more likely explanation for the explosion of interest articulation within the People's Republic of China's continuing authoritarian governance system.

Notes

1 I would like to thank Stanley Rosen and Peter Gries for including me in this volume. This chapter draws from recent research on hydropower policy in Yunnan and Sichuan (although individual interviews from this research are not cited) and industrial concentration in Wenzhou, Zhejiang, with additional interviews in Beijing. I am also grateful to Sebastian Heilmann, Lianjiang Li, William Lowry, Dorothy Solinger, and Patricia Thornton for comments on earlier versions. All errors are my own. Interviews are indicated by code below: the first two digits indicate the year, the middle letters indicate the location (Beijing is "BJ," and Wenzhou is "WZ"), and the last two digits indicate the overall interview sequence for a given locale (with A, B, C, etc. indicating the number – if more than one – of interviews with a given source).

2 See, *inter alia*, Dorothy Solinger, *Contesting Citizenship in Urban China: Peasant Migrants, the State, and the Logic of the Market* (Berkeley, CA: University of California Press, 1999); and Elizabeth J. Perry and Mark Selden, eds., *Chinese Society: Change, Conflict, and Resistance* (New York and London: Routledge, 2000).

3 On future democratization scenarios, see Bruce Gilley, *China's Democratic Future: How it Will Happen and Where it Will Lead* (New York: Columbia University Press, 2004). On local elections, see Melanie F. Manion, "The Electoral Connection in the Chinese Countryside," *American Political Science Review* 90(4) (1996), pp. 736–48; and M. Kent Jennings, "Political Pluralization in the Chinese Countryside," *American Political Science Review* 91(2) (1997), pp. 361–72.

4 Joseph Kahn, "Pace and Scope of Protest in China Accelerated in '05," *New York Times*, January 20, 2006.

5 Pierre F. Landry and Tong Yanqi, "Disputing the Authoritarian State in China," paper presented at the annual meeting of the American Political Science Association, Washington, D.C., September 1, 2005.

6 Cai Yongshun, *State and Laid-off Workers in Reform China: The Silence and Collective Action of the Retrenched* (London: Routledge, 2005); Ching Kwan Lee, "From the Specter of Mao to the Spirit of the Law: Labor Insurgency in China," *Theory and Society* 31, April 2, 2002, pp. 189–228; William Hurst and Kevin J. O'Brien, "China's Contentious Pensioners," *China Quarterly* 170 (June 2002), pp. 345–60; and Hurst, "Understanding Contentious Collective Action by Chinese Laid-off Workers: The Importance of Regional Political Economy," *Studies in Comparative International Development* 39(2) (Summer 2004), pp. 94–120.

7 *Ibid.*

8 Jim Yardley, "Chinese Riot over Handling of Girl's Killing," *New York Times*, June 30, 2008.

9 Edward Wong, "China Raises Death Toll in Ethnic Clashes to 184," *New York Times*, July 10, 2009.

10 Kevin J. O'Brien and Lianjiang Li, *Rightful Resistance in Rural China* (New York: Cambridge University Press, 2006), p. 2.

11 Joseph Kahn, "China's 'Haves' Stir the 'Have Nots' to Violence," *New York Times*, December 31, 2004.

12 Kenneth Lieberthal and Michel Oksenberg, *Policy Making in China: Leaders, Structures, and Processes* (Princeton, NJ: Princeton University Press, 1988), p. 4.

13 John W. Kingdon, *Agendas, Alternatives, and Public Policies*, 2nd edn. (New York: HarperCollins, 1995), pp. 122–3.

14 Andrew C. Mertha, *The Politics of Piracy: Intellectual Property in Contemporary China* (Ithaca, NY: Cornell University Press, 2005), ch. 5.

15 Daniel C. Lynch, *After the Propaganda State: Media, Politics, and "Thought Work" in Reformed China* (Stanford, CA: Stanford University Press, 1999).

16 Michael Büsgen, "NGOs and the Search for Chinese Civil Society: Environmental Non-Governmental Organizations in the Nujiang Campaign," master's thesis, Institute for Social Studies, Graduate School of Development Studies, The Hague, Netherlands, 2005, pp. 2–3. Scott Kennedy, *The Business of Lobbying in China* (Cambridge, MA: Harvard University Press, 2005).
17 John A. Noakes and Hank Johnson, "Frames of Protest: A Road Map to a Perspective," in Johnson and Noakes, eds., *Frames of Protest: Social Movements and the Framing Perspective* (Lanham, MD: Rowman and Littlefield), p. 8.
18 *Ibid.* See also William A. Gamson, "Political Discourse and Collective Action," *International Journal of Social Movements, Conflict, and Change* 1 (1988), pp. 219–44.
19 Hanspeter Kriesi and Dominique Wistler, "The Impact of Social Movements on Political Institutions: A Comparison of the Introduction of Direct Legislation in Switzerland and the United States," in Marco Giugni, Doug McAdam, and Charles Tilly, eds., *How Social Movements Matter* (Minneapolis, MN: University of Minnesota Press, 2002), pp. 42–65.
20 Adam J. Berinsky and Donald R. Kinder, "Making Sense of Issues through Media Frames: Understanding the Kosovo Crisis," *Journal of Politics* 68(3) (August 2006), p. 640.
21 Noakes and Johnson, "Frames of Protest."
22 E.E. Schattschneider, *The Semisovereign People: A Realist's View of America* (New York: Holt, Rinehart and Winston, 1967).
23 John A. Noakes, "Official Frames in Social Movement Theory: The FBI, HUAC, and the Communist Threat in Hollywood," in Johnson and Noakes.
24 Zuo Jiping and Robert D. Benford, "Mobilization Processes and the 1989 Chinese Democracy Movement," *Sociological Quarterly* 36, pp. 131–56.
25 Andrew C. Mertha, *China's Water Warriors: Citizen Action and Policy Change* (Ithaca, NY: Cornell University Press, 2008).
26 Of course, this has not been without controversy, as the local government offices charged with protecting IPR have cried foul that these industry associations are moving onto their turf.
27 Interview 06WZ06, December 11, 2006.
28 WLIA members that signed the statement included the following lighter and smoking paraphernalia companies: Wenzhou Nanhu, Wenzhou Baofa, Wenzhou Yaorui, Wenzhou Shengtai, Wenzhou Zhengda, Wenzhou Lucheng, Wenzhou Rifeng, Wenzhou Dongda, Zhejiang Lisheng, Wenzhou Hongda, Wenzhou Hongri, Wenzhou Tehao, Wenzhou Wangjia, Wenzhou Weili, Wenzhou Dachuan, Wenzhou Ritan, and Wenzhou Taishan corporation (internal document provided by Rifeng Lighter Corporation).
29 Interview 06WZ06, December 11, 2006.
30 Interview 07WZ04, August 8, 2007.
31 Interview 06WZ06, December 11, 2006.
32 Interview 07BJ02, August 13, 2007.
33 In the EU, lighters are subject to the general safety requirement of the General Product Safety Directive 2001/95/EC (GPSD). However, this Directive does not include specific criteria for lighters (or any other products). In order to assist businesses and national market surveillance authorities, the GPSD allows for the referencing of European standards in the *Official Journal* of the EU, thereby conferring presumption of conformity with the GPSD for those products complying with such standards. For lighters, the EN ISO 9994 standard is referenced but this standard only includes general safety specifications for lighters and does not set out CR requirements. With the adoption of EN 13869 by CEN in 2002, such CR requirements were in place but the standard was not applied by industry, nor was it enforced by the national authorities (which in the EU have the sole responsibility for undertaking market surveillance).

34 Communication with EU official, December 9, 2008.
35 Interview 07WZ04, August 8, 2007.
36 "Ministry of Commerce Takes the Lead in Convening in Wenzhou a Conference on the European Child Safety Standards for Lighters," Huainan Intellectual Property Office website, http://zscq.hn.gov.cn/popbase.asp?id=676 (accessed December 22, 2008).
37 A 2002 study on the effectiveness of the initial 1994 US legislation reported a 60 percent reduction in fires, injuries, and deaths caused by children under five, due to the enforcement of CR requirements for lighters alone. An average of one hundred lives had been saved in the US every year since 1995 due to the introduction of CR requirements.
38 This Decision (2006/502/EC) is a temporary Decision valid for periods of only one year and has to be renewed yearly. These temporary Decisions are still in place and the Commission has given a second mandate to CEN to revise EN 13869, with the aim of publishing its reference in the *Official Journal*, and subsequently stop extending the Decisions, which are not intended as a permanent measure. The revision of EN 13869 aims amongst other things to bring the definition of lighters covered by its scope in line with that of the Decision.
39 Communication with EU official, December 9, 2008.
40 Http://www.88088.com/wzpp/sjmr/2008/0909/328927.shtml (accessed December 22, 2008).
41 Http://www.mtime.com/movie/76184/plots.html (accessed December 22, 2008). The movie is based in part on Huang Fajing's story, but there has been some artistic license to incorporate a love story and other fictionalized events.
42 Peter Hays Gries, *China's New Nationalism: Pride, Politics, and Diplomacy* (Berkeley, CA; University of California Press, 2005).

4 Protest leadership in rural China[1]

Lianjiang Li and Kevin J. O'Brien

Nearly every discussion of protest leadership begins with a statement that the topic remains woefully understudied.[2] Whether it is because most social scientists shy away from "great man theories of history," favor explanations that emphasize culture or structure over agency, or are put off by the idiosyncrasies of personality, examining the people who mobilize and plan collective action has largely been left to psychologists, journalists, and activists,[3] rather than sociologists or political scientists.

Studies of contention in rural China share this general orientation. Much has been learned about the origins, dynamics, and consequences of protest, but little about the people who stand at the center of the action. For every study of grievances, petitions, or demonstrations, there are only brief passages here and there about the individuals who make it all happen.[4] This article has the modest aim of redressing this imbalance a bit. In it, we offer a series of generalizations (and examples from the field) focused on two basic questions: what do protest leaders in rural China do? And how do villagers become protest leaders? Then we turn to an area where research on the Chinese countryside may be able to make a contribution to the study of contentious politics more broadly: the relationship of repression to mobilization. Here, though we find that repression sometimes inhibits further protest (as political opportunity theorists would predict), at other times it generates outrage, enhances popular support, and boosts the determination of protest leaders to persist.[5]

Sources and research sites

What follows is based on archival materials, in-depth interviews, and remarks made on a series of surveys we conducted from 1997 to 2005. Key written sources included: government reports detailing episodes of popular contention; accounts of "peasant leaders" (*nongmin lingxiu* 农民领袖) published by journalists, policy researchers, and scholars based in China; letters of complaint and essays penned by protest leaders; and Western studies of collective action in the Chinese countryside.

Interviewees ranged from officials and researchers in Beijing, Henan, Hubei, Hunan, and Jiangxi to township officials and protest leaders in Anhui, Fujian, Hebei, Henan, Hunan, Jiangxi, and Shandong. Interviews sometimes occurred in informal settings (e.g. at banquets, in hotel rooms, on trains) and sometimes were semi-structured. The more structured encounters with protest leaders typically began with a set of questions about a person's age, education, Party membership, political positions held (if any), family background, and out-of-the-ordinary experiences (e.g. having been in the army or an urban wage worker). Afterwards, respondents were usually guided to recount: (1) how they had started challenging political power holders; (2) what specific actions they had taken and what had transpired; (3) what they had gained or lost from taking part; (4) how their family members and neighbors had reacted to their activism; (5) what they had learned about themselves, other villagers, and various levels of government; and (6) how they felt about their actions now.

One of our important sources was a series of in-depth interviews with "complainants' representatives" (*shangfang daibiao* 上访代表) in Hengyang county (衡阳县), Hunan, most of which were conducted in January and March of 2003 by Dr. Yu Jianrong (于建嵘) of the Chinese Academy of Social Sciences. Hunan, along with a number of other provinces in China's central agricultural belt,[6] has been a hotbed of popular contention since the late 1980s. Yu enjoyed exceptional access to protest organizers in Hengyang, and he invited Lianjiang Li to conduct joint fieldwork with him to explore the course and consequences of a decade-long cycle of protest. All the interviews in Hengyang were recorded and transcribed. Some were also videotaped. Given the sensitivity of the topic, the selection of respondents was done quietly through personal networking. To explore new issues that arose during the course of the fieldwork, a number of protest leaders were interviewed several times.[7]

What protest leaders do

We use the term "protest leaders" to refer to people who initiate group petitions, mass demonstrations, and other types of collective action that target political power holders. There are no reliable estimates of how many protest leaders there are in the countryside, but few doubt that their number has increased over the last decade.[8] Chinese government sources, for example, have admitted that owing to the emergence of "a small number of individuals who organize, lead, and instigate the masses," the number of "collective incidents" (*quntixing shijian* 群体性事件) has jumped tenfold in the last dozen years, from 8,706 in 1993 to 87,000 in 2005, with about 40 percent of them occurring in the countryside. Moreover, the authorities have expressed alarm that such incidents have become more organized since the mid-1990s.[9]

Protest leaders provide leadership in a number of ways. They may literally lead the charge, by appearing at a government office to lodge complaints on behalf of others, by marching in front of an angry crowd that is "demanding a dialogue" (*yaoqiu duihua* 要求对话) with local officials, or by defying their adversaries face to face. In Hengyang county, Hunan, for instance, a man concerned with over-taxation was doing housework when he heard indignant neighbors shouting "robbers" and "thieves" at some township cadres who had come to collect yet another unauthorized fee. He rushed to the scene and found that an elderly villager who refused to pay up had been knocked to the ground by the tax collectors. He began arguing with the taxmen and demanded that they cease collecting illegal fees and compensate the old man for his injuries. In short order, dozens of villagers poured out of their homes and joined him in condemning the township for excessive extraction. The dispute turned into a brawl after an official hit the protest leader on the head with a flashlight.[10]

Sometimes such leadership is close to accidental. In these cases, popular discontent may be running high, but no protests are on the horizon until one or more individuals openly confront officials, setting off a significant event. This is what happened in Cangshan county (苍山县), Shandong. The county had ordered local farmers to grow garlic-shoots but then failed to deliver the marketing assistance it had promised. Helpless garlic-growers were left to watch their hard-earned harvest rot. Public anger mounted. On a hot market day, a single irate villager and his wife suddenly charged the county government compound and demanded to see the county head. Moments later hundreds of farmers who happened to be milling about also rushed into the compound. The county head failed to appear, and the crowd became increasingly agitated. Then a few individuals smashed a glass door and ran into an office building. Many offices were ransacked, and nearly a thousand pieces of furniture and reams of government archives were destroyed. The man who initiated the incident professed no desire to set off a mass protest, let alone a riot, but his action did just this. He was later detained for "instigating a major social disturbance," but many community members thanked him for the marketing assistance that suddenly appeared once the popular action ended.[11]

A more recent episode in Jiangxi, in which hundreds of villagers raided government offices, also occurred unexpectedly. On a market day in 1999, a car owned by a township collided with a two-wheeled cart, and a man who was pulling the cart was slightly injured. His wife, who had been riding in the cart, demanded compensation, but the township officials refused on grounds that it was the couple who had been in the wrong. A quarrel ensued, in which the woman loudly explained to onlookers how the township had mistreated villagers by collecting one unapproved fee after another. Linking this critique to the incident which had just occurred, she claimed that township officials levied unlawful taxes in part to buy themselves luxurious automobiles. A number of bystanders then joined her in condemning the township officials for increasing "peasant burdens" (*nongmin fudan* 农民负担) and for their corruption. After the officials who had been in the car fled into the township complex, the crowd followed them inside. When the police tried to drive out the angry villagers, fights broke out and some villagers began to smash windows in the government building.[12]

The authorities (quite accurately) consider this type of collective action "accidental" (*oufaxing* 偶发性) and usually argue that "the masses" (*qunzhong* 群众) followed a handful of law-breakers because they "did not know the facts" (*bu ming zhenxiang* 不明真相). Of course, more often than not, villagers know exactly what is going on, and they (and their inadvertent leaders) use a random incident to express their discontent about a widespread and deeply held grievance.

In most cases, however, protest leaders, rather than acting reactively and on the moment, perform some or all of the following four tasks.[13] First, they shape individually felt grievances into collective claims. Many rural people are dissatisfied with aspects of local governance, but their complaints do not automatically jell into collective discontent. Moreover, some villagers may assume that their suffering is caused by the government as a whole and thus feel powerless before a force that is "armed with fighter planes and missiles."[14] Even when villagers sense that a problem arises from official misconduct, they may not be able to pinpoint exactly what policy or law has been violated, and therefore find it overly risky to take action. In the words of a man from Hunan: "There are many regulations regarding peasant burdens and we do not know which burdens are lawful and which are not. If we make one mistake, we'll end up breaking the law."[15] Protest leaders, by contrast, typically know exactly which regulation local officials have ignored or distorted. A protest leader in Hunan, for instance, accumulated a large trove of government documents on tax limits and used them to convince other villagers that the township had acted against central policies when it collected exorbitant fees.[16]

Much like "framing" elsewhere, protest leaders construct an interpretation of the nature and source of a grievance that can be used to mobilize people to take part in collective action.[17] Usually, they attribute villagers' woes to local violation of a central policy, thus placing the blame squarely on rural officials and identifying a powerful potential ally in the central government. This framing converts a broad, inchoate sense of being wronged into a specific claim against named officials. It also fosters a feeling of empowerment by highlighting the vulnerabilities of one's targets. In one Hunan hamlet, villagers had complained about excessive fees for a number of years but did not act until a protest leader explained that township officials had ignored a central policy.[18] Also in Hunan, a protest leader spelled out to a group of villagers while they were dining in a country eatery how they had been overtaxed by the township. His fellow diners were so grateful that they insisted on paying his bill and then used the copies of central documents he gave them to lodge complaints about over-taxation.[19]

The second task commonly undertaken by protest leaders is recruiting activists and mobilizing the public. Recruiting is differential and often rests on existing social networks, such as fellow clan members, friends, or acquaintances.[20] Protest leaders also seek out villagers who are known to have grievances against rural officials. More cautious organizers tend to avoid accepting recruits who have criminal records or other political "stains" (*wudian* 污点), to avoid offering a pretext for repression and to dispel concerns that the contention will come to naught. When collective action draws on villagers from different communities, they usually strive to ensure that each community has at least one representative as a core leader. In Hengyang, Hunan, for instance, a protest leader recruited thirteen activists, one from each natural village involved in a series of collective petitions.[21] In Ningxiang county (宁乡县), Hunan, two organizers likewise recruited one or two activists from each village in Daolin town (道林镇) and appointed them "burden-reduction supervisors" (*jianfu jianduyuan* 减负监督员).[22]

Protest leaders mobilize supporters primarily through persuasion, though they sometimes employ more heavy-handed techniques. On the one hand, they try to coax others to join in by deploying the moral authority they have acquired by taking the initiative to defend villagers' interests. A man in Shandong, for instance, was beaten repeatedly by cronies of a village party secretary for demanding a thorough auditing of the village accounts. His "sacrifice," he said, won him many devoted followers, dozens of whom he persuaded to seize the village account books, after the party secretary had entrusted them to the township for safe-keeping.[23] On the other hand, protest leaders sometimes employ the threat of violence, property destruction, and social ostracism against free riders. "Petitioners' representatives" in Hebei, for example, sought to isolate villagers who refused to join petition campaigns by boycotting their weddings and funerals.[24] Protest leaders in Hebei had followers throw stones through the windows of neighbors who were reluctant to join an effort to topple a corrupt cadre.[25] In a Shandong village, protest leaders even threatened to drive out families who refused to support a mass demonstration against county officials who had failed to compensate the village after a dam flooded its farmland.[26]

The third major role played by protest leaders is devising and orchestrating collective action. Undertaking popular contention in present-day China is always a delicate matter. Although the authorities have granted citizens the right to hold demonstrations and lodge complaints, they nearly always prohibit popular action in the name of maintaining stability. Furthermore, the State Council's "Regulation Concerning Letters and Visits" (1995, revised 2005) allows complainants to petition as a group, but does not permit them to send more than five representatives at once (Art. 12 (1995), Art. 18 (2005)). As a result, protest leaders often find themselves in a dilemma. If they pursue their claims strictly according to law, their likelihood of prevailing is slim because they cannot apply sufficient pressure on their foes. If they hope to be effective, they have to work around or brush up against the law. Protest organizers must locate a means, in other words, to balance maximizing pressure on their opponents with minimizing the risk of repression. In the last two decades, they have employed a number of strategies to do this. One is to work around the law, paying attention to its letter, if not its spirit. They may, for instance, send no more than four persons to lodge a complaint, but set up many groups, each representing a nominally different constituency.[27] Another approach is to mobilize an enormous throng and to rely on the safety of numbers for protection.[28] A third strategy is to act in a way that is acceptable to some power-holders if not to others. Protest leaders may, for example, elicit an innocuous remark such as "it is lawful to publicize central policies" from a high-ranking official and then use it as a justification to call a mass meeting in their locality to "study policies."[29] When they are confident that their followers are willing to do their bidding, they may go a step further and deliberately break the law by leading a crowd to block roads, besiege officials, hold sit-ins, or raid government buildings, burn them down, or even blow them up.[30]

In addition to choosing tactics, protest leaders make an incident occur. Orchestrating a protest often involves collecting evidence of official wrongdoing, raising money, designing slogans, deciding whether and how to negotiate with the authorities, and arranging group action. In 1999, for instance, six protest leaders in suburban Beijing staged a demonstration against corrupt village cadres at the entrance to a municipal compound. A group of villagers was instructed to take turns stationing themselves at the main gate, and a contingent of support staff was formed to bring them food and drink.[31] In actions that involve long-distance traveling, protest leaders also establish communication links and set the time and place of gatherings.[32] In 2004, for instance, protest leaders from a village in Zhangjiakou (张家口), Hebei, mobilized hundreds of villagers to trek to Beijing to lodge a complaint against a county for allowing a private, under-financed company to seize a large plot of farmland without paying the promised compensation. The county government deployed hundreds of police to stop them. The police were stationed at railway ticket counters and long-distance bus stations to question passengers, and they guarded major intersections leading into Beijing to inspect suspicious vehicles. In spite of their efforts, hundreds of petitioners made it to the capital. It turned out that the lead complainants, upon learning of the county's plan to intercept the petitioners, had divided the villagers into dozens of small teams and instructed them to travel to Beijing by bicycle. To avoid unwanted attention, teams departed at different times and took different routes. The petitioners only reassembled at a pre-set time and place after they had passed the checkpoints the county police had set up around Beijing. By the time county officials learned what had happened, hundreds of villagers had made it to the State Council's Letters and Visits Bureau. Under pressure, the county swiftly took out a loan to compensate the farmers for losing a year's harvest and returned the land to them.[33]

Lastly, protest leaders are responsible for organizing multi-village and even multi-township episodes of contention, particularly (so far) in Hunan, Hubei, Sichuan, Guizhou, Guangxi, and Shaanxi.[34] To do so, they often set up some type of organization, formal or informal. The more formal groups have names such as "burden-reduction societies" (*jianfu xiehui* 减负协会), "rights-defense societies" (*weiquan xiehui* 维权协会), "anti-corruption small groups" (*fanfu xiaozu* 反腐小组), "burden-reduction groups" (*jianfu xiaozu* 减负小组), or "peasant societies for rights-defense" (*nongmin weiquan xiehui* 农民维权协会).[35] In a Guizhou township, protest leaders established a "Peasant Alliance for Justice" (*nongmin zhengyi tongmeng* 农民正义同盟) to resist excessive local fees.[36] In Yilong county (仪陇县), Sichuan, four protest leaders set up a "County Command Center for Speaking Up for Peasants" (*quanxian wei nongmin shuohua zhihui zhongxin* 全县为农民说话指挥中心). This latter group met every ten days to "stir up the masses to resist the Party and government" and its organizers attempted (unsuccessfully) to call a county-wide meeting to study central documents that limited taxation.[37]

More cautious protest leaders often prefer to build on informal networks in order to keep their organizations invisible. In Hengyang county, Hunan, for example, protest leaders from over a dozen townships formed a loose network of mutual protection and communication. They stayed in touch through cell phones and a telephone tree, and vowed to come to each other's rescue "even if a family member had just died."[38] "Rural underground organizations" were also said to be behind unrest that broke out in Shanxi, Henan, and Hunan in late 1995, and "deliberate coordination" was evident in other clashes that occurred in Sichuan in 1993 and Hunan throughout the 1990s.[39]

These varied "mobilizing structures"[40] not only help get people out on the streets, they also facilitate allocating leadership responsibilities more efficiently.[41] In Shaanxi, protest leaders reportedly developed a complex division of labor in which different leaders specialized in planning, coordination, propaganda, communication, transportation, and negotiation.[42] In Hengyang county, Hunan, protest leaders also increased their effectiveness by sharing the tasks involved in conducting a protest campaign.[43] Some of them focused on finding and analyzing new regulations; some were in charge of collecting evidence against rural officials; some were responsible for raising funds and mobilizing supporters; some did the more mundane (but important) work of disseminating petition letters to villagers. Thanks to their coordination, protest leaders in Hengyang were able to continue making a living and sustain their contention for nearly a decade. As time passed, they also became better at applying pressure on the county government, culminating in 2003 in a single letter of complaint that challenged excessive irrigation charges, signed by representatives from 13 of 18 townships in the county.[44]

Making a protest leader

Protest leaders emerge through several channels. Some are public figures before they initiate popular contention. This group includes former village cadres, retired government officials, clan elders, school teachers, and religious figures.[45] These well-established opinion leaders usually command moral authority in their community. Villagers often call them "little sages" (*xiao shengren* 小圣人), "natural leaders" (*ziran lingxiu* 自然领袖), or "the enlightened" (*mingbairen* 明白人).[46] They are also typically known for being outspoken, upright, assertive, and knowledgeable about politics.[47] That is also why people come to them for help when they face illegal impositions or have other grievances. More often than not, such individuals are the first to stand up on behalf of other villagers, partly because they share the same grievance, partly to demonstrate their high moral standards, and partly to confirm their status as community leaders. In Henan, for example, a well-regarded former cadre was urged by fellow villagers in 1998 to lead a petition campaign against excessive fees, and he did so.[48] In many places, particularly Fujian and Jiangxi, members of the "society of senior citizens" (*laonianren xiehui* 老年人协会) and clan elders have played leading parts in organizing collective petitions against corrupt or incompetent cadres.[49]

Sometimes even incumbent village party secretaries and villagers' committee directors have become protest leaders.[50] Grassroots cadres, in some places, have played a role in devising tactics and claims-making strategies and have participated in demonstrations, rallies, or petition drives.[51] In Hunan, for instance, a newly elected villagers' committee director led a group petition against a hefty education surcharge, after dozens of angry villagers approached him for help.[52] Village authorities also sometimes side with villagers in land requisition disputes, either "because they share common interests with farmers,"[53] or because they were cut out of kickbacks or did not get as much as they believed they deserved.[54]

In many instances, community leaders do not wait to be asked and start down the road to being a protest leader by challenging a government decision or action on their own. Xiong Maisheng (熊麦生), a well-known "burden-reduction hero" in Taojiang county (桃江县), Hunan, for instance, was a successful private entrepreneur and locally renowned barefoot doctor. He enjoyed the respect of other villagers, who called him "Dr. Know-Everything" (*quanneng boshi* 全能博士). In 1997, the authorities abruptly increased township levies several-fold. Xiong, on his own initiative, immediately lodged a complaint at the county government.[55] Public figures have also acted on their own on other issues of community concern, such as village finances, grassroots elections, and land requisition.

Lone petitioners usually find it difficult to prevail, however. During their struggle with rural power-holders, some of them quickly graduate from acting on their own interests to acting on other villagers' behalf. Xiong Maisheng's contention is a good example of this. After learning of his petition to the county, township leaders first attempted to buy him off by offering a fee waiver and a 20,000 *yuan* (U.S.$2,500) bribe. When Xiong rejected the offer, a township official threatened his life. But Xiong still refused to back down. Then a group of cadres and policemen showed up at Xiong's house and threatened to beat him unless he paid the fees in full. Xiong paid up but obtained a receipt that he kept as evidence of the township's wrongdoing. Two weeks later, Xiong learned that the heads of nine nearby villages had decided to "demand an explanation" (*tao shuofa* 讨说法) of the fee hike, and Xiong volunteered to coordinate efforts to have it reversed.[56]

Sometimes a decision by individual petitioners to lead popular contention is a tactical move, designed to mobilize community support in the hope that this will elicit concessions on one's original private grievance. Cui Luokun (崔罗坤) was a prominent protest leader in Ningxiang county, Hunan, who helped mobilize a large demonstration against excessive taxation that came to be known as the Daolin Incident. Initially, however, state extraction was not his concern. In 1994, Cui, then the head of a villagers' small group, asked higher-ups at the villagers' committee and township to address a soil erosion problem. For questioning the powerful, a group of hired toughs ransacked his house and beat him badly, and the county police detained him for fifteen days. Cui then began to lodge complaints at various levels of government, seeking compensation for his property damage, his injuries, and wrongful detention. In the course of several years of futile petitioning, he bought books about the law and learned of policies calling for the reduction of peasant burdens. Cui later shifted his appeals to the issue of over-taxation, hoping to apply pressure on local authorities so that they would take his demand for compensation seriously. While speaking out on behalf of other villagers, Cui amassed a large following and became a determined "peasant leader" who led a number of collective petitions and played a pivotal role in organizing mass meetings to study tax-reduction measures.[57]

Unlike those who have enjoyed a high profile for some time, other protest leaders are newcomers to public life. These individuals are frequently male, better educated, have strong personalities, and have undergone transformative experiences, such as serving in the army.[58] Some of them feel excluded from community affairs, most often because they have poor relations with local officialdom. Others have had little interest in village politics, perhaps because they have been too busy making a living or raising a family. Some of them may have been politically active earlier in life, for example, as a Red Guard leader during the Cultural Revolution or as a school activist. Zhou Decai (周德才), a protest organizer in Henan in the early 2000s, fits in this last category. He led a demonstration in support of the student movement in 1989 and was expelled from middle school, thus losing his opportunity to take the university entrance exam.[59] Zhang Dean (张德安), the moving force behind the 1993 Renshou (仁寿) protest, is an example of the former path to leadership. In the late 1950s, he was labeled a "rightist" and expelled from the army when the Hundred Flowers era came to a sudden end.[60]

For these individuals, the journey toward leadership usually begins with an act of defiance, often following mistreatment by rural officials. In Hengyang, Hunan, one young woman tried to take her own life by drinking pesticide after township birth control inspectors confiscated all the equipment from her photo studio because she refused to pay a fine for having her first child without prior authorization.[61] Her father, an army veteran, came across a group of activists who were studying central limits on taxation while he was feverishly looking for medicine for his stricken daughter. The young woman survived, but her father refused to let the birth control inspectors go unpunished. Using what he had learned from the study group, he began lodging complaints against officials who used family planning regulations as an excuse to impose arbitrary fines.[62] Unsuccessful in this tactic, the old man later joined the other fee protesters and became a prominent "burden-reduction representative" in his community.

By standing up for themselves, assertive villagers can develop a reputation for having the derring-do and expertise to challenge power-holders. After this happens, they are frequently approached by other people who have any sort of gripe with local cadres. One protest leader, for example, was a successful businessman in rural Xiamen (厦门) until a township nearly ruined him by ending a factory lease prematurely. He then began to lodge complaints but was unable to recoup his losses. In the course of confronting the powers-that-be, the man became known for his mastery of policies and his skill at writing petition letters. Other aggrieved villagers then began to ask him for help composing their letters. Over the next few years, he set up an advisory service for rural people who felt cheated by cadres who had sold off village land without public consultation. He advised numerous villagers how to pursue complaints more effectively by combining them with popular action. Some of his clients later succeeded in obtaining compensation, and this only led more people to approach him for advice. In short order, he became one of the key protest leaders in Zhangpu county (彰浦县), Xiamen.[63]

Even if they do not suffer serious mistreatment themselves, these assertive and knowledgeable individuals are more likely than most to confront rural cadres. Here, it is knowledge of beneficial policies that typically sensitizes a person to actionable misconduct. Ling Xuewen (凌学文), a previously inactive Hunan villager, obtained some central and provincial documents from a city cadre while he was working as a bricklayer. After reading them, he immediately realized that it was unlawful for the township to collect a per capita slaughter tax irrespective of whether a farmer raised livestock. Ling successfully drove a team of township tax collectors from his home by citing these documents. He later became angry, and began to mobilize other villagers, when he learned that his younger brother, who had not heard of the policy, was forced to take out a bank loan to pay off a slaughter tax he did not owe. He copied the relevant regulation on a large piece of paper and pasted it on a wall outside the township office building. From this moment on, Ling started down what he called a "no-return road to petitioning." After spearheading a number of clashes with township officials, and joining some protest leaders from neighboring townships, by 1999 he became one of the most visible activists in Hengyang county.[64]

Heightened emotions, as in this last case, often play a role in spurring otherwise non-political individuals into action.[65] Peng Rongjun (彭荣俊), a noted protest leader in Hengyang, came across a document about reducing peasant burdens, but did not even glance at it because he was busy tending his small candy store. His wife, however, read it and started goading him into "being a man" and "struggling against" those "bastards" and "thieves" at the township. Also in Hengyang, Deng Zisheng (邓仔生), a villagers' small group leader, asked a party secretary for permission to inspect the village accounts. The secretary rudely rejected the request and dismissively claimed that he had no say over villagers' committee affairs. In the shouting match that ensued, the secretary challenged Deng to lodge complaints wherever he pleased. Shamed and outraged, Deng launched a petition campaign, first by himself and then at the head of other villagers frustrated with the lack of financial openness in their community.[66]

Finally, simple bad blood or personal rivalry between former and sitting cadres,[67] or village small group leaders and villagers' committee directors,[68] or villagers' committee directors and party secretaries,[69] and so on, may also set a person down the path toward becoming a protest leader. In 1997, Zhong Shunde (钟顺德), a former village cadre in Xuanhan county (宣汉县), Sichuan, refused to pay a small fee of 7 *yuan* (90 U.S. cents) that he felt was unlawful. The party secretary who came to collect the money dismissed his request with the words: "I don't think a flea can overturn a blanket." Insulted and humiliated, Zhong responded: "That's exactly what I want to see it do." Shortly after they exchanged words, Zhong began to lodge complaints over illicit fees, and he soon became a local "burden-reduction leader." During the next three years, he led more than twenty petition drives at the county, city, and province and staged several dozen demonstrations in his village.[70]

Repression and its effects

Nearly all protest leaders start by leading collective petitions. Initially, they call themselves "petitioners' representatives," "burden reduction representatives" (*jianfu daibiao* 减负代表), or simply "villagers' representatives" (*cunmin daibiao* 村民代表). Most are careful to avoid politically loaded terms like "leader" (*lingxiu* 领袖) or "organization" (*zuzhi* 组织) to dispel suspicions that they might be fomenting revolution or rebellion. One protest leader in Hengyang, Hunan, for example, insisted that he had no "organization," only a "troop" (*duiwu* 队伍).[71] In their contention, petitioners' representatives usually make efforts to stay within the law or at least avoid breaching it. They also tend to be deferential to those they approach for redress. Perhaps because they still are confident in the Center's ability to deliver justice,[72] they often expect to receive protection or even rewards from Beijing.[73] In the words of a protest leader from Shandong: "Some wicked officials have sealed off the Center from reality. If peasants do not lodge complaints, the emperor will never know what is going on. If I tell the emperor, he should thank me and take care of me. Anything otherwise and he would be an '*Edou Liu Chan*' (阿斗刘禅)" – referring to an emperor notorious for his lack of wisdom.[74]

At this stage, protest leaders often consider themselves to be heroic defenders of more timid and "helpless" (*pinku* 贫苦) villagers, who in their words are of "lower quality" (*suzhi jiaodi* 素质较低) or have "low political consciousness" (*zhengzhi juewu di* 政治觉悟低).[75] They may solicit donations in the community and seek co-signers for their petitions, but they do not actively mobilize others to make visits to higher levels. They claim to represent other villagers, but do not seek their endorsement, on the grounds that most people would be too afraid to express support publicly.[76] Instead, they typically base their claim to stand for others on what they do and how other villagers receive them. Explaining why he deserved to be called a petitioners' representative, one protest leader from Hunan argued that although the complaint he presented to the city government did not have many signatures, he represented many other villagers, because he had discussed the letter with them and they did not sign it only because they feared repercussions. Moreover, the villagers he met with afterwards were very respectful toward him.[77]

By stressing that they are merely representatives, petitioners' representatives convey three messages. First, they embody other villagers but do not lead them. They are simply reflecting the "opinions of the masses," not mobilizing or shaping public opinion. Second, they are not rabble-rousers but only humble petitioners. They may challenge what local officials do, but typically avoid confronting them directly. Their aim is to sound fire alarms to higher levels so that problems can be addressed before it is too late, but they do not attempt to put out fires by themselves. Lastly, because they work for the benefit of the community rather than themselves, they are not private citizens but stand at the head of a group of constituents. At this juncture, protest leaders usually have more confidence in higher authorities and in themselves than in the people they represent.

And sometimes this persistence and faith in higher levels pays off. Unlawful fees are revoked, illegal land grabs are reversed, and corrupt cadres are dismissed. But more often than not, despite their "reasonable claims" (*heli yaoqiu* 合理要求), petitioners' representatives meet with repression.[78] Public security officers raid their homes and confiscate valuables such as furniture, television sets, and even coffins. Sometimes local cadres go so far as to tear down the houses of protest leaders, partially or completely. Rural officials may beat protest leaders and their family members, illegally detain them, or have them sentenced to labor education or jail on charges such as "resisting taxes," "disturbing social order," "beating up cadres," "attacking the government," "impeding government work," "interfering with law enforcement," or "illegally instigating a disturbance."[79] Cadres in some places have used periodic strike-hard anti-crime campaigns to imprison petitioners' representatives in the name of maintaining stability and safeguarding law and order.[80] In late 1998 and early 1999, for instance, the Hengyang county government rounded up dozens of petitioners' representatives, many of whom were beaten, paraded through streets as criminals, and put up on temporary stages to be reprimanded at "ten-thousand person struggle meetings" (*wanren pidou dahui* 万人批斗大会).[81]

Repression of course often works.[82] One effective way to end an incident, at least in the short term, is to jail a protest leader. This takes "troublemakers" (*naoshi fenzi* 闹事分子) off the streets and can demoralize followers. In Hebei, one leader vowed never to petition again because he and his co-complainants were detained for two weeks by the county police after a fruitless visit to Beijing. In his words: "the Communist Party is corrupt. Lodging complaints is useless. It's not only a waste of time, energy, and money, it's also subject to repression."[83] Imprisonment of a protest leader also tests community support for further action. In Xupu county (溆浦县), Hunan, an elderly petitioners' representative had become such a "nail in the eye and thorn in the flesh" for township officials that they concluded "the government will collapse if we don't beat him down."[84] At the township's insistence, the man was sentenced to seven years in prison. Though angered by his incarceration, his followers ceased lodging complaints because they saw no hope of success. According to one of them: "If such an outrageously incorrect verdict can't be overturned under the rule of the Communist Party, who can believe that we petitioners will ever get a fair hearing?"[85]

Varieties of repression short of imprisonment (e.g. intimidation, fines, beating, property seizure, public humiliation) may also damp down protest, particularly when they appear to be (or are) condoned by higher authorities.[86] Repression also tends to be more effective on younger people, who may give up a seemingly hopeless battle and exit to cities to become migrant workers.[87] Repression, finally, can demoralize protest leaders sufficiently that they accept much less than they had hoped for. In Yiyang county (宜阳县), Henan, a man was left disabled after a beating by township officials. Everyone expected him to keep fighting now that he had little left to lose. To the dismay of fellow petitioners' representatives, he accepted an offer of 25,000 *yuan* (U.S. $3,000) compensation and dropped out of any further collective action.[88]

Effective as it often is, repression can also backfire.[89] As it does elsewhere, "repression can sometimes turn the tables on a government, exposing its brutality and undermining its legitimacy while generating public sympathy for protestors."[90] In rural China, instead of deactivating them, repression at times transforms occasional and opportunistic petitioners' representatives into dedicated and committed protest leaders. It, in other words, can steel a protest leader's resolve, not least by generating new or more intense popular support.[91] Harsh repression by officials who are widely believed to be corrupt or predatory may convince attentive bystanders that protest leaders are truly taking action on their behalf. A villager in Hengyang, for instance, said that he was not paying much attention to the activities of a group of complainants until he saw thugs hired by the township beat up a protest leader's wife. That the activists had borne such a cost persuaded him that they must be doing a "favor" (*hao shi* 好事) for villagers like himself, so they deserved his backing. He soon joined up and became a petitioners' representative himself.[92] With new backers, the main protest organizer was able to continue lodging group complaints and publicizing central policies after six of his thirteen initial recruits withdrew.

Even jailing protest leaders may not put as final an end to contention as rural officials might hope. In fact, imprisonment can enhance the prestige, honor, and social recognition of people who are willing to "hazard time, liberty and even life against powerful, sometimes ruthless foes."[93] On the day a 73-year-old protest leader from Yibin county (宜宾县), Sichuan, was due to be released after three years in jail, nearly 20,000 of his supporters gathered for a welcome-home ceremony. They had raised nearly 8,000 *yuan* (U.S. $1,000) to buy fireworks for the celebration.[94] In Hunan, one of the men behind the Daolin Incident received a hero's welcome when he was released from prison in 2004, with villagers dispatching seven vehicles to pick him up in Changsha (长沙) and setting off fireworks when he and his entourage reached his home town.[95] The boost in prestige that jailing produces can translate into a new episode of popular action, when a protest leader becomes more determined both to persist and to not let his followers down. In Hengyang, Hong Jifa (洪吉发) was jailed for three years for "disrupting social order." His incarceration, however, did not diminish his standing, but instead brought him public acclaim as a "good man" and a "hero" from his comrades and fellow villagers. Immediately after being released, Hong rejoined a group of petitioners' representatives and became a "daring vanguard" (*ji xianfeng* 急先锋) in subsequent protests. This case corroborates an observation made by three Xinhua reporters: "some grassroots cadres think that the reason their localities are unstable is that a tiny number of 'peasant heroes' (*nongmin yingxiong* 农民英雄) are 'up to no good' (*gao gui* 搞鬼). So they believe that stability will be restored if only those individuals are arrested and jailed. But the outcome is often just the opposite of what they wish."[96]

Other than enhancing social standing, repression may generate two other types of popular support. First, it can increase a protest leader's credibility, thereby making it easier to raise funds.[97] Repression suggests to some onlookers that protest leaders are public spirited or even altruistic, that donations will not be pocketed, and that a small contribution may help them hang on long enough to obtain intercession from above. Second, repression can prompt community members to offer protection to their champions. This can involve offering them meals and places to hide, tipping them off when the police are nearby, or serving as lookouts.[98] In many places, particularly Hunan, Sichuan, Jiangxi, Anhui, and Hebei, large numbers of villagers have clashed with local officials and police while trying to defend protest leaders or rescue them after they were detained.[99] Rural people in parts of Hunan, Henan, Fujian, and Shandong have also volunteered to serve as bodyguards for protest leaders.[100] One protest leader from Shandong quite proudly said that he always had several unpaid bodyguards accompanying him when he went to the township or county to lodge complaints.[101]

With support, the likelihood of success may seem high enough for a protest leader to continue pursuing a claim. Retreat can also become difficult because social recognition nearly always comes packaged with high expectations. Once they begin, protest leaders often find it hard to retreat, partly out of fear they will be considered half-hearted cowards by their supporters and partly because they may be mocked by other protest leaders as shameless "traitors" (*pantu* 叛徒) to their own cause.[102]

Repression also generates yet another compelling motive not to give up. By inflicting humiliation, property damage, injuries, or other losses on protest leaders, repression can increase the costs of withdrawal by adding a new grievance to the list – why was I repressed and how will I be compensated for my losses? This new reason for discontent is often even more deeply felt than the grievance (public or private) that originally precipitated action. In the words of a protest leader in a Hebei village, who refused to stop petitioning after he was beaten by some thugs hired by the township: "You either don't start it or you pursue it to the end. If I quit now, I have suffered a serious beating for nothing."[103] Some protest leaders conclude that they have lost so much that they have little left to lose. One man in Hengyang admitted that petitioning was a sure road to bankruptcy, but he refused to give up because he had already used up all his savings, was deep in debt, and his house had been damaged by township officials. He was not sure what might await him if he continued to lead group petitions, but he felt he had no other choice but to persist.[104]

Besides cementing a person's determination to continue petitioning, repression may also lead to radicalization and make a protest leader more prone to adopt tactics that entail popular mobilization and open confrontation. In Hengyang, one long-time protest leader admitted that he broke into tears after learning of a county-wide crackdown that came to be known as the Zhajiang Incident (渣江事件). He said that he had never believed that the authorities could be so "cruel" (*canren* 残忍) as to break the arm of a 70-year-old protester and nearly beat him to death; neither had he thought the masses would be so "defiant" (*bu fu* 不服) as to throw stones at (and drive away) officials during a mass meeting to denounce protest leaders. According to him, this crackdown was a turning point, after which he and his associates relied more and more on publicizing policies and directly confronting tax collectors, because it was obvious that "petitioning by itself was useless."[105] According to three Xinhua reporters, other protest organizers have been similarly radicalized. Based on an investigation of six Hunan counties, they concluded that "many 'peasant leaders' are even willing to go down together with rural officials, if that's the only choice."[106]

When repression continues or intensifies, protest leaders may become completely disillusioned with the regime and begin to act like movement entrepreneurs.[107] Wanted by the police or fearing further retaliation, some activists from rural Henan and Hunan have gone into hiding or departed for urban areas. They work only to scratch out a living and spend much of their time seeking foreign media attention or the support of reform-minded NGOs inside and outside China.[108] Some protest leaders have even edged toward becoming revolutionaries. In Hunan, for instance, Huang Guoqing (黄国卿) reportedly said "kings, lords, and generals are not determined by birth," quoting Chen Sheng, one of the leaders of the rebellion that brought down the Qin Dynasty.[109] Zhou Decai, another well-known protest leader and essayist from Henan, vowed in 2002 to launch a democratic revolution to end one-party rule.[110]

Conclusion

Protest leaders in rural China perform a number of tasks. Among others, they lead the charge, shape collective claims, recruit activists and mobilize the public, devise and orchestrate acts of contention, and organize cross-community struggles. Protest leaders emerge through several channels. Long-time public figures initiate popular action on their own or in response to requests from other villagers; ordinary villagers evolve into protest leaders after efforts to seek redress (largely for personal grievances) fail. The making of protest leaders is a joint product of self-selection, public acclaim (and pressure), and heavy-handed attempts to suppress dissent, which sometimes backfire.

Rural officials may attempt to co-opt or buy off protest leaders, but more often they turn to repression. Although cracking down can inhibit further contention, at other times it firms up the determination of organizers and makes them more likely to adopt confrontational tactics, partly because it enhances their popular support and partly because it increases the costs of withdrawal. Detaining or jailing a protest leader may put an end to contention or inspire more spirited defiance. Public humiliation, threats, fines, beatings, and property destruction likewise have uncertain consequences. Why do some instances of repression demobilize protest leaders and their followers while others fire them up? The earliest political opportunity theorists suggested that repression by and large works. Others, more recently, have pointed out that repression can backfire, or that the relationship between it and a new round of popular action is complex and conditional.

In rural China, whether repression backfires appears to depend on three factors. In general, repression authorized by township or county leaders, who do not have much popular trust,[111] is more apt to backfire than that authorized by higher levels. The effect of repression also depends on the amount of social capital a protest leader possesses. Crackdowns are less likely to meet popular outrage if a protest leader has alienated community members by, for example, collecting compulsory "donations" or refusing to pay for restaurant meals. Lastly, repression is much more likely to backfire when a protest leader can somehow attract the attention of higher levels or sympathetic journalists, lawyers, and public intellectuals.

Protest leaders are admittedly only a small fraction of the rural population, but their prominence of late is an indicator of wider discontent. The appearance of "peasant leaders," "peasant heroes," and "rights defenders" in many places would not have been possible unless aggrieved villagers sought them out or enthusiastically followed them once they took up a cause. Moreover, protest leaders would find it difficult to persist and organize new episodes of contention in the face of repression without support in the community. That rural people often hold in high esteem those whom officials wish to see isolated and ostracized is perhaps the main reason why the authorities find the presence of protest leaders in the countryside so alarming. So far the government has relied primarily on repression (combined with moderate concessions) to silence protest leaders. But repression has costs, too. It undoubtedly discourages people from organizing protests, but also rewards the adventurous few with considerable moral authority and community influence.

Notes

1 For helpful comments, we would like to thank Yongshun Cai, Feng Chen, Xi Chen, David Meyer, Rachael Stern, Sidney Tarrow, Guobin Yang, and the anonymous reviewers of this paper. Special note should be made of Prof. Yu Jianrong of the Chinese Academy of Social Sciences, who kindly shared some of his interview transcripts with us. Generous financial support was provided by the Harry Frank Guggenheim Foundation, the Research Grants Council of Hong Kong, and the Institute of East Asian Studies at the University of California-Berkeley.

2 See Ron Aminzade, Jack A. Goldstone, and Elizabeth J. Perry, "Leadership Dynamics and Dynamics of Contention," in Ronald R. Aminzade, Jack A. Goldstone, Doug McAdam, Elizabeth J. Perry, William H. Sewell Jr., Sidney Tarrow, and Charles Tilly, *Silence and Voice in the Study of Contentious Politics* (New York: Cambridge University Press, 2001), pp. 126–8; Colin Barker, Alan Johnson and Michael Lavalette, "Leadership Matters: An Introduction," in Colin Barker, Alan Johnson, and Michael Lavelette, eds., *Leadership and Social Movements* (Manchester: Manchester University Press, 2001), p. 2; Aldon D. Morris and Suzanne Staggenborg, "Leadership in Social Movements," in David A. Snow, Sarah A. Soule, Hanspeter Kries, eds., *The Blackwell Companion to Social Movements* (Malden, MA: Blackwell, 2004), p. 171; Alberto Melucci, *Challenging Codes: Collective Action in the Information* Age (New York: Cambridge University Press, 1996), p. 332; Sharon Erickson Nepstad and Clifford Bob, "When Do Leaders Matter? Hypotheses on Leadership Dynamics in Social Movements," *Mobilization* 11(1) (March 2006), p. 1.

3 For a perceptive organizer's perspective, see Saul D. Alinsky, *Rules for Radicals* (New York: Vintage, 1971).

4 For discussions of leadership, see Yongshun Cai, "The Resistance of Laid-off Workers in the Reform Period," *China Quarterly*, no. 170 (June 2002), pp. 327–44; Yongshun Cai, "Collective Ownership or Cadres' Ownership? The Non-agricultural Use of Farmland in China," *China Quarterly*, no. 175 (September 2003), pp. 662–80; Patricia Thornton, "Comrades and Collectives in Arms: Tax

Resistance, Evasion, and Avoidance Strategies in Post-Mao China," in Peter Hays Gries and Stanley Rosen, eds., *State and Society in 21st Century China: Crisis, Contention, and Legitimation* (New York: Routledge, 2004), pp. 87–104; and especially Thomas P. Bernstein and Xiaobo Lü, *Taxation without Representation in Contemporary Rural China* (New York: Cambridge University Press, 2003); Yu Jianrong, "Conflict in the Countryside: The Emerging Political Awareness of the Peasants" [translated by Thomas Michael], *Social Research* 73(1) (Spring 2006), pp. 141–58; Yu Jianrong, *Dangdai Zhongguo nongmin de weiquan kangzheng: Hunan Hengyang kaocha* (Farmers' Struggle to Defend Their Rights in Contemporary China: An Investigation of Hengyang, Hunan) (Beijing: Zhongguo wenhua chubanshe, 2007); and Wu Zhang, "Peasant Power in China: A Comparative Study of Peasant Protest in Hunan in the 1990s," paper presented at the 101st Annual Meeting of the American Political Science Association, September 1–4, 2005, Washington, D.C. On "rebel" and "mandarin" styles of leadership in Maoist China, see Aminzade, Goldstone, and Perry, "Leadership Dynamics," pp. 133–42.

5   On the debate over how repression affects mobilization, see Jennifer Earl, "Repression and the Social Control of Protest," *Mobilization* 11(2) (June 2006), p. 129; Christian Davenport, Hank Johnston, and Carol Mueller, *Repression and Mobilization* (Minneapolis, MN: University of Minnesota Press, 2005).

6   Bernstein and Lü, *Taxation without Representation,* p. 6. In central agricultural provinces popular protest is much more common in some counties than in others. Younger and better-educated county party secretaries are more likely to seek promotion by launching expensive development projects, which often increase peasant burdens and provoke popular protests. By contrast, county party secretaries who are near retirement or who do not have sufficient education to justify further promotion often choose to accord highest priority to maintaining stability.

7   Many of the Hengyang interviews are available in Yu Jianrong's book *Dangdai Zhongguo nongmin de weiquan kangzheng: Hunan Hengyang kaocha* (当代中国农民的维权抗争：湖南衡阳考察, *Farmers' Struggle to Defend Their Rights in Contemporary China: An Investigation of Hengyang, Hunan*) (Beijing: Zhongguo wenhua chubanshe, 2007).

8   Our 2005 survey in 100 villages suggested that protest leaders were active in much of the countryside. Of 96 villages where data were collected, 58 had protest leaders. The 100 villages were randomly sampled in 50 townships of 25 counties in Fujian, Hebei, Jilin, Jiangsu, and Sichuan. Data were not collected from four villages in two Hebei townships, where county officials did not allow the questionnaire to be administered.

9   On collective incidents, see Gonganbu disi yanjiusuo "quntixing shijian yanjiu" ketizu, "Woguo fasheng quntixing shijian de diaocha yu sikao" (Investigation and reflection on collective incidents in our country), *Neibu canyue (Internal Reference)*, no. 31 (10 August 2001), pp. 18–25; Zhongyang zhengfawei yanjiushi, *Weihu shehui wending diaoyan wenji (Collected Essays on Maintaining Social Stability)* (Beijing: Falü chubanshe, 2001). On the number of collective incidents in 2005, see "Gonganbu zhaokai xinwen fabuhui tongbao 2005 nian shehui zhi'an xingshi ji huozai xingshi" (The Public Security Ministry holds a news conference on the public security and fire disaster situation in 2005), http://www.mps.gov.cn/cenweb/brjlCenweb/jsp/common/article.jsp?infoid=ABC00000000000001018; accessed 14 August 2006.

10 Interview, petitioners' representative, Hengyang, Hunan, 2003. A riot then broke out, during which two government jeeps were overturned. The man who initiated the action was ultimately sentenced to three years in jail for "gathering a crowd to disturb social order" (*Criminal Court Verdict*, no. 66, 1999, People's Court of Hengyang county, Hunan Province).

11 See Li Cunbao and Wang Guangming, *Yimeng jiuzhang (Nine Chapters on Yimeng)*, *Renmin wenxue (People's Literature)*, no. 11 (November 1991), pp. 73–7; Song Zhenyuan, "Zouxiang shichang – xie zai Cangshan 'suantai shijian' fasheng shinian zhihou" (Marching toward the market: a note written ten years after the "garlic-shoots incidents" in Cangshan), *Shichang bao (Market)*, 23 December 1998, p. 7; Ding Xiguo, Wang Jinye, and Song Zhenyuan, "Yi zhua keji, er zhua liutong: Nongye jiegou tiaozheng caifang zhaji" (First to use new technologies, second to improve circulation – notes on agricultural restructuring), *Renmin ribao (Huadong xinwen) (People's Daily, East-China News)*, November 1, 2000, p. 1.

12 Interview, rural researcher in Jiangxi, 2001.

13 On leadership tasks more generally, see Aminzade, Goldstone, and Perry, "Leadership Dynamics," pp. 126–54; Morris and Staggenborg, "Leadership in Social Movements," pp. 171–96; Melucci, *Challenging Codes*, pp. 339–40; Nepstad and Bob, "When Do Leaders Matter?," pp. 1–22.

14 Interview, villager, Hebei, 1994.

15 Yu Jianrong, *Yuecun zhengzhi (Politics in Yue Village)* (Beijing: Shangwu yinshuguan, 2001), p. 499.

16 Xiang Jidong, "Cong 'xianfa guanhuai' tan qi" (About "constitutional concerns"), in Zhang Yinghong and Qi Zuliang, *Zhongguo nongmin yu dangdai zhengzhi (Chinese Peasants and Contemporary Politics)* (Beijing: Zhongguo wenshi chubanshe, 2005), p. 222.

17 Hank Johnston and John A. Noakes, *Frames of Protest: Social Protest and the Framing Perspective* (Lanham, MD: Rowman and Littlefield, 2005).

18 Yu, *Politics in Yue Village*, p. 554.

19 Interview, petitioners' representative, Hengyang, Hunan, 2003.

20 On recruitment using networks, see Mario Diani and Doug McAdam, eds., *Social Movements and Networks: Relational Approaches to Collective Action* (Oxford: Oxford University Press, 2003).

21 Yu, *Politics in Yue Village*, p. 554.

22 Liu Jian, Jiang Shan, Lü Guoqing, Chen Xianfa, and Duan Xianju, "Nongcun wending: yige ningzhong de huati" (Rural stability: a grave topic), *Banyuetan (neibuban) (Fortnightly Chats) (Internal edition)*, no. 4 (April 1999), p. 10; Duan Xianju, Tan Jian, and Chen Peng, " 'Yingxiong' hai shi 'diaomin'?" (" 'Heroes' or 'shrewd, unyielding people'?"), *Banyuetan (neibuban) (Fortnightly Chats) (Internal edition)*, no. 2 (February 2000), p. 10.

23 Interview, petitioners' representative, Hengyang, Hunan, 2003. For more reports on this man, see Xu Zhiyong, "Xuanju zhi hou – Liji cun cunmin zizhi diaocha" (After the election: an investigation of villagers' self-government in Liji village), *Zhongguo gaige (nongcun ban) (China's Reforms) (Rural edition)*, no. 2 (February 2003), pp. 10–14; Huang Kaitang and Dong Lanfang, "Cunweihui tao gongzhang zhuanggao zhen zhengfu" (A villagers' committee sues the township government to obtain the village chop), *Zhongguo gaige (nongcun ban) (China's Reforms) (Rural edition)*, no. 9 (February 2003), pp. 35–7; Zhu Ling, *Hui cun ji shi – caogen minzhu yu qian guize de boyi (Stories of Hui Village: A Game of Grassroots Democracy and Hidden Rules)* (Shanghai: Dongfang chuban zhongxin, 2004).

24 Yang Shouyong and Wang Jintao, " 'Wending cun' weihe chule da luanzi?" (Why did a big disturbance occur in a "stable village?"), *Banyuetan (neibuban) (Fortnightly Chats) (Internal edition)*, no. 1 (January 2001), p. 42; Zhang Jun, "Xiang zhengfu yuanhe zao chongji" (Why was the township government attacked?), *Minzhu yu fazhi (Democracy and Legality)*, no. 1 (6 January 2001), p. 41.

25 Kevin J. O'Brien and Lianjiang Li, "The Politics of Lodging Complaints in Rural China," *China Quarterly*, no. 143 (September 1995), p. 775.

26 Interview, rural researcher from Beijing, 1999. For a similar case in Anhui, see Xu Jingping, "'Xiaoji wending' niang eguo" ("Negative stability" leads to disastrous consequences), *Banyuetan (neibuban) (Fortnightly Chats) (Internal edition)*, no. 12 (December 2000), p. 40.

27 Interviews, petitioners' representatives, Hengyang, Hunan, 2003.

28 O'Brien and Li, "The Politics of Lodging Complaints," pp. 773–4; Carl Minzner, "Xinfang: An Alternative to the Formal Chinese Judicial System," *Stanford Journal of International Law* 42(1) (Winter 2006), pp. 103–79; but cf. Yuen Yuen Tang, "When Peasants Sue En Masse: Large-Scale Collective ALL Suits in Rural China," *China: An International Journal* 3(1) (March 2005), pp. 46–9.

29 Interviews, petitioners' representatives, Hengyang, Hunan, 2003; rural researcher in Henan, 2004. Yang Hao, "Nongmin de huhuan" (Cries of peasants), *Dangdai (Modern Times)*, no. 6 (November 1999), p. 79; Yu, *Politics in Yue Village*, pp. 548–9; Jiang Zuoping and Yang Sanjun, "Chuanhuan si wei 'lingxiu' niang cheng yi chang fengbo" (Subpoenaing four "leaders" results in an incident). *Banyuetan (neibuban) (Fortnightly Chats) (Internal edition)*, no. 2 (February 2000), p. 16.

30 Interviews, petitioners' representative, Hengyang, Hunan, 2003; rural researcher in Jiangxi, 2006; Duan Xianju, "Jujiao jiuyi nongmin de minggenzi" (Focusing on the life-roots of 900 million farmers), *Banyuetan (neibuban) (Fortnightly Chats) (Internal edition)*, no. 1 (January 2002), p. 5; *Ibid.*, p. 245.

31 *Ibid.*, p. 66.

32 *Ibid.*, pp. 98, 153, 221, 324.

33 Interview, rural researcher in Beijing, 2006.

34 Zhongyang zhengfawei, *Collected Essays*, pp. 245, 262, 277, 302.

35 Zhao Shukai, "Shequ chongtu he xinxing quanli guanxi – guanyu 196 feng nongmin laixin de chubu fenxi" (Community conflicts and a new type of power relationship – a preliminary analysis of 196 letters of complaints by farmers), *Zhongguo nongcun guancha (China Rural Survey)*, no. 2 (March 1999), p. 45; Yu Jianrong, "Zhuanxing Zhongguo de shehui chongtu – dui dangdai Zhongguo weiquan kangzheng huodong de guancha" (Social conflicts in transitional China – observation of rights-defense activities by workers and peasants in contemporary China), *Gaige neican (Inside information on reform)*, no. 34 (1 December 2004), p. 18; Zhou Yuan and Wang Yanping, "Minjian liliang guanli minjian" (Let civil forces manage communities), in Zhou Yuan (ed.), *Nongmin! Nongmin! (Peasants! Peasants!)* (Guangzhou: Huacheng chubanshe, 2004), p. 140.

36 Zhongyang zhengfawei, *Collected Essays*, p. 277.

37 Jiang and Yang, "Subpoenaing four 'leaders'," pp. 15–16.

38 Interview, petitioners' representative, Hengyang, Hunan, 2003.

39 Zhonggong Sichuan shengwei zuzhibu ketizu, "Zenyang zhengque chuli quntixing tufa shijian" (How to correctly handle collective and abrupt incidents), *Banyuetan (neibuban) (Fortnightly Chats) (Internal edition)*, no. 1 (January 2002), pp. 29–32; Bernstein and Lü, *Taxation without Representation*, pp. 155–6.

40 Sidney Tarrow, *Power in Movement*, 2nd edn. (New York: Cambridge University Press, 1998), ch. 8.

41 Zhongyang zhengfawei, *Collected Essays*, p. 277.

42 *Ibid.*, p. 302.

43 On one person rarely having the full complement of skills needed to organize contention, see Aminzade, Goldstone, and Perry, "Leadership Dynamics," p. 152.

44 Interview, rural researcher in Beijing, 2004.

45 Bernstein and Lü, *Taxation without Representation,* p. 149; O'Brien and Li, "The Politics of Lodging Complaints," pp. 767–8; Zhang, "Peasant Power," passim;

Yang, "Cries of Peasants," p. 79; Zhongyang zhengfawei, *Collected Essays*, p. 277. Our 2005 survey showed that of 991 ordinary villagers randomly selected in 96 villages, 55 (5.8 percent) had in the previous decade taken the lead in: (1) petitioning; (2) going to Beijing to petition; (3) rejecting illegal fees; (4) demanding dialogues with government leaders; or (5) blocking traffic. Of 441 purposively selected incumbent village cadres and heads of villagers' small groups, 22 (5.0 percent) had done the same. Of 209 purposively selected "public figures," e.g. former village cadres, former candidates of villagers' committees, clan elders, religious leaders, and former members of a village election steering committee, 20 (9.6 percent) had done the same.

46 Interview, petitioners' representative from Zhangpu, Xiamen, 2004; Bao Yonghui, "Dui nongcun sige zhongda wenti de zai renshi" (Reflections on four major rural issues), *Xiangzhen luntan (Township Forum)*, no. 7 (July 1991), p. 15.
47 On the personality traits of rural protest leaders, see Xiaolin Guo, "Land Expropriation and Rural Conflicts in China," *China Quarterly*, no. 166 (June 2001), p. 432; also Zhang, "Peasant Power," pp. 43–4; O'Brien and Li, "The Politics of Lodging Complaints," pp. 767–71; Lianjiang Li and Kevin J. O'Brien, "Villagers and Popular Resistance in Contemporary China," *Modern China* 22(1) (January 1996), pp. 28–61; Kevin J. O'Brien and Lianjiang Li, *Rightful Resistance in Rural China* (New York: Cambridge University Press, 2006), Appendix A.
48 Interview, rural researcher in Henan, 2004.
49 Interview, rural researcher in Jiangxi, 2001; Interview, rural researcher at Beijing University, 2005.
50 Interview, petitioners' representative from Shandong, Guangzhou, 2003. Bernstein and Lü, *Taxation without Representation*, pp. 152–3; Lucien Bianco, *Peasants without the Party: Grass-roots Movements in Twentieth Century China* (Armonk, NY: M.E. Sharpe), pp. 250–1; Thornton, "Comrades and Collectives in Arms," pp. 90, 97–8; Li Junde, "'Jianfu yingxiong' za cheng le fanzui xianyiren" (How did peasant burden-reduction heroes become crime suspects), *Banyuetan (neibuban) (Fortnightly Chats) (Internal edition)*, no. 2 (February 2000), pp. 13–14; Zhang Cuiling, "Zenyang duidai zheli de nongmin shangfang – Anhui Chengzhuang shijian diaocha baogao" (How to deal with peasants lodging complaints? An investigative report on Anhui's Chengzhuang incident), *Fazhi yu xinwen (Legality and News)*, no. 1 (January 2002), pp. 4–8.
51 Thornton, "Comrades and Collectives in Arms," p. 98.
52 Lianjiang Li, "Elections and Popular Resistance in Rural China," *China Information* 16(1) (2002), pp. 89–107.
53 Yu Jianrong, "Social Conflict in Rural China Today: Observation and Analysis on Farmers' Struggles to Safeguard Their Rights," *Social Sciences in China* (Autumn 2005), p. 130.
54 Interview, rural researcher at the Development Research Center of the State Council, 2006; Interview, rural researcher in Beijing, 2006.
55 Li Xuexiang and Xiao Qing, "Cong 'jianfu yingxiong' dao 'zhengfu jianduyuan'" (From a "burden-reduction" hero to a "government supervisor"), *Zhongguo gaige (Nongcun ban) (China's Reforms) (Rural edition)*, no. 9 (September 2003), p. 40.
56 Li and Xiao, "From a 'burden-reduction hero'," p. 41.
57 Duan *et al.*, "'Heroes' or 'shrewd, unyielding people'?," pp. 10–11.
58 O'Brien and Li, "The Politics of Lodging Complaints," p. 768; O'Brien and Li, *Rightful Resistance in Rural China*; Bernstein and Lü, *Taxation without Representation*, p. 148; Ethan Michelson, "Climbing the Dispute Pagoda: Grievances and Appeals to the Official Justice System in Rural China," *American Sociological Review* 72(3) (2007), pp. 459–85; Ethan Michelson.

"Justice from Above or Justice from Below? Popular Strategies for Resolving Grievances in Rural China," *China Quarterly*, no. 193 (March 2008), pp. 43–64; Zhao Shukai, "Shangfang shijian he xinfang tixi: Guanyu nongmin jin jing shangfang wenti de diaocha fenxi" (Petitioning incidents and the letters and visits system: Investigation and analysis of the issue of farmers who lodge complaints in Beijing), *Sannong Zhongguo 2003 (Chinese Agriculture, Countryside, and Farmers*, 2003), pp. 115–25. Yu, *Politics in Yue Village*, p. 565; Yu, "Social Conflict," p. 129. Our 2005 survey corroborated some of these observations. A weighted multiple logistic regression showed that, among ordinary villagers, the better educated were significantly more likely to be protest leaders (p < .01). Veterans of the People's Library Army split, with those who were party members significantly less likely to lead popular protests, whereas those who were not party members were significantly more likely to do so (p = .05). Older villagers were marginally more likely to be protest leaders than younger people, and men were more likely to be protest leaders than women (p < .10).

59 Zhou Decai, "Geren jianli" (A short autobiography), mimeograph, 2002.

60 In October 1975 Zhang Dean was jailed on what he considered a trumped-up charge. On his release date in 1977, Zhang refused to leave the prison at first and demanded an explanation of why he had been detained for fifteen months. He told a reporter in 2001: "I have personally tasted the bitterness of losing the basic rights of a citizen, so I cherish those rights." See Xiwu Lapa, "Zhengce he falü shi nongmin de baohushen – nongmin Zhang Dean de jianfu shijian yu sikao" (Policy and law are farmers' guardians – reflections on burden-reduction practices of farmer Zhang Dean), *Zhongguo gaige (Nongcun ban) (China's Reforms) (Rural edition)*, no. 1 (January 2002), p. 7.

61 Interviews, petitioners' representatives, Hengyang, Hunan, 2003.

62 Interview, petitioners' representative, Hengyang, Hunan, 2003.

63 Interview, petitioners' representative from Zhangpu, Xiamen, 2004. This protest leader was arrested in 2005 and charged with plotting to abduct two county officials. He vehemently denied the charge. To coerce a confession and deprive him of sleep, the police shined bright lights in his cell around the clock. Despite numerous collective petitions by villagers, he was sentenced to seven years in prison. Personal communication with a rural researcher in Fujian, December 26, 2005.

64 Interview, petitioners' representative, Hengyang, Hunan, 2003.

65 Ronald R. Aminzade and Doug McAdam, "Emotions and Contentious Politics," in Aminzade *et al.*, *Silence and Voice*, pp. 14–30.

66 Interview, petitioners' representative, Hengyang, Hunan, 2003.

67 Jiang Zuoping, Li Shuzhong, and Yang Sanjun, "Jianfu zuzhi wajie ji" (The Dissolution of a Burden-Reduction Organization), *Banyuetan (neibuban) (Fortnightly Chats) (Internal edition)*, no. 4 (April 2001), pp. 73–4; O'Brien and Li, "The Politics of Lodging Complaints," p. 769.

68 Interview, petitioners' representative, Hengyang, Hunan, 2003.

69 Interview, petitioners' representative from Shandong, 2003.

70 Jiang *et al.*, "The Dissolution," p. 73.

71 Interview, petitioners' representative, Hengyang, Hunan, 2003.

72 Lianjiang Li, "Political Trust in Rural China," *Modern China* 30(2) (April 2004), pp. 228–58; but cf. Ethan Michelson, "Connected Contention: Social Resources and Petitioning the State in Rural China," unpublished paper, 2 March 2006. On declining faith in the Center, see also O'Brien and Li, *Rightful Resistance in Rural China*, Ch. 4.

73 One protest leader in Hengyang expected to receive an official commendation for his efforts. Another said he was qualified to be a provincial governor. A third believed he could be a good county head. Interviews, petitioners' representative,

Hengyang, Hunan, 2003; petitioner from Henan, Beijing, 2005; petitioners' representative from Shandong, Guangzhou 2004.

74 Interview, petitioners' representative from Shangdong, 2003.

75 Interviews, petitioners' representatives, Hengyang, Hunan, 2003.

76 On the reluctance of bystanders to take action owing to fear of village cadres and their allies in the township government, see Guo, "Land Expropriation," p. 433.

77 Interview, petitioners' representative, Hengyang, Hunan, 2003.

78 Individual petitions are, of course, most often ignored. That is much more difficult to do for collective complaints that have five or more signatures. Sometimes rural officials also try to buy off protest leaders by offering them a village position or a financial inducement. In Hubei, one villager organized a collective petition demanding lower taxes and fees. But he abandoned his efforts immediately after the township offered to lease him a fishpond at a below-market price. Interview, rural researcher in Wuhan, Hubei, 2006. See also Bernstein and Lü, *Taxation without Representation*, p. 150.

79 Xiang, "About 'constitutional concerns,'" p. 222; Zhang, "How to deal with peasants," p. 8; Guo Yukuan, "Taishi cun: yichang meiyou shengli zhe de duikang" (Taishi village: a confrontation without winners), *Gaige neican (Inside Information on Reform)*, no. 33 (20 November 2005), p. 28; Yu, *Politics in Yue Village*, pp. 555–6.

80 Interview, petitioners' representatives, Hengyang, Hunan, 2003; interview, rural researcher in Hunan, 2004.

81 Anonymous, "Wushi renquan jingyong jizuo fangshi bangjiao duixiang bei kunbang guapai" (Without regard for human rights, people who should be educated were bound up and publicly exposed in extreme leftist fashion), *Hengyang ribao (Hengyang daily)*, 18 October 1999, p. 3. Interviews, petitioners' representatives, Hengyang, Hunan, 2003.

82 On this more generally, see Earl, "Repression and Social Control," p. 134.

83 Interview, petitioners' representative, Hebei, 1999.

84 Xiang, "About 'constitutional concerns'," p. 222; interview, rural researcher in Hunan, 2004.

85 Interview, rural researcher in Hunan, 2004. On undermining a collective lawsuit by suppressing a small group of informal leaders, see Tang, "When Peasants Sue," p. 47.

86 In Hebei, a township party secretary ordered the police to "hang" (*diao qilai*) a petitioners' representative on a telephone pole, facing the sun, with his hands held high. Anticipating that the legality of this punishment would be challenged, the secretary claimed that the county had advised him to be firm in dealing with troublemakers. In a further attempt to preempt a legal challenge, he also threatened to sue the petitioner for tampering with the village's electricity transformer. The man then gave up his petitioning. Interview, township party secretary, Hebei, 1994.

87 A number of protest leaders in Hengyang, who were under 35 years of age, simply left the countryside after a multi-village, collective complaint in 1996 failed to produce relief. Interviews, petitioners' representatives, Hengyang, Hunan, 2003.

88 Interviews, rural researcher in Henan, 2004; petitioners' representatives, Hengyang, Hunan, 2003.

89 In China, see Bernstein and Lü, *Taxation without Representation*, p. 149; Tang, "When Peasants Sue," p. 48. On repression backfiring elsewhere, see Jack A. Goldstone and Charles Tilly, "Threats (and Opportunities): Popular Action and State Response in the Dynamics of Contentious Action," in Aminzade *et al.*, *Silence and Voice*, pp. 80–1; David Hess and Brian Martin, "Repression,

Backfire, and the Theory of Transformative Events," *Mobilization* 11(2) (June 2006), pp. 249–67.

90 Nepstad and Bob, "When Do Leaders Matter?," p. 15.

91 Some protest leaders, of course, overestimate the social support they enjoy. In Hengyang, one long-time protest leader was so confident that he would win a villagers' committee election in 2005 that he did not campaign. But he lost badly. Even the main protest leader in the county failed (by a narrow margin) to win in his village, partly because of the township's efforts to de-legitimize his candidacy, and partly because he did not start soliciting votes until a few days before the election. Prior to the balloting, both men assumed that they would sail to overwhelming victories. Interview, rural researcher in Beijing, 2006.

92 Interviews, petitioners' representatives, Hengyang, Hunan, 2003.

93 On the enhanced status and recognition that Nelson Mandela, Aung Saan Suu Kyi, Vaclav Havel, and Daniel Berrigan won as a result of being jailed, see Neptstad and Bob, "When Do Leaders Matter?," pp. 5, 9.

94 Yang Xianhong, "Zhuanfang Liu Beixing: jianzheng Sichuan nongmin lingxiu nao geming" (An interview with Liu Beixing: witnessing a peasant leader in Sichuan fomenting a revolution), http://www7.chinesenewsnet.com/gb/MainNews/Sino News/Mainland/2006_7_20_19_43_40_62.html (accessed 21 July 2006).

95 Interview, rural researcher in Hunan, 2004; also Zhang, "Peasant Power," pp. 29–30.

96 Duan *et al.*, " 'Heroes' or 'shrewd, unyielding people'?," p. 12. For more on what he calls "peasant champions," see Ian Johnson, *Wild Grass: Three Stories of Change in Modern China* (New York: Pantheon Books, 2004), ch. 1.

97 Duan *et al.*, " 'Heroes' or 'shrewd, unyielding people'?," p. 9.

98 Li and Xiao, "From a 'Burden-Reduction Hero'," p. 42; Liu *et al.*, "Rural stability," p. 10; Duan *et al.*, " 'Heroes' or 'Shrewd, Unyielding People'?," p. 12.

99 Liu *et al.*, "Rural Stability," pp. 10–11; Duan *et al.*, " 'Heroes' or 'Shrewd, Unyielding People'?," p. 11; Yu Jianrong, *Politics in Yue Village*, pp. 568–9; Yu Jianrong, "Nongmin you zuzhi kangzheng jiqi zhengzhi fengxian" (Organized peasant resistance and its political risks), *Zhanlue yu guanli (Strategy and Management)*, No. 3 (June 2003), p. 2; Jiang and Yang, "Subpoenaing Four 'Leaders'," pp.15–16.

100 Duan *et al.*, " 'Heroes' or 'Shrewd, Unyielding People'?," pp. 9–10.

101 Interview, petitioners' representative from Shandong, 2003.

102 Interview, petitioners' representative from Shandong, 2003; interview, petitioners' representative from Shandong, 2003.

103 Interview, petitioners' representative, Hebei, 1994; also Zhang, "Peasant Power," p. 28.

104 Interview, petitioners' representative, Hengyang, Hunan, 2003.

105 Interview, petitioners' representative, Hengyang, Hunan, 2003.

106 Duan *et al.*, " 'Heroes' or 'Shrewd, Unyielding People'?," p. 12.

107 For more analysis, see Lianjiang Li, "Political Trust and Petitioning in the Chinese Countryside," *Comparative Politics* 40(2) (2008), pp. 401–19.

108 Interviews, rural researchers in Beijing, 2004.

109 *Ibid*, p. 11. The quotation may sound innocent, but it implies that Huang favors dynastic change and the overthrow of Communist rule. The logic is that since "kings" are not determined by birth, everyone can be a king.

110 Zhou Decai, "Zhi zhongyang bangongting, guowuyuan bangongting, rendaihui bangongting bing Jiang Zemin zongshuji, Zhu Rongji zongli, Li Peng weiyuanzhang" (A letter to the general offices of the Central Party Committee, the State Council, and the National People's Congress and to General Secretary Jiang Zemin, Premier Zhu Rongji, and Chairman Li Peng), mimeograph, 2002.

111 See Li, "Political Trust in Rural China."

5   Tenuous tolerance in China's countryside[1]

Teresa Wright

I trust in the Party and the central government to bring justice to us ordinary people; otherwise I wouldn't be here.

(Zhao Guangjun, 43, a farmer traveling to Beijing to petition
for redress after local officials took his land)[2]

In many ways, Zhao Guangjun is typical of China's rural residents. Often sorely wronged by local officials, farmers have suffered as a result of their lack of economic and political power. Simultaneously, China's rural residents are a contentious bunch, showing a great willingness to fight back against the injustices that they have suffered. They also have a clear sense of "rights" (*quanli* 权力) – including the right to land. And, as with farmer Zhao, they have tended in the post-Mao era to have faith that central Chinese Communist Party (CCP) elites are on their side. With this combination of characteristics, China's farmers thus far have not posed a serious threat to the ruling regime, yet they remain a volatile force that is far from politically quiescent.

Around the world, farmers typically have not played the role of a democratic vanguard. In most countries that have experienced social pressures for democratization, urban socioeconomic sectors – such as private capital holders, urban factory workers, and intellectuals – have led the charge for democratic change. Yet in China, the potential democratic role of farmers cannot be discounted. To begin, they comprise China's largest socioeconomic sector. As of late 2006, 737 million (56 percent) of China's 1.3 billion residents resided in the countryside and engaged in agricultural work.[3] Even with continued urbanization and migration, China's farming population is expected to drop to no lower than 40 percent by 2030.[4] Beyond their sheer numbers, Chinese farmers have a long history of rebelliousness. Along with playing a major role in supporting the revolutionary ascension of the CCP, China's peasants were politically engaged and active during the Maoist era. Further, in the reform period, farmers have been extremely restive. Rural protests have comprised a major portion of the tens of thousands of yearly "mass disturbances" (*daguimo saoluan* 大规模骚乱) that have appeared since the early 1990s. Farmers also have submitted hundreds of thousands of collective petitions to government authorities.

Yet despite their activism in the late post-Mao era, China's peasants have shown little proclivity toward challenging the existing CCP-led political system. As with former state-owned enterprise employees and rank-and-file private sector workers, farmers have evidenced sometimes great disdain for local officials, yet remarkable trust in the central government. When they have engaged in protest, they have appealed to national leaders to enforce what in the farmers' view are benevolent and well-intentioned laws. Even so, there have been signs that peasant support for the central regime may be declining. Further, relative to other socioeconomic sectors, farmers have appeared more open to fundamental political change.

The political attitudes and proclivities of China's peasants have been influenced by their perceptions of socioeconomic mobility, relative socio-economic status, dependence on the party-state, and political options. In turn, these perceptions have been shaped by farmers' experiences of the CCP's post-Mao economic reforms. Overall, the configuration of these factors has led China's twenty-first-century farmers to be restless, and only tenuously tolerant of the political status quo.

Post-Mao rural economic reforms

Beginning in the late 1970s, China's entirely state-controlled rural economic system was dismantled, and market forces were allowed to shape peasants' economic decisions and outcomes. During the Mao era, rural land was collectivized, and all produce was bought and sold through supply and marketing cooperatives that were owned and operated by the party-state. Beyond ostensible government assurance that peasants would be provided with basic sustenance, resources were allocated to individuals based on the number of work points that they had accrued through their labor during the year. In most cases, very little was left after the basic needs of the collective were met.[5]

With the death of Mao and the ascension of Deng Xiaoping to the helm of the ruling CCP, dramatic changes transpired in the countryside. By the mid-1980s, a new "household responsibility system" was in place nationwide. The communes were broken up, and plots were leased to farm families by the state.[6] After fulfilling their contractual obligation to make a fixed pay-ment of grain or other agricultural items at a below-market price, house-holds were allowed to use or sell any additional produce from the plot as they pleased. Meanwhile, local rural governments were encouraged to develop Township and Village Enterprises (TVEs). Reflecting a continued socialist emphasis on state ownership and collective labor, these firms were collectively owned by the village or township. Because the household responsibility system stipulated that land rights could be maintained only if the household met the state's agricultural quotas, all village enterprise employees and most township enterprise employees worked in the firm only part time, and remained engaged in farming.[7] The success of TVEs was made possible by China's opening to the global capitalist economy via the establishment of Special Economic Zones (SEZs). In villages located within or near such zones, access to supplies and markets was eased, and new opportunities arose to fulfill labor-intensive and low-tech needs within the production process. Consequently, although most villages tried to establish TVEs, these enterprises were most prominent and successful in coastal provinces, and much less so in central and western areas.

In some poor regions, township and village officials responded to their shortage of funds by adding to legally sanctioned taxes various supplemental fees, assessments, fines, and forced contributions. Peasants were forced to pay for government services such as licenses and birth registration, and were penalized for both minor and major infractions – including fines of up to 5,000 *yuan* (more than the average peasant's yearly income) for having a second child within five years of the first. In addition, compulsory assessments were exacted for school and road construction, water projects, power station building and maintenance, medical facilities, and public security.[8] When peasants resisted making payments, officials sometimes used force against them. According to central government accounts, local authorities "ransack[ed] homes, taking grain, furniture or livestock," and bullied and beat peasants – sometimes seriously injuring them or even causing their death.[9]

To address the deteriorating political situation in the countryside, central authorities took steps to democratize and enhance the power of local Village Committees (VCs). In doing so, CCP elites did not wish to diminish the Party's ability to direct the political system and the economy, but rather to strengthen the Party's ability to implement its policies at the local level and ensure social stability.[10] In late 1987, an Organic Law gave village residents the right to nominate and elect VC members, who would serve three-year terms. In turn, VCs were made answerable to Village Assemblies made up of all adult residents.[11] By 1990, "rudimentary" VCs had been established in virtually every Chinese village.[12] Yet, only about 15 percent of all VCs were estimated to be operating "reasonably well" (*xiangdang bucuo* 相当不错) in accordance with the standards outlined in the Organic Law.[13]

Since the early 1990s, China's farmers have been ever more directly impacted by market forces deriving from China's late entry into the global capitalist system. Following Deng Xiaoping's 1992 "Southern Tour" (*nanxun* 南巡), the capital cities of all inland provinces and autonomous regions were opened to international trade and investment, and scores of free trade zones, economic and technological development zones, and high-tech industrial development zones were established in medium and large cities.[14] In 2000, the central regime's "Go West" (*xibu dakaifa* 西部大开发) policy further opened China's interior areas to foreign investment and industrial development. As free-trade and foreign investment zones have spread, the expanding job market has given peasants new opportunities to find wage work and earn income through non-agricultural pursuits. Simultaneously, the Party has eased internal migration restrictions, thus increasing peasants' ability to seek off-farm work.

Yet diminished party-state control and increased market influence over the economic fate of rural residents have not been entirely beneficial to China's farmers. For along with greater opportunities for economic advancement has come increased competition. Continued party-state direction of farmers' economic pursuits via local government directives to develop particular rural industries and enterprises has only exacerbated this trend. Although TVE output increased between the late 1980s and late 1990s, as TVEs proliferated, competition rose, with the result that profit did not grow commensurately. To deal with the dual problem of too many TVEs and too little profits, local officials privatized virtually all small and/or marginally profitable TVEs. The end of formal government ownership in these enterprises subjected employees to the vicissitudes of the market, allowing enterprise managers previously constrained by popular views of employment rights in collective enterprises to fire workers, to demand more stringent work conditions, and to reduce wages.[15] At the same time, competition among rural *hukou* (户口) holders rose as official constraints on internal migration diminished.

In the middle part of the first decade of the 2000s, this trend began to abate, as unskilled labor shortages appeared in some coastal provinces. The result was a slight improvement in wages and working conditions in these areas. However, this positive development for peasants seeking wage work proved to be short-lived. In part, this was due to the mobility of capital. While some factories responded to the dearth of cheap unskilled labor in coastal areas by moving inland within China, many others simply packed up and left the PRC.[16] Additionally, the disappearance of unskilled labor shortages was fueled by the economic crisis of the United States (the major importer of Chinese exports) that began in late 2008. As of 2009, the combined result has been a contraction of job opportunities for unskilled workers, such as peasants in search of wage work.

Similarly, sideline production schemes among peasants have been both encouraged and hampered by the combination of state direction and market forces. In countless cases, township or village officials have decided that profits may be made through a particular product, such as bricks, mushrooms, gloves, plastic, cable, or fertilizer. Subsequently, local authorities have ordered households and villages to sink money into this new enterprise. The consistent result has been increased demand for inputs and increased supply of outputs, such that the price of inputs has risen, and the value of the final product has declined. Often the peasants have been left worse off than they were when they started, owing to their sunken investment costs.[17]

In addition, China's increasing immersion in the global economy has subjected peasants to severe fluctuations in agricultural prices. While government policies such as tariffs on agricultural imports and domestic agricultural subsidies have kept competition with foreign suppliers somewhat at bay, the diminution of state purchases of grain at fixed prices has meant that an increasing portion of the crops produced by China's peasants has been affected by domestic and international market forces. When domestic harvests were good (as was the case in 1991, 1992, and 1997), crop prices fell dramatically.[18] Further, when world crop prices plummeted in the late 1990s, crop prices in China dropped by more than one-third.[19] Since China's ascension into the World Trade Organization in 2001, farmers have become only more vulnerable to global price fluctuations, as China's agricultural tariffs have dropped by about 20 percent, and export subsidies have been discontinued.[20] In 2007–8, rising crop prices made farming more profitable. Yet, even so, international market forces have constrained the potential gains of China's farmers. Because the household responsibility system allots peasants only small and scattered plots of land, China's peasants have had limited ability to compete with the large-scale and mechanized farm complexes that predominate in major agricultural exporters such as the U.S.

In localities with fewer opportunities for successful non-agricultural pursuits, these problems were compounded in the 1990s by further increases in local government financial extractions from the peasantry.[21] Yet in the first decade of the 2000s, the trend toward ever-increasing rural exactions was not only halted, but reversed. Beginning in 2000, central authorities initiated pilot projects to gradually phase out rural taxes and fees in some provinces. In 2002, Party leaders announced national reforms requiring that all formal taxes and informal charges be phased out by 2006.[22] Further, national authorities made concrete efforts to ensure that this new policy would be realized. Provinces were given centrally prescribed benchmarks, which were then handed down to township and village leaders.[23] With promotion clearly tied to the fulfillment of these benchmarks, local leaders readily complied. In addition, in some provinces each household was sent a letter explaining the new tax and fee reforms, and told to sign it.[24] With peasants made aware of the new central policies, it was difficult for local leaders to ignore or circumvent them. As a result, the pace of implementation was surprisingly rapid. By 2004, virtually all rural taxes and fees had been abolished.[25]

Although peasants have enjoyed a reduction in government exactions as a result of this reform, the broader impact of this change has varied by location. In wealthier coastal areas where market opportunities have been more abundant and local authorities have been less reliant on agricultural taxes, local enterprises have provided adequate revenue to make up for the decline in tax funds. In many of these localities, the peasant tax burden was negligible even prior to the first few years of the 2000s tax reforms. In such cases, local governments have continued to pay cadre salaries and provide public services and benefits.

In more remote and economically undeveloped localities, conditions have deteriorated. For the structural flaw that led to increasing farmer burdens in the first place – insufficient funds for cadre salaries and public services at the township and village levels – has only worsened. Although the central government increased budget transfers to compensate for local revenue shortfalls, very little of this money has trickled down as it has passed through the provincial and county governmental levels. In a 2003–4 study of twenty townships, for example, only three received transfer funds, and even they got only enough to provide a small supplement to pay some cadre salaries.[26] As a result, large numbers of township and village governments have been in debt since the first few years of the 2000s. To pay cadre salaries and provide centrally mandated services such as education, most have borrowed money. When the local government's credit rating has been so poor that loans have not been forthcoming, individual cadres even have taken out personal loans to pay for collective expenses. Still, funds have been inadequate in most central and western localities. In the 2003–4 study referenced above, only seven of the twenty surveyed townships were able to pay cadre salaries in full and on time. Many owed two or three months' back pay to their staff, and some were behind by as much as two years. The situation at the village level typically has been even worse.[27] Because scarce township and village funds have gone almost entirely to salaries in poor rural areas, public services have withered.[28] In 2004, central authorities issued a new rural policy document that attempted to address the problem. Most importantly, the document instituted a five-fold increase in rural spending.[29] As of 2009, this policy appears to have done little to ameliorate the depressed conditions of poor villagers. However, it has at least given peasants the impression that the national regime is concerned about their plight.

Meanwhile, the twenty-first century has witnessed an increase in the requisitioning of peasant land for non-agricultural development. Although this practice already was common in the late 1990s, since the first few years of the 2000s it has been pandemic in rural areas that are close to urban zones.[30] In the first half of 2004 alone, government sources reported nearly 47,000 cases of "illegal land activities" (*tudi weifa huodong* 土地违法活动) nationwide.[31] Between 1990 and 2002, an estimated 66.3 million farmers had their land confiscated.[32] The impact of land requisitions on the peasantry has been uneven. In some locations, land revenues have been used to provide public services, or even give villagers regular stipends that provide them with a higher and more stable income than they had earned from farming.[33] Yet in many cases, peasants have received little compensation.[34] For example, a 1999 study of a township in Yunnan province found that county and township governments took 60–70 percent of all income from land sales, village governments received 25–30 percent, and farmers were given only 5–10 percent. In one particular sale, the land had sold for 150,000 *yuan* (元) per *mu* (亩) of land, but villagers received only 28,000 *yuan* per *mu*.[35] In 2006, central officials attempted to address this problem by directing provincial governors and local leaders to reduce government requisitions of land that had been allocated to rural residents.[36] As of 2009, this directive appears to have had little impact. Yet, as with the 2004 rural policy document mentioned above, it has indicated to peasants that Party elites are on their side.

Peasant perceptions

The combination of beneficial and harmful developments that have arisen since the early 1990s has had a similarly mixed impact on peasant perceptions of socioeconomic mobility, relative socioeconomic status, dependence on the state, and political options. On the whole, farmers have experienced upward mobility. Using 2003 as a baseline, between 1989 and 2005, the yearly real per capita income of rural residents rose by 300 percent – from approximately 1,000 to 3,000 *yuan* (roughly U.S.$125 to 375).[37] Similarly, China's rural residents have enjoyed many more consumer goods. Between 1985 and 1998, per capita consumption of meat, eggs, and fish increased by roughly 50–100 percent. During the same period, the number of washing machines per 100 rural households climbed from 1.9 to 22.81, the number of refrigerators from .06 to 9.25, color TV sets from .8 to 32.59, and motorcycles from .1 to 13.52.[38] In a nationwide survey undertaken by Han and Whyte in 2004, which is reinforced by Whyte in Chapter 6, relative to other major socioeconomic sectors, farmers exhibited some of the highest levels of optimism.[39]

Yet these general trends mask great variation in the lived experiences of China's peasants since the early 1990s. In more developed rural areas where residents have been less reliant on agriculture for their income, virtually all have expressed the belief that they have moved upward materially. In a 2000 survey conducted in the prosperous southern region of Jiangsu (江苏) province, for example, close to 90 percent of villagers reported that their standard of living had "noticeably improved" (*mingxian gaishan* 明显改善).[40] As one peasant said in the late 1990s, "We get food from our farm, and profits from our factory. Everything that townspeople have, we have too. Houses, modern furniture, TVs, fridges, we've got them all. We've got a phone, too, so we can get through to anywhere in the country. How could I not be satisfied?"[41]

In marked contrast, peasants who have continued to depend on agriculture "have experienced absolute, not just relative, declines in their standard of living" in the late reform period.[42] Although the tax reforms of the first few years of the 2000s lightened the tax burdens of poor peasants, most farmers have remained at a subsistence level. In one poor village, as late as 2000, residents lived in caves that were roughly 3 meters wide and 7 meters long. Until the late 1990s, they had no electricity, and as of 2000 they had no electrical appliances aside from a light. In 2000, their kitchen was outdoors, consisting of a cooker made of mud bricks and two burners. A typical resident consumed only 2–4 catties (2.6–5.2 pounds) of cooking oil and 1–2 catties (1.3–2.6 pounds) of meat per year. On most days, breakfast was noodle soup, lunch consisted of wheat flour gruel (sometimes with a few home-grown vegetables), and dinner was a soup made of millet or corn, and some steamed buns.[43] For agriculturally reliant peasants whose land has been expropriated with little compensation in the late reform period, even this kind of bare survival has not been assured. In addition, to the extent that the late post-Mao era has witnessed a withering of government-funded services such as education, infrastructure, and utilities in poor villages, residents' living standards have suffered.

Relative to other groups, peasants' socioeconomic status has declined since the early 1990s. From 1997 to 2003, for example, per capita average annual rural income reportedly rose 25 percent, but urban incomes increased by 65 percent.[44] From a ratio of 2.1:1 in 1990, the urban–rural income gap grew to 3.3:1 in 2007.[45] If the social welfare benefits of urban residents are included, the economic disjuncture between urban and rural residents has been even larger.[46] In another illustration of this disparity, as of 1999, 25 percent of the rural population consumed less than U.S.$1 per day, as compared with 0.5 percent of urban dwellers.[47]

Among rural residents, material disparities shifted somewhat in the late reform period. In the 1990s, the income gap between those predominantly engaged in agriculture and those relying primarily on other sources of income grew larger. In the first few years of the 2000s, tax reforms ameliorated this imbalance somewhat, as the poorest peasants who had paid the highest proportion of taxes relative to their income received the most economic relief. In addition, in the latter years of the first decade of the 2000s, the rise in agricultural commodity prices was a boon to China's farmers. Further, although coastal villages remain far more prosperous than those in China's interior, the spread of specially designated development zones and loosening of migration restrictions since the early 1990s have decreased the degree of inter-provincial rural inequality.[48]

Within villages, however, economic inequality has increased over the course of the late reform period.[49] As in the early post-Mao era, the most politically well-connected households in a locality have been the most prosperous. Able to occupy upper-tier jobs close to home, they have earned healthy incomes without having to migrate in search of work. Meanwhile, the poorest and least politically connected families have remained engaged only in farming. Most of those with a middling level of connections and resources have sent some family members out in search of off-farm work, leaving the less able-bodied at home to tend to the farm.[50] As in the early reform period, material inequalities that correlate with the unequal distribution of political power have been a major source of peasant discontent. As Manion finds in multi-village surveys conducted in 1990 and 1996, "against an historical background of Maoist egalitarianism, many [peasants] associate growing inequality with the low moral scruples of those with wealth and power."[51]

Reflecting the economic inequalities and local budget shortfalls that have appeared in rural areas in the reform era, village elections increasingly have been dominated by the relatively wealthy. As Levy notes, because many localities have been unable to pay cadre salaries, only those with independent income have been able to afford to serve. In addition, village governments and residents increasingly have relied on the resources of prosperous villagers.[52] In one famous case from the first few years of the 2000s, the winning candidate actually paid each villager 1,800 *yuan* (roughly U.S.$225) – roughly two-thirds of the average rural resident's annual income![53]

Meanwhile, the late reform era has witnessed further increases in peasants' economic independence from the party-state. To begin, the power of rural officials to control the issuance of residence permits has declined.[54] Similarly, the tax reforms of the first few years of the 2000s have made farmers more autonomous vis-à-vis local authorities. Yet peasants have continued to be economically tied to the state for their land. Peasants also have had to abide by the party-state's grain quota and price stipulations. Among those whose land has been requisitioned in the late post-Mao period, this tie has been severed. For peasants who subsequently have received regular payments from the local government, a new and more appealing form of economic dependence has taken its place. For these individuals, systemic political reform holds little material appeal. Contrarily, farmers who have been bereft of both land and government support have become completely independent of the party-state for their livelihood. Within this group, political discontent has run high.

At the same time, the configuration of political options in the post-Mao period has undercut the potential interest of peasants in opposing the overall political system. As in the early reform period, farmers have been able to submit petitions or request government hearings. In addition, relative to the first half of the post-Mao era, village elections have become more meaningful. In 1998, the Party promulgated a new Organic Law regarding village governance. Among other things, the law stipulated that VCs should allow Village Assemblies to discuss and decide on matters such as village expenditures and revenues, applications, plot allocations, family planning actions, and collective contracts. The law also instructed VCs to publicize local government allocations and decisions. In addition, the new law gave all adult villagers the right to run for election, to directly nominate candidates, and to recall VC members before their term of office was complete.[55] According to various reports, the quality of village elections has improved. While in 1990, the Ministry of Civil Affairs estimated that only about 15 percent of Village Committees nationwide were operating in accordance with central policies, in 2003 a Carter Center report found that this was true in 40 percent of China's villages.[56] Similarly, in a comparison of elections in rural Shaanxi (陕西) province in 2000 and 2004, Kennedy found "clear improvements in the quality of village elections regarding the nomination of candidates and the competitiveness of elections." In addition, Kennedy reports that "once [village] elections are fully implemented, it is difficult to revert to semi-open elections or no elections."[57] Also in the first few years of the 2000s, Levy found that village government transparency had increased, particularly in more wealthy areas. In the late 1990s, for example, a county official in a moderately economically developed area estimated that "20 to 30 percent of villages did their transparency work well, 60 percent satisfactorily, and 10 to 20 percent poorly." According to Levy, the situation in this county had improved by the first few years of the 2000s.[58] To the degree that these institutionalized political mechanisms have increased the system's responsiveness to the demands and interests of peasants, challenging the CCP-led political system has not been an appealing option.

Political attitudes and behavior

Peasant perceptions of economic mobility, relative socioeconomic status, dependence on the state, and political options in the late reform era have in some areas bred extensive political dissatisfaction with local elites. At the same time, peasants have evinced a generally favorable view of the central regime. Even so, in comparison with other socioeconomic sectors, peasant support for continued CCP rule in the late reform period has been tenuous and declining.

Since the early 1990s, farmers have been quite restless. In 1993, central authorities reported well over 6,000 cases of "turmoil" (*dongluan* 动乱) in the countryside. In nearly 1,000 of these instances, 500 or more protestors were involved. In all, more than 8,000 deaths were incurred, and 200 million *yuan* worth of property was destroyed. In 1995 and 1996, similar waves of peasant uprisings occurred.[59] In 1997, nearly 900,000 peasants in nine provinces participated in collective petition efforts and public demonstrations that in many cases involved violent confrontations with the authorities. In 1999 roughly five million farmers participated in such political activities, and in 2003 nearly two million did the same.[60] Since 2005, government statistics on the frequency of popular unrest have not been forthcoming, but both official media reports and independent observations suggest that peasant uprisings have remained frequent and widespread.

In addition to street protests, millions have participated in collective petition efforts. Although data since 2006 are not available, the total number of petitions skyrocketed in the first half of the first decade of the 2000s.[61] In 2003, the government petition office received over 10 million petitions. In 2005, this number rose to 13 million. Official and scholarly reports estimate that approximately 60–80 percent of these petitions were initiated by peasants, and related to land disputes.[62]

The content and geographic distribution of peasant grievances shifted over the course of the 1990s and 2000s. Between the early 1990s and the first few years of the 2000s, the major peasant concern was excessive taxes. As Bernstein and Lu report, discontent with tax and fee burdens during this period was "widespread and chronic."[63] Because local government exactions were much steeper in central and western provinces than in coastal zones, peasants in the former reported much higher levels of dissatisfaction, and also displayed a much greater proclivity to engage in contentious collective action.[64] Since the tax reforms of the first few years of the 2000s, protests and petition efforts revolving around excessive taxation virtually have disappeared, and China's western and central villages have been relatively quiet. Meanwhile, peasant discontent and unrest seem to have increased in China's coastal provinces, where most cases of land requisitions have occurred. In 2004, 87 percent of known cases of rural disturbances reportedly arose from land disputes.[65]

Despite these shifts in grievances and geography, peasants' basic political attitudes have been remarkably consistent between the mid-1990s and the latter years of the first decade. In Michelson's 2002 survey of five provinces and the municipality of Chongqing (重庆), farmers reported general satisfaction with the ability of local leaders to resolve most basic villager problems.[66] Yet when it has come to tax disputes and land requisitions, peasants often have expressed grave discontent with local authorities. In these cases, farmers have insisted that their outrage is not simply due to the material hardship that local government actions have caused. Rather, their dissatisfaction has derived from their view that tax and land revenues have gone almost entirely into the pockets of local political leaders and their cronies. Meanwhile, peasants have displayed faith in the central government. In surveys conducted by Li between 1999 and 2001, a substantial majority of villagers expressed the belief that the national government was well intentioned, but that, when it came to tax disputes, local authorities thwarted the capacity of the Center to implement its benevolent policies. As a farmer engaged in tax protests in the late 1990s stated, "Damn those sons of bitches [township and village cadres]! The Center lets us ordinary people have good lives; all central policies are very good. But these policies are all changed when they reach lower levels. It's entirely their fault. They do nothing good, spending their whole day wining and dining. The only thing they don't forget is to collect money."[67] Myriad studies and interviews have uncovered an identical frame of mind among rural protestors. Indeed, research on rural tax and land conflicts universally has concluded that what has encouraged peasants to undertake collective action in the first place has been their belief that local authorities have not been implementing central policies designed to protect peasants' interests.[68] In like manner, O'Brien and Li's 2003–4 survey found that 78 percent of respondents agreed or strongly agreed that "the Center is willing to listen to peasants who tell the truth and welcomes our complaints," and 87 percent agreed or strongly agreed that "the Center supports peasants in defending their lawful rights and interests."[69]

Still, compared to other socioeconomic groups, peasant support for the CCP-led political system has appeared weak. First, farmers have shown relatively little interest in joining the CCP or participating in its affiliated organizations. As of 2006, only 3.07 percent of those living in the countryside were Party members, as opposed to 8.9 percent of urban residents.[70] Although these numbers also reflect the Party's lack of interest in recruiting new peasant members (particularly since the advent of Jiang Zemin's "Three Represents" [*sange daibiao* 三个代表] policy in 2002), even farmers who are CCP members have shown little enthusiasm for maintaining this status. This is most clearly illustrated when rural Party members migrate to the city in search of wage work. As Dickson relates, most of these individuals decline to register with the Party branch in their new urban neighborhood or workplace, as doing so requires attendance at meetings and study sessions, as well as the payment of dues.[71] Consequently, rural migrants who are CCP members generally are so in name only.

Further, farmers have appeared more likely than other socioeconomic sectors to believe that "the well-being of the country should depend on the masses instead of state leaders."[72] When they feel wronged, peasants have reported less reluctance than urban residents to argue with the political authorities. In addition, farmers have shown more support for free-market capitalism, and a greater belief in core democratic values such as free and fair elections, and freedom of speech and expression.[73]

The future trajectory of peasants' political attitudes and behavior may depend on the extent to which the central regime succeeds in promoting mechanisms within the existing political system that satisfactorily address peasant grievances. One key indicator is the degree to which village elections are meaningful. As Manion finds, high-quality local elections seem to promote both public trust in government, and government trustworthiness.[74] Although Kevin O'Brien and Rongbin Han note that procedural improvements have been more impressive than have been changes in the actual exercise of power, free and fair village elections do seem to have become more prevalent over time.[75] To the extent that this trend continues, one might expect that peasant support for the existing political system will only rise in the future. Of course, to the degree that meaningful local elections become the norm in China, the political system will in reality be more democratic than is currently the case.

Similarly, the perceived responsiveness of the petition and hearing systems is important. Heurlin and Whiting's 2005 survey of seventeen provinces found that in 68 percent of petition cases (virtually all of which concerned land compensation), the government either refused to increase the peasants' compensation (36 percent) or took no action at all (32 percent).[76] Li's 2003–5 survey of villagers in two provinces uncovered even more disturbing results: over 60 percent of petitioners had been subjected to one or more forms of local repression, including being subjected to fines (28.2 percent); having their homes demolished or destroyed (21.8 percent); having their homes ransacked, properties confiscated, and valuables taken away (31.4 percent); being beaten, or having their family members beaten (46.8 percent); and being detained, arrested, and sent to labor camps (41.1 percent). Still, in Li's survey roughly 40 percent reported satisfaction with the result of their petitioning effort.[77] In Heurlin and Whiting's research, among the 32 percent of cases where petitions resulted in increased compensation, 12 percent of respondents were satisfied with the amount.[78]

Not surprisingly, Li found that peasants who have had good experiences with petitioning have expressed increased trust in the central government, while those with bad experiences have displayed diminished faith in and lowered support for the ruling regime.[79] Yet interestingly, regardless of a person's assessment of the outcome, those who had petitioned central authorities in Beijing reported reduced trust in the national regime. As a whole, these petitioners were roughly 31 percent less likely than other peasants to agree that the Center truly cared about farmers, nearly 41 percent less likely to agree that the Center welcomed farmers petitioning, and approximately 47 percent less likely to agree that petitioning Beijing was very useful.[80] Thus, even though beneficent national laws and pronouncements have encouraged peasants to take action within existing political structures, when their efforts have come to naught, they have become disillusioned with the political system as a whole. As one petitioner relates, "when we returned [home], seven of us were detained for a few weeks. It's useless to seek justice. Opposing graft and corruption means time in prison. There is no place to look for justice."[81]

For some, the response has been despair. Among Li's respondents, more than 13 percent of unsuccessful petitioners said that they would give up. But for most others, the reaction has been rage and determination.[82] In Li's survey, roughly 82 percent of failed petitioners said that they would continue petitioning until their goals were achieved; approximately 74 percent asserted that they would publicize policies and mobilize the masses to defend their lawful rights; slightly more than 45 percent said that they would "do something that cadres would be afraid of"; and nearly 56 percent said that they would establish an organization to defend farmers' lawful rights.[83] Although not common, some even expressed the desire to bring down the regime. In the words of one peasant whose repeated collective petition efforts had failed, "If we do not get the expected response in a given period of time, then we will go all out to mobilize the masses to struggle for a peasant's right to life and democratic rights by starting a democratic revolutionary movement."[84]

It must be emphasized that the vast majority of peasants in the late reform era have not petitioned the government or engaged in protests. As of the middle part of the first decade of the 2000s, only about 1.4 percent of China's rural residents undertook petition efforts, and only .25 percent participated in public "disturbances" (*saoluan* 骚乱).[85] Yet to the extent that the number of these actions continue to rise and the government's response is not seen as satisfactory, peasant discontent may be expected to become more widespread and deep. Given that most unsuccessful petitioners have not given up, but rather have continued their activism – often in a more confrontational way – peasant-based challenges to the ruling regime are likely to increase.

Conclusion

On balance, China's farmers are tolerant of the political status quo, but only tenuously so. Despite the central Party leadership's attempts to ameliorate the most severe problems faced by rural residents – including exorbitant and arbitrary fees in the 1990s and illegal land requisitions in the first decade of the 2000s – farmers have continued to suffer abuse at the hands of local officials. When rural residents press for redress through petitioning, they often face further harassment, detention, and violence. To the extent that these problems continue, or worsen, China's farmers are likely to lose what faith they have in the national regime.

Seemingly aware of this, in the fall of 2008 the CCP Central Committee passed a resolution on "Rural Reform and Development" (*nongcun gaige he fazhan* 农村改革和发展) that would effectively end rural migration restrictions and enable peasants to transfer land use rights. The central Party leadership's hope is that these measures will restrict the ability of local officials to requisition rural land, and enable rural residents to increase their incomes.[86] Even so, a basic quandary will remain. To the extent that continued economic growth requires that agricultural land be developed, farmers must be displaced. Yet the party-state cannot afford to provide their sustenance, and the market offers insufficient opportunities for unskilled labor.

At the same time, central elites face a quandary regarding rural petitioners. As illustrated by this chapter's opening quotation from Zhao Guangjun, many farmers believe that the national leadership is well intentioned, and that if local problems are only brought to the Center's attention, national elites will step in to save the day. Of course, Party leaders have an interest in perpetuating such popular beliefs. Yet simultaneously, central elites do not wish to encourage petitioning, and seem content with allowing local authorities to achieve "stability" (*wending* 稳定) in whatever ways they see fit. As a result, national authorities generally turn a blind eye when local officials follow petitioners to Beijing, kidnap them, and bring them home. Even worse, Beijing police are widely known to pick up petitioners and take them to "black prisons" (*heijianyu* 黑监狱) in the capital. The relevant local authorities are then contacted to retrieve the petitioners. If the petitioners refuse to recant their grievances, they suffer even more. Along with continued illegal detention, many are "beaten, tortured or sent to extra-judicial 're-education through labor' camps . . . for daring to tarnish the names of officials."[87]

Working in a more positive direction for China's farmers, and possibly undercutting the ability of local authorities to abuse those in their jurisdiction, are village elections. Over the course of the past twenty years, these elections have indeed "begun to change the way in which village authorities gain power."[88] In almost every province, voters are able to nominate their own candidates, and in roughly half of all villages, free and fair voting procedures are the norm. In these localities, the quality of local leadership has improved, and peasant dissatisfaction has declined. Further, it seems clear that these trends are unlikely to be reversed.

That said, rural experts such as O'Brien and Han caution that advances in village elections have not always succeeded in changing the way that local authorities *exercise* power.[89] Elected village leaders often are treated as subordinates by officials at the township or provincial level, and village-level Party organizations and leaders frequently dominate Village Committees.[90] At the same time, Village Committees in some localities have been subject to coercion by gangsters and "black societies."[91]

The realities faced by farmers demonstrate the wide variation that exists in China today. Truly, politics in contemporary China is pluralized, such that it is impossible to say anything definitive about the polity or its people as a whole. In the countryside, beyond the universal de-collectivization of land and advent of village elections, there is no common experience. For every village with legitimate, competent, autonomous, and benevolent leaders, there are many with endemic corruption and abuse. And for every wealthy village, there are others in which living conditions are bleak. Similar inequalities cut across virtually every axis. Urban residents are wealthier than rural; villages in the east are more prosperous than those in the center and the west; villages that are closer to cities are better off than those that are more remote; and more well-connected residents of a village have higher living standards than their neighbors. Moreover, both inequalities and injustices are constantly in flux. Whereas in the 1990s China's poor interior villages were the site of great unrest due to excessive taxes and fees, since the first few years of the 2000s these areas have been relatively peaceful, while relatively prosperous coastal localities have exploded.

For the analyst, such extreme variation renders prediction difficult. For China's ruling elites, it presents a never-ending challenge. As of the time of this writing, national leaders have been able to provide peasants with sufficient support and political opening to prevent the rise of organized opposition to the overall political system. However, this state of affairs is exceedingly fragile, and is unlikely to persist in perpetuity.

Notes

1 Adapted from *Accepting Authoritarianism: State–Society Relation's in China's Reform Era*, by Teresa Wright © 2010. Board of Trustees of the Leland Stanford Jr. University. By permission of the publisher, www.sup.org.

2 Jamil Anderlini, "Punished Supplicants," *Financial Times*, March 5, 2009.

3 "NBS: China's Rural Population Shrinks to 56% of Total," *Xinhua*, October 22, 2006. As of 2000, 70 percent did not earn regular incomes from non-farm wage labor, and only 2.5 percent had registered individual family enterprises. *Zhongguo tongji nianjian 2000 [China Statistical Yearbook 2000]* (Beijing: Zhongguo tongji chubanshe [China Statistical Bureau Press], 2000), p. 369; Zhongguo xiangzhen qiye nianjian 2001 [China Rural Enterprise Yearbook 2001] (Beijing: Zhongguo nongye chubanshe [China Agricultural Bureau Press], 2001), p. 95.

4 "Urbanization is Reducing China's Rural Population," *People's Daily*, February 23, 2006. In 1990, 74 percent of China's citizens were rural residents; in 2001 64 percent lived in rural areas ["NBS: China's Rural Population Shrinks to 56% of Total"].

5 For a more detailed discussion of this period, see Jean C. Oi, *State and Peasant in Contemporary China: The Political Economy of Village Government* (University of California Press, 1989).

6 Originally, the lease period was fifteen years; it was lengthened to thirty years in 1998.

7 Jean C. Oi, *Rural China Takes Off: Institutional Foundations of Economic Reform* (Berkeley: University of California Press, 1999), p. 78.

8 Thomas Bernstein and Xiaobo Lu, "Taxation without Representation: Peasants, the Central and the Local States in Reform China," *China Quarterly* 163 (September 2000), p. 743.

9 *Ibid.*, pp. 746–7.

124   *Teresa Wright*

10 Lianjiang Li and Kevin O'Brien, "The Struggle over Village Elections," in Merle Goldman and Roderick MacFarquhar, eds., *The Paradox of China's Post-Mao Reforms* (Cambridge: Harvard University Press, 1999), pp. 129–44.
11 In situations where the village population is too large or scattered to meet regularly as a group, some provinces allowed for the establishment of Village Representative Assemblies consisting of representatives of each household [O'Brien, "Implementing Political Reform," pp. 42–3; Susan Lawrence, "Democracy, Chinese Style: Village Representative Assemblies," *Australian Journal of Chinese Affairs* 32 (July 1994), p. 61].
12 Kevin O'Brien, "Implementing Political Reform in China's Villages," *Australian Journal of Chinese Affairs* 32 (1994), pp. 41–3; Susan Lawrence, "Democracy, Chinese Style: Village Representative Assemblies," *Australian Journal of Chinese Affairs* 32 (July 1994), p. 61.
13 This estimate comes from the Ministry of Civil Affairs. See O'Brien, "Implementing Political Reform," p. 51.
14 "Opening to the Outside World: Special Economic Zones and Open Coastal Cities," China Internet Information Center (under the auspices of the State Council Information Office), http://www.china.org.cn/e-china/openingup/sez.htm (accessed May 25, 2008).
15 James Kung, "The Evolution of Property Rights in Village Enterprises," in Jean Oi and Andrew Walder, eds., *Property Rights and Economic Reform in China* (Stanford: Stanford University Press, 1999), pp. 95–122.
16 "China May Face Labor Shortage in 2010," *China Daily*, May 14, 2007.
17 For numerous specific examples of this process, see Cao Jinqing, *Huanghe biande Zhongguo* (New York: Routledge, 2005).
18 Jean C. Oi, "Two Decades of Rural Reform in China," *China Quarterly* 159 (September 1999), p. 619.
19 Dwayne Benjamin, Loren Brandt, and John Giles, "The Evolution of Income Inequality in Rural China," *Economic Development and Cultural Change* (2005), pp. 770–1.
20 "The U.S.–China WTO Accession Deal," *FAS online* (U.S. Department of Agriculture), February 9, 2000, http://www.fas.usda.gov/info/factsheets/China/deal.html (accessed May 25, 2008).
21 Bernstein and Lu, "Taxation without Representation."
22 Ran Tao and Ping Qin, "How Has Rural Tax Reform Affected Farmers and Local Governance in China?," *China and World Economy* 15(3) (2007), pp. 20–1.
23 Linda Chelan Li, "Working for the Peasants? Strategic Interactions and the Unintended Consequences in the Chinese Rural Tax Reform," *The China Journal* 57 (January 2006), p. 102.
24 Jean Oi and Shukai Zhao, "Fiscal Crisis in China's Townships: Causes and Consequences," in Elizabeth Perry and Merle Goldman, *Grassroots Political Reform in China* (Cambridge: Harvard University Press, 2007), p. 82.
25 Ran Tao and Ping Qin, "How Has Rural Tax Reform Affected Farmers and Local Governance in China?," *China and World Economy* 15(3) (2007), pp. 19–32; Oi and Zhao, "Fiscal Crisis." According to a 2005 survey undertaken by the Center for Chinese Agricultural Policy, total rural exactions declined by more than 50 percent between 2000 and 2004 [Tao and Qin, "How Has Rural Tax Reform . . .," p. 23]. A 2004 report by the National Bureau of Statistics states that the peasant tax burden declined by over 27 percent between 2003 and 2004 [Oi and Zhao, "Fiscal Crisis," p. 82].
26 Oi and Zhao, "Fiscal Crisis," p. 80.
27 *Ibid.*, pp. 83–6, 90.
28 Oi and Zhao note that this expenditure priority results from the fact that unpaid cadres are more likely to rebel than are ordinary peasants deprived of government

services. And, in order to protect their chances of job retention and promotion, township cadres must prevent local instability or protests that might come to the attention of political higher-ups [Oi and Zhao, "Fiscal Crisis," pp. 89 and 94–5].

29 Andrew Yeh, "Rural Policy: New Leaf or Old Hat?," *China Economic Quarterly* Q1 (2004); and Matt Forney, "Trouble in the 'New Socialist Countryside'," *China Economic Quarterly* Q1 (2006), pp. 53–5.

30 A 2003–4 study by the Institute of Rural Development at the Chinese Academy of Social Sciences found that between 1990 and 2002 more than 60 million farmers lost their land. The study's authors assert that this number has increased in more recent years. See Zhao Ling, "Significant Shift in Focus of Peasants' Rights Activism," China Elections and Governance online, http://www.chinaelections.net/PrintNews.asp?NewsID=3123 (accessed May 28, 2008). Technically, land is under the collective ownership of the village, and as such is subject to VC control. Yet VCs do not have the power to expropriate land for compensatory use. Rather, this power is held by the county government. In most cases, it appears that land expropriation is initiated by the township, which then appeals to the county for approval, and also attempts to convince the relevant VC to relinquish the land [Xiaolin Guo, "Land Expropriation and Rural Conflicts in China," *The China Quarterly* 166 (2001), pp. 424–6].

31 Ling Zhao, "Significant Shift in Focus of Peasants' Rights Activism," China Elections and Governance online (interview with Jianrong Yu), http://www.chinaelections.net/newsinfo.asp?newsid=3123 (accessed May 24, 2008).

32 Http://www.rurallandlaw.cn/shidaiqianyan/904775.htm.Cited in Cheng Li, "Hu Jin Tao's Land Reform: Ambition, Ambiguity, Anxiety," *China Leadership Monitor* 27 (Winter 2009), p. 6.

33 Oi and Zhao, "Fiscal Crisis," p. 93.

34 Since 1999, compensation fees for the loss of crops on expropriated land have been six to ten times the value of the average annual output of the land over the prior three years [Xiaolin Guo, "Land Expropriation and Rural Conflicts in China," p. 427].

35 *Ibid.*, pp. 427–28. One *mu* is roughly equal to one-sixth of an acre.

36 Yeh, "Rural Policy"; Matt Forney, "Trouble," pp. 53–5.

37 Albert Park, "Rural–Urban Inequality in China," in Shahid Yusuf and Anthony Saich eds., *China Urbanizes: Consequences, Strategies and Policies* (New York: World Bank Publications, 2008), p. 42.

38 Yiguo Zhang and Yuanheng Yang, "The Evaluation of People's Living Level of China," Shandong Province Statistical Bureau of China, http://isi.cbs.nl/iamamember/CD2/pdf/542.PDF (accessed May 19, 2008).

39 Chunping Han and Martin King Whyte, "The Social Contours of Distributive Injustice Feelings in Contemporary China," in Deborah Davis and Feng Wang, eds., *Creating Wealth and Poverty in Contemporary China* (Stanford: Stanford University Press, 2008), pp. 193–212.

40 Zhong Yang, "Democratic Values among Chinese Peasantry: An Empirical Survey," *China: An International Journal* 3(2) (2005), p. 197.

41 Cao, *Huanghe biande Zhongguo*, p. 82.

42 Benjamin *et al.*, "The Evolution . . . ," pp. 770–1.

43 Cao, *Huanghe biande Zhongguo*, pp. 226 and 232–3.

44 Yeh, "Rural Policy," p. 26, citing Chen Xiwen, deputy director of China's Central Financial Work Leading Group.

45 *Zhongguo tongji nianjian* [*China Statistical Yearbook*], various years.

46 Renwei Zhao, "Increasing Income Inequality and Its Causes," in Carl Riskin, Renwei Zhao, and Shi Li, eds., *China's Retreat from Inequality* (New York: M.E. Sharpe, 2004), pp. 25–43.

47 Roy Prosterman and Brian Schwarzwalder, "From Death to Life: Giving Value to China's Rural Land," *China Economic Quarterly* Q1 (2004), p. 20.
48 Benjamin *et al.*, "The Evolution . . . ," pp. 791–7.
49 *Ibid.*, p. 799.
50 Lei Guang and Lu Zheng, "Migration as the Second-Best Option: Local Power and Off-Farm Employment," *China Quarterly* 181 (2005), p. 44.
51 Melanie Manion, "Democracy, Community, and Trust: The Impact of Elections in Rural China," *Comparative Political Studies* 39(3) (April 2006), p. 314.
52 Lei Guang and Lu Zheng, "Migration as the Second-Best Option," p. 30.
53 It should be noted that this candidate later lost his position. Although there was some debate as to whether or not he had engaged in bribery (since he paid all villagers, and not only his supporters), the city Discipline Department ruled that the election was invalid [Richard Levy, "Village Elections and Anticorruption," in Elizabeth Perry and Merle Goldman, eds., *Grassroots Political Reform in Contemporary China* (Cambridge: Harvard University Press, 2007), p. 35].
54 An Chen, "The Failure of Organizational Control: Changing Party Power in the Chinese Countryside," *Politics and Society* 35(1) (March 2007), pp. 145–79; Tom Miller, "Hukou Reform: One Step Forward," *China Economic Quarterly* Q3 (2005), pp. 34–7.
55 Organic Law of the Villagers Committees of the People's Republic of China, http://www.china.org.cn/english/government/20729.htm (accessed May 29, 2008). Recall proceedings may be initiated by a petition signed by one-fifth of all villagers. The matter then goes to a vote, and a simple majority prevails. It should be noted that the law also states that VCs should include "an appropriate number of women" (Article 9).
56 Josephine Ma, "Create a Uniform System for Village Polls, Says Jimmy Carter," *South China Morning Post*, September 9, 2003, p. 5. Similarly, a study of rural Jiangsu province in 2000 found that 40 percent of village elections were free, fair, and competitive [Jie Chen, "Sociopolitical Attitudes of the Masses and Leaders in the Chinese Village," *Journal of Contemporary China* 14(44) (August 2005), p. 453]. A 2004 survey of village elections in Shaanxi province reports that 80 percent of villages had conducted competitive elections, but that the quality of the nomination process varied widely [John James Kennedy, "The Implementation of Village Elections and Tax-for-Fee Reform in Rural Northwest China," in Perry and Goldman, eds., *Grassroots Political Reform* (Cambridge: Cambridge University Press, 2007), p. 60]. A 1999 Ministry of Civil Affairs report found that 66 percent of village elections met national standards [Xinhua, July 11, 1999, SWB-FE 3585, p. G4, July 13, 1999 and *South China Morning Post*, July 13, 1999. Cited in Bernstein and Lu, "Taxation without Representation," p. 762].
57 Kennedy, "The Implementation . . . ," pp. 55 and 72.
58 Levy, "Village Elections and Anticorruption," pp. 38–9.
59 Bernstein and Lu, "No Taxation without Representation," pp. 753–4; *Cheng Ming*, in Thomas Bernstein, "Unrest in Rural China: A 2003 Assessment," *Center for the Study of Democracy Paper* 13 (2004), pp. 3–4.
60 *Cheng Ming*, in Bernstein, "Unrest in Rural China," pp. 3–4.
61 "Petition Cases Rise 23.6% Last Year in China," *Xinhua*, March 9, 2005.
62 Zhao, "Significant Shift in Focus of Peasants' Rights Activism."
63 Bernstein and Lu, "No Taxation without Representation," p. 756.
64 In a 2002 survey of rural households in six provinces, Michelson found that 85–90 percent of villagers in the central provinces of Hunan and Henan reported at least one grievance, as opposed to only 22–26 percent of villagers in coastal Shandong and Jiangsu provinces [Ethan Michelson, "Climbing the Dispute Pagoda: Grievances and Appeals to the Official Justice System in Rural China,"

American Sociological Review 72 (June 2007), p. 475]. On the geographic distribution of collective disputes in the 1990s and first few years of the 2000s, see Bernstein and Lu, "No Taxation without Representation" and Zhao, "Significant Shift in Focus of Peasants' Rights Activism."

65 Peasants' major complaints are that land is illegally or forcefully confiscated, or that compensation is too low [Zhao, "Significant Shift in Focus of Peasants' Rights Activism"].

66 Ethan Michelson, "Justice from Above or Below? Popular Strategies for Resolving Grievances in Rural China," *China Quarterly* 193 (2008), pp. 43–64.

67 Anshun Zhu, "Ruci jian fang wei na ban?" [Why did they build new houses?], in Shukai Zhao, ed., *Noncun, nongmin* [*The Countryside and the Peasantry*], Qinghua University, 1999 (unpublished paper), p. 384. Cited in Kevin J. O'Brien and Lianjiang Li, *Rightful Resistance in Rural China*, New York and Cambridge: Cambridge University Press, 2006, p. 43.

68 For examples, see Bernstein and Lu, "Taxation without Representation"; O'Brien and Li, *Rightful Resistance*; Guo, "Land Expropriation and Rural Conflicts in China"; Zhao, "Significant Shift in Focus of Peasants' Rights Activism"; and Tangbiao Xiao, "Ershinian lai dalu nongcun de zhengzhi wending zhangkuang" [The Stable Conditions of Mainland Peasants During the Last 20 Years], *Ershiyi Shiji* [*The 21st Century*] 4 (2003).

69 O'Brien and Li, *Rightful Resistance*, p. 45.

70 In 2006, of a total of 73 million CCP members, an estimated 50.37 million (69 percent) were urban residents, and 22.6 million (31 percent) were rural residents. The total urban population in 2006 was roughly 563 million, and the total rural population was roughly 727 million.

71 *Ibid.*

72 Yang Zhong, "Democratic Values among Chinese Peasantry: An Empirical Study," *China: An International Journal* 3(2) (September 2005), p. 203.

73 *Ibid.*, pp. 194, 200, 203, 207; Bernstein and Lu, "Taxation without Representation," p. 759.

74 Manion, "Democracy, Community, and Trust," p. 319.

75 Kevin O'Brien and Rongbin Han, "Path to Democracy? Assessing Village Elections in China," *Journal of Contemporary China* (forthcoming).

76 Christopher Heurlin and Susan Whiting, "Villagers Against the State: The Politics of Land Disputes," paper presented at the annual meeting of the American Political Science Association, Chicago, August 30, 2007, p. 20; Li, "Political Trust and Petitioning in the Chinese Countryside," *Comparative Politics* 40(2) (January 2008), pp. 209–26.

77 Li, "Political Trust and Petitioning."

78 Heurlin and Whiting, "Villagers Against the State," p. 20.

79 In Li's survey, successful petitioners became 45.7 percent more likely to agree that the central government truly cared about farmers and 63.7 percent more likely to agree that petitioning Beijing was very useful. Conversely, "local repression had a negative correlation with trust in the Center" [Li, "Political Trust and Petitioning"].

80 Li, "Political Trust and Petitioning."

81 Lianjiang Li, "Political Trust in Rural China," *Modern China*, Vol. 30, No. 2 (2004), p. 247.

82 See also O'Brien and Li, *Rightful Resistance*, ch. 4.

83 Li, "Political Trust and Petitioning."

84 Li, "Political Trust in Rural China," p. 247. For similar quotes, see Jianrong Yu, "Conflict in the Countryside: The Emerging Political Awareness of the Peasants," *Social Research* 73(1) (Spring 2006), p. 149; and Cao, *Huanghe biande Zhongguo*, p. 253.

85 If one assumes that 80 percent of the roughly 13 petitions submitted in 2005 related to land disputes (and therefore were initiated by peasants), then roughly 10.4 million of China's 737 million peasants submitted a petition. In 2003, roughly 2 million of China's roughly 800 million peasants participated in public protests.
86 See Cheng Li, "Hu Jintao's Rural Land Reform," available at http://www. brookings.edu/~/media/Files/rc/articles/2009/01_china_land_reform_li/01_china_ land_reform_li.pdf.
87 Anderlini, "Punished Supplicants."
88 O'Brien and Han, "Path to Democracy?," p. 360.
89 *Ibid.*
90 *Ibid.*, pp. 367–74.
91 *Ibid.*, p. 375.

6 Do Chinese citizens want the government to do more to promote equality?

Martin King Whyte

China has sustained an extraordinary growth rate for the three decades since market reforms were launched in 1978, but this record has produced at least one very worrisome consequence. As state employment and bureaucratic allocation have given way to markets and competition, income differences have widened considerably. Although the average standard of living has risen sharply, losses of jobs and benefits have plunged large numbers of Chinese families into poverty even as, at the other end of the social scale, the reforms have produced many new millionaires living in guarded and gated mansion compounds. The research project reported in these pages is devoted to trying to understand how Chinese citizens view the complex inequality trends in their society. Do most Chinese feel gratitude for the general improvements in living standards that have occurred since 1978 and perceive growing income and other gaps as either regrettable but of minor importance, unavoidable, or perhaps even as necessary and desirable? Or is the majority sentiment instead that the switch from socialist to market principles and rising income gaps are signs of a social order that has become fundamentally unjust? Do many Chinese harbor nostalgic feelings for the presumed greater equality of the Mao era and want the government to take more active steps to reduce current inequalities?

In recent years many analysts have depicted Chinese society as increasingly rocked by anger and protest activity in response to rising inequalities. For example, official police statistics state that the number of "mass protest incidents" (*daguimo kangyi shijian* 大规模抗议事件) in China increased from 8,700 in 1993 to 87,000 in 2005, with commentators suggesting that rising anger about inequality was a prime factor behind this surge.[1] A poll of senior officials conducted by the Central Party School in 2004 concluded that the income gap was China's most serious social problem, far ahead of crime and corruption, which were ranked two and three.[2] On a similar note, a summary of the 2006 "Blue Book" published by the Chinese Academy of Social Sciences (an annual assessment of the state of Chinese society) stated, "The gini coefficient, an indicator of income disparities, reached 0.53 last year, far higher than a dangerous level of 0.4."[3] Reports such as these have led some analysts to conclude that China is becoming a "social volcano," with rising anger about inequality and distributive injustice a threat to political stability.[4]

An additional element of this kind of conventional account of Chinese social trends is the assumption that if China is headed toward a social volcano, the eruptions will mostly come from reform-era losers – those left behind and disadvantaged by recent trends, even as growing middle and propertied classes are relatively satisfied with the status quo. While migrants, the poorly educated, residents of interior provinces, and other relatively disadvantaged groups are assumed to be unhappy with current inequalities, it is China's rural population that is often seen as most angry. A recent edition of the *Economist* magazine declares, "A spectre is haunting China – the spectre of rural unrest,"[5] while *Time* magazine's Asian edition declared at about the same time, "Violent protests . . . are convulsing the Chinese countryside with ever more frequency," and continued its report with phrases such as "seeds of fury" and "the pitchfork anger of peasants."[6]

The Hu Jintao and Wen Jiabao leadership that took command in China in 2002–3 has taken the threat posed by anger over increasing inequality quite seriously. In recent years they have announced a number of dramatic policy changes designed to make China a more "harmonious society" (*hexie shehui* 和谐社会), particularly measures aimed at alleviating rural poverty. For example, rural taxes and fees were limited and then the grain tax was phased out entirely, rural school fees are being eliminated, and moves are underway to create a new if modest village medical insurance system in all rural communities (to replace the cooperative medical insurance plans that collapsed early in the reform era) and to implement in rural areas a version of the minimum livelihood stipend (*dibao* 低保) system that heretofore has only been implemented in urban areas. It seems clear that China's leaders hope that through interventions such as these they can respond to popular desires for greater equality and thereby reduce the possibility that the "pitchfork anger of peasants" might threaten Communist Party rule.

However, we need to stop and ask whether these analyses of popular attitudes in China today are correct or not. Are Chinese very angry about what they feel are excessive inequalities in their society? Would they prefer a social order characterized by much greater social equality? Do they think the Chinese government should be playing a more active role in limiting and redressing current inequalities? And within Chinese society, is it disadvantaged groups in general, and farmers in particular, who have the strongest desires for greater equality? These are questions this essay considers by using data from a 2004 China national survey on these issues. In the sections that follow, I first describe the data used here and measurements of key dimensions of preferences for greater equality and for a more active government role in redistribution from the rich to the poor. I then evaluate how Chinese citizens feel about these issues and compare their perceptions with the responses of citizens in other societies. Next, I examine the variations within

Chinese society in preferences for greater equality. Finally, I interpret the findings and discuss some of their implications.

The 2004 China national survey on attitudes toward inequality

This essay's empirical analyses come from the 2004 national China Survey on Inequality and Distributive Justice, which was conducted by a collaborative research team.[7] Part of the inspiration for this survey came from previous surveys on inequality and distributive injustice attitudes in other societies, and particularly from the International Social Justice Project (ISJP), which carried out two rounds of national surveys on these issues, in 1991 and in 1996, in several Eastern European societies making the transition from socialism to capitalism, as well as in several advanced capitalist societies.[8] The 2004 China survey questionnaire included a large number of translations of questions used in such earlier surveys as well as many new questions about distinctive features of China's current patterns of inequality. The 2004 survey used an innovative sampling method, spatial probability sampling,[9] to identify and interview a nationally representative sample of Chinese citizens ranging in age from 18 to 70, with a response rate of about 75 percent, yielding a final sample of 3,267 cases.[10]

Chinese preferences for equality and government redistribution

The 2004 China questionnaire covered a broad range of attitude questions regarding inequality and distributive injustice issues. For the purposes of the present analysis, I focus on only a limited portion of this terrain. Specifically, I examine here distinct aspects of views about whether current inequalities are excessive, about the desirability of more equal distribution, about the preferred role of the government in promoting equality and providing basic services to Chinese citizens, and about desires to limit the ability of the wealthy to purchase better lives for their families.[11]

First, to see how Chinese citizens perceive the size of current inequalities, we asked whether respondents think current income differences nationally are too small, somewhat too small, about right, somewhat too large, or too large. Our summary statistics show that a substantial majority of respondents (71.7 percent) feel that the gaps are to some degree excessive (see the first row of Panel A in Table 6.1). However, when we additionally asked respondents about income differences within their own work units and in the neighborhoods in which they live, the proportion who said that such "local" income differences are excessive was much smaller – only 39.6 percent and 31.8 percent, respectively (see rows 2 and 3). Indeed, for these latter two questions, the most common response was that income differences within the work unit and the neighborhood are about right. So these responses contain mixed messages. Clearly most Chinese feel that income differences in the entire nation are larger than they should be, but when they are asked

Table 6.1 Chinese preferences regarding equality and inequality

Table 6.1A: Views on current income gaps (row %)

	too small	somewhat small	about right	somewhat large	too large	N
National income gaps	1.4	4.4	22.5	31.6	40.1	3254
Work unit income gaps	1.6	8.9	49.9	27.1	12.5	2107
Neighborhood income gaps	1.9	10.2	56.1	26.6	5.2	3264

Table 6.1B: Views on egalitarian distribution (row %)

	strongly disagree	disagree	neutral	agree	strongly agree	N
Equal distribution is most fair	10.6	34.1	26.3	22.9	6.2	3262
Redistribution to meet needs	8.1	29.8	32.5	24.2	5.3	3259
Extra help to poor	1.0	6.8	30.2	45.6	16.3	3252

Table 6.1C: Views on government efforts to promote equality (row %)

	strongly disagree	disagree	neutral	agree	strongly agree	N
Government limits top income	7.9	26.8	31.5	24.0	9.8	3262
Government reduces rich–poor gap	1.8	10.3	30.6	34.2	23.1	3260
Government guarantees jobs	0.5	3.9	20.0	45.6	30.1	3261
Government guarantees minimum living standard	0.5	2.7	16.1	39.4	41.4	3263

about people in their local environment – those who more realistically would be used as their reference groups – then only about one respondent in three says that current income differences are excessive.

Since at least some Chinese citizens have objections to the size of current inequalities, it is worth considering how they would feel about a much more equal distribution of income and other resources and about government redistribution as a method of achieving such a result. Several questions relating to these issues are displayed in Panels B and C of Table 6.1. First, we have responses to the statement, "Distributing wealth and income equally among people is the fairest method." As we can see from the first row of Table 6.1B, opinions are divided on this issue, but with more respondents disagreeing with this statement than agreeing. Evidently a strictly egalitarian distribution is not desired by most Chinese. Nor is need-based redistribution very popular, as seen in the similar pattern of reactions to the second question shown in Table 6.1B: "There should be redistribution from the rich to the poor in order to satisfy everyone's needs." However, judging from the third row in Table 6.1B, there is much more popular approval of affirmative action efforts to help the poor, with 61.9 percent of respondents agreeing with the statement "It is fair to give people from lower social strata extra help so they can enjoy more equal opportunities."

The next four questions, whose response patterns are displayed in Panel C of Table 6.1, all inquire about whether the government should take additional measures to reduce inequality. It is apparent that most Chinese do not favor limits on the maximum income individuals should be able to earn (see the first row in Table 6.1C), with the pattern of responses very similar to the first two rows in Table 6.1B. However, there is much more support for the other three possible government actions, with 57.3 percent approving government efforts to reduce the gap between high and low incomes, 75.7 percent favoring government guarantees of jobs for everyone willing to work, and 80.8 percent advocating the government guaranteeing a minimum standard of living for everyone.

Taken together, these responses suggest that the predominant view among Chinese citizens is that the ideal society would differ from the status quo mainly by having poverty eliminated through government-sponsored job and income guarantees, but without setting limits on the income and wealth of the rich or redistributing from the rich to the poor. (Respondents were not asked to explain how the government could help the poor without extracting more from the rich.) This appears to be a formula for a market-oriented welfare state, not a socialist society,[12] and there is little evidence here that most citizens are very angry about current inequalities or harbor strong resentments against China's newly emerging class of entrepreneurs, millionaires, and, yes, capitalists.

Governments in any society can promote social equality in a variety of ways, and not simply by redistributing from the rich to the poor. In particular, the government can finance and provide basic services to citizens – public goods – rather than requiring citizens to purchase such services in the market. Other things being equal, a society in which the provision of public goods is extensive will be more equal than a society in which such distributions are more limited.[13] It is worth asking, then, whether Chinese citizens in general would like their government to have the major responsibility for providing services in such areas as health care, education, housing, and care for the elderly. Our questionnaire contained a series of six questions about the provision of a range of such services, asking respondents to say for each whether individuals should be fully responsible for providing it, mainly responsible, share the responsibility equally with the government, or whether

Table 6.2 Chinese view on equality versus inequality in social service provision

Table 6.2A: Views on who should provide basic services (row %)

	individual fully	individual mainly	equally	the state mainly	the state fully	N
Responsibility for health care	5.9	12.9	50.8	19.2	11.1	3265
Responsibility for primary and secondary education	7.3	15.5	33.9	26.4	16.9	3263
Responsibility for university education	5.4	14.6	49.1	20.5	10.5	3262
Responsibility for employment	6.5	19.7	44.2	19.6	9.9	3265
Responsibility for housing	18.1	35.4	32.5	9.5	4.5	3264
Responsibility for care for elderly	10.6	18.0	38.4	19.5	13.3	3263

Table 6.2B: Views on the rich purchasing better services (row %)

	strongly agree	agree	neutral	disagree	strongly disagree	N
Fair, rich children get better schooling	20.1	44.1	21.5	11.5	2.7	3257
Fair, rich buy better housing	15.2	42.8	25.8	13.1	3.0	3254
Fair, rich get better health care	12.0	35.2	25.3	19.1	8.5	3246

it should be mainly or fully the responsibility of the government. The pattern of responses to these questions is displayed in Table 6.2A.

These responses yield a mixed picture. Primary and secondary education is the arena we inquired about that respondents are most likely to feel is mainly or entirely the government's responsibility (43.3 percent), while housing is at the other end of the scale, with only 14 percent of respondents feeling the government is or should be mainly or fully responsible for its provision. However, for all of these services except housing, the most common response was that responsibility should be shared between the government and individuals (with figures for category 3 ranging from 32.5 percent to 50.8 percent). Even though only in regard to housing did more respondents feel the service was an individual rather than a governmental responsibility (by 53.5 percent versus 14 percent), for the other services except primary and secondary education, the gap between the proportions favoring government responsibility versus individual responsibility is not that large (3–11 percent).

These figures lend themselves to a variety of interpretations. Three of these realms (medical care, housing, and care for the elderly) are at present mainly the responsibility of, and are financed primarily by, individuals and families rather than by the government.[14] So these figures could be interpreted as showing a desire for the government to do more than at present to provide and pay for medical care and care for the elderly, although not in the realm of housing. However, the roughly normal-curve shape of the distribution of these responses and the predominance of views that individuals should share the responsibility in each of these service areas undermine the view that Chinese citizens would generally prefer a stronger state role in promoting social equality through distributing social services as public goods. Insofar as individuals play a significant role in the provision and distribution of these services, variations in income and other resources will obviously produce differential access and unequal consumption levels.

Further insight into how Chinese citizens view the unequal access that results from at least partial reliance on individuals and families to provide and finance basic services comes from three other questions included in our survey. We asked each respondent to respond on a five category scale, ranging from strongly agree to strongly disagree, to three statements: "It is fair for rich people to pay for better schooling for their children"; "It is fair that rich people can purchase better housing than other people"; and "It is fair that rich people can enjoy better health care than other people." The pattern of responses to these three statements is shown in Table 6.2B. There is much more agreement than disagreement with each of these statements, with the largest gap on paying for better schooling (64.2 percent vs. 14.2 percent) and the smallest on paying for better medical care (47.2 percent vs. 27.6 percent). In other words, not only do most survey respondents not favor primary reliance on the government to provide and finance basic social services, but a majority of Chinese citizens also accept the inegalitarian distribution of housing, schooling, and medical care that results when responsibility is shared between the government and individuals. So in regard to the provision of basic services, our findings echo the responses to earlier questions. We don't see in these results a strong popular desire for the Chinese government to do a lot more to promote social equality.

Chinese views on promoting equality in comparative perspective

As mentioned earlier, some of the questions used in the 2004 China survey were replications of questions asked in the ISJP surveys in the 1990s.[15] Two rounds of surveys were carried out by the ISJP, in 1991 in both advanced capitalist and formerly socialist societies (Bulgaria, Czech Republic, Estonia, Germany [East and West], Holland, Hungary, Japan, Poland, Russia, Slovenia, the United Kingdom, and the United States), and in 1996 only in selected Eastern European transitional societies (the former East

Germany, Hungary, Russia, Bulgaria, and the Czech Republic). For the purpose of comparison with our Chinese survey results, in instances where surveys were conducted in a country both in 1991 and 1996, we consider only the latter, and also to keep our tables from becoming unwieldy, we omit the 1991 survey results for Estonia, Slovenia, and Holland. That procedure yields the following nations whose citizen attitudes we compare to China: Russia, Bulgaria, Hungary, the Czech Republic, East Germany in 1996 and Poland in 1991 as the Eastern European transitional societies, and the United States, the United Kingdom, West Germany, and Japan in 1991 as the advanced capitalist countries. Table 6.3 presents cross-national comparisons of selected measures of equality preferences.[16]

Panel A of Table 6.3 summarizes the percentages of those who say that income gaps nationally are too large or somewhat too large. While, as noted earlier, a majority of Chinese respondents (71.7 percent) think that China's national income gaps are too large, it turns out that this figure is actually on the *low* side in comparative perspective. With the exception of Poland in 1991 and the former East Germany in 1996, citizens in every other post-socialist transitional society agree in substantially larger numbers that income gaps in their country are excessive, with about 95 percent of respondents in both Hungary and Bulgaria in 1996 expressing this view. In fact, the tendency of Chinese citizens to see national income gaps as excessive is roughly parallel with the responses in the capitalist countries included in the 1991 ISJP surveys, with only citizens in the United States somewhat less likely to express this sentiment (65.2 percent versus 71.7 percent). In short, the comparative evidence indicates that Chinese citizens are if anything *less* likely than citizens of other societies to perceive current national income gaps as excessive.

The next set of questions concerns preferences for more egalitarian distribution patterns and government efforts to promote greater equality. Did the Mao-era extreme promotion of egalitarianism, at least at the rhetorical level, leave an imprint on Chinese popular attitudes today? The Chinese and comparative responses to six questions in this realm are displayed in Table 6.3, Panels B and C. In these panels the percentages given are simply the sum of "agree" (*tongyi* 同意) and "strongly agree" (*feichang tongyi* 非常同意) responses to the statements read out to respondents. In none of the countries covered here do more than a minority of respondents say it would be fairest to give everyone in society equal shares, and China (at 29.1 percent agreeing with egalitarian distribution) is right in the middle of the pack. (Japan stands out as the country with the strongest support for egalitarian distribution, with 37.5 percent favoring this approach.) China is more distinctive in that *fewer* citizens favor redistribution from the rich to the poor in order to satisfy everyone's needs than in most of the other locales – only 29.5 percent favor this approach, compared to 36.8–72.8 percent in Eastern Europe and 45–75.7 percent in the three Western capitalist countries. (Curiously, Japanese are about as unlikely as Chinese to favor this approach, at 30 percent, even though they are the ones most likely to favor

Table 6.3 Chinese views on equality in comparative perspective

Table 6.3A: Views on national income gaps (% somewhat large and too large)

	China 2004	Russia 1996	Bulgaria 1996	Hungary 1996	Czech Republic 1996	East Germany 1996	Poland 1991	U.S. 1991	Great Britain 1991	West Germany 1991	Japan 1991
National income gaps	71.7	86.3	95.6	94.9	78.6	72.1	69.7	65.2	75.0	70.8	72.6

Table 6.3B: Views on egalitarian distribution (% agree and strongly agree)

	China 2004	Russia 1996	Bulgaria 1996	Hungary 1996	Czech Republic 1996	East Germany 1996	Poland 1991	U.S. 1991	Great Britain 1991	West Germany 1991	Japan 1991
Equal distribution is most fair	29.1	28.6	32.4	18.9	12.7	24.8	19.1	19.2	28.9	21.3	37.5
Redistribution to meet needs	29.5	44.9	36.8	64.0	39.2	72.8	50.9	45.0	46.7	75.7	30.0
Extra help to poor	61.9	76.1	76.2	54.6	61.3	n.a.	88.0	82.1	79.5	n.a.	75.0

Table 6.3C: Views on government efforts to promote equality (% agree and strongly agree)

	China 2004	Russia 1996	Bulgaria 1996	Hungary 1996	Czech Republic 1996	East Germany 1996	Poland 1991	U.S. 1991	Great Britain 1991	West Germany 1991	Japan 1991
Government limits top income	33.8	39.5	43.7	55.4	21.7	53.1	44.3	16.7	37.9	31.7	33.4
Government guarantees jobs	75.7	93.2	88.8	89.2	74.3	88.9	86.2	50.4	66.2	70.6	84.5
Government guarantees minimum living standard	80.8	90.8	92.5	70.1	85.6	87.8	85.3	55.9	82.1	83.9	80.6

Table 6.3D: Views on rich purchasing better services (% agree and strongly agree)

	China 2004	Russia 1996	Bulgaria 1996	Hungary 1996	Czech Republic 1996	East Germany 1996	Poland 1991	U.S. 1991	Great Britain 1991	West Germany 1991	Japan 1991
Fair, rich children better schools	64.2	60.0	60.1	39.0	22.9	31.0	67.9	65.2	56.3	51.9	50.9
Fair, rich buy better housing	58.0	60.8	57.0	59.4	n.a.	47.2	n.a.	n.a.	n.a.	n.a.	n.a.
Fair, rich better health care	47.2	41.5	21.0	11.2	n.a.	6.4	n.a.	n.a.	n.a.	n.a.	n.a.

egalitarian distribution.) The next question (row 3 in Table 6.3B) concerns affirmative action. Respondents were asked whether it is fair to give extra help to the disadvantaged so they can enjoy more equal opportunities. Most respondents in all locales favor affirmative action, but Chinese citizens are again on the low side in regard to this opinion. Only 61.9 percent of Chinese respondents agree or strongly agree with the desirability of giving extra help to the disadvantaged, a figure a little higher than in the Hungarian and Czech surveys, but much lower than the 75–88 percent who favor such measures both in other Eastern European post-socialist and in advanced capitalist societies.

The three rows in Table 6.3C are responses to statements about things the government might do to promote greater equality. Government-provided minimum income guarantees and the government as the last resort provider of jobs to the poor are popular in most of the included countries except the United States, and China's level of approval of these two approaches (80.8 percent and 75.7 percent) is not particularly low or high compared to all the other countries included. The final measure covered, government-imposed limits on the maximum income a person can make, tends to be favored more in the Eastern European transitional societies (with the exception of the Czech Republic) than in the capitalist countries, and the pattern of China's responses is closer to the latter than to the former. Specifically, only about one-third of Chinese favor upper income limits, compared to about 40–55 percent in most Eastern European societies (but only 17–38 percent in the capitalist societies included in this comparison).

Chinese citizens experienced a period of more egalitarian rhetoric and policy than their counterparts in Eastern Europe in the late Mao era.[17] One might have thought that this experience would produce broader support for social equality today than in other state socialist societies. However, perhaps unpleasant memories of the egalitarian experiments and rhetoric of the Mao era have produced, in reaction-formation fashion, more ardent rejection of egalitarian distribution than in other post-socialist societies. Is either of these speculations borne out by the data in Table 6.3, panels B and C? Perhaps Chinese are *less* likely than citizens in most other societies to favor redistribution from the rich to the poor to meet popular needs or to favor affirmative action to help the poor, and they are also more like residents of established capitalist than of other transitional societies in being unenthusiastic about the government imposing maximum income limits. However, they respond similarly to respondents in Eastern European countries as well as Japan in being *more* likely than their counterparts in Western capitalist societies to favor the government providing jobs for the poor. On balance Chinese citizens today certainly do not appear unusually egalitarian, compared to citizens of other countries, and in some respects (e.g. regarding affirmative action and maximum income caps) they appear more skeptical of egalitarian policies. So these data provide more support for the "reaction against," rather than the "legacy of" the Maoist egalitarianism argument, but the distinctiveness of Chinese response patterns here is relatively muted.

Table 6.3, Panel D, shows responses to questions about the acceptability of the rich keeping and enjoying their advantages and passing them on to their children. This is a domain in which current policies and rhetoric in China ("it is good for some people to get rich first" 让一部分人先富起来) constitute a very sharp break with the Mao era, when pursuit of personal advantage and even slightly conspicuous consumption was politically dangerous. The three questions ask whether it is fair for the rich to get better education for their children, better housing, and better medical care. Unfortunately we only have responses to the first of these three questions in several of the surveys. In general, though, the figures in Table 6.3D show as much or more approval of the rich enjoying the fruits of their success in China as in the other countries surveyed. The most distinctive contrast concerns the ability of the rich to enjoy better medical care than others. Evidently respondents in some other post-socialist societies (although we only have data for Russia, Bulgaria, Hungary, and the former East Germany) tend to see access to medical care more as a basic social right rather than a market-distributed good, and they thus express strong disapproval of this statement. However, Chinese citizens are less likely to share this view, with close to a majority agreeing that the rich should be able to obtain better medical care than others.

In general these comparative figures from the ISJP surveys help us place results from the 2004 China survey in perspective. How the Chinese responses compare with the other countries examined here varies from question to question. However, in general Chinese citizens have views that are either similar to their counterparts in other societies or which indicate a *weaker* desire for social equality.[18] To phrase the matter in another way, the conventional view that most Chinese citizens view the inequalities within which they live today as excessive and unfair appears to be incorrect. On balance most Chinese have come to terms with and accept these inequalities, rather than feeling that the government should take active steps to reduce them. There does not appear to be a groundswell of demands for making China a more equal society.[19] So the simple answer to the question posed in the title of this paper, "Do Chinese citizens want the government to do more to promote equality?," is "not particularly".

Variations in desires for equality and government redistribution

Although the most common responses to our survey indicate greater acceptance than anger about current inequalities, there are nonetheless substantial variations in the views of respondents. A substantial minority of respondents feel that equal distribution would be best (29.1 percent), that upper limits should be placed upon incomes (33.8 percent), that the state should be mainly or fully responsible for caring for the elderly (32.8 percent), and that it is wrong for rich families to purchase better health care for their families (27.6 percent). Is the conventional wisdom correct that in general it is disadvantaged groups, and farmers in particular, who are most likely to express such a desire for greater equality and want the government to do more to promote it? In this section we investigate the social background sources of variations in preferences for more equality and for government redistribution.

Measures of preferences for equality and government redistribution

First, in order to tap the sentiment that current inequalities are too large, I use responses to the first question displayed in Table 6.1A and refer to this measure as "Excessive inequality."[20] On a similar note, the three questions about preferences for equality (favoring egalitarian distribution, advocating redistribution to aid the poor, and approval of affirmative action measures to help the disadvantaged – see Table 6.1B) could not be combined into a reliable composite scale, so I examine here only the social contours of agreement versus disagreement with the first of these statements: "Distributing wealth and income equally among people is the most fair method."[21] I refer to this measure as "Prefer equality."

Third, from three of the four questions concerning the role of the government in promoting increased equality in Table 6.1C, I constructed a composite scale I refer to as "[preference for] Government leveling." The three included items asked respondents to state agreement or disagreement with the following statements: "The government should assure that every person is able to maintain a minimum standard of living"; "The government should provide an opportunity to work for every person willing to work"; and "The government has the responsibility to shrink the gap between high and low incomes."[22]

Fourth, in order to tap desires for the government to take the major responsibility for health care, education, care for the elderly, and other services, I constructed a summary scale from the six questions displayed in Table 6.2A. I refer to this as the "Government services" scale, with a low score indicating a desire for individual responsibility and a high score indicating a desire for government responsibility for providing basic social services.[23] Finally, for the fifth measure I constructed a summary score from the three questions about views on rich people using their wealth to purchase better lives for themselves and their children (see Table 6.2B): "It is fair for rich people to pay for better schooling for their children"; "It is fair that rich people can purchase better housing than other people"; and "It is fair that rich people can enjoy better health care than other people;" again with the response categories varying from strongly agree to strongly disagree. This summary measure thus indicates opposition to the rich using their wealth to purchase better lives, and I refer to this summary measure as "Oppose rich transmit status" (or "Vs. rich transmit" for short).[24]

Social background predictors of preferences for equality

Thus we have five distinct measures of attitudes reflecting different aspects of preferences for equality and for government efforts to promote equality: Excessive inequality, Prefer equality, Government leveling, Government services, and Vs. rich transmit. The following pages describe a range of background characteristics that I use to try to explain variations in attitudes on these five scales.[25]

I use a wide range of objective occupational and residential status categories, other objective demographic and socioeconomic characteristics, geographic location measures, and subjective status variables as potential predictors of variations in attitudes toward promoting inequality. Many but not all of the background predictors I use in this analysis are designed to test the idea that those who currently have advantages or have been "winners" as a result of market reforms are more satisfied with the status quo and thus have less desire for greater equality than those with low status or who have been "losers" in the reforms.

Objective characteristics: occupations and residential status categories

Since in China occupational categories are entangled with another even more important status cleavage – between those with urban versus rural household registration (*hukou* 户口) status – I constructed a set of twelve occupational/residential status categories as predictors of inequality attitudes, four of which involve current agricultural household registrations – farmers, rural non-agricultural workers, migrants, and rural "others" (e.g. rural residents not in the labor force) – and eight categories involving non-agricultural registrations – unskilled/semi-skilled workers, skilled workers, the self-employed (including private business owners), routine non-manual workers, professionals, managers/administrative cadres, the urban unemployed, and urban "others" (again mainly those not in the labor force).[26] According to the conventional wisdom, we would expect to find the most desire for greater equality among the lowest status groups – particularly among farmers, migrants, the urban unemployed, and urban unskilled/semi-skilled workers.

Objective characteristics: demographic and socioeconomic traits

In the analyses that follow I employ a range of other measures of objective characteristics of respondents which might have some association with variations in preferences for equality: gender (with female = 1; male = 0), age of respondent, the age of respondent squared (divided by 100),[27] number of years of education, marital status (married = 1; all others = 0), ethnicity (Han Chinese = 1; all others = 0), the logarithm of the respondent's household income in 2003 (self-reported in response to our survey questions), Chinese Communist Party membership (yes = 1; no = 0), whether the respondent was currently or had before retirement been employed in a state-owned enterprise (SOE) (yes = 1; no = 0), and a summary measure of the respondent's exposure to unofficial communications.[28] If the conventional wisdom is correct, then individuals with advantaged social status (high education, high family income, Party membership, etc.) would be expected to have low desires to promote further equality, while those who are or were employed in state-owned enterprises or who have access to a range of unofficial sources of information might be expected to have more critical and egalitarian attitudes.[29]

Objective characteristics: geographic location measures

I assume that the attitudes of individuals toward various aspects of inequality and distributive injustice are affected not only by their personal and family background characteristics, but also by where they live and work. It has often been suggested, for example, that individuals located in the booming parts of the Chinese economy, such as in Shanghai or in the Pearl River Delta in the Southeast, will tend to feel optimistic and accepting about the shape of current inequalities, while those located in distant interior locales or in areas that are more troubled economically, such as the "rustbelt" cities of China's Northeast, will have much more critical attitudes. Furthermore, in his work G. William Skinner stressed that measuring location simply in terms of provinces is a very poor guide to almost any social variation, since within any province or region there is a large gap between those located in the urban core and those in the distant rural periphery.[30]

In order to tap the geographic location factors that may influence attitudes toward inequality issues, I utilize three different measures. First, I classify our respondents in terms of the conventional division of China by provinces into Eastern, Central, and Western provinces as defined by China's National Statistics Bureau.[31] Second, reflecting an attempt to respond to Skinner's criticisms, I classify each respondent in terms of how distant they live from a prefectural or higher level city, using a scale of eight categories ranging from 0 = resides in a prefectural or higher level city to 7 = resides 200 or more kilometers from the nearest prefectural or larger city.[32] Finally, in order to try to capture the observation that some provinces have been much more affected by market reforms and the economic activity they have spawned, I utilize research conducted by scholars in China[33] to categorize the relative degree of market transformation of all the provincial units in which our respondents are located, with the values ranging from 3.61 for Ningxia to 9.74 for Guangdong (out of a maximum possible of 10).[34] In the conventional account we expect to find more desire for equality and redistribution in Central and Western provinces, in locales far from any city, and in provinces that are "backward" in terms of the impact of market reforms.[35]

Subjective indicators

Research in other societies indicates that subjective perceptions of personal and family status and of improvement or deterioration in these circumstances sometimes have as much or more influence on attitudes about inequality and distributive injustice as objective socioeconomic characteristics of respondents.[36] With this consideration in mind, in trying to explain variations in preferences for equality and government redistribution, I also use as predictors a variety of measures of subjective status and experiences. Four such subjective measures are employed in this analysis: (1) responses to a question about how the respondent's family's living standard compares with five years earlier (i.e. in 1999), ranging from 1 = much worse to 5 = much better; (2) a summary measure of relative social status compared to local reference groups;[37] (3) a summary scale of inequality-related bad personal or family experiences during the past three years, which I call simply "bad experiences";[38] and (4) a scale constructed to reflect a belief that current differences between rich and poor people are more due to society's unfairness than to the variable merits of individuals, which I refer to as the "unfair inequality" scale.[39] In the conventional view respondents who report that their families are doing better than five years earlier and better as well than local people they compare themselves with will tend to accept current inequality patterns, while those who have had many negative personal or family experiences or feel that current inequalities are based upon societal unfairness are likely to desire greater equality and redistribution.

Statistical results

The results of analyses of background variations in preferences for equality among Chinese citizens are reported in the correlation and regression statistics displayed in Table 6.4.[40] In examining a table as complex as Table 6.4, it does not make sense to scrutinize and try to explain each individual statistical coefficient. The issue here is whether there are some general tendencies for survey respondents of particular types to express unusually strong preferences for social equality while others have weaker egalitarian preferences. In order to answer this question, it is necessary to scan across the rows and columns of Table 6.4 to look for evidence of such general tendencies. As we do so we notice that, for the Vs. rich transmit scale, in general the statistical coefficients are weak and the percentage of variance in that scale explained by all of our predictors taken together (as shown in the R-squared statistic in the final row of the table) is also very low. Since we are unable to explain much about the pattern of who objects to rich people buying better lives for their families (which, as we saw in Table 6.2B, most Chinese

Table 6.4 Variations in views on equality and government equality promotion (correlations and regressions)

	Excessive inequality		Prefer equality		Government leveling		Government services		Vs. rich transmit	
	r	β	R	β	r	β	R	β	r	β
Objective: occupation/hukou										
farmer	-.12***	-.10*	.12***	.10*	-.14***	-.08**	-.21***	-.19***	.03	-.03
rural non-farm	-.04*	-.06*	-.01	.03	-.05**	-.08***	-.07***	-.11***	-.00	-.03
migrant	.08***	.07*	.02	.05	.02	.01	-.02	-.09***	-.03	-.04
rural others	-.12***	-.12***	.05**	.05*	-.14***	-.11***	-.07***	-.11***	-.01	-.04
urban others	.05**	-.00	-.03	.02	.08***	.03	.14***	-.03	-.01	-.08*
urban unemployed	.07***	.04	-.02	-.01	.09***	.05*	.12***	.02	-.05**	-.08**
unskilled/semiskilled worker	.05**	omitted	-.06***	omitted	.05*	omitted	.12***	omitted	.03	omitted
skilled worker	.04*	-.01	-.04*	.02	.08***	.02	.06***	-.03	.01	.01
self-employed	.01	-.01	-.02	.00	.03	.01	.04*	-.01	-.01	.01
routine non-manual	.07***	.03	-.09***	-.03	.08***	.04	.08***	.00	-.01	-.01
professionals	.07***	.03	-.06***	.01	.06***	.00	.05**	-.02	.00	-.01
managers/cadres	.02	.01	-.09***	-.01	.04*	-.01	.03	-.02	-.01	-.02
Objective: demographic/SES										
female	-.04*	-.02	.05**	.02	-.08***	-.04*	-.03	-.02	.00	.02
age	-.00	-.06	.05**	.18	-.01	.01	.05**	.04	.01	-.27
age-squared/100	-.00	.06	.04*	-.19	-.01	-.01	.05**	.04	.02	.30*
years of education	.14***	.14***	-.20***	-.16***	.21***	.15***	.19***	.08**	-.01	.05
married	-.00	.00	.01	-.01	.01	.03	-.04*	-.02	-.04	-.04
Han ethnicity	.10***	.09***	-.02	.00	.14***	.08***	.07***	.01	-.07***	-.07**
log of household income	.08***	.02	-.15***	-.04	.14***	.04	.12***	-.05*	-.04*	.00
CCP member	.07***	.04*	-.08***	-.02	.09***	.04*	.03	-.02	.01	.01
SOE employment	.12***	.06**	-.13***	-.06**	.12***	-.00	.18***	.08***	.01	.01
access to unofficial information	-.00	-.10***	-.09***	.03	.09***	-.04	.16***	.04*	-.05**	-.09***

Objective: geographic

	r	β	r	β	r	β	r	β	r	β
East region	−.07***	omitted	.05**	omitted	.02	omitted	.15***	omitted	.04*	omitted
Central region	.13***	.11^{ns}	−.09***	−.14^{ns}	.11***	.09^{ns}	−.09***	−.15^{ns}	−.10***	−.20***
West region	−.08***	−.00	.06**	.01	−.18***	−.06	−.10***	−.05	.09***	−.08^{ns}
distance to city	−.10***	.06*	.04*	−.11***	−.20***	.02$^{\wedge\wedge\wedge}$	−.23***	−.10^{ns}	.07***	−.02
province marketization	−.02	.01	.02	−.05	.08***	.06^{ns}	.09***	−.03	−.05**	−.17^{ns}
Subjective predictors:										
5-year SOL trend	−.02	.01	−.05**	−.02	−.02	.04*	−.11***	−.03	−.03	−.03
relative social status	−.06**	−.09***	−.06***	.02	−.05**	−.08***	−.01	−.02	−.07***	−.08***
bad experiences	.01	.04	.12***	.06**	.02	.06**	.02	.07***	−.01	−.03
unfair inequality scale	.14***	.11***	−.01	.03	.22***	.16***	.25***	.18***	−.02	−.01
R-squared		.10		.08		.15		.17		.04

Note: *** = $p <= .001$; ** = $.001 < p <= .01$; * = $.01 < p <= .05$.
r are bivariate correlation statistics; β are standardized regression coefficients from ordinary least squares regressions.
^{ns} = coefficient no longer statistically significant after correction for case clustering
$^{\wedge\wedge\wedge}$ = statistically significant beyond $p = .001$ level after correction for case clustering.

approve of), I concentrate discussion here on variations in the other four measures of preferences for equality and of government efforts to promote such equality.[41]

As we scan across Table 6.4, the findings for farmers are particularly striking. Farmers are significantly more likely than the comparison group (urban unskilled and semi-skilled workers) to say that the fairest general distribution method would be to give everyone an equal share. However, on the three other measures (Excessive inequality, Government leveling, and Government services), farmers are significantly *less* likely than the comparison group to see current inequalities as excessive and to desire the government to intervene to reduce inequality and provide basic social services, patterns that are contrary to the conventional wisdom. Rural non-farm workers and the "rural others" category show similar if slightly less consistent tendencies. Migrants, however, show a different response pattern. They share with their rural brethren a preference for individuals rather than the state supplying social services, but in other respects their views are more like other residents of cities, and the Excessive inequality regression model shows that migrants are more likely than any other occupational group, rural or urban, to feel that national income gaps are too large.

The urban occupational groups display the obverse pattern from farmers. The correlation columns show that in general the urban categories are opposed to the principle of equal distribution, but on the other hand they are likely to view current national income gaps as excessive and desire a more active government role in limiting inequality and in distributing social services. The regression columns show that in comparison with unskilled and semi-skilled workers, there are virtually no significant differences in these attitudes for the other urban groups.[42] In other words, this tendency to be concerned about national income gaps and desire more active efforts by the government to promote equality (despite opposing the principle of equal distribution) is a general tendency of all urban groups, whether of low or high social status.

In terms of the demographic and socio-economic predictors of egalitarian attitudes shown in the second panel of Table 6.4, the most striking pattern is that the highly educated show the same pattern of responses as urbanites – to oppose egalitarian distribution, but to be concerned about national income gaps and prefer a more active role by the government in promoting social equality. To some extent individuals who work or have worked in state-owned enterprises, Chinese Communist Party (CCP) members, and members of the Han ethnic group show similar but somewhat less consistent responses. From the correlation column it appears that high family income is also associated with the same pattern, but once other predictors are controlled for in regression models, these associations are sharply reduced, and in the case of Government services reversed, so that respondents from rich families have a net tendency to be somewhat *less* likely than others to favor government provision of social services.

In their own way these findings about the effects of education, CCP membership, SOE affiliation, and Han ethnicity are as surprising as the obverse patterns for China's farmers. Ordinarily, and to a considerable extent in research in other societies,[43] we expect that disadvantaged groups will favor redistribution and government provision of social services, while advantaged groups will be less supportive of such measures. For China in 2004, we find instead a pattern in which urban people in general as well as respondents with certain kinds of status advantages (after controlling for urban versus rural status) are more egalitarian, while rural people in general and farmers in particular are less so.[44] How to understand and explain these counter-intuitive patterns is a challenge to which we return later, after scanning the remainder of Table 6.4.

The pattern of associations for geographic predictors, as shown in the third panel of Table 6.4, is difficult to interpret. Quite a few of the correlation coefficients are statistically significant, although they point in different directions, rather than toward a consistent tendency for disadvantaged locales to have stronger preferences for social equality. Once we control for the influence of other predictors in our regression models and correct for the clustering tendency shared by the geographic predictors,[45] many of these associations are no longer statistically significant, and some show a reversal of the direction of the association. The regression results that are statistically significant continue to defy easy interpretation. There are net tendencies for those living far from any city to be more critical of national inequalities and to prefer government efforts to limit inequalities, but at the same time such respondents are less likely to favor equality as a principle of distribution. The only regional effect that survives our scrutiny is for residents of provinces in Central China to be less critical than residents of Eastern provinces of rich people purchasing better lives for their families, the opposite of the expected pattern. None of the marketization associations remain statistically significant in our regression analyses. So on balance geographic location doesn't help us much in explaining variations in preferences for equality.

Finally, the coefficients for the subjective factors displayed in the fourth panel of Table 6.4 are not entirely consistent, but they give some hints of patterns that do fit the conventional wisdom. How respondents feel their families are doing compared to five years earlier does not have much impact on these measures of preferences for equality, but there is some (expected) tendency for those who judge they are better off than those they compare themselves with to be less supportive of equality and government redistribution, while those whose families have had multiple inequality-related bad experiences within the past three years are likely to favor egalitarianism. The clearest pattern, however, involves the unfair inequality scale. Those who feel that the main reason why some people are rich and others are poor in China today is an unfair social order (rather than, say, variations in individual effort or talent) are significantly more likely than others to see current national income gaps as excessive, to favor government efforts to limit inequality, and also to favor government provision of basic social services. So in the realm of subjective measures, those who feel somewhat disadvantaged and are critical of current inequalities are likely to favor equality and government redistribution. But in terms of objective background characteristics it is a different and more counter-intuitive story, as we have seen in discussing the first two panels of Table 6.4.

Interpretations and conclusions

In earlier sections of this essay I reviewed evidence from a national survey conducted in China in 2004 to determine the preferences of Chinese citizens for greater social equality and support for government efforts to produce a more equal society (both by directly limiting inequality and by providing basic social services without regard to ability to pay). The conventional wisdom is that rising inequality unleashed by market reforms is contributing to anger and protest activity, that most Chinese would prefer greater social equality achieved through government redistribution, and that these sentiments are particularly strong in disadvantaged groups and locales. China's top leadership since 2002 has introduced a number of new policy interventions based upon these assumptions, but the evidence from our survey suggests that the conventional wisdom is wrong on all counts.

China's citizens are not especially angry about current inequalities, and a majority are opposed to measures such as limiting top incomes or adopting egalitarian distribution principles, while they also favor allowing the rich to purchase better lives for their families. Insofar as they favor increased equality, it is by way of affirmative action measures designed to help the poor, not via redistribution and limits aimed at "leveling down" the rich. In other words, Chinese preferences for equality are somewhat mild and not that different from the sentiments shared by many Americans and other citizens in advanced capitalist societies, and they do not involve a demand for a dramatic departure from the status quo.

This conclusion is bolstered by comparisons with surveys conducted in other countries, as reported in Table 6.3. In general the evidence in that table shows that Chinese citizen preferences for equality are more similar to the attitudes found in advanced capitalist societies than to those held by citizens in most other post-socialist societies included in the ISJP surveys. In some respects (regarding redistribution and affirmative action to help the poor), Chinese are even less sympathetic toward equalizing measures than famously individualistic Americans. As discussed earlier, as of 2004 we see little evidence of the presumed widespread outrage over growing inequality or popular demands that the government intervene to promote greater equality.

The findings reported in the last section of this paper represent an even more dramatic challenge to the conventional wisdom, as well as to findings of surveys on inequality attitudes in other societies. We find that disadvantaged groups (rural residents in general, and farmers in particular), who by the conventional wisdom should have the strongest demands for greater equality, are in fact significantly *less* likely than others to express such demands in responding to our survey questions. At the same time, some advantaged groups (urbanites in general, the well-educated, CCP members, members of the Han ethnic group, people with SOE ties) are significantly *more* likely to express preferences for equality and for government intervention to make China a more egalitarian society. How can we explain the paradox that already advantaged groups favor policies that would appear to threaten their vested interests, while those who could most benefit from such interventions are less likely to want them?[46]

The key to answering this puzzle is to understand the nature of social stratification in the Mao era and what the post-socialist transition means in the case of China. To the extent that Chinese socialism promoted social equality, it did so primarily within local work units and communities.[47] Across the boundaries of organizations and locales, however, things were very unequal, and government policies and socialist institutions often aggravated, rather than controlled or reduced, those gaps. Chinese urbanites in general, and particularly those working in large and high status work organizations, were well provided for and favored by the workings of the socialist system. At the other end of the social scale, China's farmers were bound to the soil as essentially "socialist serfs" with miserly and generally declining state investment and development priority, while being exhorted by the state to pull themselves up out of poverty via bootstraps-style "self-reliance" (*zili gengsheng* 自力更生). Even the vaunted advances in health care and education achieved in rural areas during the socialist era were primarily the result of "unfunded mandates" financed by rural residents and communities, rather than through funding provided by the state. In other words, contrary to popular images and slogans of the period, Chinese socialism was a highly stratified and very inegalitarian social order in which those favorably situated in the state-controlled bureaucratic system had much better lives and opportunities than those located toward the periphery of that system.[48]

Given this context, market reforms have had quite different implications for individuals who had different locations within the socialist bureaucratic hierarchy. Those who had been favored by socialist bureaucratic allocation have been threatened by the loss of benefits and security that had been doled out by the state and its subordinate agencies, the most dramatic example being the millions of employees of state-owned enterprises who have seen their incomes, health insurance and other benefits, and even their jobs jeopardized as a result of the "smashing of the iron rice bowl" (*fensui tiefanwan* 粉碎铁饭碗) reforms of the late 1990s.[49] If you have been favored by the paternalism the socialist state bestows on favored sectors and locales, it is not surprising that you will fear that you will not be able to do as well by "going down into the sea" (*xiahai* 下海) of market competition. You are likely to try to hold on to the advantages and security you have derived from close relations with the state, and if so you are likely to view rising inequalities that result from market reforms critically and wish the government would do more to counteract them. In short, urbanites in general and many kinds of high status individuals can still be seen today as "supplicants to the socialist state,"[50] and in terms of our survey questions this stance translates into responses that appear as relatively strong preferences for equality and government redistribution.

From the perspective of those at the other end of the status hierarchy (the majority of the Chinese population living in rural villages and relying on farming for subsistence), things looked quite different under socialism. The state was high above and far away, and quite miserly in its provision of resources, while at the same time very strict in limiting peasant options. Commune members generally had to devote their lives to farming (primarily growing grain), without much ability to engage in the supplementary activities that Chinese farmers had for centuries undertaken in order to survive – handicrafts, construction, trading, family-run businesses, etc. – and without any real ability to migrate elsewhere in search of better opportunities. In some sense, then, China's farmers were victims of "socialist equality" since state policies and institutions locked them into fairly uniform impoverishment.

For China's farmers the combination of market reforms, agricultural de-collectivization, and the loosening of migration restrictions provided potential for genuine "liberation" from socialist serfdom. They were no longer bound to the soil, nor were they prevented from diverting their energies away from field cultivation into other potentially more lucrative economic activities. They had no secure state-provided patronage to lose, and so in a sense they had nowhere to go but up.[51] At any point in time in recent years, well over 200 million Chinese villagers have been engaged in non-farming pursuits, particularly via jobs in rural factories or as migrant labor in cities, a human wave that would have been unimaginable in the late Mao period.[52]

Obviously most of those who are still engaged in farming in China today remain at or near the bottom of the status and income hierarchy, but market reforms have introduced many new (or perhaps old and familiar, since they existed prior to the 1950s) options and possibilities that socialism had blocked off. Given this history, it is not particularly surprising that China's rural residents in general, and farmers in particular, tend to hold relatively favorable views of the wider income gaps that have arisen as a result of the reforms and look with more suspicion than urbanites on suggestions that the state should place limits on the rich or take greater responsibility for supplying basic social services. China's farmers were in no position under socialism to be supplicants to the socialist state, and they don't have as much desire as their urban counterparts today to rely on the government to promote greater equality.[53]

In sum, the puzzle about why advantaged groups and urbanites in general give "egalitarian" responses to our survey questions while farmers and rural people in general show weaker preferences for equality and government redistribution can be understood by recognizing that China is still not a fully developed capitalist society organized in terms of occupation-based social classes competing in national labor markets. Instead China is still profoundly affected by the state socialist system that has been only gradually dismantled since 1978. This is a system in which many who benefited by their close relations with the state in the socialist era still lament the loss of their privileged status, while those who suffered from their caste subordination under socialism may see current inequalities as manifestations of their present or potential future liberation.[54] Given this history, there is an understandable tendency for those who were successful supplicants to the socialist state to express stronger preferences for equality than those at the bottom of the social order, who may feel it would be better if the state just got out of the way and let them compete freely for available opportunities.[55]

The results of our 2004 survey indicate that the conventional wisdom that there is a large and growing desire in China for greater equality, and that this desire is strongest among disadvantaged groups, is basically incorrect. There is more acceptance than anger about current patterns of inequality, and the strongest preferences for greater equality are expressed by urbanites and the well-educated, groups that are hardly disadvantaged. These results should not be interpreted, however, as indicating that China's leaders can now relax and not worry at all about growing inequality or rural discontent. The focus in our survey was specifically on issues of distributive injustice. Other recent studies of rural discontent[56] can be interpreted as showing that many rural people are very angry about their current situation, but more as a result of abuses by local officials and other *procedural* justice issues, not because of the growing inequalities spawned by market reforms.

It is also unclear how durable or unstable the attitude patterns reported here may be. My interpretation of the 2004 survey results has suggested that patterns of the socialist past are still shaping Chinese attitudes today, and if that is the case, then we might expect only gradual evolution and thus relative stability in the attitude patterns described here. However, strictly speaking, our survey responses pertain to only one point in time, in 2004. Perhaps there was a relatively favorable public mood in China at that time, shaped by both 26 years of rapid economic growth and new government initiatives launched after 2002 to promote a "harmonious society," such as by reducing the taxes and fees faced by villagers and building new village medical insurance plans.[57] If that is the case, could Chinese popular attitudes about inequality patterns have turned sour since 2004? The global financial crisis that erupted in 2008, in which Chinese exports contracted, millions of (mostly migrant) workers lost their jobs, and economic growth slowed markedly, may have produced growing popular discontent and feelings that current inequalities in China were excessive and unfair. Rather than assume that this is the case, however, it will require new surveys of Chinese popular attitudes to determine whether or not Chinese citizens now have stronger preferences for equality and government redistribution than they expressed in 2004.[58]

Notes

1 Jae Ho Chung, Hongyi Lai, and Ming Xia, "Mounting Challenges to Governance in China: Surveying Collective Protestors, Religious Sects, and Criminal Organizations," *The China Journal* 56 (2006), pp. 1–31; Murray Scot Tanner, "We the People (of China) . . . ," *Wall Street Journal*, February 2, 2006, p. A10. Since 2005 Chinese media have ceased publishing annual reports on national protest totals, and some Western analysts suspect that by 2009 the total was considerably higher.
2 "Survey of Chinese Officials' Opinions on Reform: Beijing Daily," *Xinhua News Bulletin*, November 29, 2004.
3 Josephine Ma, "Wealth Gap Fueling Instability, Studies Warn," *South China Morning Post*, December 22, 2005. According to the World Bank (*Sharing Rising Incomes: Disparities in China* (Washington, DC: World Bank, 1997), the Gini coefficient of national income distribution in 1981 was .29. Recent estimates by foreign analysts imply a substantial increase since, but not to a level as high as claimed in the 2006 CASS report. Björn Gustafsson, Li Shi, and Terry Sicular, eds., *Inequality and Public Policy in China* (Cambridge: Cambridge University Press, 2008) report a figure of .45 for the Gini for China in both 1995 and 2002. For comparison purposes, the United Nations Development Report for 2007–8 (available online at hdr.undp.org/en/statistics/) gives a Gini for China of .469, compared to .408 for the United States, .249 for Japan, .368 for India, .334 for Bangladesh, .57 for Brazil, and .578 for South Africa.
4 He Qinglian, "A Volcanic Stability," *Journal of Democracy* 14 (2003), pp. 66–72.
5 "How the Other 800m Live," *Economist*, March 22, 2006, p. 12.
6 "Seeds of Fury," *Time Asia*, March 5, 2006.
7 The present author was principal investigator of the project, and the research team consisted also of Albert Park (economics, then at the University of Michigan, now at Oxford), Pierre Landry (political science, Yale), Wang Feng (sociology, University of California-Irvine), Jieming Chen (sociology, Texas A&M University-Kingsville), and Chunping Han (sociology, University of Texas at Arlington, formerly a doctoral student in sociology at Harvard), with our primary PRC collaborator and director of survey fieldwork Shen Mingming (political science, Peking University, Director of the Research Center for Contemporary China at Beida). Primary funding for the survey came from the Smith Richardson Foundation, with supplementary funding provided by the Weatherhead Center for International Affairs at Harvard, the Center for the Study of Democracy at University of California at Irvine, and Peking University. Research assistance from Chunping Han, Maocan Guo, Edward Weihua An, and Dong-Kyun Im made possible the analyses presented here.
8 See James Kluegel, David Mason, and Bernd Wegener, eds., *Social Justice and Political Change* (New York: Aldine de Gruyter, 1995); David Mason and James Kluegel, eds., *Marketing Democracy: Changing Opinion about Inequality and Politics in East Central Europe* (Lanham, MD: Rowman and Littlefield, 2000).
9 Pierre Landry and Mingming Shen, "Reaching Migrants in Survey Research: The Use of the Global Positioning System to Reduce Coverage Bias in China," *Political Analysis* 13 (2005), pp. 1–22. Most probability sample surveys in China

to date have used household registration (*hukou*) records as the basis for draw-ing samples. However, those records are more and more inaccurate due to the increased mobility of Chinese – Landry and Shen found in a 2001 Beijing survey that about 45 percent of the respondents selected by spatial probability sampling in that city were not residing in the places where they were officially registered. Spatial probability sampling involves using maps of population density and Geographic Positioning System devices to select actual physical points on the ground in China with probability proportional to population size, and then to interview one adult per household in each household located within a designated square around each point.

10 The project sampling plan included an over-sampling of urban places in order to yield enough cases for examination of variations within urban areas. Therefore when I present the overall pattern of responses to various questions in the pages that follow, I use sampling weights to correct for this over-sampling in order to produce figures designed to show responses that are representative of all Chinese adults between the ages of 18 and 70.

11 Our questionnaire also included questions about perceptions of the shape and fair-ness or unfairness of current inequalities, whether current inequalities promote positive incentives, how much opportunity there is for people to improve their standard of living, and other aspects. These other aspects of citizen attitudes toward inequality issues will not be considered here but are addressed in other project publications, such as Han Chunping and Martin K. Whyte, "The Social Contours of Distributive Injustice Feelings in Contemporary China," in D. Davis and Wang Feng, eds., *Creating Wealth and Poverty in Post-Socialist China* (Stanford: Stanford University Press, 2009); Martin K. Whyte and Maocan Guo, "How Angry Are Chinese Citizens about Current Inequalities? Evidence from a National Survey," *Social Transformation of Chinese Societies* (forthcoming); Martin K. Whyte, *Myth of the Social Volcano: Perceptions of Inequality and Distributive Injustice in Contemporary China* (Stanford: Stanford University Press, forthcoming).

12 It should be noted that the egalitarianism of the Mao era (particularly during the Cultural Revolution) consisted primarily of measures to limit the incomes, bonuses, and other advantages of intellectuals, officials, and other high status groups, rather than to provide income and job guarantees to the poor. See Martin K. Whyte, "Destratification and Restratification in China," in G. Berreman, ed., *Social Inequality: Comparative and Developmental Approaches* (New York: Academic Press, 1981). The Cultural Revolution approach to achieving equality by "leveling down" evidently has little appeal in China today.

13 A primary factor explaining the greater inequality of the United States in com-parison with most continental European societies is the more limited extent of government-provided goods and services in America. And of course state social-ist societies, including China during the Mao era, tended to provide a broader range of public goods, and to have a more limited range of things distributed by markets, than is the case in capitalist societies.

14 The case of medical care is complicated, since most provision of medical care continues to take place in government-run hospitals. However, the large major-ity of the population have lacked medical insurance coverage since the onset of market reforms (at least until the effort, only starting at the time of our survey in 2004, to create new village medical insurance plans in China's rural areas), so that most medical care has been provided on a fee-for-service basis. with payments borne by individuals and families, even when government-employed doctors are providing the care.

15 Kluegel *et al.*, eds., *Social Justice and Political Change*; Mason and Kluegel, eds., *Marketing Democracy*.

16 Several of the questions in Tables 6.1 and 6.2 were designed especially for the China survey, so no comparative ISJP results are available: the questions about inequalities within the work unit and neighborhood from Table 6.1A, the question about reducing the gap between the rich and the poor in Table 6.1C, and the questions about individual versus government responsibility for providing basic services in Table 6.2A.

17 William Parish, "Destratification in China," in James L. Watson, ed., *Class and Social Stratification in Post-Revolution China* (Cambridge: Cambridge University Press, 1984); Martin K. Whyte, "Destratification and Restratification in China," in G. Berreman, ed., *Social Inequality: Comparative and Developmental Approaches* (New York: Academic Press, 1981). For example, in Eastern Europe, as in the Soviet Union, material incentives were stressed as motivational devices, but they were denounced in China after the launching of the Cultural Revolution in 1966. Similarly, the use of clothing styles to convey relative status or even gender was taboo in China in the late Mao era, and regular campaigns were launched to send the educated and elites down to serve at manual labor posts in industry and agriculture, "leveling down" measures that Mao's critics in the Soviet camp viewed as bizarre.

18 It might be objected that the timing of the ISJP surveys so early in the post-socialist transition in Eastern Europe, in 1991 and 1996, biases these comparisons, since the "big bang" approach to dismantling central planning produced economic depressions in the early 1990s throughout the former Soviet bloc. However, more limited comparisons with data from recent surveys in Eastern Europe and a comparison of comparable surveys conducted in Beijing in 2000 and Warsaw in 2001 show very similar contrasts to those reported here (see Martin K. Whyte and Chunping Han, "Popular Attitudes toward Distributive Injustice: Beijing and Warsaw Compared," *Journal of Chinese Political Science* 13 (2008), pp. 29–51; Dong-Kyun Im, "Beliefs and Attitudes toward Economic Inequality in Contemporary China: What Do Cross-National Data Tell Us?," unpublished seminar paper, Harvard University Department of Sociology, 2009). More recent ISJP surveys (conducted in Hungary in 2005 and in the Czech Republic and the former East and West Germany in 2006) show attitude patterns that do not, in fact, differ much from the 1990s results shown for those countries in Table 6.3 (Bernd Wegener, personal communication). So the timing of the surveys cannot explain the contrasts with China shown in Table 6.3.

19 Related analyses using other attitude measures from the 2004 survey come to a similar conclusion, undermining the claims that China is a social volcano about to explode as a result of feelings of distributive injustice. See, for example, Han and Whyte, "The Social Contours of Distributive Injustice Feelings in Contemporary China"; Whyte and Guo, "How Angry Are Chinese Citizens about Current Inequalities?"

20 The questions displayed in rows 2 and 3 of Table 6.1A were not used to construct a composite scale of Excessive inequality because generally only urban respondents answered the question about inequalities within their work units. The Excessive inequality measure varies from 1 = current inequalities are too small to 5 = current inequalities are too large, and in statistical analyses it is treated as if it were a continuous variable. We performed ordered logistic regression analysis and obtained results very similar to the ordinary least squares regression that will be reported here, so for the sake of simplicity and comparability we report only the latter.

21 Responses were recorded in the familiar five-category scale, ranging from strongly agree to strongly disagree, with the values reversed so that 5 = strongly agree. In statistical analyses I treat this measure as a continuous variable. Again the results of ordered logistic regression were very similar but will not be reported here.

22 Again the response categories for each statement were recorded on a five-point scale ranging from strongly agree to strongly disagree, and then reversed so that 5 = strongly agree. The reliability for this scale is $\alpha = .65$. The scale was constructed from the factor scores reflecting the common content of these three items, and then converted to values ranging from 1 to 100. The reader should note that the tenor of these statements involves the view that the government should promote a more equal distribution mainly by "affirmative action" policies, or "leveling up" – by providing jobs and minimum incomes to the poor – rather than by "leveling down" as stressed during China's Cultural Revolution. The one question included in Table 6.1B that was not included in the Government leveling scale concerned approval of the government placing a maximum income limit on the population – in effect, a "leveling down" measure. That item did not have high enough associations with the other three items to be included in a reliable expanded scale.

23 The reliability of the Government services scale is $\alpha = .82$. The scale was constructed from the factor scores reflecting the common content of these six items, and then converted to values ranging from 1 to 100.

24 Again I constructed the summary measure from the factor scores reflecting the common content of the constituent items, rescaled to vary from 1 to 100. The reliability of the Vs. rich transmit scale is $\alpha = .71$.

25 Excessive inequality, Government leveling, and Government services are positively and significantly correlated with one another, but the other two measures (Prefer equality and Vs. rich transmit) are not so correlated, so it makes sense to retain all five measures. Specifically, here is the pattern:

Equality scale inter-correlations

	EI	PE	GL	GS	VRT
Excessive inequality	1				
Prefer equality	−.17**	1			
Government leveling	.31**	−.10**	1		
Government services	.17**	−.03	.33**	1	
Vs. rich transmit	−.02	.00	−.07**	−.06**	1

** = relationship significant below .01 level (2-tailed test)

26 Note that migrants are treated as a separate category, no matter what type of urban job they are performing or even whether they are employed at all. In the statistical analyses that follow I use these twelve categories to create twelve "dummy variables" that are used in computing correlations and regression coefficients. I use the unskilled/semi-skilled urban worker category as the omitted reference group in regression models.

27 The age-squared term is used in our statistical calculations in an effort to detect curvilinear relationships between age and inequality attitudes. I suspect that the most critical attitudes may be held by respondents who are middle aged, as those most affected negatively by the disruptions of the Cultural Revolution – China's "lost generation" – and if so I expect to find a positive association between age and a particular critical attitude toward inequality but a negative association with age-squared (the division by 100 makes the resulting age-squared coefficients more comparable to those computed for age alone). In other words, positive and negative coefficients for the age and age-squared terms, respectively, would suggest that the relationship between age and the attitude in question resembles a parabola or inverted U shape.

28 The access to unofficial information scale was computed from a series of seven questions, each of which asked the respondent to rate their cosmopolitanism or exposure to outside or unofficial influences on a scale from 1 = never to 4 = frequently: domestic travel within China; travel outside China; exchange information about society's current events with relatives and/or friends within China; exchange information about society's current events with relatives and/or friends outside China; learn news from international periodicals, television, or radio; learn information other than news from international books, magazines, television programs, or movies; and use the internet. So a higher score indicates more or multiple kinds of exposure to a range of sources of information beyond the official news media.

29 There are contradictory expectations that derive from affiliation with an SOE. During the socialist era, SOE employees were favored compared to urbanites in collective enterprises, not to mention rural residents. However, in recent years many SOEs have had trouble adapting to market reforms, with many downsizing and laying off personnel or even going out of business. The discussion in the text assumes that the latter tendency is dominant, but this is an empirical question.

30 See, for example, G. William Skinner, "The Spatial Logic of Uneven Development in Contemporary China," unpublished paper, 2005.

31 In regression analyses, the East region serves as the omitted reference category.

32 Prefectural cities are cities intermediate in the Chinese urban administrative hierarchy between county capitals and provincial capitals. Obviously using this measure all of our urban respondents in medium or larger cities receive a score of zero, with only the remainder of the respondents residing in smaller cities and towns or rural areas filling the other seven categories as appropriate.

33 See Fan Gang and Wang Xiaolu, *Zhongguo shichanghua zhishu – Gediqu shichanghua xiangdui jincheng 2004 niandu baogao* (Marketization indexes for China: Report on relative progress toward marketization in various localities in 2004) (Beijing: Economic Science Press, 2004).

34 Fan and Wang use twenty-three distinct indicators, each ranging from 0 to 10, to measure different aspects of marketization of a province, and the measure we use here is simply the mean of these twenty-three separate indicators. Their data refer to 2002, two years prior to our survey, the most recent figures available.

35 However, we face a special problem in the statistical analysis of the associations between these geographic measures and our preference for equality measures. We will be employing ordinary least squares (OLS) regression to disentangle the impact of various predictors on these attitude measures. However, our geographic measures violate a core assumption of OLS regression, that the values of one respondent in a locale are independent of the values of other respondents in the same locale, since all of the respondents in one sampling unit (80 were used in our survey) will have the same value for each of our three geographic measures. If we don't take into account this clustering tendency, the statistical significance of our geographic measure regression coefficients would tend to be exaggerated. In order to correct for this clustering effect I employ an arcane technique called multilevel analysis (thanks to Dong-Kyun Im for showing me the ropes) to correct for this problem and estimate unbiased standard errors and statistical significance levels for the geographic predictor regression coefficients, with the modifications indicated by special notations in the resulting table of results.

36 See, for example, James Kluegel, "Economic Problems and Socioeconomic Beliefs and Attitudes," *Research on Social Stratification and Mobility* 7 (1988), pp. 273–302; Martin Kreidl, "Perceptions of Poverty and Wealth in Western and Post-Communist Countries," *Social Justice Research* 13 (2000), pp. 151–76.

37 The relative social status measure is computed from the mean of four questions about how the respondent would rank their current living standard compared to

four alternative local reference groups: relatives, former classmates, co-workers, and neighbors. In each case the response categories ranged from 1 = much worse to 5 = much better, so the resulting mean scale also ranges from roughly 1 to 5.

38 We asked respondents about whether in the past three years they or any members of their family had had the following experiences: being seriously ill, suffering physical injury or economic loss due to artificial or natural disasters, being laid off or becoming unemployed, having difficulty paying for medical care, dropping out of school because of inability to pay the fees, having to borrow money to cover basic living expenses, and being treated unfairly by local officials. For each experience we recorded a 1 if the respondent said they had experienced it and 0 otherwise, and then the bad experiences scale is simply the sum of these separate scores, thus ranging from 0 to 7.

39 The Excessive inequality scale concerns whether the gap between the rich and poor is too large or not, not whether the differences are based upon societal unfairness. Unfair inequality is a scale designed to measure the latter perception. This scale was constructed from the common factor in items ranking discrimination, lack of equal opportunity, and problems in the economic structure high as explanations for poverty, and dishonesty, having special connections, having extra opportunities, and unfairness of the economic structure as explanations for wealth (reliability $\alpha = .74$).

40 The bivariate correlation statistics (r) tell us what the association is between a particular social background predictor (displayed by row) and one of our five measures of equality preferences (displayed by column) without controlling for the influence of any of the other predictors. However, since those predictors are themselves interrelated in complex ways (for example with farmers having less education and lower incomes generally than urban residents), we perform regression analysis to determine the net association between a particular predictor and each equality preference measure, once we control for the effects of all of the other predictors simultaneously. The standardized ordinarily least squares regression coefficients are indicated by column headings of β. (Standardized coefficients are displayed in Table 6.4 in order to reveal the relative strength of the net associations of different predictors.) The R-squared statistic at the bottom of each column of regression statistics shows how much of the variation in a particular equality preference measure is explained by all of the predictor variables taken together. (Preliminary analyses were carried out involving regression models with separate subsets of predictor variables, but since those analyses didn't reveal substantial differences from the full regression models presented in Table 6.4, in the interests of simplicity those preliminary regression results are not displayed here.)

41 The few significant associations for Vs. rich transmit are also somewhat puzzling and contradictory. We see there an expected tendency for those with high relative social status and members of the dominant Han ethnic group to be significantly less likely than others to oppose rich people buying better lives for their families, while the elderly are more likely to do so. However, we also see here unexpected and surprising patterns – with urbanites who are not working, residents of Central provinces, and those with access to unofficial sources of information also significantly less likely to oppose rich people buying better lives.

42 The lone exception is a slightly higher preference for government leveling among the urban unemployed, a result that could be the result of chance factors (since any time you examine more than 20 statistical coefficients, you expect to find at least one that is significant beyond the .05 level).

43 For the United States, see James Kluegel and Eliot Smith, *Beliefs about Inequality: Americans' Views of What Is and What Ought to Be* (New York: Aldine de Gruyter, 1986); for Russia, see Martin Ravallion and Michael Lokshin, "Who Wants to Redistribute: The Tunnel Effect in 1990s Russia," *Journal of Public*

Economics 76 (2000), pp. 87–104; for East and West Germany, see Albert Alesina and Nicola Fuchs-Schündeln, "Good-Bye Lenin (or Not?): The Effect of Communism on People's Preferences," *American Economic Review* 97 (2007), pp. 1507–28. My thanks to Weihua An for bringing these last two studies to my attention.

44 Note that the Prefer equality measure isn't part of this pattern, since rural people score high on this measure and urbanites and other advantaged groups low. The fact that our Prefer equality question is tapping an attitude that is quite different from Excessive inequality, Government leveling, and Government services explains the negative correlations between these measures shown earlier (see note 25).

45 See note 35.

46 Most of the new social policy interventions enacted since 2002 in the effort to make China into a more "harmonious society" have involved measures to remove financial burdens from, and provide financial resources to, rural residents and communities, even though by the evidence of our survey, rural preferences for government egalitarian intervention are relatively weak.

47 See, for example, the discussion in Andrew Walder, "The Remaking of the Chinese Working Class, 1949–81," *Modern China*, 10 (1984), pp. 3–48; Yanjie Bian, *Work and Inequality in Urban China* (Albany, NY: SUNY Press, 1994); Kam Wing Chan, *Cities with Invisible Walls* (New York: Oxford University Press, 1994); Dorothy Solinger, *Contesting Citizenship in Urban China* (Berkeley: University of California Press, 1999); Wang Fei-ling, *Organizing through Division and Exclusion: China's* Hukou *System* (Stanford: Stanford University Press, 2005); Wang Feng, *Boundaries and Categories: Rising Inequality in Post-Socialist Urban China* (Stanford: Stanford University Press, 2008); Martin K. Whyte, *One Country, Two Societies: Rural–Urban Inequality in China* (Cambridge: Harvard University Press, 2010).

48 These generalizations apply to other centrally planned socialist systems as well, not just to China. The classic statement of these tendencies is Milovan Djilas, *The New Class: An Analysis of the Communist System* (New York: Praeger, 1957). See also Ivan Szelenyi, *Urban Inequalities under State Socialism* (New York: Oxford University Press, 1983). Those of us who live in capitalist welfare states tend to assume that when the government intervenes in the distributive system, the goal is to foster greater equality. However, Szelenyi convincingly demonstrated for Eastern Europe during the 1970s that government policies in regard to housing and other social services systematically benefited those who were already favored by their close relations with the state, rather than the poor and disadvantaged.

49 It is important to emphasize that market reforms in urban areas occurred later than in rural areas, and that the state and *danwei*-provided iron rice bowl of material security survived for most urban residents until the mid-1990s. Thus the attitudes we tapped in our 2004 survey reflected recent experiences for such individuals, not things that happened 25 years earlier as the reforms were launched.

50 See Deborah Davis, "Urban Families: Supplicants to a Socialist State," in D. Davis and S. Harrell, eds., *Urban Families in the Post-Mao Era* (Berkeley: University of California Press, 1993).

51 There are, however, troubling exceptions to this generalization. In particular, de-collectivization resulted in the collapse of cooperative health insurance systems in virtually all Chinese villages. Even though these systems had relied on local resources, rather than state funding, their collapse led to health care reverting to a fee-for-service system in which major medical problems could impoverish a rural family. Rural secondary school enrolments also plummeted during the 1980s, with some recovery in more recent years.

52 Rural industries did exist within the people's commune system, but they had to operate under severe restrictions and were mainly supposed to produce goods for the local community (farm tools, cement, basic chemical fertilizers), so they could not employ more than a very limited number of villagers. See Dwight Perkins, ed., *Rural Small-Scale Industry in the People's Republic of China* (Berkeley: University California Press, 1977).

53 My thinking about these issues has benefited from the discussion in the doctoral thesis written by Chunping Han ("Rural–Urban Cleavages in Perceptions of Inequality in Contemporary China," unpublished doctoral dissertation, Department of Sociology, Harvard University, 2009), which considers a much broader range of attitude questions from the 2004 survey than examined here.

54 Other research shows similarly counter-intuitive contrasts between the attitudes of urbanites and rural residents in China. For example, in all developing societies previously studied in a research program launched in the 1960s by Alex Inkeles, urban residents have more "modern" attitudes (a syndrome that includes things like a sense of personal efficacy and a reliance on science to solve problems) than rural residents. However, a survey conducted in the Greater Tianjin area in 1990 found just the opposite, with city residents having more "traditional" attitudes than residents of surrounding villages, particularly those working in rural factories. See the discussion in Alex Inkeles, C. Montgomery Broaded, and Zhongde Cao, "Causes and Consequences of Individual Modernity in China," *The China Journal* 37 (1997), pp. 31–59; for a similar analysis, see Yasheng Huang, *Capitalism with Chinese Characteristics: Entrepreneurship and the State* (New York: Cambridge University Press, 2008). The dependency orientations fostered in urban work units under socialism help to explain this counter-intuitive finding, as they help explain ours.

55 Our findings provide confirmation of the view that trying to explain social behavior and attitudes by relying only on the current status characteristics of the individuals being studied without taking into account their past histories will lead to impoverished or misleading explanations. See the discussion in Paul Pierson, *Politics in Time: History, Institutions, and Social Analysis* (Princeton: Princeton University Press, 2004). It should also be noted that China's villagers are still disadvantaged in multiple ways in market competition currently, particularly as a result of the household registration (*hukou*) system, which prevents them from enjoying the rights and opportunities that urbanites enjoy. See the discussion in Solinger, *Contesting Citizenship in Urban China*; Wang, *Organizing through Division and Exclusion*; Whyte, *One Country, Two Societies*.

56 E.g. Thomas Bernstein and Xiaobo Lu, *Taxation without Representation in Contemporary Rural China* (Cambridge: Cambridge University Press, 2003); Kevin O'Brien and Li Lianjiang, *Rightful Resistance in Rural China* (Cambridge: Cambridge University Press, 2006).

57 Our questionnaire included a question about what had happened to rural taxes and fees compared to three years earlier, an issue that had been a big source of contention in the late 1990s (see Bernstein and Lu, *Taxation without Representation in Contemporary Rural China*). In fact, 70.3 percent of our respondents indicated that their taxes and fees in 2004 had been reduced compared to their levels in 2001.

58 The author is directing an effort to conduct a follow-up national survey in the fall of 2009 on popular attitudes toward inequality and distributive injustice issues in order to examine whether and how Chinese views on these issues may have changed. That survey, involving basically the same research team and procedures as employed in the 2004 survey, will be the focus of future reports.

7 Chinese youth and state–society relations[1]

Stanley Rosen

Reflecting the increasing pluralization of Chinese society after more than thirty years of reform, Chinese youth today are far from unified in belief systems or behaviors. A broad understanding of the attitudes and behaviors of Chinese youth has thus proved elusive for observers, both inside and outside China. Up until mid-2008, it was common to find youth under attack in the Chinese media, characterized as the "me generation" (*wo shidai* 我世代) and criticized for being "reliant and rebellious, cynical and pragmatic, self-centered and equality-obsessed," as well as "China's first generation of couch potatoes, addicts of online games, patrons of fast food chains, and loyal audiences of Hollywood movies."[2] The Sichuan earthquake of May 12, 2008 seemingly changed everything: The same media outlets that had written off such youth now reversed themselves to extol their virtues, while noting, not just in passing, that their altruistic behavior was not surprising because they had learned the virtues of "great compassion, benevolence, and gallantness" from imbibing traditional Chinese culture, and that, after all, they had "fully enjoyed the achievements of China's 30 years of reform and opening up."[3] Still, it is difficult to reconcile these compassionate youth with those who have been labeled anything from "angry youth" (*fenqing* 愤青) to "neocon nationalists."[4] Indeed, reflecting the continuing influence of the recent past, some Chinese critics have referred to Internet-savvy nationalists as "online Red Guards" (*wangluo hongweibing* 网络红卫兵) infected by a "populist virus"[5] (*mincuizhuyi bingdu* 民粹主义病毒).

It seems clear that there are competing and often contradictory influences shaping the attitudes and values of young Chinese today, particularly in the wealthy coastal areas. They have become very *internationalist* in their outlook, and are strongly affected by global trends. Likewise, they are very *pragmatic* and *materialistic*, largely concerned with living the good life and making money. The third competing influence, most often called *nationalism* in its more extreme form, represents a broader impulse and encompasses not only the defense of China against perceived enemies from abroad, but also the kind of love of country and self-sacrifice in support of those most in need that was evident in the volunteerism that followed the earthquake. Chinese youth have shown that they are capable of exhibiting all of these tendencies at different times, depending on the circumstances, or even at the same time. As some interviewees noted, even those youth who felt they had to "show patriotism" by honoring the short-lived attempt to boycott Carrefour, the French superstore, in response to French interference with the Olympic torch relay during its Paris run, made sure to use up all their discount coupons and finish their shopping prior to the May 1 boycott.[6]

While public opinion surveys have certainly revealed the importance of money and material things in the lives of Chinese youth, and have shown the prevalence of instrumental values,[7] at the same time, they suggest a young generation desperate to believe in something and very willing to make sacrifices *if* they are persuaded that the cause is just. Thus, an opportunity such as the Sichuan earthquake presented an occasion to demonstrate their idealism. This idealism is not new; it was also there in the Maoist period, as well as during the Tiananmen Square demonstrations and hunger strike in May 1989, although those were, of course, different generations of youth with very different belief systems. In the late 1980s, internationalism appeared to be far stronger than patriotism, and some conservative cultural critics in China such as Wang Xiaodong labeled student attitudes in those days as "reverse racism" (*nixiang zhongzu zhuyi* 逆向种族主义) as the students often dismissed much of Chinese culture and government policy and adopted a naïve, pro-Western outlook, ranging from almost total belief in Western media reports from the BBC and Voice of America to a fascination with Western philosophers such as Jean-Paul Sartre, Friedrich Nietzsche, and Sigmund Freud.[8] Ironically, the more the Chinese government limited information about the West entering China, the more the students, who knew their government was lying about so many developments within China, believed uncritically the Western reporting.[9]

For youth today, the unabashed, uncritical internationalism of the late 1980s has been replaced by what Yongming Zhou has called a new interpretive framework that acknowledges the pursuit of national interest as the ultimate goal of international relations. From this perspective, information emanating from Western media sources is viewed skeptically by well-educated, well-informed young Chinese, who assume that such reporting is merely attempting to further a pro-Western agenda.[10]

This chapter will examine how the pluralization of Chinese society and its attendant influence on youth values and behaviors have complicated the efforts of the state to mobilize youth in pursuit of state goals. In the complex interaction that marks state–society relations, the state has often been compelled to respond to a rapidly changing popular culture initiated from below. Thus, the ubiquity of "idol" worship, particularly among teens and "tweens," has led directly to officially mounted and/or sanctioned fan websites dedicated to Chinese leaders. At the same time, society has creatively responded to top-down state initiatives considered undesirable, leading to the fascinating development of widespread "spoofing" (*egao* 恶搞), with youth very much in the forefront of this "movement." The (in)famous mythical beast known as the "grass-mud horse" (*cao ni ma* 草泥马), introduced on the Internet as a reaction and commentary against Web censorship, and discussed below, is the most recent prominent example of this phenomenon. Indeed, official youth league journals have devoted considerable attention to spoofing.[11]

The argument will also highlight and seek to reconcile a number of seeming contradictions, not least in the minds of Chinese authorities. For example, survey data consistently show patriotism and love of country ranking at or very near the top of the value system for Chinese youth, yet surveys also reveal a surprising admiration for some key attributes of the American political system, most notably the separation of powers, which is often seen as a better check on the abuse of official power than the Chinese party-state model. The admiration for "things foreign" is even more pronounced when one examines cultural issues. It is therefore important to understand – despite the dismay of those responsible for youth socialization – that patriotism and love of country must be separated from support for party or government policy initiatives. In a real sense, Chinese youth, particularly students at elite universities, can trace their revolutionary credentials all the way back to the May 4 Movement of 1919, two years before the founding of the Chinese Communist Party. Mao Zedong did not hesitate to tap into this tradition when he called on China's youth to "be concerned with the great affairs of state" (*guanxin guojia dashi* 关心国家大事) and become Red Guards against his entrenched party opposition during the Cultural Revolution. The data presented below suggest that the "youth elite" in the coastal cities, at elite universities, and soon to become members of the rising middle class – in short, the beneficiaries of the reform program since the crushing of the student movement of 1989 – still feel empowered to challenge state authority. However, as the conclusion will note, thus far Chinese youth have primarily pursued a pragmatic, success-oriented approach, placing their public lives in the service of their private ambitions. So long as the political leadership remains unified, and state policies further the rise of China in world affairs and the rise in the standard of living of these elite youth, it is unlikely that such youth will take any overt political risks. But the political legacy of youth activism and the increasing importance of public opinion expressed through modern technological tools must remain a crucial concern for the party-state.

"Post-1980s youth" and their critics

Until quite recently it was common to refer to age groups in China as "generations" (*dai* 代), with those coming of age before 1949 constituting the First Generation and those growing up after 1989 the Fifth Generation. However, in another sign of the influence of global trends on China, the Chinese media now refer to generations based on their date of birth, using a concept that originated in *Time* magazine and was introduced through

Chinese literature. Discussions of Chinese youth focus on the "post-1980s generation" (*baling hou* 八零后), representing the roughly 200 million Chinese born between 1980 and 1989.[12] Given the apparent contradictions that mark youth attitudes and behaviors, it is interesting to contrast the assessment of these youth by other generations with their own subjective evaluation. One interesting survey asked those born in the 1960s and 1970s to assess their successors. Table 7.1 presents the findings, which, not surprisingly, show quite clearly for each of the categories listed that earlier generations see the post-1980s youth as more superficial, self-centered, and materialistic than members of that generation see themselves. These findings are highly congruent with many other surveys published in the Chinese media and with my own interviews. Some informants noted, in pointing to some prominent cases widely publicized on the Internet, that there is a common desire for instant success and for using one's "fame" to earn money. They also noted that the influence of their parents has been crucial, since parents are said to be less interested in what their children do and more interested in how successful they are. A fascinating documentary film on a democratic election in a primary school in Wuhan, in which the parents push their eight-year-old children to lie, cheat, and even publicly humiliate their opponents, suggests that the youngest generation might not be an improvement.[13] In this regard, the war of words between post-1980s youth, who are just beginning to mature and take their place in Chinese society, and the next generation, the "post-1990s youth," that has been well documented in the Chinese media and in online videos, further suggests either the vindication of the familiar expression "Each generation is worse than the last" (*yidai buru yidai* 一代不如一代) or, more likely, that each new generation is eager to push its reluctant predecessors offstage.[14]

The post-1980s generation has been surveyed extensively in the Chinese media, with some of the most interesting surveys addressing political participation and attitudes toward Western culture. Although published studies of political attitudes and participation are of widely varying quality – it is common for pragmatic youth to report politically correct responses – read carefully these surveys can suggest some intriguing behavioral patterns. For example, in its annually published investigation of youth in Beijing, the Beijing Municipal Communist Youth League was very pleased to note that in 2005–6 around 75 percent of youth expressed a willingness to participate in politics. In previous years, the number had not reached 50 percent. Looking more closely at the findings, however, one finds that only 10 percent were enthusiastic about such participation. More telling was what "participation" actually meant to the respondents. When asked what form such participation had taken, 72.5 percent noted that they had not actually participated at all; 11.1 percent said that participation meant expressing their opinions to family members or friends, followed by 5.8 percent who participated by expressing their opinions in Internet discussions. Only 0.6 percent said that

Table 7.1 The "post-1980s generation" in their own eyes and in the eyes of previous generations

Attributes of the "post-1980s generation"	How "pre-1980s generations" see them (%)	How the "post-1980s generation" sees itself (%)
Their circle of friends is very large, but their family circle is very small	48.6	31.4
They had their first sexual experience before the age of twenty	43.9	24.9
They've been deeply influenced by Japanese anime	59.7	31.1
They never drink straight hot water, but only bottled sweetened beverages	41.0	10.9
They pay attention to outer appearance and are fussy about how they dress	73.2	59.3
From an early age they've grown up eating at Kentucky Fried Chicken and McDonald's	32.3	6.4
Their life can't be separated from their great love of the Internet, QQ (instant messaging), and surfing the Web	78.3	48.2
They never watch the news or read books	36.2	7.5
They don't sleep at night; they're not awake during the day	51.5	37.2
They always consider themselves the center of attention	61.4	28.7
They don't like to cooperate with others	41.6	20.7
They don't want to take on any responsibilities	53.1	22.4
They don't like to take the lead in doing things, but always want others to take care of it	54.6	29.0
They never defer to others, but always feel that they're really great	64.2	29.9
Their concepts of morality, right and wrong, and sense of responsibility are not at all strong	61.4	18.5
They always have a high assessment of their own abilities	64.2	28.1
They often waste time at entertainment venues such as karaoke parlors and bars	45.1	12.0
When they buy things they only look at the appearance; they're not concerned with practical value	54.2	23.2

Source: http://news.sina.com.cn/c/2006-04-03/03598595630s.shtml, published in Jiang Fangbing, "Dui 'baling hou' yidai jiaose piancha wentide tiren yu fansi" [Views and Reflection on Role Deviation of the "Post-1980s" Generation], in Zhongguo qingnian yanjiu [China Youth Study] No. 6, June 2007, p. 25. Details of this survey first appeared in Zhongguo qingnian bao [China Youth Daily], April 3, 2006 where it was noted that the survey arm of the newspaper collaborated with Sohu News Center and Sina Women's Channel beginning on March 26, 2006 to do an online survey with a sample size of 3,457 pre-1980s netizens and 6,010 post-1980s youth.

they would contact either a party or youth league organization to express an opinion, suggesting how far the party-state apparatus has retreated in the daily lives of most youth.[15]

Another area that is frequently examined is motivation to join the Communist Party. The results often depend on how the question is asked. For example, if asked why they joined the party, respondents are likely to give a politically correct answer. Some surveyors have dealt with this issue by offering a series of choices, ranging from politically correct to instrumental and offering the possibility of choosing up to three reasons, thus allowing the respondent to choose the politically correct answer as well as the "real" reason. Other surveyors have simply asked respondents why they joined and why they thought others around them were joining, with a predictably wide variation dividing their own relatively pure intentions from the self-serving motivations of their comrades.[16] More recent surveys, presumably reflecting the post-1980s generation's belief that individual desires no longer need to be camouflaged, have elicited what appear to be more honest responses. Party membership is widely desired and considered to be valuable for one's future success, most notably in finding a well-paid job and good housing in a major city, and many youth noted that they were under pressure from their parents to join. In a survey of over 2,000 students from various universities in Xi'an, only 11.5 percent said they wanted to join the party because they believed in communism; other surveys and interviews have revealed that most applicants have little knowledge or even interest in most party activities and goals.[17]

A major theme in survey research on youth attitudes and behaviors is the inroads that Western culture has made into the belief systems of Chinese youth. One of the more revealing surveys was conducted among 629 history students at thirty-three universities throughout China by the World History Institute of the Chinese Academy of Social Sciences (CASS). The findings were considered too sensitive to be published in the open press and appeared in one of the internal journals published by CASS. Only some of the twenty-one topics queried can be addressed here. As Table 7.2 demonstrates, in terms of belief systems, 72.7 percent chose "individual struggle" and another 10 percent "did not know" their belief system. Only 17.2 percent opted for "struggle to achieve communism." More than 94 percent acknowledged that they had been influenced by Western culture, and even though more than 82 percent agreed that Western video products propagate Western political ideas and a Western lifestyle, fewer than 12 percent expressed a willingness to negate such products. Most directly, more than 51 percent identified themselves with American cultural concepts, while around 32 percent said, in effect, it was a "non-issue" (*wusuowei* 无所谓). Only 17 percent said they did not identify with these concepts. The surveyors were surprised to discover that more than 61 percent identified with liberalism (*ziyouzhuyi* 自由主义) and found it to be a concept of universal moral significance, despite the fact, as the surveyors put it, that everyone knows

166   *Stanley Rosen*

Table 7.2 Chinese youth attitudes toward Western "cultural penetration"

Question 1: "On the issue of belief systems"	%
"Strive to realize Communism"	17.2
"Strive for individual success"	72.7
"Don't know"	10

Question 2: "Do Western visual culture products directly or indirectly propagate Western political concepts and lifestyles?"

"Yes"	82.2
"No"	11.6
"Not certain"	6.2

Question 3: "On attitudes toward the American cultural concepts being propagated by American visual culture"

"Identify with them"	51.2
"Don't identify with them"	17.2
"It makes no difference" (*wusuowei* 无所谓)	31.7

Note: N = 629, from 33 Chinese universities (conducted by the Institute of World History, Chinese Academy of Social Sciences).

Source: "*Dui woguo qingnian xuesheng zai xinyang deng 21 ge zhongda wentishang de wenjhuan diaocha ji jianyao fenxi*" [A Brief Analysis of Responses to a Survey Questionnaire on Belief Systems and 21 other Important Questions given by Young Chinese Students], in *Lingdao canyue* [Reference Reading for Leaders] No. 19, July 5, 2007, pp. 24–28. The title of the survey was "The Influence of Western 'Cultural Penetration' and our Countermeasures."

that liberalism is part of Western political thought and the basis of the "democratic system" associated with Western capitalism. In like manner, the surveyors were dismayed that close to 36 percent of respondents endorsed the concept of "separation of powers" (*sanquan fenli* 三权分立) associated with Western political and legal systems, while more than 20 percent said they were "uncertain" whether they endorsed it: only 44 percent expressed opposition to the concept.

On a number of questions, the results surprised, even "shocked" (*lingren chijing* 令人吃惊), the surveyors, and suggested that the students were clearly deviating from their lessons. For example, when the students were asked to rank the ten greatest historical events of the twentieth century, the breakup of the Soviet Union and the changes in Eastern Europe ranked third, right behind the Second World War and the founding of the People's Republic of China. The 1917 Russian Revolution ranked only seventh. As the surveyors lamented, the Russian Revolution marked the opening of the confrontation between capitalism and socialism, which still exists, while the disintegration of the Soviet Union and the changes in Eastern Europe should not be seen as a new demarcation point in this confrontation. They were also dismayed to discover that, when asked to rank nineteen Western academic authorities and Chinese Marxist thinkers, the students found the works of the Marxist historians and philosophers far less influential on their own ideas than those from the capitalist world. The biggest shock was the ranking of China's first Marxist theorist, Li Dazhao, second from the bottom. Nor were the surveyors pleased when only 40 percent of the students objected to "spoofing" or "poking fun" (*xishuo* 戏说) at history. Even the "obvious fallacy" (*miulun* 谬论) of the Western-promoted concept of universal human rights found support among almost one-third of the students of history. On a more positive note, when asked to choose the ten greatest thinkers in world history, Confucius was named on 86.5 percent of the ballots and Karl Marx was chosen on 82.3 percent. No one else received as much as 40 percent.[18]

The results of this survey are consistent with a number of other surveys that address similar questions, although, to be sure, given the sensitivity of these issues, they do not appear in unaltered form in the open media. This is particularly the case with surveys conducted among university students at the leading universities in Beijing, reflecting the greater willingness of these students to seek solutions to the longstanding problems that have plagued Chinese governance. For example, a detailed survey of over 500 students at five of Beijing's best colleges, including Beijing and Qinghua universities, by Chen Shengluo, a professor at the China Youth University for Political Sciences (*Zhongguo qingnian zhengzhi xueyuan* 中国青年政治学院), discovered that the students' admiration for the American system far exceeded (*yuanyuan chaoguo* 远远超过) their support for the Chinese model. Chen was particularly surprised to find that around 75 percent of his sample either greatly liked (31.7 percent) or comparatively liked (43 percent) the Western model of the separation of powers. Adding those who said it was "okay" (*yiban* 一般), the figure comes to 95.8 percent. The remaining 4.2 percent chose "comparatively dislike" and not a single student (out of 505) chose "completely dislike."[19] Chen interpreted the results to suggest that the students felt that the leadership's anti-corruption campaigns had been unsuccessful and that the American system had been more effective in rooting out this problem. He also saw the results as an indication of the limits of the patriotic education campaign, discussed on pp. 170–171.

Chinese authorities appear to be well aware of the attraction of the Western model and have sought to counter it. The seductiveness of this model was brought home particularly forcefully with the unexpected and high profile opposition of Charter 08[20] and the published journals of former Premier and Party General Secretary Zhao Ziyang. Indeed, Zhao recalled Deng Xiaoping's firm and repeated opposition to the separation of powers and multiparty systems of the West, and even to Zhao's moderate attempts to expand political participation.[21] On June 5, 2009, a day after the twentieth anniversary of the suppression of the 1989 student movement, the major party media organs introduced the "Six Whys," offering a defense of the Chinese political system as superior to its Western counterparts. Not coincidentally, one of the "whys" explained why China practiced a "system of people's congresses" instead of the "separation of powers," and another explained the necessity of continuing the Chinese model of "cooperation and consultation of various parties with the CCP," rather than the "Western multi-party system."[22]

Openly published surveys have reinforced a number of these findings, particularly in terms of the penetration of American and Western popular culture into the social life of Chinese youth. One national survey of approximately 2,800 individuals ranging in age from 18 to 60 showed clearly that the celebration of American holidays correlated directly with age, ranging from a high of 57 percent of those aged 18–25 to a low of less than 13 percent for those 56–60 years of age.[23] Interviewees noted, in keeping with the widespread perception of the post-1980s generation, that Western holidays provided a convenient pretext to have a party. In addition, surveys commonly reveal a preference among youth for Hollywood films over those produced domestically.[24]

These results raise a number of larger issues that affect China's relationship to the international community. While a full discussion of this question is clearly beyond the scope of this chapter, it is nevertheless important to address those aspects that touch upon the role of Chinese youth as a factor in state–society relations. We can begin with what may appear to be a paradox. Interview and survey data reveal a high level of patriotism and love of country among Chinese youth, while at the same time suggesting a strong attraction toward the West, along with a lack of confidence when dealing with Westerners. A survey and analysis in *China Youth Daily* dealt with this issue directly. It began by noting that public opinion polls in the West had discovered that as many as 93 percent of Frenchmen, 90 percent of Americans, 88 percent of Italians, 87 percent of Germans, 87 percent of Englishmen, and 86 percent of Spaniards thought that China was the second most powerful country in the world. By contrast, an Internet survey in China found that 80 percent of the netizens thought that China was still not a powerful country. Moreover, an online survey of more than 2,500 youth conducted by the newspaper in conjunction with sina.com found that more than 59 percent felt that the large majority of Chinese "worshipped and had blind faith in foreign things" (*chongyang meiwai* 崇洋媚外); close to 56 percent felt that Americans were the world's most confident people; more than 76 percent thought that such confidence was closely tied to a nation's economic power; and almost 50 percent thought that Chinese lacked confidence when face to face with citizens from advanced Western countries.[25]

It is helpful to consider these results when examining the widely reported phenomenon of China's "angry youth." While that image has tended to dominate discussions in the Western media, it has been difficult to determine the relative numbers of such youth, or even their influence within China. However, such angry youth and former angry youth who are still angry at middle age have been associated with high profile examples of societal reaction to this perceived sense of Chinese inferiority. Ostensibly strongly critical of Western arrogance and dominance, there is a not so hidden subtext in their writings offering criticism of Chinese elites for insufficiently defending the nation's interests and accepting a second-class status in world affairs, despite China's obvious economic success and new importance internationally.

A highly publicized recent debate that reveals the complexities associated with the angry youth phenomenon and its relative impact on state–society relations surrounded the book *Unhappy China*, published in March 2009, and written by "five grassroots intellectuals."[26] Extensively analyzed in both the Chinese and Western media, *Unhappy China* can be considered a sequel to the 1996 best-seller *China Can Say No*.[27] While overtly dismissive of Western efforts to resist China's rise within the international community, both books also direct their "anger" at those *within* China who have not sufficiently defended China's interests. As one of the authors of both volumes, Song Qiang, noted in an interview after the publication of *Unhappy China*, the book "depicts the decline of a school of ideas that has existed in China for three decades and has dominated the world-views of the country's political elites, government economists, cultural elites, editors-in-chief and even some military chiefs."[28] In challenging the views of these "political elites" (*zhengzhi jingying* 政治精英) Song notes that China's economic success and growing national strength since the publication of *China Can Say No* in 1996 should have emboldened those who still are currying favor with the West.[29]

The debate within China over *Unhappy China*, as with most cutting-edge contention, has taken place primarily in cyberspace, with commentators in some of China's English language publications and on such "liberal" online forums as douban.com overwhelmingly critical.[30] Although some of the critical sources reported that the book had been placed on "inconspicuous shelves" of bookstores and that "it does not sell well," other sources note that it has "occupied the top spot on all categories of the weekly best seller lists of dangdang.com, one of China's largest online bookstores," and that online surveys at sites such as sina.com show a more even division of opinion, ranging from the 54.4 percent who agreed that "China should seize the best opportunity created by the financial crisis and stand out as a leader," to the 41.3 percent who believed that "this radical nationalism must be brought under control, and we should adopt a more rational and realistic thinking."[31]

State initiatives and youth responses

As the previous section suggested, a decade into the new millennium the Chinese state has often been compelled to be *reactive*, to respond to initiatives coming from society below. However, this should not obscure the state's often very *proactive* role in seeking to guide and tame a sometimes unruly youth.

In the aftermath of Tiananmen in 1989, Chinese leaders realized that they had to find a solution to their legitimacy crisis, particularly among rebellious youth. In moving even further from a legitimacy based on ideological criteria to a legitimacy based on performance indicators, "socialism with Chinese characteristics" expanded significantly to embrace cultural and economic forms from the West that previously had been unacceptable to the Communist Party. The strategy has been to make China rich and powerful, raising the standard of living so as to enable increasing numbers of Chinese to enter the middle class while positioning China to be a world-class leader in a variety of areas, including education and science. Youth had to feel that their life chances, particularly in terms of income, employment, housing, and other measures of personal and family success, were steadily improving, and that their country was playing an important role in world affairs. Because performance, unlike ideology, is measurable, Chinese citizens could monitor the state's success in realizing these goals. Many indicators suggest that China has done very well to this point, particularly among urban, well-educated youth, the stratum that posed the greatest threat to regime stability in 1989.[32] At the same time, in seeking to appease the ambitions of the rising middle class and the new generation of post-1980s and post-1990s youth, who will support state policies *if they work*, a number of contradictions arising out of these policies have surfaced. Given space considerations, only some representative examples of these new policies and the ensuing reactions can be explored.

In education, at the university level, the Ministry of Education has sharpened the distinctions that divide the best schools from the very good, the good, and the mediocre, and it has designated a small number of elite schools, headed by Tsinghua (*Qinghua* 清华) and Peking (*Beijing* 北京) universities, to receive the level of funding that will enable them to achieve world-class status.[33] At the secondary level as well, classes are often tracked by ability, fostering competition and promoting entrepreneurial skills. Moreover, as part of a wide-ranging policy to educate citizens for the twenty-first century, there has been an ongoing curriculum reform. The most public controversy has been over the revision of high school history textbooks, with the case of Shanghai widely discussed, to de-emphasize such familiar issues as class struggle, socialist ideology, and the historical role played by individual revolutionary leaders in favor of more attention to economics, science and technology, and global trends. At the same time, however, since 1991, there has been an ongoing and, judging from openly published survey research, apparently quite successful "patriotic education campaign," with discourse focusing on the national humiliations of the past, to foster love of the motherland.[34]

There have also been attempts to promote political education in a manner that might appeal to technology-savvy youth, with rather mixed results. For example, in the survey conducted by Chen Shengluo cited earlier, when students in his sample were asked whether they liked their compulsory political education classes, only 2.2 percent rated these courses highly, and another 15.8 percent said they were comparatively good, for a total of 18 percent. Not surprisingly, there was a high positive correlation between those who favorably assessed these courses and support for China's political system, and an inverse correlation between a positive assessment of these classes and support for the American political model.[35]

On the other hand, in September 2008, following the positive images generated by the Sichuan earthquake and the success of the Olympic Games, *People's Daily* launched an official fan site dedicated to the president and premier, seeking to provide patriotic cyberyouth with a "cool place to visit,"[36] a strategy that – judging solely by the number of "hits" – appears to have been more successful. Indeed, following that success, a private citizen set up the "PRC Officials' Fan Circle" website, www.zhongguofans.com, to celebrate the achievements of top leaders in various provinces and municipalities.[37] It has since been censored and closed.

Another strategy has been the marketing of computer games to the online world that substitute model Communist soldiers such as Lei Feng or other acceptable historical figures for heavily armed superheroes and reward players for doing good deeds instead of gunning down evildoers; response has reportedly also been "cool," but not in the positive sense.[38] In keeping with many surveys and interviews that suggest the values of contemporary youth run toward individualism and resistance to such prepackaged, politically correct role models, those who have achieved "idol" status include "Supergirl" (*chaoji nüsheng* 超级女声) contest winner Li Yuchun, chosen in an "open" election. Although she was criticized by establishment voices for her quirky personality, mediocre voice, and androgynous appearance, these same attributes were considered positives by the more than 3.5 million voters who chose her. Another popular youth icon is Han Han, a handsome 26-year-old writer and race car driver whose rebellious attitude, conspicuous consumption, and witty posts have made him the "ultimate symbol of instant individual gratification" and his blog on sina.com the most accessed.[39] This resistance to authoritative voices is common in other areas, including the widespread use of "spoofing," in which youth transform popular or well-known media content into something politically or culturally subversive.[40]

One recent example of spoofing offers a helpful window onto the complex interaction that governs state–society relations. In January 2009, with little fanfare, a mythical creature dubbed the "grass-mud horse," seeking to defend its desert turf (*gebitan* 戈壁滩) from the encroaching "river crabs" (*hexie* 河蟹), appeared on a Chinese Web page. In short order, a YouTube children's song drew 1.4 million viewers, with cartoons, documentaries, and learned treatises by intellectuals on the strange creature's struggles against the river crabs widely disseminated on the Internet. Since "grass-mud horse" and the name of the desert both sound like obscenities, albeit written with different Chinese characters, and "river crab" sounds very much like the ubiquitous "harmony" Hu Jintao and the leadership are perpetually extolling – in fact, "to harmonize" a post is to censor it – there is no doubt that the spoof was meant to ridicule the efforts of the propaganda apparatus to police the Internet, and to suggest that such efforts were no match for China's enterprising netizens.[41]

Conclusion

This overview of youth attitudes and behaviors in the context of evolving state–society relations has perhaps raised as many questions as it has answered. We cannot definitively assess, for example, the balance between the materialistic and the patriotic, other than to note that both remain core values for Chinese youth. During "normal" times, materialism and the pursuit of individual and familial success will overwhelm other values; however, patriotic (and nationalistic) surges will arise during "abnormal" times, when there is a perceived outside threat or insult to China (the bombing of the Chinese Embassy in Belgrade, Yugoslavia, by NATO forces in May 1999; the interference with the Olympic torch relay in France in 2008; the visit of a Japanese prime minister to the Yasakuni Shrine) or a domestic challenge to the moral sense of Chinese youth (the tragedy of the Sichuan earthquake; the outrageous official abuse of power, as documented through the visual images made possible by modern technology). The political authorities have of course based their legitimacy on both the material and the spiritual (i.e. patriotism and nationalism), with considerable success thus far. Success in the future requires the continuing expansion of middle-class opportunities for youth as they enter the workforce, a strong and credible commitment to eliminate official abuses, and the expected rise of China to world power status, particularly since, as surveys show, despite the lack of confidence noted above, a majority in China expect their country to overtake the United States at some point as the world's leading superpower.[42]

A second question – and one that is addressed throughout this volume – is the relationship between state policies and societal demands. Is the state primarily responding to initiatives from below, or is society merely reacting to the cues emanating from the political system? This chapter, and the volume more generally, has suggested, through a number of cases, that disentangling the complex state–society relationship is extraordinarily difficult, with elements of both the top-down and bottom-up models often present and interacting. The grass-mud horse creation was a societal response to Internet censorship. But increasing Internet censorship is of course a response to the use of the Internet to promote values and goals contrary to state aims.

Despite such hedging and ambiguity, there are a number of conclusions that can be stated more assertively. First, we have seen and will continue to witness the "secularization" of youth attitudes and behaviors. With the communist ideal receding ever further into the background, we can expect the political authorities to continue to reinterpret "socialism with Chinese characteristics" less and less "ideologically." As Bruce J. Dickson revealed in Chapter 1, the party has continued to adapt in order to survive, and, as we have shown in this chapter, youth pursue party membership as a necessary investment to increase their chances of getting a good job and leading a comfortable middle-class life. This is not their grandfather's (or even their father's) Communist Party. If youth are not joining the party for political reasons, their "participation" in politics more generally has in effect been a private participation, through friends, family, and in anonymous Internet activities.

This suggests a second conclusion. When the year 2009 began it was frequently noted by Western scholars as well as the Western and Chinese media that, as "the year of anniversaries," 2009 would be particularly sensitive, and would usher in "a peak period for mass incidents" (*quntixing shijian* 群体性事件).[43] However, as suggested above, the pursuit of a pragmatic, success-oriented approach by the post-1980s generation and their successors in the post-1990s generation has meant that the multiple anniversaries of significant past events have not posed any immediate threat to the regime. There are few indications that these current youth generations will take any overt political risks, particularly if the leadership remains unified.

At the same time, however, given the increasing politicization of protests and the potential for economic problems to call heightened attention to social inequalities and tensions that have simmered just below the surface, party leaders monitored these anniversaries closely, seeking to ensure that "idealistic" youth did not link up with disgruntled migrant and other laid-off workers, while stepping up their control of the Internet and other new technologies. In the longer term, the rising expectations of China's youth and the middle class, and the still relevant legacy of youth activism, will continue to pose challenges for a government that has staked its legitimacy on deliverable performance criteria.

Notes

1 This chapter is a revised and substantially expanded version of an article entitled "Contemporary Chinese youth and the state" that originally appeared in the *Journal of Asian Studies* 68(2) (May 2009), pp. 359–69. I am grateful to the journal and to Cambridge University Press for permission to reprint material from that article.

2 "The 'Me Generation'," *Beijing Review* No. 9, February 28, 2008 (online). A similarly titled article, written by Simon Elegant, had appeared in *Time* magazine on June 26, 2007 and had attracted considerable attention on Chinese blogs. See the original article and translations of several blog posts in *EastSouthNorthWest*, August 1, 2007.

3 "Complete New Appraisal of the Post-80's Generation," *People's Daily* (English, online), June 4, 2008. The publication of this favorable appraisal of contemporary Chinese youth on June 4 was presumably not coincidental.

4 Evan Osnos, "Angry Youth: The New Generation's Neocon Nationalists," *New Yorker*, July 28, 2008, pp. 28–37.

5 "Why Grandpa Wen Has to Care; Populist Politics in China," *Economist*, June 14, 2008 (online). The original source is a long two-part article in *Zhongguo qingnian bao* on April 2, 2008 by Wu Jiaxiang.

6 On the struggle by Chinese youth to forge an identity, see Ian Weber, "'*Shanghai Baby*': Negotiating Youth Self-Identity in Urban China," *Social Identities* 8(2) (2002), pp. 347–68.

7 For example, one 2007 survey reported in a leading Communist Youth League publication asked the purpose of friendship and found that 45.9 percent of youth said that "friends were a kind of capital" (*pengyou shi yizhong ziben*). See Zhang Bona, "The Change in the Concept of Association among Youth during the Thirty Years of Reform," *Zhongguo qingnian yanjiu* [China Youth Research], no. 1 (January 2008), p. 23.

8 Shi Zhong, "Chinese Nationalism and the Future of China," translated in Stanley Rosen, ed., "Nationalism and Neoconservatism in China in the 1990s," *Chinese Law and Government* 30 (6) (November–December 1997), pp. 8–27. A shorter version of this article had appeared in Hong Kong's *Mingbao yuekan*, No. 9, September 1996. Shi Zhong is the penname of Wang Xiaodong, who was also in the lead in criticizing the film "*Lust, Caution*" (*se, jie*) for its defamation of patriotic students, among other ills, and most recently was one of the authors of the 2009 volume *Unhappy China*, discussed on p. 169. Indeed, showing a considerable degree of continuity, one of the critiques of Chinese elites and Chinese foreign policy that the authors of *Unhappy China* highlight is the persistent refusal to challenge the West, even after Chinese economic success and Western decline.

9 This assessment is based on travel and interviews throughout China, particularly on college campuses, throughout the 1980s.

10 Yongming Zhou, "Understanding Chinese Internet Politics," in *China and Democracy: A Contradiction in Terms?*, Woodrow Wilson International Center for Scholars Asia Program Special Report, no. 131 (June 2006), pp. 21–5.

11 See the cover story and a series of articles entitled "'Spoofing': A Type of Youth Culture Phenomenon," *Zhongguo qingnian yanjiu* [China Youth Research], no. 6 (June 2008), pp. 4–24, referenced more fully in note 40.

12 The expression is now used for virtually all areas of Chinese life to refer to individuals (e.g. "a post-1980s poet") or phenomena (as in "a post-1980s Web site or magazine"). See Zhao Feng, "The Evolution from 'Generations' to 'Post'," *Zhongguo qingnian bao*, July 6, 2008, p. 3.

13 See Chen Weijun, director, "*Please Vote for Me*" (55 minutes, China, 2007); the DVD is available from First Run Features. The popular TV series "Who Determines My Youth" (*Wode qingchun shei zuozhu*), about three mothers in their fifties and their daughters born in the late 1980s, offers a rather different window onto the generation gap. See Chen Nan, "When Worlds Collide," China Daily e-clips, May 22, 2009. Another TV series, *Fen Dou* (Working Hard), follows the lives of seven twenty-something friends.

14 Zhang Wei, "The War between Two Labels: A True Record of the 'Post-80's' and 'Post-90's' Attacks," *Zhongguo qingnian bao*, May 7, 2008, p. 10. In fact, the Chinese media have also begun referring to a "post-1985 generation," suggesting generational change every five years. See "The Evolution from 'Generations' to 'Post'," op. cit. Some interviewees born around 1990 suggested that there was a generation gap every *three* years. Technology has been an important driving force for generational distinctions. As one 19-year-old interviewee noted, while she had QQ (instant messenger) in the sixth grade, her 10-year-old cousin began using it in the third grade. In the Internet and blog "wars," the post-1980s youth are sometimes called "the strawberry generation" because they look good on the outside but become rotten after you touch them (*waibiao guangxian, yipeng jiu huai*). A recent survey, conducted from August to November 2007, assesses the behavioral patterns of the "post-1990s" youth. See *90 hou qunti wenhua he xiaofei qushi yanjiu baogao* [A Research Report on the Group Culture and Consumption Trends

among "Post-1990s" Youth] (Beijing: Horizon Research, 2008). Unfortunately, the purchase price is 36,000 *yuan* (about U.S.$5,300). For a free summary, see Yuan Yue, "Sighing with Emotion Today: 2008, the First Adult Year of the 'Post-1990s Generation'," sina.com blog, November 3, 2008 (http://blog.sina.com.cn/ victory). For an interesting comparison of post-1970s, post 1980s, and post-1990s youth, in which exposure to the Internet and their differing life experiences help explain their attitudes and behavior, see the post by ytwhych at http://iask. games.sina.com.cn/b/8633989.html?from=related (March 28, 2007).

15 *Beijing qingnian fazhan baogao* [Report on the Development of Beijing Youth], 2005–6 edition (Beijing: Renmin chubanshe, 2007), pp. 331–8. There were 742 respondents for this part of the survey.

16 Stanley Rosen, "The Victory of Materialism: Aspirations to Join China's Urban Moneyed Classes and the Commercialization of Education," *The China Journal*, no. 51 (January 2004), pp. 42–6.

17 Wang Xingjia, "An Investigation and Analysis of the Ideological and Political Situation of Young Students," *Zhongguo qingnian yanjiu*, no. 7 (July 2007), pp. 54–6. For a study in Beijing that points up a wide variety of "erroneous views" with regard to motivation for Party membership, see Feng Haiyan, "An Investigation into the Motivations for Party Membership among Contemporary University Students," *Zhongguo qingnian yanjiu*, no. 6 (June 2008), pp. 55–7. These findings are congruent with the recent research on the subject by Bruce Dickson and Gang Guo. See Bruce J. Dickson, "Who Wants to Be a Communist? The Appeal of Party Membership in Contemporary China," paper presented at the annual meeting of the Association for Asian Studies, Chicago, March 29, 2009; Gang Guo, "Party Recruitment of College Students in China," *Journal of Contemporary China* 14 (May 2005), pp. 371–93. For an overview of the changes in membership structure of the party in urban China in the 1990s that argues that the development of marketization has made it easier for the younger generation to achieve socioeconomic success without joining the party, thus compelling the party to adjust its recruitment strategy to appeal to these well-educated, professionally qualified youth, see Hiroshi Sato and Keiya Eto, "The Changing Structure of Communist Party Membership in Urban China, 1988–2002," *Journal of Contemporary China* 17 (November 2008), pp. 653–72.

18 CASS Institute of World History Special Topics Group, "A Brief Analysis of a Survey of Young Students with Regard to Belief Systems on 21 Important Questions," *Lingdao canyue* [Reference Reading for Leaders], no. 19, July 5, 2007, pp. 24–8. The other great thinkers chosen, in order, were Mencius, Einstein, Kant, Nietzsche, Darwin, Newton, Hawking, and Durkheim.

19 Chen Shengluo, "*Zhongguo daxuesheng dui zhongmei liangguo zhengzhi zhidu de kanfa diaocha yanjiu: yi beida, qinghua deng beijing wusuo zhongdian daxue weili* (An Investigation of the Views of Chinese University Students with Regard to the Chinese and American Political Systems: Taking Five Elite Universities in Beijing, Including Beijing and Qinghua as Examples), unpublished manuscript, to be translated in a future issue of *Chinese Education and Society*. The survey was conducted in June 2007.

20 "Charter 08," a document released on December 10 and signed by more than 2,000 Chinese citizens, including some middle-level government officials, advocated the elimination of one party rule and its replacement by a democratic system that would protect human rights. The party's strong reaction suggested that they saw this document, and the willingness of so many individuals to sign their names openly, as a warning of additional challenges to come in 2009. For a translation of the Charter and government reaction, see Perry Link, "China's Charter 08," *New York Review of Books* LVI(1), January 15, 2009, pp. 54–6.

21 Bao Pu, Renee Chiang, and Adi Ignatius, eds. and trans., *Prisoner of the State: The Secret Journal of Premier Zhao Ziyang* (New York: Simon & Schuster, 2009). See Part VI, "How China Must Change," pp. 247–73.

22 The "Six Whys" have been translated by the China Media Project at Hong Kong University. See David Bandurski, "Because Forsaking Marxism Means Toppling the Great Wall," posted on June 19, 2009 (http://cmp.hku.hk/2009/06/19/1668/). It has been widely disseminated on the web by the China Digital Times (http://Chinadigitaltimes.net).

23 "American Holidays: They're Only a Reason to Pass on Good Wishes," *Di yishou*, No. 1043, June 24, 2008 (http://www.horizonkey.com/showart.asp?_id=787&cat_id=6).

24 Stanley Rosen, "Film and China's Youth Culture," *Education About Asia* 13(3) (Winter 2008), pp. 38–43.

25 Xiao Shunan and Zhou Qin, "Why Do Sixty Percent of Youth Think That Chinese People Worship and Have Blind Faith in Foreign Things?" *Zhongguo qingnian bao* [China Youth Daily], December 14, 2007, p. 2. Some interviewees from elite senior highs in Beijing confirmed the accuracy of these results, noting that graduates who went to study abroad instead of at a Chinese university were held in higher esteem, and citing the better treatment from teachers for those who had been admitted by top American universities.

26 Song Xiaojun, Wang Xiaodong, Huang Jisu, Song Qiang, and Liu Yang, *Zhongguo bu gaoxing: da shidai, da mubiao; ji women de neiyou waihuan* [Unhappy China: The Great Time, Grand Vision and Our Challenges] (Nanjing: Jiangsu renmin chubanshe, 2009).

27 Song Qiang, Zhang Zangzang (Zhang Xiaobo), and Qiao Bian, *Zhongguo keyi shuo bu: lengzhan hou shidai de zhengzhi yu qinggan jueze* [China Can Say No: Political and Emotional Choices in the Post-Cold War Era] (Beijing: Zhonghua gongshang lianhe chubanshe, 1996). Song Qiang and Zhang Xiaobo were active in the writing and editing of both books.

28 "Unhappy Misunderstanding," BeijingReview.com.cn, no. 15, April 16, 2009.

29 *Ibid.* and Li Li, "Happy or Unhappy Is the Question," BeijingReview.com.cn, April 16, 2009. One of the authors of *Unhappy China*, Wang Xiaodong, has long been critical of these dominant elites for their deference toward the West. This assessment is based on my interviews with Wang in the early and mid-1990s, when he was young enough to still qualify as an "angry youth." As noted above (see note 8), his writings after 1989 had accused Chinese students in the late 1980s of "reverse racism"; privately, he was just as critical of the party's reform faction.

30 The critical English language publications include peopledaily.com.cn (April 15, 2009), shanghaidaily.com (March 27, 2009), and xinhuanet.com (March 25, 2009). Some English language sources have offered a more complex picture, with competing analyses, ranging from dismissive (chinadaily.com, March 25, 2009) to more balanced (chinadaily.com, April 18, 2009, and beijingreview.com.cn, April 17, 2009).

31 The argument against the book's popularity can be found at http://news.xinhuanet.com/english/2009-03-25/content_11072198.htm# and the opposite view can be found at http://www.bjreview.com.cn/quotes/txt/2009-04-17/content_191457.htm.

32 Recent surveys by CASS suggest that there are about 4–5 percent of Chinese currently in the middle class (meeting the criteria from several different indicators), with about 10 percent in the cities and 12–15 percent in the large cities. Perhaps most importantly, many more people subjectively view themselves as already middle class than the objective indicators would suggest, a sign of government success. See *Lingdao canyue* [Reference Reading for Leaders], no. 34, December 5, 2007, pp. 16–20. One survey found that while over 80 percent did not currently

view themselves as middle class, over 43 percent thought there was a very real possibility that they would enter the middle class in the next ten years. See *Zhongguo qingnian bao*, December 24, 2007, p. 2.

33 On the debate over what constitutes a "world-class university" in the context of Beijing University, see the translations in Stanley Rosen, ed., "The Beida Reforms (I), (II), and (III)," in *Chinese Education & Society* 37(6) (November–December 2004), 38(1 and 2) (January–February and March–April 2005).

34 On the controversy over high school history textbooks, see Joseph Kahn, "Where's Mao? Chinese Revise History Books," *New York Times*, September 1, 2006. For the backlash against this new emphasis, see "Shanghai History Textbook Controversy, Revisited," *Shanghaiist*, September 14, 2007 (http://shanghaiist.com/2007/09/14/shanghai_histor.php). For an argument that suggests that the campaign has not been successful, that in fact "pragmatism, not patriotism, is the religion of the contemporary PRC," see Julia Lovell, "It's Just History: Patriotic Education in the PRC," at http://thechinabeat.blogspot.com/2009/04/its-just-history-patriotic-ed. . . . , posted on April 22, 2009.

35 Chen Shengluo, "Zhongguo daxuesheng . . . ."

36 *South China Morning Post*, September 9, 2008.

37 See Peh Shing Huei, "Beijing Turns on the Charm Online," *Straits Times*, January 12, 2009 (online).

38 Ching-Ching Ni, "Will China's Youth Play Virtuous Virtual Game?," *Los Angeles Times*, November 4, 2005, p. A5.

39 Surveys and discussions on "idol worship" are featured heavily in academic journals and the mainstream press. Horizon Research has done a series of surveys over the last ten years examining role models, film and sports stars, and other admired personages in China and the West. While not intended as a longitudinal panel study, the results are nevertheless quite revealing. In an extensive survey of junior and senior high school students in five coastal cities conducted in 1999, which asked the students to choose the person, living or dead, they considered most successful, the males chose Bill Gates, followed by the richest man in Hong Kong, Li Ka-shing. For the females, the top choices were former Premier Zhou Enlai and a favorite teacher; Gates and Li were relegated to fifth and sixth places. It is also interesting to note that Gates was the overwhelming favorite at the senior high level, but scored poorly among junior high students, even below George Washington, who came in at number ten. See the research report *Xun Cool yi dai* [Looking for the Cool Generation] (Beijing: Horizon Research, December 15, 1999), pp. 21–3. More recent Horizon surveys have shown the decline of Bill Gates in favor of movie stars. For example, a 2005 survey found Hong Kong superstar Andy Lau a clear winner, and even Mao Zedong edged Gates, although Gates was comfortably above Deng Xiaoping. See *"Renshi weilai de xiaofei zhuliu* [Understanding Future Consumer Trends], *Di yi shou* [First Hand], February 5, 2007.

40 On spoofing, see the series of articles entitled *" 'Egao': yizhong qingnian wenhua xianxiang"* ['Spoofing': A Type of Youth Culture Phenomenon] in *Zhongguo qingnian yanjiu* [China Youth Research], no. 6, June 2008, pp. 4–24. For a brief account in English, see Ashley Esarey and Xiao Qiang, "Political Expression in the Chinese Blogosphere," *Asian Survey* 48(5) (September–October 2008), pp. 764–5. The influence of blogs, including Tencent's Q Zone, Douban, Tianya.cn, 80 Hoo, and the Sina and Sohu blog portals on Chinese youth could form a separate article. I am grateful to Rebecca Mackinnon and Xiao Qiang for introducing me to some of these blogs. Also see Yunxiang Yan, "Little Emperors or Frail Pragmatists? China's '80ers Generation," *Current History*, September 2006, pp. 255–62.

41 Michael Wines, "Mythical Beast (a Dirty Pun) Tweaks China's Web Censors," *New York Times*, March 12, 2009, pp. A1, 12; http://www.youtube.com/watch?v =T2Fl3q5gZNC.
42 *The Pew Global Attitudes Project: China Survey*, July 22, 2008, pp. 19–20.
43 Dong Ruifeng, "Early Warning about Mass Incidents," *Liaowang xinwen zhoukan* [Outlook Weekly], No. 1, 2009, online; Ariana Eunjung Cha, "As China's Jobless Numbers Mount, Protests Grow Bolder: Economic Woes Shining a Light on Social Issues," *Washington Post*, January 13, 2009, p. A07; "The Year of Living Dissidently," *Economist*, January 17, 2009, pp. 42–3; Rosen, "Contemporary Chinese Youth and the State." The anniversaries include the May 4 Movement (May 4, 1919), the Tiananmen Square Protests and the subsequent bloody military assault (April–June 4, 1989), and the bombing of the Chinese Embassy in Belgrade by NATO forces (May 7, 1999).

8 Censorship and surveillance in Chinese cyberspace

Beyond the Great Firewall

Patricia M. Thornton

On June 20, 2008, President Hu Jintao marked the 60th anniversary of the founding of the *People's Daily* (*Renmin ribao* 人民日报), the official voice of the Chinese Communist Party (CCP), by paying a formal visit to the central offices of the newspaper. Congratulating those assembled for their service to the people, Hu called upon the staff to do an even better job of "performing its function as the organ of the Party's Central Committee guiding public opinion." Shortly thereafter, in a move indicative of just how vital new information technologies have become in renegotiating the boundaries between the Chinese state and society, Hu used a computer terminal to hold the first ever online chat between a reigning president and the Chinese people on the popular online portal of the *People's Daily*, the "Strong Nation Forum" (*qiangguo luntan* 强国论坛).

Hailing the chatroom participants as his "netizen-friends" (*wangmin pengyou* 网民朋友), the president extended his "sincere regards and best wishes" to all before taking questions. With the floor open, the first question fielded by the secretary-general was whether he often had occasion to go online. Hu responded that, despite his demanding work schedule, he tried to find time to go online as often as possible, and that he did frequent the *People's Daily's* "Strong Nation Forum" during his forays on the Web. In response to the second question, Hu revealed that he used the Web primarily to read domestic and international news, to better understand which problems or issues were of concern to his "netizen-friends," and in hopes of learning their opinions and suggestions regarding the workings of the party-state. Finally, in responding to the last question, Hu reassured his public that the leaders of the party-state "pay extremely close attention" to the opinions and recommendations of "netizen-friends," because "the people are fundamental":

> We govern on the peoples' behalf, and consequently in considering problems, implementing policy, and handling issues, we all wish to hear the broad range of the opinions of the masses, and gather together their wisdom. The Internet is one important channel through which we can understand popular sentiment, and assemble the collective wisdom of the people.[1]

Perhaps even more revealing than the exchange itself was the manner in which it was reported, both at home and abroad. Whereas Xinhua's English language news service proudly proclaimed "Chinese President Holds First Ever Web Chat with Citizens," and *China Daily* boasted "Hu Makes History with Online Chat,"[2] Western news outlets were not only more reserved in their assessment, but openly skeptical as well. In London, the *Guardian* reported that " 'Boss Hu' Ducks Tricky Question in Online Chat," and emphasized the mediated nature of the exchange, pointing out that the forum host doctored the manner in which some of the questions were addressed, and the fact that the president, "who is widely seen as stiff and distant," did not type his own responses, but dictated them instead.[3] The *Guardian*'s chief rival, *The Times*, claimed that Hu's appearance was in fact a public relations attempt "intended to polish Mr. Hu's rather stilted image," and summed up the visit with a headline designed to emphasize the social distance between the Chinese party-state and its citizens: "Hu Pokes His Head over 'Great Firewall' to Seek the Opinions of 221m Netizens."[4]

The concept of China's "Great Firewall," a term likely first coined by Geremie Barmé and Sang Ye in an article written for *Wired* magazine in 1997,[5] has taken on a life of its own among scholars, journalists, and pundits. Often connected to the "Golden Shield" program of Web surveillance originally proposed the following year, the "Great Firewall" conjures images of an ill-fated xenophobic regime struggling to erect and maintain technologically advanced barriers of censorship to limit access to information by its per-petually restive subject population. Such references hearken back to the Cold War imagery of iron and/or bamboo curtains, deployed to great effect by Ronald Reagan just after June 4, 1989, when the former president wishfully observed, "The biggest of Big Brothers is increasingly helpless against com-munications technology. Information is the oxygen of the modern age. It seeps through the walls topped by barbed wire, it wafts across the electrified, booby-trapped borders. . . . The Goliath of totalitarian control will be brought down by the David of the microchip."[6] Just over a decade later, Thomas Friedman of the *New York Times* likewise boasted that "the Internet and globalization are acting like nutcrackers to open societies and empower" pro-democracy forces under illiberal regimes by providing them with "artillery" in the form of the Internet.[7]

The belligerent undertones that drive the policy debate over Internet access in mainland China have likewise pervaded popular discussions on the English language Web, triggering angry protests against Western companies like Google and Yahoo that have been accused of cooperating with Chinese censors in order to preserve their access to the vast mainland Chinese mar-ket.[8] Wry net activists have launched a downloadable open-source Firefox module that promises users outside the Chinese mainland the opportunity to "take an unforgetable [sic] virtual trip to China and experience the tech-nical expertise of the Chinese Ministry of Information Industry" to screen and block information in real time on their own computers.[9] One popular site that regularly reports on Web-related developments derisively refers to the booming mainland Chinese blogosphere as "China's Censoredsphere."[10] References to China's "Great Firewall" have even spawned a pop paean to impregnability by the British indie rock band Honeytrap.[11]

The roiling controversy over Chinese cyberspace is fraught with moral indignation on both sides of the issue. In May 2005, on Slashdot.com, the popular English language forum that bills itself as "news for nerds," speculation that Google had agreed to cooperate with Chinese censors stimulated a heated discussion regarding the operation of the "Great Firewall." One post in English addressed to the "Citizens of China" offered links to five pages presumed to be blocked in China, including speculation regarding genocide in Tibet and a summary of Jasper Becker's *Hungry Ghosts*, a book that documents the famine that followed in the wake of communization during the 1958 so-called "Great Leap Forward." Concluding with a link to the famed photo of the "Tank Man," a Chinese citizen who faced down a line of People's Liberation Army (PLA) tanks near Tiananmen Square on June 4, 1989, the message concluded with the charge: "Freedom starts with you." This provoked an immediate response from "HungWeiLo," a reader who argued that the Chinese people with whom s/he came into frequent contact

> are already quite knowledgeable about all the information provided in the links above, and most do not hesitate to engage in discussions about such topics over lunch. The fact that you feel all 1.6 billion Chinese are most certainly blind to these pieces of information is a direct result of years of indoctrination of Western (I'm assuming American) propaganda.[12]

In a similar vein, Liu Kang recently observed that "tales of China's political repression and terror have more to do with the political, ideological, and commercial objectives of the Western media than with what really happens in China today."[13]

The propensity of the Western media to sensationalize Internet censorship was recently highlighted when two well-known Chinese bloggers celebrated for their irreverence, Massage Milk (*anmo ru* 按摩乳) and Milk Pig (*nai zhu* 奶猪), posted the following statement on their webpages: "Due to unavoidable reasons with which everyone is familiar, this blog is temporarily closed." The BBC's Sebastian Usher quickly filed a report linking the closures to an upcoming annual session of National People's Congress, taking an opportunity to observe that the Chinese government "administers the most sophisticated system of Internet censorship and control anywhere in the world," one that "is tightened even further" during key political junctures.[14] Within hours, Reporters Without Borders issued a statement condemning the closures. The following day, the two blogs were back on-line: in his first post, Wang Xiaofeng of Massage Milk admitted staging the closure of the blog "to give foreign media a lesson that Chinese affairs are not always the way you think," and castigated Western media outlets for their "irresponsible" reportage of the ambiguous statement posted on the Web.[15]

Driving much of the hand-wringing that occurs in the West over the "Great Firewall" is what Joshua Kurlantzick has identified as the "pervasive myth" that "the Internet is a powerful force for democracy," and the deeply held suspicion that attempts to restrict full access to the Web slow inevitable progress toward political liberalization.[16] Wang Jisi, Director of the Institute of American Studies of the Chinese Academy of Social Sciences (CASS), argues that such predictions likely stem from a persistent "propensity to view Chinese politics (as well as politics in other 'undemocratic states') as a constant division and tension between 'the authorities,' which are preconceived as hostile to the West, and 'the people,' who must be friendly to the United States and its allies."[17] Yet empirical evidence is mounting that the link between democracy, political liberalization, and Internet adoption is tenuous at best. First, at the heart of much concern about China's so-called "Great Firewall" is the suspicion that techniques of censorship and surveillance employed by authoritarian regimes like the CCP discourage Internet use, either directly or indirectly.[18] This is clearly untrue: the most recent statistics released by the Chinese Internet Network Information Center (CNNIC) show that, by the end of June 2008, the number of netizens, or Internet users, in China reached 253 million, surpassing the number of U.S.-based netizens, and making China the nation with the largest number of Internet users in the world.[19] Second, despite the rhetoric and speculation to the contrary, the "Great Firewall" is not impenetrable. While evading surveillance and censorship can be tricky, Internet proxy use in mainland China has risen in recent years. A 2007 CASS survey of Internet users in seven Chinese cities found that over one quarter of Chinese netizens regularly turned to proxy servers in order to surf the Web.[20] Statistics collected by Dynamic Internet Technology, one of the many companies that provide a free proxy service to mainland-based Web users, show that during momentous events like the SARS outbreak, the number of mainlanders regularly relying on proxies to access Websites normally not available in mainland China rise by at least 50 percent. After the outbreak was contained, traffic on proxies remained high, with the overwhelming majority of proxy users originating in mainland China.[21] Third, popular constructions of the "Great Firewall" presume that mainland Chinese users, given their druthers, would elect to have uncensored and unfiltered access to the Web. This is also untrue. A 2007 Pew Center survey carried out in mainland China by CASS found that 80 percent of mainland respondents agreed that the Internet should be controlled or managed, and 85 percent of those respondents asserted that the Chinese government should be the entity in charge of controlling or managing it.[22]

With the foregoing caveats in mind, at least some of the assumptions underlying the "Great Firewall" may be open to qualification. Without denying that censorship and surveillance of the Chinese Internet does occur or suggesting that its effects are not significant, some have pointed to the increasingly robust realm of Chinese cyberspace as an "incipient but yet dynamic"[23] form of civil society characterized by a "greater diversity" of online spaces than are readily available in the offline public sphere.[24] Zhao Yuezhi notes that "although one cannot overstate the pervasiveness and draconian nature of this regime, nor its efficacy in social control," what she finds most striking in her research of traditional and Web-based Chinese media today is "the ever more thunderous drumbeat of opposition" to repression and control, and the impressive variety of forms that such opposition takes.[25]

This chapter seeks to map some of the rich and varied terrain of the online public sphere beyond the so-called "Great Firewall of China," and to demonstrate that, censorship notwithstanding, mainland Chinese netizens indeed make extensive use of the Internet to reflect upon, debate, and contest political matters. One 2000 survey conducted by Guo Liang and Bu Wei found that nearly 63 percent of the mainland Chinese respondents surveyed regarded the Internet as the best medium for "expressing personal opinions or viewpoints, or publishing self-authored work," as compared to 22.7 percent and 14.6 percent for newspapers and magazines, respectively.[26] Following Michael Warner, whose analysis of public discourse focuses on "the kind of public that comes into being only in relation to texts and their circulation . . . part of the common repertoire of modern culture,"[27] this chapter seeks to replace the popular conception of a singular "virtual public sphere" tightly bounded by a "Great Firewall," with a more internally diverse and porous aggregation of shifting groups of netizens that are primarily constituted by their collective attention to a particular text or issue.[28] Likewise, Nancy Fraser points out in her work on the public sphere that, despite assumptions to the contrary, the historically bounded bourgeois public sphere described in the work of Jürgen Habermas was defined in large part by its exclusivity. Nonetheless, Fraser emphasizes the role of collective deliberation in the formation of publics and counterpublics in the public sphere, arguing that it is the process of discursive interaction, and not unrestricted access, that defines the public sphere as such.[29] The remaining sections of this chapter will focus on a series of recent debates centered in Chinese cyberspace on the nature of the contemporary Chinese state, the on-going process of market reform, and popular concern about the nature of post-socialist Chinese society.

Debating the state

In late September 2008, on the eve of the PRC's 59th National Day, one of China's most popular newspapers, *Southern Weekend* (*Nanfang zhoumo* 南方周末), invited its readers to take the opportunity to "quietly consider" what type of relationship they, as citizens, actually had with their country. The editors noted that the word "country" (*guojia* 国家) had two meanings in Chinese: first, one that corresponds roughly to the English meaning of the term, and refers to a land and its people; and, second, a term that signifies the power of the state, and the organs of government. In particular, the editors at *Southern Weekend* sought answers to four questions from their broad readership: "What do I do for my country? What does my country do for me? What can I do for my country? And, what can my country do for me?"[30]

The selection of responses *Southern Weekend* published on its Website were by no means uniformly positive. Several of the responses refer directly to contemporary social ills, such as unemployment and the steeply rising cost of school tuition, or to recent scandals that reflect poorly on the regulatory capacity of the state, such as the sale of melamine-tainted milk powder by the Sanlu corporation. A small handful convey a sense of hopelessness, cynicism, or disappointment about rising unemployment, diminishing social welfare benefits, or political corruption.[31]

However, the invitation from *Southern Weekend* elicited a much broader response than appeared on the newspaper's site. Chinese netizens posted and circulated widely a variety of responses, stimulating frank and sometimes heated exchanges regarding the relationship between the nation and its citizens. Paris-based Xiong Peiyun, author of a widely read blog and erstwhile contributor to *Southern Weekend*, offered the following on his blog in response to the second and fourth questions:

> (What does my country do for me?) Defamation is not [a sign of] sound moral character, I decided before I had any positive recollections I would refuse to answer this type of question. But my conscience is clear: if, in my life I have some beautiful memories, that is by no means due to what the country has done for me, nor is it due to what the country has not done for me.
>
> (What can my country do for me?) The state works too hard, and should take a break. For the past fifty years, the state has fucked up our minds pretty badly (*guojia wei women ba xin dou cao huaile* 国家为我们把心都操坏了). The people of this generation are self-reliant and independent, and in many ways don't want to burden the country. Since the state doesn't have a collective stomach with which to digest food for me, I would ask the state not to use the collective brain it doesn't have to think for me. If this were a lecture hall, I would "politely" exhort the state back to its seat, so that I could finish speaking.[32]

One of the most frequently cross-posted responses on the Chinese language Web, worth quoting in full, was offered by a netizen who goes by the name Wuyuesanren (五岳散人):

> (What have you done for your country?) When I was a student, with respect to my country (and here I should say "the government"), I was an excellent if embryonic little screw,[33] that subsequently became scrap

metal (*youxiu luosi dade chuxing, houlai baofale* 优秀螺丝钉的雏形，后来报废了). In the first six years of my working life as an electrical engineer in a state-owned factory, I think I contributed my meager bit of surplus value. Afterwards, as a reporter, other than paying my taxes, I wrote as much as could be reported about the dark side of things; and about that which I was not allowed to report, I couldn't do anything. Now as a commentator, I remit the tax that I genuinely owe in the form of speech – and this I offer to my true country.

To my true country, please allow me this modest boast: I have done what I could, and I plan to keep doing it. And to those few persons who have confused their identities with the country, please also allow me to brag a bit: you have not succeeded, or at least not completely. I also intend to keep it up.

(What has the country done for me?) The country (and here I mean the true nation) gave me the color of my skin, my language, and my cultural foundation: for instance, I always think that Chinese food is the best, and that English tea is dogshit. Aside from these things which are innate, or which I had to accept before I was capable of making my own choices, the country did nothing for me.

But in another sense, the country just did so much for me, giving me piles of textbooks full of dogshit, telling me how to take pride in devoting myself to the state-owned factory, after which I discovered that most of my co-workers who also believed this had been laid off, always looking at the Ministry of Truth documents telling me what I'm not allowed to report, and even so many things that I can't say on the Internet. And so on, and so on, and so on. And now I just discovered that the milk I have been drinking has a problem. Is that enough for you?

(What else can you do for your country?) This question also does well to raise the two divergent meanings of "country" (as a matter of fact, you can refer to my answer to the first question). As long as I have hands that can type, a brain that still works, the things that I am doing now is what I plan to keep on doing. Lian Yue once said, "We are the system," Li Ao said, "This is my country, and I want to make her free." I have neither their profundity nor their passion. What I will say is: "When I see something wrong, there is no one who can shut me up!"

(What else can the country do for you?) To this country now called the Peoples' Republic of China, formerly known as the country of the Tang, Song, Yuan, Ming and Qing [dynasties]: I have the things you have given me, I live on your soil, you have already given me all that you can. That which you cannot give me, I wish to give to you.

The best thing about other countries is not what they can do *for* me, but rather that they understand better what they cannot do *to* me. If you knew what you could not do, that would be doing more for me; and if you do not know that, that is what I will make you understand.[34]

As the above responses make clear, the public that formed in dialog with the questions posted by *Southern Weekend* increasingly focused on parsing the various meanings associated with the Chinese word for country or nation (*guojia* 国家), and, in particular, how to separate the institutions and apparatuses of state power from the more durable and inclusive concept of the nation. Harvard-trained Professor Ding Xueliang addressed precisely this aspect of the emerging debate in his responses to the four "difficult questions" on his blog, observing that the Chinese term for "country" actually combined the meanings of four English words: "state," "country," "land," and "nation," "the differences between which are not easy to discern: the term 'country' emphasizes the national territory and its people; whereas 'state' primarily refers to the political power of the government."[35] Within days, Chang Ping, a regular commentator in the pages of *Southern Weekend*, composed an essay entitled "What Is a Country?" sparked in part by the four questions. Chang noted that, at first, "I felt I didn't know how to respond, since I didn't know to what these various [references to] 'country' were referring." Citing Ding's nuanced response, however, Chang proposed likewise to decouple the concept of the "nation" that encompasses "a sovereign territory and its people" from that of its "ruling institutions," noting that the latter can clearly act in ways that do not accord with the interests of its citizens. Noting that the esteemed Chinese Academy of Science had just released a National Health Report that ranked the PRC in first place among "responsible nations," and the U.S. last, Chang expressed his puzzlement at how the concept of "national responsibility" might be addressed in global and historical terms, and to whom the "nation" might be held responsible.[36]

Censorship notwithstanding, the original invitation by *Southern Weekend* created at least a virtual space within which some frank exchange of views among netizens could and did take place. The cross-posting of particularly critical posts, like that offered by Wuyuesanren, in numerous fora broadened the discussion and likely stimulated other, like-minded contributions and reflections across the Web. Further, Chang Ping's commentary, building upon Ding Xueliang's ruminations, illustrates the interpenetrability of cyberpublics, and, as the following example will underscore, the revolutionary capacity of Chinese cyberspace to knit together specialized, academic discussions with popular concerns in a manner that creates recombinant effects across social strata.[37]

Contesting the market: neoliberalism and the "Lang Xianping Storm"

During the summer of 2003, a group of mainland Chinese academics turned their attention to the question of neoliberalism and its impact on market reform in China. CASS established a Research Group on Neoliberalism, which convened a conference and ultimately produced a 2004 volume entitled *Neoliberalism: Commentaries and Analyses* (*Xin ziyouzhuyi yu pinglun* 新自由主义与评析). The contributors to the volume collectively argued in part that neoliberalism represented nothing less than the "theoretical expression of the ideology of globalization of the international monopoly capitalist class, the essential aim of which is to dismember the nation-state in order to create more space for monopoly capital."[38] Shortly thereafter, in August 2004, *Guangming ribao* published an article, "Beware the Neoliberal Thought Tide," that was later reposted by interested users on a Xinhua Website. The article reportedly received 9,800 hits and over 500 tags in a mere three and a half days after its migration to the Xinhua news Web.[39]

Also in August 2004, Lang Xianping (Larry Lang), a professor of finance at the Chinese University of Hong Kong who holds a Ph.D. in Economics from the University of Pennsylvania's Wharton School, gave a lecture at Fudan University in Shanghai in which he charged that many state-owned enterprises (SOEs) – including well-known Chinese companies like Greencool, Kelon, and Haier – were using management buyouts (MBOs) to seize state assets and defraud the public. Although similar objections to the stripping of state assets had been raised previously by a small handful of others, Lang presented detailed data that described precisely how Greencool had privatized public assets, publishing the results of his study under the provocative title, "A Bacchanalian Feast as the 'State Retreats and the People Advance'."[40] In a separate article published online on the same day, Lang publicly addressed seven key questions about the leveraged MBOs staged by Greencool, marshaling an impressive series of graphs and tables that raised serious ethical questions about the conglomerate, concluding that if Gu Chujun, the chairman of the board of Greencool, "is a model Chinese entrepreneur, then I genuinely weep for China's future."[41] Whereas the CEOs of Kelon and Haier remained relatively indifferent to Lang's attack, Gu responded by threatening to file suit against Lang in a Hong Kong court of law.

By way of response, Lang moved to mobilize public opinion in his favor. With a letter from Gu's lawyer in hand, on August 17 Lang logged on to one of the most vibrant and popular chatrooms in Chinese cyberspace, sohu.com, to make his case, triggering what has since become known as the "Lang Xianping Storm" (*Lang Xianping jufeng* 郎咸平飓风) or "Lang Cyclone"(*Lang xuanfeng* 郎旋风). On August 30, Sohu established a special site entitled "The Great Debate on SOE Property Rights Reform," which quickly became the locus of a heated debate among netizens – one count by Sohu claimed as many as 30,000 Internet posts addressing the topic.[42] On August 31, the online financial information portal of *Dongnan Morning News* (*Dongnan zaobao* 东南早报) reported that over 40,000 netizens had read Lang's online critique of the Greencool MBOs, and that 90 percent of them indicated their support for Lang's position on the perils of privatization.[43] In summing up the online debate in retrospect, the *China Daily* noted that the "overwhelming majority" of opinions posted supported "the neoleftists headed by Lang."[44]

A counterpublic soon formed, with a group of defensive mainstream economic analysts and wealthy entrepreneurs at its core. Picking up on the debate in cyberspace, the *21st-Century Business Herald* published a trenchant critique of Lang with the headline "The Direction of SOE Property Rights Reform Must Not Be Changed." Noted Beijing University economist Zhang Weiying offered a heated rebuttal of the "new leftist" camp in an interview with the *Economic Observer* on August 28. The editorial department of *Beijing Youth Daily* rushed to defend Zhang and others, charging that "it is unfair for many people to criticize mainstream economists for speaking on behalf of the propertied class or for their own self-interests. If he had not believed in a grand principle, Zhang Weiying could not have braved the tide."[45] For his part, Zhang continues to argue that economic policymakers need to remain insulated from public opinion, particularly as it is circulated on the Internet, because Chinese netizens are easily misled.[46]

By September 15, Lang's trenchant criticism of not only leveraged MBOs, but neoliberal market reform, had marshaled sufficient public attention that ten well-known mainland Chinese academics issued a formal statement supporting Lang and criticizing the "neoliberal views" that lay behind China's efforts to restructure SOEs. Within days, three economists – Zuo Dapei, Yang Fan, and Han Deqiang – wrote a letter to the Chinese leadership demanding an investigation of the three companies researched by Lang, calling for hearings on the attrition of state assets through unmonitored privatization, and urging the leadership to rethink the entire process of state enterprise reform.[47]

However, the public that formed on the Internet to debate the issue continued to widen, ultimately adding an impressive diversity of voices to what had begun chiefly as an academic exercise. On September 23, 2004, a netizen referring to himself as "Mr. Yundanshuinuan," a laid-off worker in his fifties, commented that the discussion on the *People's Daily* "Strong Nation Forum" struck him as "odd" insofar as "the sole missing voice is that of the workers." Forum participants responded with the following comments:

- State enterprise workers have no right to speak; their only right is to be laid off.
- Where are the political leaders of the people? Come out and speak a word of justice for the proletariat and do one good thing.
- I appeal, with my blood, to the Central Committee to immediately stop and reexamine a process of state enterprise reform that is dominated by power and money!
- Who is listening even if workers are speaking out?
- Where can workers speak out?
- The reform should enrich workers and farmers. Why not?
- How many super-rich individuals have been created through the plundering of state assets?!

- How much say have the masses of workers had in the more than 10 years of SOE reform? Oh, government, who do you represent?
- This is easy to understand. The industrial working class is no longer the leading class today. Their words have no weight. It is not that they are not speaking; it is that nobody listens to them.
- In the eyes of the elite, workers and farmers are superfluous . . .
- This strange phenomenon clashes with our Constitution and the nature of our state! This is so inconsistent with the working-class political party of ours!![48]

Meanwhile, in real time, workers at a former military factory in Chongqing staged a strike that began on August 18, 2004, just as the "Lang Xianping Storm" was brewing in cyberspace. The Chongqing 3403 Factory, which workers claimed was worth nearly 200 million *yuan*, was sold to a private entrepreneur for a mere 22 million *yuan*, with 20 million of the down payment offered in the form of a loan. Naide, the corporation that made the purchase, was a former SOE that had been privatized and acquired by factory director Lin Chaoyang in 1998 under the Chongqing government's SOE privatization program. Lin targeted the 3403 Factory, 30 kilometers away. When the 3403 Factory was on the verge of declaring bankruptcy, Lin became its designated "backdoor" purchaser, in part through colluding with the 3403 factory manager, whom he later rewarded with a handsome sinecure. When the workers learned of the situation, they mobilized to purchase the factory themselves for 30 million *yuan*, but Chongqing officials dragged their feet in responding to the offer. On August 25, 2004, more than 300 police officers stormed the factory, and five days later more than 1,200 police were sent in to put down the strike. On August 28, 2004, *China and the World* published an article signed by "Ordinary Workers at the Chongqing 3403 Factory and Chongqing Naide Industrial Corp." that charged mainstream economists and researchers like those attacking Lang Xianping with making false and groundless claims. They were, furthermore, "sucking up the sweat and blood of the people on the one hand and illegally receiving bribes from those who got rich instantly from the reforms on the other." On the "Protagonist Forum," one netizen began a new subject thread with the header "Chongqing 3403 Factory: 200 million yuan worth of state assets sold for 22 million yuan; workers demanded democratic management and production for self-salvation, bloody conflict ensues," which generated the following responses between August 28 and August 31, 2004:

- Can the good leading comrades within the party who are said to exist in large numbers, especially those respected senior leaders, contact the workers in the factory? . . .
- Why can't old and new leftists mobilize 10 percent of the energy they mobilized for the petition to commemorate Mao's anniversary, to support the real struggles of Chongqing workers?

- This issue revealed that after more than several decades of revolution, some people still have answers to questions such as who creates wealth and who sustains whose life upside down. How can such individuals call themselves communists and become leaders? . . .
- This article was posted at Century Solon Forum. It attracted more than 100 hits within 10 minutes, and the Webmaster quickly deleted it . . .
- I propose . . . a petition to support 3403 Factory . . .
- May this material be gathered together and be integrated with our support for Lang Xianping, so as to stop SOE property rights reform?
- I appeal to the entire working class in Chongqing with industrial workers as its core force, to unite and oppose privatization.[49]

As the foregoing comments clearly demonstrate, publics and counterpublics in Chinese cyberspace not only remain fully cognizant of the censorship and surveillance to which they are subjected on the Web, but even openly discuss their frustration with the limitations placed upon public discourse in cyberspace. Yet perhaps even more intriguing, as the next examples demonstrate, is the manner in which the dynamics of censorship have come to be internalized by Chinese netizens, who have banded together over time to exercise their own form of social control by using the Web as a form of grassroots policing of moral conduct.

Confronting society: human flesh search engines

Perhaps one of the most vibrant foci of recent debates in Chinese cyberspace is the rise of new social forces and social phenomena in the post-Mao era. To the extent that disturbing new trends are seen as the products of market reform and/or the gradual "retreat" of the state, some of these debates have powerful political overtones, and offer implicit critiques of the Party and its current leadership. Equally telling is the extent to which Chinese netizens have been making use of the Internet not merely to engage in public deliberation about such social phenomena, but also to organize, from the bottom up, to exact social justice on those who have been accused of transgressing social norms.

On February 26, 2006, a netizen named "Glass Shard" (*cui boli zhazi* 碎玻璃渣子) entered a post on the discussion board of Mop magazine (*maopu luntan* 猫扑论坛) under the heading "Outrage: bloodthirsty middle-aged hottie slaughters small animal." The post included a photo of a provocatively dressed middle-aged woman trampling a kitten to death with her stiletto heels, which the poster said had been excerpted from a longer video. The clip that finally circulated in Chinese cyberspace showed an elegantly dressed woman in a scenic public park who briefly cuddled a small kitten before putting it on the ground and stomping it to death with her stiletto heels. The shocking footage elicited outrage from Chinese netizens, who quickly spread the footage across all of the major fora in Chinese cyberspace, demanding to know who she was. Netizens gathered at the Mop discussion board, not only to express their outrage and disgust, but also to exchange information gleaned from the film clip. Within days, the video was traced back to a user calling herself "Gainmas," registered on the Website of a Hangzhou-based company, www.crushworld.net, who was also found to have used the same name to purchase a pair of high-heeled shoes on eBay the previous year. Enraged netizens launched a denial of service attack that paralyzed the crushworld Website. While the mystery woman in the video was temporarily dubbed the "Kitten Killer of Hangzhou," netizens quickly discovered that the public park in which the scene was filmed was in Heilongjiang, and closed in. The name of the cameraman was revealed by a netizen who posed as a potential buyer of the film; other Luobei County residents identified the woman in the video as a nurse who worked at the pharmacy of a local hospital. She had also registered with QQ, a popular mainland Chinese message service, where she posted of herself: "I furiously crush everything to do with you and me."[50] It took netizens a total of six days to uncover the true identity of the culprit, who issued a lukewarm apology blaming the incident on her despondence following a marital separation. It did little to mollify an enraged cyber-public. Despite the apology and the fact that there was no applicable law in the PRC prohibiting cruel treatment of animals, both she and the cameraman who filmed the episode lost their jobs.

What emerged from the incident was a phenomenon that has since become known as the "human flesh search engine" (*renrou sousuo yinqing* 人肉搜索引擎), in which self-organized publics of Chinese netizens collectively mobilize their power on the Internet to investigate issues or incidents of interest to them. In the wake of the "kitten killer" incident, a "human flesh search engine" sprang into attack against a 52-year-old farmer, Zhou Zhenglong, who submitted a photo he claimed to have taken in his backyard of the supposedly extinct wild South China tiger. Zhou received 20,000 *yuan* from excited officials at the Shaanxi Department of Forestry for the photo, who quickly staged a major press conference to announce the tiger's discovery. Forums across Chinese cyberspace filled up with posts accusing Zhou of fraud; a few weeks later, netizens traced the photo to an old Lunar New Year poster, leading to Zhou's arrest. On September 27, 2008, he was sentenced to two and a half years in prison for fraud.

More recently, Jiang Yan blogged privately about her devastation after discovering her husband's infidelity shortly before jumping to her death from the couple's 24th-floor apartment. Following the dramatic suicide, a friend of the victim established a memorial Website to which she uploaded the diary posts, and some photographs of the once-happily married couple. Outraged Chinese netizens determined that they would seek a form of posthumous justice for Jiang. Within only days, photos of the unfaithful husband, an advertising executive at Saatchi & Saatchi in Beijing, along with his mistress, were posted on various Internet sites, along with their phone numbers, addresses and national ID numbers. Enraged netizens defaced both his home and the home of his parents with slogans accusing him of causing his wife's death, and flooded Saatchi & Saatchi with harassing phone calls until the firm decided to fire him.

Last spring, Wang sued Zhang Leyi, the friend of his deceased wife, for uploading her diary. He also sued leading Chinese Internet portals Tianya and Daqi for violation of his privacy and defamation of character. In December 2008, the Chaoyang District Court in Beijing fined Daqi.com and Zhang Leyi a total of 8,000 *yuan* (about U.S.$1,100).[51]

In April 2008, a 21-year-old Duke University student from Shandong province named Grace Wang tried to mediate between rival groups on the Duke campus engaged in a "Free Tibet" protest. Wang's involvement was posted to the Internet, where she was quickly labeled a "race traitor." "Human flesh search engines" quickly uncovered her address and phone number in the U.S., as well as her parents' address in Shandong, resulting in a stream of death threats to all involved, and an incident of vandalism in which a pot of human excrement was left on her parents' doorstep.[52]

As the foregoing case suggests, "human flesh search engines" have the capacity to train their collective attention on policing not only social mores, but political issues as well. In October 2008, Lin Jiaxiang, a party secretary in the Shenzhen Maritime Administration, was caught on the closed-circuit security camera at a restaurant asking an 11-year old girl, who was dining with her parents at the time, for directions to the washroom. When Lin appeared confused by the directions, she offered to escort him. The young girl claims that when they got to the door of the washroom, Lin grabbed her by the neck and forced her into the room in an apparent attempt to molest her. The restaurant camera shows that moments later the girl ran back to her parents to report the incident. During the argument that ensued between Lin, the child's parents, and restaurant staff, Lin is clearly heard to exclaim: "Do you know who I am? I was sent here by the Beijing Ministry of Transportation, my rank is the same as your mayor. So what if I pinched a little child's neck? Who the fuck are you people to me?! Do you dare fuck with me? Just watch how I am going to deal with you!" After the story appeared online, and the footage of the incident was posted on YouTube,[53] netizens identified Lin and his position within the Shenzhen Maritime Administration. Lin was subsequently fired from his job and it was reported that he would be "severely punished."[54]

Two months later, Nanjing city Jiangning district Housing Administration director Zhou Jiugeng was relieved from duty for "expressing inappropriate opinions to the media without authorization, which caused negative social effects," and for "using public funds to purchase high-priced cigarettes." The dismissal came after an incident in which, against considerable public opinion, he actually fined two real estate developers in the city for lowering their prices in a slow real estate market. He argued in the local press that he had taken the action "for the people" of Nanjing, the vast majority of whom naturally welcomed the price drop. His assertions led angry netizens to uncover a photo of Zhou with a high-priced brand of cigarettes on his desk and a Constantin watch worth 10,000 *yuan* on his wrist, items no honest public servant in the PRC could reasonably afford to purchase.[55]

On January 18, 2009, the Jiangsu People's Congress Standing Committee approved the Xuzhou City "Computer Information System Security Protection Regulations," a set of local ordinances designed to delimit some of the potentially harmful effects of human flesh search engines. The regulations criminalize the disclosure and sharing of private information about others on the Internet without their permission. Both originators and propagators may face a fine of up to 5,000 *yuan*, and, in more serious cases, offenders may be barred from using a computer or accessing the Internet for six months. Not surprisingly, news of the regulation triggered an avalanche of commentary on the Web, with an estimated 90 percent of the posters on "People's Net" opposed, because they claimed such restrictions "worked against the monitoring of government officials by grassroots citizens." One netizen commented that "corrupt officials must love this piece of legislation." NetEase ran a survey on the same day, asking, "Are you worried about being the target of a human flesh search?" More than 80 percent of the netizens selected the response, "I am not worried because I haven't done anything wrong." Another 15 percent, however, expressed concern, and wanted laws banning the activity.[56]

The following day, the leader of the Xuzhou People's Congress Standing Committee clarified that the law was not intended to be a total ban on "human flesh search engines," because state law permitted "netizens . . . [to] expose bad social behavior, or report the illegal activities of leaders and cadres, or criticize uncivilized behavior in society." Furthermore, "it is the right of the public to monitor the government." Citing the case of the former Quanshan district party secretary Dong Feng, who was denounced on the Internet such that the party disciplinary committee was alerted and he was ultimately prosecuted, the representative pointed out that the regulations were not intended to ban public reporting of illegal conduct on the part of officials."[57]

On QQ.com, news of the regulations elicited a wave of comments from netizens, one of whom noted:

> This type of corrosive behavior falls in the space between law and morality, which, when deliberately used to exert influence, [shows] our society is devoid of a value system based upon genuine justice. This is also a kind of mob action that can cast a permanent shadow on a victim. Therefore, presently among a people whose moral thought lacks sufficient quality (*suzhi* 素质), the appearance of this law will certainly have a positive use. Only the manner of its execution begs improvement.[58]

194   *Patricia M. Thornton*

Conclusion

When Deng Xiaoping famously shut the door on debating reform in 1992,[59] the introduction of the Internet to the PRC two years later opened a small but widening window through which sporadic "contentious conversations" over a wide variety of issues – political, economic, and social – do take place. Western concern over the power and prevalence of the PRC's vast Internet censorship regime – which is now said by some to employ at least 30,000 full-time cybercops to monitor online conversations and delete "offensive" and "inappropriate" messages[60] – is by no means unjustified. The recent spate of arrests over the circulation of "Charter 08," which calls for greater freedom of expression and free elections, and the publication of which was timed to coincide with the 60th anniversary of the Universal Declaration of Human Rights, attests to the validity of such concerns. Even more troubling is the possibility that Chinese authorities may be enticing netizens seeking to circumvent censorship into using bogus proxy servers, known as "honey pots," allowing Internet censors not only to monitor viewing patterns, but also to entrap would-be cyberdissidents before banned content is distributed or, in some cases, actually downloaded.[61] Official monitoring of TOM-Skype, a Web-based communications tool established as a joint venture involving a Chinese high-tech firm and eBay, has already been uncovered.[62]

Yet, as the preceding examples have demonstrated, it is misleading to imagine that Chinese netizens have been paralyzed or silenced by the operation of Chinese censors. Instead, the Chinese language Web has emerged as a vital node not only for popular contention and far-ranging debate about a variety of political topics, the progress of market reform, and decline of social mores, but even as a vehicle through which Chinese netizens police social conduct on the part of ordinary citizens as well as that of authorities. Moreover, the extent and nature of Internet censorship itself are frequent topics of discussion on the Web; as of early 2009, at least one high-ranking official in the Beijing Internet Propaganda Management Office found himself targeted by a "human flesh search engine" for allegedly receiving bribes.[63]

Western fascination with the existence and operations of the "Great Firewall" has tended to enhance the perceived division between the censorial power of the party-state, on the one hand, and the discursive power of the Chinese cyberpublic, on the other. Yet, as we begin to contemplate the implications of new research on the historical emergence of the bourgeois public sphere in the West that shows it to have been both more exclusive and more internally heterogeneous than some have imagined,[64] we may end up coming around to a fuller appreciation of how public spheres may develop in other contexts and in other times, even those that appear to thrive beneath the censor's gaze.

Notes

1 吴绮敏，孙承斌，"唱响奋进凯歌，弘扬民族精神－记胡锦涛总书记在人民日报社考察工作，" 人民日报 (2008/06/21). On the renaissance of "public opinion" in post-Mao China, see Stanley Rosen's "Public Opinion and Reform in the People's Republic of China," *Studies in Comparative Communism* 22(2/3) (1989), pp. 153–70, and "The Rise (and Fall) of Public Opinion in post-Mao China," in Richard Baum, ed., *Reform and Reaction in Post-Mao China* (New York: Routledge, 1991), pp. 60–83.

2 Xinhua General News Service, "Chinese President Holds First Web Chat with Citizens," June 20, 2008; and Chinadaily.com.cn, "Hu Makes History with Online Chat," June 21, 2008, accessed via LexisNexis.

3 Jonathan Watts, " 'Boss Hu' Ducks Tricky Questions in Online Chat," *Guardian* (London), June 21, 2008, p. 22.

4 Jeremy Page, "Hu Pokes His Head over 'Great Firewall' to Seek the Opinions of 221m Netizens," *The Times* (London), June 24, 2008, p. 29.

5 Geremie R. Barmé and Sang Ye, "The Great Firewall of China," *Wired* 5.06 (June 1997), available at http://www.wired.com/wired/archive/5.06/china.html (accessed January 28, 2008).

6 Karin Davies, "Reagan Pays Tribute to Chinese Demonstrators," United Press International, June 13, 1989, accessed via LexisNexis.

7 Thomas L. Friedman, "Censors Beware," *New York Times*, July 25, 2000, p. 25. Friedman's comment was directed at the liberalizing force of the Internet in Jordan.

8 Cisco Systems, Silicon Valley's largest company and a supplier of hardware to China, recently faced an investor revolt when 29 percent of shareholders voted for a motion that demanded that it should report on how its products were being used to limit free speech. Rhys Blakely, "How Long Can Great Firewall of China Last?," *The Times* (London), May 18, 2007, p. 71. Paul Buchheit, former Google employee and inventor of gmail, is also credited with initiating the "Google, don't be evil" campaign, inspired in part as an employee protest against Google's co-operation with Chinese censors in 2001.

9 The module is called "The China Channel Firefox Add-on," and can be downloaded at http://chinachannel.hk/ (accessed January 28, 2009). A variety of Websites, like WebSitePulse (http://www.Websitepulse.com/help/testtools.china-test.html), also provide real-time testing of individual URL addresses in the PRC.

10 See Bloggers' Blog at http://www.bloggersblog.com/censorship/ (last accessed January 29, 2009).

11 The song appears on the album "Follies in Great Cities" (Tough Love Records, 2008); the band's myspace Webpage can be viewed at http://www.myspace.com/honeytraponmyspace (accessed January 28, 2009).

12 The exchange appears on http://slashdot.org/article.pl?sid=05/05/11/2258207&tid=217 (accessed January 28, 2009).

13 Liu Kang, *Globalization and Cultural Trends in China* (Honolulu: University of Hawaii Press, 2007), p. 82.

14 Sebastian Usher, "China Shuts Down Outspoken Blog," March 8, 2006, accessed January 28, 2009 at http://news.bbc.co.uk/1/hi/world/asia-pacific/4787302.stm.

15 Geoffrey A. Fowler and Juying Qin, "Chinese Bloggers Stage Hoax Aimed at Censorship Debate," *Wall Street Journal*, March 14, 2006. p. B.3. The blogs in question can be viewed at Wang Xiaofeng's (王晓峰) blog "Massage Milk 按摩乳," which can be viewed at http://lydon.ycool.com/; Yuan Lei's (袁蕾) blog, "Milk Pig 乳猪," is at http://milkpig.ycool.com/.

16 Joshua Kurlantzick, "Dictatorship.com," *New Republic*, April 5, 2004, p. 21.

17 Wang Jisi, "The Internet in China: A New Fantasy?," *New Perspectives Quarterly* 18(1) (Winter 2001), http://www.digitalnpq.org/archive/2001_winter/Internet.html (accessed January 29, 2009).
18 See, for example, Mauro F. Guillén and Sandra L. Suárez, "Explaining the Global Digital Divide: Economic, Political and Sociological Drivers of Cross-National Internet Use," *Social Forces* 84(2) (December 2005), pp. 687–9.
19 China Internet Network Information Center, "Statistical Survey Report on the Internet Development in China (Abridged Edition)" (July 2008), p. 10. http://www.cnnic.cn/download/2008/CNNIC22threport-en.pdf (accessed October 10, 2008).
20 Center for Social Development, Chinese Academy of Social Sciences, "Surveying Internet Usage and Its Impact in Seven Chinese Cities" (November, 2007), www.markle.org/downloadable_assets/china_Internet_survey_11.2007.pdf (accessed January 28, 2009).
21 Bill Xia, "The Coming Crash of the Matrix," *China Rights Forum* 3 (2004), p. 43.
22 Center for Social Development, Chinese Academy of Social Sciences, "Surveying Internet Usage and Its Impact in Seven Chinese Cities."
23 Guobin Yang, "The Coevolution of the Internet and Civil Society in China," *Asian Survey*, 43:3 (May/June 2003), p. 406.
24 Guobin Yang, "The Internet and Civil Society in China: A Preliminary Assessment," *Journal of Contemporary China* (August 2003) 12(36), p. 465.
25 Zhao Yuezhi, *Communication in China: Political Economy, Power, and Conflict* (Lanham, MD: Rowman and Littlefield, 2007), p. 62.
26 郭良, "2000 年北京、上海、广州、成都、长沙－互联网使用状况及影响的调查报告" (2001 年4月), available online at http://ec.youth.cn/itre/. The statistic in question appears in Table 3-4-1, at http://ec.youth.cn/itre/text6.htm.
27 Michael Warner, "Publics and Counterpublics," *Public Culture* 14(1) (2002), p. 50.
28 Walter Lippman famously argued, "the public is not . . . a fixed body of individuals. It is merely those persons who are interested an affair . . . The membership is not fixed . . . it changes with the issue." See *The Phantom Public* (New York: Macmillan, 1925), pp. 77, 110.
29 Nancy Fraser, "Rethinking the Public Sphere: A Contribution to the Critique of Actually Existing Democracy," in Craig Calhoun, ed., *Habermas and the Public Sphere* (Cambridge, MA: MIT Press, 1992), pp. 109–42.
30 南方周末评论部, "国庆，我们一起想想'我和我的国家'," September 28, 2008, accessed January 28, 2009 at http://www.infzm.com/content/18048.
31 Selected responses to the three questions can be viewed at http://www.infzm.com/content/18049, http://www.infzm.com/content/18053, and http://www.infzm.com/content/18050, respectively (accessed January 28, 2009). Posted responses to the first and second questions have been translated into English on the blog at http://www.zonaeuropa.com/20081004_1.htm and http://www.zonaeuropa.com/20081002_1.htm, respectively (accessed January 28, 2009).
32 熊培云, "2008 年，国庆，答《南方周末》评论周刊问," October 3, 2008. , accessed on January 28, 2009 at http://www.sixiangguo.com/.
33 Here the author refers a oft-repeated phrase from the campaign to emulate Lei Feng, a Mao-era model solider who purportedly wrote in his diary that he modestly sought to have only the "spirit of a screw" 螺丝钉的精神 in service to the vast machinery of the party-state.
34 五岳散人，回答一下《南方周末》的问题, October 3, 2008, accessed October 15, 2008 at http://www.bullog.cn/blogs/yaobo/archives/185512.aspx. Excerpts of his responses have also been translated into English at http://chinadigitaltimes.net/2008/10/answering-those-questions-on-the-southern-weekend/ (last accessed January 28, 2009). The above translations are my own.

35 丁学良回答《南方周末》的艰难问题, October 11, 2008, accessed January 28, 2009 at http://blog.sina.com.cn/s/indexlist_1350338334_5.html.
36 "长平专栏：'国家'是什么," 南方都市报 (2008年10月11日, AA31) 网友评论. Chang's essay was posted on numerous blogs and in various fora across the Web. Accessed January 29, 2009 at http://epaper.nddaily.com/A/html/2008–10/11/content_594976.htm.
37 On the recombinant potential of the Internet, see Jonathan Bach and David Stark, "Link, Search, Interact: The Co-Evolution of NGOs and Interactive Technology," *Theory, Culture & Society* (2004) 21(3), p. 101.
38 "国际垄断资产阶级关于全球化意识形态的理论表现，其根本目标是肢解民族国家，为垄断资本提供更多的空间。" 李瑞英, "警惕新自由主义对我国的影响," 《光明日报》, June 14, 2004, http://www.cas.cn/html/Dir/2004/06/14/0314.htm.
39 韩强：经济现象的哲学思考 – 评新自由主义 (2004年11月19日), accessed January 28, 2009 at http://finance.sina.com.cn.
40 郎咸平, "在'国退民进'盛筵中狂欢的格林柯尔," accessed January 28, 2009 at http://finance.sina.com.cn.
41 郎咸平, "七问顾雏军曝光格林柯尔并购神话" 21世纪经济报导 (2004年8月16日), accessed January 29, 2009 at http://business.sohu.com/20040816/n221548398.shtml.
42 Zhao Yuezhi, *Communications in China* (New York: Routledge, 2008), pp. 291, 305. Zhao provides an excellent analysis of the Lang Xianping incident in Chapter 6 of the volume cited.
43 企业舆论环境十年来最坏？, 东南早报 (2004年8月31日) accessed January 29, 2009 at http://www.qzwb.com/gb/content/2004–8/31/content_1343625.htm.
44 "Revamp Rules to Promote Equality," *China Daily*, January 7, 2005, accessed January 30, 2009 at http://www.chinadaily.com.cn/chinagate/doc/2005–01/07/content_406928.htm.
45 Zhao Yuezhi, *Communications in China,* pp. 317–18.
46 Personal communication with Professor Zhang Weiying, January 12, 2009.
47 Joseph Fewsmith, "China Under Hu Jintao," *China Leadership Monitor* 14 (2005), p. 5.
48 Zhao Yuezhi, *Communications in China*, pp. 307–9.
49 Zhao Yuezhi, *Communications in China*, pp. 309–10, 314–15.
50 Richard Spencer, "Just Who Is the Glamorous Kitten Killer of Hangzhou?," *The Telegraph*, March 4, 2006, accessed January 30, 2009 at http://www.telegraph.co.uk/news/worldnews/asia/china/1512082/Just-who-is-the-glamorous-kitten-killer-of-Hangzhou.html.
51 Peh Shing Huei, "Cyber Hunters in for Crash Landing: Online Harassment and Exposure of 'Public Enemies' May Soon Be Made Illegal in China," *Straits Times* (January 3, 2009); see also "People at the Mercy of an Online Mob," *South China Morning Post*, September 8, 2008, both accessed via Nexis UK.
52 Sim Chi Yin, "Ugly Side of Online Nationalism in China," *Straits Times*, April 26, 2008, accessed via Nexis UKs; Grace Wang later published an editorial describing the experience. See Grace Wang, "Caught in the Middle, Called a Traitor," *Washington Post*, April 20, 2008, p. B1.
53 Last accessed February 3, 2009 at http://www.youtube.com/watch?v=noRiR4ZzXgQ.
54 "深圳海事局书记涉猥亵女童被停职" 南方都市报 (2008年11月01日), last accessed February 2, 2009 at http://www.nanfangdaily.com.cn/epaper/nfds/content/20081101/ArticelA01002FM.htm.
55 王斯莉, "房产局长抽天价烟续：网友曝其弟为房产老总," 每日经济新闻, December 18, 2008, last accessed February 04, 2009, at http://sc.people.com.cn/news/HTML/2008/12/18/20081218094432.htm.

56 "人肉搜索禁令保民不保官：举报贪官、揭露丑恶现象等人肉搜索行为均不在徐州立法禁止之列，"南方都市报 (2009年1月21日), accessed February 2, 2009 at http://epaper.nddaily.com/A/html/2009-01/21/content_691558.htm.

57 "人肉搜索禁令保民不保官，"南方都市报 (2009年1月21日).

58 Posted on QQ.com discussion board under discussion headed, 江苏徐州立法禁止人肉搜索 最高可罚5000元, January 22, 2009, accessed February 3, 2009 at http://comment5.news.qq.com/comment.htm?site=news&id=18116733#reload.

59 邓小平文选 (北京：人民出版社, 1993), pp. 374–5.

60 This number is an oft-cited and much-disputed figure. See, for example, Nicholas D. Kristof, "In China It's ******* vs. Netizens," *New York Times*, June 20, 2006; but also Tim Johnson, "Misconceptions about China's Internet," Knight Ridder Washington Bureau, September 28, 2007, both accessed via NexisUK.

61 David Wilson, "Beware the Treachery behind Proxy Servers," *South China Morning Post*, February 25, 2003, p. 7.

62 Matt Hartley, "How a Canadian cracked the Great Firewall of China: Forgotten Password, Creative Hacking Lead Toronto-based Researcher to Stumble onto Surveillance Network Tracking Chinese Dissidents," *Globe and Mail* (Canada), October 3, 2008, p. A3.

63 See, for example, 张涛, "张涛：网管办的陈华是个什么样的共产党员？,"中国报道周刊 (2009年01月22日), last accessed January 28, 2009 at http://www.china-week.com/html/4680.htm.

64 On the exclusionary practices that delimited the public sphere's emergence in the West, see Joan Landes, *Women and the Public Sphere in the French Revolution* (Ithaca: Cornell University Press, 1988); Mary Ryan, "Gender and Public Access: Women's Politics in Nineteenth Century America," and George Eley, Nations, Publics, and Political Cultures: Placing Habermas in the Eighteenth Century," in Craig J. Calhoun, ed., *Habermas and the Public Sphere* (Cambridge, MA: MIT Press, 1993).

9 The politics of art repatriation

Nationalism, state legitimation, and Beijing's looted zodiac animal heads[1]

Richard Kraus

At the February 25, 2009 Christie's auction in Paris, two Chinese zodiac heads (*shoushou* 兽首), the rabbit and the rat, came up for sale. They were part of the collection of the late French fashion designer Yves Saint Laurent.[2] The sale arose at a time of tense relations between France and China, focused partly on Beijing's unhappiness with French support for the Dalai Lama (达赖喇嘛). Chinese officials demanded the return of the zodiac heads, which it declared were Chinese "national treasures" (*guobao* 国宝) looted by the British in the nineteenth century. Chinese lawyers sought to block the sale in a French court. Pierre Bergé, Saint Laurent's partner and seller of the massive art collection, further fueled the dispute by offering to give the two statues to China – in exchange for human rights reforms and Tibetan freedom. When the sale went ahead, China announced sanctions against Christie's designed to hurt its business with Asian customers.[3]

China had purchased the boar head rather quietly in 2003, and in 2007 Macao casino magnate Stanley Ho (何鸿燊) bought the horse head and gave it to the nation. Thus there was reason to imagine that in this sale a Chinese buyer would emerge to make another patriotic donation. But what happened at the Paris auction was quite different. A mystery telephone bidder's offer of U.S.$40 million was the high price. But Cai Mingchao (蔡铭超), a Xiamen (厦门) art dealer, disclosed several days later that his bid had been insincere, that "I shall not pay the money. I did the bidding just to stop the auction, and I did it on behalf of the whole Chinese people."[4] Cai claimed that he had acted without the knowledge of the Chinese government, which apparently feared that the heads had been purchased by a foreign collector. Nonetheless, doubts were strengthened by the fact that Cai was an (unpaid) advisor to the National Treasures Fund, which is affiliated with the Ministry of Culture.[5] Adding to the confusion was a rumor that Cai's fake offer was higher than the real bid of a London-based Chinese business executive who had intended to donate the statues to his homeland.[6]

Reaction in China was mixed: was Cai was a fool who had damaged China's reputation? Or was he a patriot who had challenged an unjust international system for dealing in plundered national treasures? Had China's Ministry of Culture been involved? If so, why? Why should the Chinese government be so sensitive to the international trade in Chinese artifacts?

The magic of political legitimacy

Political legitimacy is a kind of public illusion, a shared and often fragile understanding that a regime is somehow appropriate, fitting, and in some vague sense a part of the natural order of things. Because legitimacy is ultimately a cultural concept, it is understandable that its claims often center upon specific cultural objects. These can be art works whose history may be imagined to represent the nation's, and which are surrounded by an aura that may extend its magic to the possessor of the art.[7]

Students of Chinese politics can easily identify moments when the magic of legitimacy was questioned or refashioned around some object which might be famous or otherwise remain obscure: peasant rebels who raid the costume trunks of opera troupes for the "imperial gown" which will make a rebel resemble an emperor; Cultural Revolutionary (*wenhua dageming* 文化大革命) struggles over physical possession of a bureaucratic seal, believed to be the talisman of office; Tang Taizong's (唐太宗) decision to take to his grave China's most celebrated piece of calligraphy – Wang Xizhi's (王羲之) *Orchid Pavilion Preface*; Hua Guofeng's (华国锋) embrace of the oil painting of Mao Zedong (毛泽东) assuring him that *With You In Charge, My Heart is at Ease*. In none of these instances can one specify how much "legitimacy" was conveyed by the cultural object in question, yet political actors certainly behave as if legitimacy is at stake.

Political legitimacy must be won on two fronts. Not only must domestic populations believe in their rulers' right to occupy office, but foreign states must recognize these same rulers' authority through diplomacy, if the nation is to participate fully and conventionally in international affairs.

When political legitimacy is imagined to derive from objects which reside outside the nation, a peculiar combination of politics arises. Internally, the object becomes the subject of the nationalist politics of popular indignation, yet externally, the object is associated with the far more refined elite political world of fine arts and diplomacy. For instance, after World War II, the United States was in possession of Hungary's Crown of St. Stephen. A gift from the pope to Hungary's king a thousand years earlier, the crown was the nation's most visible emblem of national continuity and political legitimacy. By refusing to return it to Hungary, the United States withheld a key symbol of legitimacy from a communist government with which it had otherwise normal relations. Émigrés who understood the meaning of the crown protested President Carter's decision to transfer the crown from Fort Knox to Budapest, even as the communist government celebrated in its recovery.

Art stolen from China during the long era of imperialist plunder arouses indignant patriotism in China. Yet while it evokes little concern in most foreigners, it is of great interest to the elite world of fine arts. I will use one such act of plunder, the 1860 sack of Beijing's *Yuanming Yuan* (圆明园), as a starting point for exploring China's relationship to its purloined past. In brief, the story is about the use of state power to return a set of statues to

China. But this success in overcoming the national shame of imperialist plunder is eroded by China's continuing position as an exporter of newly plundered art treasures for foreign collectors. While China's successful repatriation of one set of statues may have some legitimizing symbolism within China, the looting of archeological sites remains a serious problem.

The zodiac statues of the Garden of Perfect Brightness

The 1860 sack of the "Garden of Perfect Brightness" (*Yuanming Yuan* 万园之园) stands out among the many contemptuous gestures of European imperialism toward a weakened China. Located some five miles to the northwest of Beijing, this elaborate garden was constructed over several decades beginning in 1709 as a retreat for China's Manchu rulers.[8] The *Yuanming Yuan* is often known in English as the "Old Summer Palace," to distinguish it from the present Summer Palace, which was imagined to have been built as its replacement. In fact, the "new" Summer Palace (*Yihe Yuan* 颐和园) began as a part of the older garden, and the *Yuanming Yuan* was never a summer palace, but the favored residence and political center for the Qing emperors.

The Garden of Perfect Brightness featured many architectural delights modeled upon the styles of the wealthy and sophisticated lower Yangzi region. The cosmopolitan Qianlong emperor (乾隆皇帝) added several European style buildings in this garden, under the supervision of the Italian émigré artist Giuseppe Castiglione. Castiglione, well known in China as "Lang Shining" (郎世宁), was a Jesuit who worked in China from 1715 until his death in 1766. As painter and architect, he introduced Sinified Western styles to Chinese court circles.[9]

For the *Yuanming Yuan*, Castiglione worked under the inspiration of Versailles, fashioning elaborate stone buildings set amidst colorful walkways. In front of a large building known as the *Haiyantang* (Seafood Banquet Hall 海晏堂), he designed an elaborate fountain. Twelve animal heads, representing the figures of the Chinese zodiac, were cast from bronze and placed atop life-size human bodies which were arranged alongside a pool of water. Every two hours a different animal spouted water, so that the fountain served also as a clock. At noon, all twelve animals joined in an expectorating ensemble. The complex mechanism broke down in 1786, never to be repaired.

In October 1860, French and British troops destroyed the *Yuanming Yuan* as punishment for Chinese recalcitrance in settling the Second Opium War. The immediate rationalization was the claim that Chinese had killed European prisoners, but the broader political purpose was to press a reluctant Chinese government to accept European terms. The British took the lead in destruction, putting wooden structures to the torch, demolishing as much of the stone structures as they could, and of course, seizing as much loot as they could carry. According to Captain Charles ("Chinese") Gordon, later famous as imperialism's martyred general in Sudan, "Everyone was wild for plunder." "You can scarcely imagine the beauty and magnificence of the places we burnt. It made one's heart sore to burn them; in fact, these palaces were so large, and we were so pressed for time, that we could not plunder them carefully."[10]

The British leader was the 8th Earl of Elgin, and son of the notorious thief of the Parthenon Marbles (known in London as the Elgin Marbles, but not in Greece).[11] Perhaps it was a family tradition, or a genetic disorder (*his* son, the 9th Earl, was Viceroy of India 1895–99, and no doubt also managed to take some nice things home to Britain). China had declined sharply from its power and prosperity of the previous century, and was unable to repel the European forces. The First Opium War (1838–42) began a long cycle of humiliation at the hands of European armies whose military superiority only increased with each year. At the same time, China was torn by the massive disruption of the Taiping Rebellion (太平天国), a civil war which cost some twenty million lives over two decades.

The *Yuanming Yuan* was rich in symbolic potential; it was there in 1793 that the British emissary, Macartney, was received by the Qianlong emperor, causing a crisis when he refused to kowtow.[12] But the British commanders seemed unaware of the coincidence, although they took back to England several cannons which had been presented to the emperor by George III.[13]

Among the treasures looted by the European soldiers were the decapitated animals of Castiglione's zodiac fountain. Their plunder included other work with a distinctive international character, such as a set of engravings of Qing military victories over the Western Mongols. Sketches from the field in the eighteenth century had been turned into paintings, which were sent to France to be engraved on copper plates from 1766 to 1775. The Qianlong emperor had later inscribed poems upon the engravings.[14]

As cultural property, the loot from the *Yuanming Yuan* is awash in symbolism. European usurpation of the emperor's treasures and destruction of his palaces denoted a new stage in relations in which Chinese were forced to confront their defeat and humiliation. That these were the emperor's personal belongings heightened the injury to China's sovereignty.[15]

The *Yuanming Yuan* remained a shattered ruin for many years, a visible scar in Beijing to remind all Chinese of their government's weakness and of the West's might. While before 1860 the garden had been a private pleasure palace for the Emperor, after its sack it became a public spot, with contending interpretations inscribed upon its ruins.

When reformers such as Kang Youwei (康有为) and Liang Qiqiao (梁启超) saw objects looted from the imperial garden on public display in Paris and New York, they were humiliated by their nation's weakness, and strengthened in their resolve to overthrow its tottering Qing dynasty.[16] It was not until after the dynasty's fall in 1911, that the radical May 4 movement began to spread a popular awareness of national shame from the West's plunder of Chinese art.[17] In response to growing nationalist resentment, in 1930 the Kuomintang (国民党) government legislated to limit the participation of foreigners in archeological digs and prevent them from purchasing relics.[18]

In the People's Republic, the grounds of the former imperial garden have been turned into a public park, with the ruins a major center of attraction, where young people pose to have their photos taken with scenic fractured columns in the background. The government displays these relics in a rather subdued manner. Instead of indignant displays of the history of their destruction, a long signboard reproduced in their entirety the unequal treaties forced upon China by Britain, France, the United States, Russia, Japan, Germany, and lesser imperialist powers, joined by a simple notice urging visitors "never forget national humiliation" (*wuwang guochi* 勿忘国耻). The signboard was removed in the midst of the new century's first decade, allegedly because its decay posed a public danger, although this may also reflect a political decision to ratchet down the theme of national disgrace.[19]

A semi-official compendium for Overseas Chinese of the basic elements of Chinese culture includes the *Yuanming Yuan*, focusing on its role as seeking to synthesize Chinese and Western architecture. The implication is clear, that the 1860 destruction of the palace by European imperialists demonstrated that such a synthesis was difficult, and premature.[20]

Today the *Yuanming Yuan* is being partially restored; a stone gazebo, situated at the heart of a maze, was the first to be rebuilt in 1999. One developer has proposed to restore the site, beginning with the Chinese palaces, to be fitted out with ethnic restaurants.[21] But even if it were possible to reconstruct the entire collection of buildings, walks, fountains, and waterways that constituted the palace in its days of glory, one imagines that the government would be averse to give up such a potent symbol of victimhood.[22] Yet this victimhood is often missed by non-Chinese: a group of American university students in Beijing in 1987 visited the *Yuanming Yuan* and reported that they had seen with their own eyes the Cultural Revolution's infamous Red Guard (*hongweibing* 红卫兵) vandalism.

For Europeans, the booty's symbolism has been malleable. As memories of war faded, looted objects became heirlooms only loosely associated with some ancestor's Eastern service. Crusted with a vague imperial nostalgia, the pieces became commodities, offered up for sale as curiosities, rather than as art.[23] Some of the loot never even left China, but was auctioned off in Beijing immediately after the sack of the palace.

Among the pieces which did leave China were several of the zodiac statues (or rather, the heads of these statues, which are the only parts to survive). The monkey and pig were auctioned in October 1987 in New York. In London, in June 1989, Sotheby's sold the tiger, horse, and ox. Three of the zodiac heads ended up in private Taiwan collections late in the twentieth century. Four of the dozen bronze heads are missing. In the spring of 2000, the tiger, ox, and monkey heads were offered at twin auctions in Hong Kong by the leading international art dealers Christie's (monkey and ox) and Sotheby's (tiger).[24] Sotheby's also sold a large hexagonal vase which was looted from the *Yuanming Yuan*, but this piece attracted much less attention than the zodiac sculptures.[25] The companies did not deny that the art was looted, and marked the pieces as coming from the *Yuanming Yuan*. The Chinese government was appalled, and urged the auction houses to hold the sales elsewhere, rather than embarrass China by a public reminder on its own territory of its century of shame.[26] The Ministry of Culture's Cultural Relics Bureau claimed that it would be "insulting and deeply painful to the Chinese people to have these things sold before their eyes."[27] The two auction houses denied violating any treaty or law, and announced that the sale of the offending items would go on, despite growing unease among Hong Kong Chinese. The crisis left a Bureau of Cultural Relics official to mutter, "We will take measures soon. We will not leave the matter as it is."[28]

The Chinese army rescues monkey, tiger, and ox

The successful bidder for the three heads was the Poly Group, a Beijing company which operates a small museum, and which is intimately connected to the People's Liberation Army. The Poly Art Museum described its purchase (for U.S.$4 million) as a patriotic adventure:

> Half an hour before the sale, the leaders of the China Poly Group (中国保利集团) felt profoundly that control was about to be lost over these treasures of the nation, that they might once again suffer calamity and be carried away, and that the sale by auction in Hong Kong of national treasures was a great blow to the interests of the nation, not only impinging on a century of national sentiment on the part of the Chinese people, but further bearing on the prosperity and stability of Hong Kong. As a state-owned enterprise, it is naturally right that the thoughts and concerns of the state should also be our thoughts and concerns. Whilst seeking direction from the relevant state organs and those of the Beijing municipality, the leaders of the Poly Group thereupon instructed the Hong Kong representative of the Poly Art Museum to attend the auction and rescue the national treasures.[29]

Of special interest are the role of the Chinese army and the assertion that the three zodiac heads are "national treasures."

The highest bidder for the three zodiac statues at both auctions was Yi Suhao, the Poly Group's representative.[30] The Poly Group is a state-owned corporation with many financial ventures, but its wealth is rooted in arms exports. Given its specialized business, it is not surprising that the leadership of the corporation is intimately connected to top army leadership, including its general manager, He Ping (何平), Deng Xiaoping's (邓小平) son-in-law. The corporation has become wealthy through the international arms trade, much like its U.S. counterparts General Dynamics, Rockwell, or General

Motors. And like these counterparts, Poly has lots of former military officers on its staff, and prides itself on its patriotism. The English name "Poly" may refer to diversified holdings in real estate and high technology as well as arms. But it also is homophonous with the Chinese name *Baoli* (保利), which means "protect interests."

There is a nice historical symmetry to art plundered by British troops being repatriated by the cash of China's army, and the quotation above certainly suggests that the People's Liberation Army wants to present itself as the heroic rescuer, undoing the shame of a Qing dynasty army which lost the art to foreign troops. It is clear that Poly's purchase was closely co-ordinated with top national leaders. The regime which won their return claims a kind of legitimacy in its act of restoring trophies to a place of honor in their nation of origin.

The recovered statues were exhibited in Beijing's Poly Museum, established in 1998 and headed by a former director of Beijing's Palace Museum. One might imagine that an army art collection would feature large oil paintings of battle scenes. But the Poly Museum has none of these. Instead, the three zodiac heads joined a small but select collection which otherwise features only two types of objects. One gallery displays perhaps a hundred bronzes from the Shang, Zhou, and Han dynasties. A second gallery features a collection of forty exquisite Buddhist figures, from the Northern Wei through the Tang dynasties. The objects appear to be of very high quality, and are very effectively displayed by overhead spotlighting.[31] The Poly Museum apparently also has an unexhibited collection of paintings.

In a Chinese context the army's role is a little less odd than it might be in the West. China's armed forces have long been involved in arts and entertainment. There are many military ensembles which perform popular music, as well as military opera troupes, literary magazines, publishers, and an arts school. The Poly Museum is on the second floor of the popular Poly Theater building. The lobby of the Poly Theater advertises concerts of chamber works with harpsichord, the "Trovatore Bar" (游吟诗人酒吧) invites guests, as does a small book shop, whose titles included the expected works on Napoleon and the German army, but also books on courtesy (including Lord Chesterfield), fiction (including "literary" novels by such contemporary authors as Su Tong 苏童), a guide to raising dogs, and, most surprisingly, a study of politically persecuted poets.[32]

But the Poly Art Museum does not merely add a layer of refinement to the tough core of the Chinese army. It also responded to a state directive in 1999, when the fifty-three top state-owned enterprises were instructed to set aside funds for culture, in order to prepare for an onslaught from Western cultural industries after membership in the World Trade Organization.[33] With its museum, Poly was already well positioned to help be a bastion for national art. And with the national treasures under its control, Poly was also able to exhibit them to promote its real estate subsidiary in Shenzhen (深圳).[34]

The mystique of national treasures

Zodiac statues are repatriated as "national treasures." The concept of national treasures is borrowed from Japan, apparently via Taiwan. In Japanese practice, the term denotes a specially protected category of art works. In 1998, Japan had 1,048 works designated as national treasures which cannot be exported.[35] In China, on the other hand, "national treasure" is not an official category, but a subjective one, applied to works that someone believes to be essential to defining China's national spirit.[36]

The animal heads are prized as "national" treasures for political, not aesthetic reasons. The legitimacy of the ruling Communist Party is rooted in ending a "century of humiliation, blood and tears"(*yige shijide xueleishi* 一个世纪的血泪史) and the return of the plundered heads symbolizes the success of the revolution in winning international status.[37]

There is no strong argument to be made for the zodiac heads on aesthetic grounds. One art historian has likened them to garden ornaments, of no special interest even to the Qianlong emperor. They were certainly not the best art plundered from the *Yuanming Yuan* by Lord Elgin's troops.[38] And the failure of Chinese budgets for arts conservation and the simplest protection against looters and thieves to keep pace with growing national prosperity suggests that this flamboyant purchase may not have been the best way to spend money in support of Chinese culture. Indeed, after the failed 2009 auction purchase, some opined that the zodiac heads are not really national treasures, but mere "faucets", not worth the cost in light of such burdens as housing destroyed by earthquake and real estate development.[39]

Are the zodiac heads really Chinese at all? They were executed by Chinese craftsmen in accord with the rather Westernized conceptions of an Italian artist who was honestly attempting to satisfy his Chinese patron. One of the heads, a tiger, looks remarkably like a bear. The bear is not in the Chinese zodiac, and one imagines that Castiglione had little experience with tigers as he was completing the fountain.

As symbols, the three heads are not ideal emblems of a rising China overcoming decaying Western imperialism. It might be more aesthetically and politically satisfying if the auction houses had tried to peddle a more unambiguously Chinese and universally respected piece of plunder. But symbols cannot be matched ideally with their causes, and objects often become symbolic by happenstance.

Yet the zodiac statues have some advantages as emblems. They are easily recognizable by the artistically unsophisticated, in contrast to many ink paintings which might well be better appreciated by connoisseurs. Indeed, a 1982 Chinese film, *The Burning of the Imperial Palace* (*Huoshao Yuanming Yuan* 火烧圆明园) uses a quick view of a (reconstructed) zodiac fountain to signal that the action had moved to the *Yuanming Yuan*, so sure was its director that his audience would recognize these figures as emblems of the garden's impending destruction.[40] The zodiac animals' status as "national treasures" is enhanced by the monumentality of bronze, perhaps strengthening the status of statuary, which is not the most prestigious of premodern Chinese art forms.

Moreover, the bronze statues are relatively sturdy, making it easier for their new owners to move them around the nation for patriotic display. The Chinese state quickly exploited the return of its long-lost objects to spur nationalist sentiment. The three heads were sent around the nation on tour. Immediately after the purchase, a large crowd came to inspect them in the Hong Kong Art Museum. They were also put on display in Shenzhen, Guangzhou, Chongqing, Chengdu, Tianjin, and Beijing. The whole episode of the zodiac statues is scripted to bolster the legitimacy of the regime which repurchased the statuary. From 1860 plunder, through 140 years in which the statues wandered abroad like a set of homeless ghosts, to the army-backed purchase, and finally the triumphant display across China is a rather emphatic example of art as an instrument of statecraft.

An unspoken background for the zodiac statue drama was the collection of art housed in Taipei, the National Palace Museum. This superb collection of art once owned by China's emperors is a much better candidate than the zodiac heads to be the emblem of political legitimacy.

Revolutions are often occasions for massive transfers of art objects. Cromwell sold many of the paintings assembled by Charles I, and the Louvre was founded on the art collection of the late Bourbon ruling family. The Soviet Union quietly disposed of many pieces from the Czar's collection, selling some to Andrew Mellon, who set them up in the United States National Gallery of Art. The Chinese revolutionary century has been no different in reminding us of the mobility and liquidity of fine art objects.

The emperors of China included many connoisseurs, and the imperial collections of art were unrivaled. When the empire collapsed, the last emperor, Pu Yi (溥仪), treated the collection as his personal property, despite efforts by various republican regimes to claim the art as national patrimony. Aware of the controversy, the young Pu Yi slipped pieces out by his brother to sell for money. When Pu Yi became Japan's puppet ruler of Manchukuo (*wei manzhouguo* 伪满洲国), he hauled more art treasure with him to the northeast.[41]

Amidst this drainage by the emperor, Chiang Kai-shek's (蒋介石) new national government moved the remaining pieces to the new capital in Nanjing. But with the approach of Japanese invaders, Chiang divided and concealed the collection. It was not reassembled at the end of the war, but much was shipped, with American help, to Taiwan along with the retreating Kuomintang army.[42]

As seen from Beijing, Taiwan is an art-poor and culturally marginal province which was for fifty years a Japanese colony; yet it has possession of the deepest cultural symbols of political legitimacy. For Chiang Kai-shek, the possession of these treasures was a marker of the viability of his claim to rule the entire nation. For the Kuomintang, possession of the imperial art collection denoted right to rule, even from temporary quarters in Taiwan.

The Kuomintang government also deployed objects from the Imperial collection in its diplomatic rivalry with the mainland. But when some four hundred pieces were sent on exhibition to the United States in 1996, five hundred people sat in for two days in front of the museum, demanding that the government reduce the scale of the tour in order to protect the objects. One banner demanded: "Museum is no Foreign Ministry, don't take top art treasure to work for national diplomacy."[43]

Yet Taiwan's former Democratic Progressive Party (DPP) (*minjindang* 民进党) government had a different attitude toward these symbols than its Kuomintang predecessor. For the DPP, Taiwan is home, and the National Palace Museum is another bastion of mainlander power. Indeed, when Chen Shui-bian (陈水扁) was elected president in 2000, he made three symbolic gestures to reassure Taiwan's mainlander population: he placed flowers at the Chiang Kai-shek Memorial Hall, he visited Chiang Ching-kuo's (蒋经国) widow, Faina Chiang (蒋方良), and he visited the National Palace Museum in suburban Taipei. But there was some discussion in Taiwan of splitting the collection, establishing a new museum in southern Taiwan, the base of DPP support.[44] A government decision to build a branch in Chiayi (嘉义) was accompanied by discussion of changing the museum's name, leading the Kuomintang to complain that the DPP government was seeking to remove cultural symbols that are not Taiwanese.[45] One can imagine the collection becoming a bargaining chip as Taiwan and the mainland work out their relationship.

The zodiac heads have a role to play in Taiwan–mainland relations. At the end of 1991, following a visit to Taiwan by Poly Group head He Ping, the zodiac statues went to Taipei, as part of a three-month exhibit of over 100 pieces from the Poly Museum collection.[46] The repatriation of imperialist plunder provides a medium by which all Chinese, not only the citizens of the People's Republic, can be proud of their improved status in the world.

New plunder replaces the old

The story of the army rescuing national treasures from the clutches of foreign collectors may be read with many meanings. The appeal to Chinese national pride is obvious enough, as is the Communist Party's desire to be seen as the inheritor of a revolutionary tradition of standing up to foreign exploitation. But this drama was also staged for the benefit of foreign arts firms in Hong Kong. Patriotic bravado helped China deal with its embarrassment that Hong Kong continues to be a center for the sale of artistic plunder from China, while it put the Hong Kong art market on notice that China expected its activities to be low key, at least superficially legal, and to avoid causing public awkwardness for China's rulers.

The fact that two foreign auction companies offered these works for sale in Hong Kong was problematic. The zodiac statues came to Hong Kong soon after China regained sovereignty over the city in 1997. They became one of a series of contests by which Hong Kong and Beijing are working out how

Chinese sovereignty should apply to the former British colony.[47] Beijing has generally tried to rule with a light hand through its formula of one country, two systems. Despite (some might say because of) a steady stream of alarms from the neocolonial Hong Kong elite, and a barrage of Western press accounts warning of the loss of Hong Kong's "autonomy," Beijing has generally treated Hong Kong quite loosely. In this instance, as in most, Hong Kong law prevailed over the frustrated State Cultural Relics Bureau.

Perhaps some in Beijing fantasized about simply sending the army in to seize the controversial fountain heads. After all, Hong Kong is a city which still honors the looter of the emperor's garden with the name of Elgin Street. But Beijing has generally been patient with Hong Kong, resisting any temptation to fill the former colony's map with "People's Avenues" (*renminlu* 人民路) and "May First Squares" (*wuyi guangchang* 五一广场) to replace markers of British imperialism. To put the matter more sharply, Hong Kong itself was repatriated imperialist booty.[48]

Nevertheless, it might have been prudent for Christie's and Sotheby's to put obviously stolen works up for sale in another country. But they did not, and China's use of troops armed with money (Hong Kong's weapon of choice) to recover the art by purchasing it enabled Beijing to claim the moral high ground.

One reason for the auction houses to disregard Beijing's warnings is that these are companies with long traditions of arrogance toward China. Christie's first sold loot from the *Yuanming Yuan* in May, 1861, and has been profitably churning this stock for 140 years.[49] Why should it stop, or even alter its plans after such a long run of success?

A second reason is commercial, and even more compelling. A Hong Kong sale promised greater publicity and higher prices than other venues. As China has prospered, an indigenous class of collectors has emerged, and Christie's and Sotheby's want to profit from its new purchasing power and cultural interest. Christie's and Sotheby's handled 90 percent of the world art business in the 1990s, when both firms opened offices in China. They employed relatives of high officials to promote sales mostly held outside of China.[50] New Chinese auction houses have also arisen, with close ties to families from the political elite. Late President Liu Shaoqi's (刘少奇) daughter, Liu Tingting (刘亭亭), headed the Sungari International Auction Company (中贸圣佳国际拍卖有限公司), while former Party head Zhao Ziyang's (赵紫阳) daughter, Wang Yannan (王雁南), was vice-president of the Guardian Auction Company (嘉德国际拍卖有限公司).[51]

On the eve of the zodiac statues auction, Sotheby's was trying to stimulate similar interest in art auctions among younger members of Hong Kong's wealthy elite. The firm organized a "practice" (*yanxi* 演练) auction for charity, in order to familiarize Hong Kong's golden youth with the conventions of the fine arts auction. Often educated abroad, the young rich of Hong Kong typically cannot read calligraphy, or understand the poetry in a painting's inscription. Sotheby's sought to institutionalize the provision of expertise to meet such deficiencies.[52]

An expanding global art market, eager to recruit wealthy Chinese into its embrace, needed Hong Kong in 2000. Hong Kong remains the prime site where mainland, Hong Kong, and Southeast Asian collectors of Chinese fine arts can conveniently assemble. It is not surprising that this trend in the sales of Chinese art led to a clash with a self-consciously ascending Chinese state.

The clash was made more likely by Hong Kong's role in the supply of new plunder for the world market. Hong Kong's prosperity rests on its role as a commercial intermediary between the People's Republic and the outside world. In the fine arts, this has made Hong Kong a major center for the distribution of freshly plundered art objects. China is unable to control art theft, despite ample criminal penalties. Grave robbing is an ancient profession in China, which is littered with unexplored underground burial sites. Many peasants find it more profitable to "harvest" items from tombs than from their own fields. And many officials have been caught selling objects from museum collections. Massive corruption smoothes the way to market. The most desirable items end up for sale in an export market, for which Hong Kong remains a central point for smuggling, a place it has held since the establishment of the People's Republic. Increased Chinese shipping from other ports facilitates smuggling from other cities, but Hong Kong is likely to remain important for some time.

State efforts to combat archeological plunder are so inadequate that the failures have elicited protests from legislators. The site of Zhejiang's (浙江) Liangzhu (梁祝) culture has been particularly hard hit. Although China designated the area for special protection in 1996, there have since been at least 57 instances of robbery, leaving a residue of 127 pits dug by robbers. Moreover, this archeological site shared its "protected zone" with twenty-three rock quarries. In June, 2000, nearly a hundred members of Zhejiang's Political Consultative Conference visited the site to demand stronger measures by the state.[53] Further evidence of the political frustration with the art-theft problem is found in the serious penalties which befall those who are apprehended. Zhang Guohua (张国华), leader of a gang which blasted its way into a tomb of the Western Han dynasty (206 B.C. to 24 A.D.), was sentenced to death in Henan (河南) province.[54]

The zodiac rescue alarmed many in the Hong Kong fine arts world, who fear restrictions on their ability to export freshly plundered art. Many Hong Kong collectors were understandably concerned that they could not document the origin of each piece in their collections. In some cases the art has been obtained from dubious sources. The Hong Kong legislature considered amending local law to restrict the sale of smuggled goods, but decided this would be disruptive to the local arts market.

The role played by Sotheby's and Christie's is not particularly noble. A price-fixing scandal forced resignations from the leadership of both companies (and the 2001 conviction of former Sotheby chairman Alfred Taubman), suggesting that they conspired to form an international criminal organization.[55]

Despite the social register connotations of the international arts trade, this business depends upon stirring up customer demand with the titillation of new goods, which it then sends agents to find. This can mean casting an indifferent eye at the origins of the goods they sell.[56] A 1997 article criticized Chinese auction firms for "unprofessional and unethical behaviour" (*weifan zhiye daodede xingwei* 违反职业道德的行为) which limits "the Chinese art market's bid for international respectability."[57] However accurate the assessment, the point seems ill placed in light of the New York conviction of Taubman and the agreement to restore U.S.$0.5 billion to the customers he cheated.

As the zodiac statue controversy escalated, and China's commitment began to become evident, Beijing's claims began to be treated with more seriousness. Hong Kong's chief English language newspaper, for instance, stopped putting "looted" art in ironic quotation marks. Anthony Lin of Christies warned that pressure from China might lead to Hong Kong art sales moving to other venues.[58] But such defiant responses were replaced by calmer words, as the auction houses were reportedly shaken by Beijing's tough attitude. An aide to Hong Kong Chief Executive Tung Chee-hua (董建华) characterized the double sale as a "commercial activity that could not be more stupid." But he said there was no need for new legislation to ban such sales (as Beijing had demanded), because the auction houses would not do it again.[59]

The zodiac heads controversy thus led to no legal changes for Hong Kong's fine arts economy. Although Beijing participates in the 1970 UNESCO convention against illegal export and transfer of cultural property, the Basic Law which governs Hong Kong does not allow its application in Hong Kong. However, the zodiac rescue mission was more than symbolic, to the extent that it raised consciousness of China's position in an international distribution of fine arts. In 1997, when China joined the Unidroit Convention to help repatriate lost art, Beijing announced that it did not give up its right to claim art stolen prior to signing the treaty.[60] On May 21, 2000, at the height of the controversy, China announced the formation of a recovery team to lead the effort to repatriate more of the nation's plundered national treasures.[61]

The international distribution of art objects as a measure of global inequality

While many citizens of the West deplore the sale of stolen art objects, wealthy nations tend to resist measures to remedy it, taking the view that countries such as China should limit the supply, instead of having Britain, the U.S., or Japan limit demand. At one level the situation is of course scandalous, with art-importing nations blaming their suppliers and victims as they try to sustain a status quo which permits easy smuggling and lower prices for collectors and museums. There is a parallel in approaches to the drug trade, with wealthy importing nations seeking to regulate supply, while poorer, supplying nations often argue that European and North American governments should control their domestic consumers.

From a somewhat colder perspective, the trade may be seen as an unavoidable leakage, by which China participates in the international cultural economy. National wealth and power are manifest in several dimensions. Military might and quality of health care are two quite different indicators of international standing. Another, less frequently noticed measure is the international distribution of art objects. Items of beauty, at least a beauty recognized in global markets, tend to flow from poorer to richer nations.

The fact that the distribution of beautiful objects is rather more uneven indicates that we do not take very seriously our own rhetoric about art as the common heritage of all humanity. In a more equal world there would not only be pre-Columbian statues in New York, but American abstract impressionist paintings in Peru and Guatemala. There would be Cambodian Buddhist sculptures in Paris and canvases by Delacroix and Manet in Pnomh Penh, batik in Argentina and totem poles in Senegal. However, this is not what happens. Not only is the art unevenly distributed in terms of economic value, but it is difficult to "exchange" art among Africa, Asia, and Latin America without the mediation of wealthy nations. For instance, in 1999 Shanghai displayed seventeen cases of antiquities from ancient Egypt. Yet the art came from Britain, not Egypt. The items were from the British Museum, sent on tour to Asia during its recent remodeling.[62] Egypt cannot easily afford to mount such a show, and when it can, the art is typically shown in wealthy nations which have helped finance the exhibition.

A crude classification misses out on subtleties, but suggests an underlying dynamic in the international cultural economy. Some nations are unusually art-rich, often because they occupy land where their ancestors (or someone else's ancestors) left abundant architectural and monumental artifacts. Other lands are art-poor, often because they were never the locations for great civilizations of the past, or fewer artifacts have survived, or because indigenous arts have not been discovered by the international market. Italy, China, Peru, and Turkey are examples of art-rich nations, while the United States, New Zealand, Namibia, and the Dominican Republic are relatively art-poor.

Some of the art-rich nations are also economically wealthy, such as Italy, Japan, or France, but others are not. And some of the art-poor nations are also economically prosperous. The United States, for instance, has used some of its wealth to create an indigenous art, and to acquire art works from other nations. The historic pattern has been for the American robber baron to decorate Cleveland or St. Louis with renaissance oils purchased from downwardly mobile Italian aristocracy.

How art-rich is China? China has been losing art for longer than many nations have made it.[63] The Liang dynasty's Yuandi (元帝 (r. 552–54) assembled 240,000 scrolls of paintings, books, and calligraphy in his palace collection. As Western Wei armies attacked the capital, he burned the lot, of which only 4,000 scrolls survived. Sui Yangdi's (隋炀帝) achievements as emperor (r. 605–17) included the Grand Canal and a fine art collection. When the emperor traveled on these canals with a spectacular flotilla, he liked to carry his pieces of calligraphy and painting with him. On one of these journeys a boat loaded with art treasures capsized and sank. Through this accident the greater part of the imperial collection was lost. The Emperor Taizong of the Tang dynasty was crazy for the calligraphy of Wang Xizhi, collecting 2,290 pieces in the imperial palace collection; none survives, except as copies. This is not to justify foreign plunder by arguing that the Chinese have been beastly toward their own art, but to remind us that China has been producing phenomenal amounts of art for millennia.

The point is not that it is immoral for Americans to have collections of Chinese art, but that there is an asymmetry in our exchange by which few Chinese citizens have access to American or other Western art. The present distribution of art objects, like the distribution of brain surgeons, ballistic missiles, and top-rate universities, is uneven.

The maldistribution of art is rarely regarded as an issue in wealthy nations.[64] But it is an issue for poor countries, where artists and art students are deprived of opportunities to understand the techniques behind entire genres. The history of oil painting in China, for instance, is partly a history of limited access. There are no great Western oils in China; traveling shows have brought some paintings, but often of a very inferior quality. The lack of Western art in third world nations is not a trivial issue. China not only has no great Western paintings, but it is even difficult to find books with first-class reproductions of Western paintings. This scarcity made it easier to shut off access altogether during the Cultural Revolution. It is striking how the modern history of oil painting in China gives such a prominent role to key individuals who helped introduce techniques, such as the Russian expert Maximov in the 1950s, or who arranged exhibitions of actual Western paintings, such as the American tycoon Armand Hammer in the 1980s.

No one would argue that the citizens of poor nations are about to riot for a more just redistribution of objects of beauty ("Dozens hurt as Karachi mob demands impressionist paintings and Toltec carvings"). But when art works become associated with all the emotions of nationalism, people do get excited, as did the angry crowd in Hong Kong outside the zodiac heads auction.

Arguments against the current international distribution come most frequently from those nations which have been plundered. The classic case is Greece's persistent demands that the British return the Parthenon Marbles. In 1799 the 7th Lord Elgin was British Ambassador to Turkey. Caught up in a craze for Greek things, Elgin took along his architect, with an eye to redecorating his mansion in Scotland. Elgin set his eye on Athens' Parthenon. Greece was not yet independent of Turkish rule, and British influence in the Eastern Mediterranean was high after Nelson's victory over the French at the Battle of the Nile. The Turks permitted Elgin to remove any sculptures which did not interfere with the walls of the Parthenon. By 1806 Elgin had shipped two hundred crates of Greek national heritage to Scotland aboard British warships.

Byron and others demanded that the statues be returned to the Greeks. When Greece gained independence in 1832, the refurbishing of the Parthenon as a national symbol began a long and still unsuccessful campaign to repatriate the Marbles. Elgin eventually sold the statuary at a great loss to the British government. They now reside in London's British Museum, where they are known as the "Elgin Marbles," to give an edge to British claims of legitimate ownership.

The Parthenon Marbles case is of interest to any nation which has lost art through plunder and hopes to regain possession. The British responses to Greece set the pattern for all plunder cases.[65]

First, there is the argument of legal ownership. British claims that the Turkish government approved Elgin's removal of the Parthenon friezes is not very convincing to Greece. But plunder-hosts utilize the complexity of international law to sow confusion about counter-claims to art whose acquisition has come under question. Such art can include items which were purchased in perfectly straightforward and honorable sales, those which were stolen outright, and those extracted under unfair conditions, which can in no way be called free exchange.

Second is the argument about care and protection, that the Marbles would have suffered physical loss if not destruction if not for the watchful care of the British Museum, which is protecting the art on behalf of all humanity. Similar arguments have been made about Chinese art in foreign collections – at least they were protected against Red Guard violence. The argument has lost its appeal, however, in light of information that the British Museum damaged the Marbles in the 1930s, and has covered this up until recently. One might also point to the German "protection" of Dunhuang (敦煌) treasures lost to bombing in World War II.[66]

A third argument looks with horror at the purported implications of returning the Marbles. This is deemed likely to initiate a ceaseless demand for restoration of art works to their nations of origin. And who would want to see a world in which the only Greek art was in Greece, and the only Chinese art in China? This would be culturally damaging to us all. This is of course a red herring, as return of a specific piece of art does not require creating a global harmonization of nationalities and art.[67] Indeed, the growing "world heritage" movement, which draws moneyed tourists to view restored art and architecture in its national setting, offers an alternative path to the status quo.

Unsurprisingly, Western legal scholars interested in the trade in cultural objects have developed a neoliberal critique of the state-centered approach favored by China and some other third world nations.[68] Self-styled "cultural internationalists" argue that China and similar states need to expand, not restrict, the trade in cultural artifacts. There should be fewer restrictions, which are said to encourage theft and black markets. For poor nations, old objects must be desacralized and newly regarded as secular items which can be sold by peasants for economic advantage as the objects "pass from the cultural to the economic sphere."[69]

Neoliberals say that China should have a process of judicious selection that may result in the export of all but the most culturally significant items. "The developing art-rich nations should treat cultural property as an exploitable national resource, not to be hoarded absolutely, but to be 'mined' as a source of income." Funding would somehow thus be assured for preservation efforts. In one optimistic projection, "scientists would replace thieves."[70]

These arguments resemble a brief for Western museums and art dealers. Murphy's informative book on China dismisses much protection out of hand: "the 'protected' resources are very often unowned – indeed, unexcavated – relics rather than identifiable owned objects." Murphy tarnishes those who favor tighter regulations by associating them with takers of bribes who seek "to protect the illicit income."[71] A country's comparative poverty becomes an argument against, rather than for, stricter national controls. In general, the approach is to blame the victims, who may not choose to regard artifacts of their cultures as objects to be mined. "Mining" art from the ground devalues the objects into the rawest export commodities, rather than allowing value to be added by the nation of origin.

The Western fine arts world is inevitably intertwined with the world of big money and high finance. For instance, the invaluable Internet resource Artnewspaper.com announces that it is available on Bloomberg terminals, which exist chiefly to convey stock market figures and other information for investors. Sotheby's and Christie's may recently have been administered by scoundrels, but the auction houses are inevitably drawn into the realm of international commerce.[72] At the same time, in nations which have been plundered, the recovery issue is likely to fall in the political arena, with a risk that it will become the realm of political adventurers, manipulating patriotic appeals for career advantage.

The zodiac heads controversy pitted Western dealers who regarded the heads as fine arts commodities against a Chinese state which was not yet willing to see them "pass from the cultural to the economic sphere." In addition to helping buttress the Communist Party's claim that its authority is just, the zodiac statues helped provide a practical focus for energetic and potentially disruptive nationalist emotion throughout China. In addition, they also provided Hong Kong citizens an opportunity to display their own rather tentative patriotic sentiments.

Of course much art has been returned to China. For example, the National Gallery of Canada recently returned a plundered arhat which was first sold outside China by Sotheby's in 1970.[73] And a Japanese museum returned a piece stolen in 1994.[74] China and other Asian nations may take some encouragement from the recent turn of respectable opinion in the West about art plundered by the Nazis. Much has been found to have been resold to private collectors or museums after the war, fueling a movement to restore art works to the heirs of their owners, many of whom were Jews killed by Germany.[75] But slow as this restoration has been, it has been eased by the fact that it is primarily an intra-Western phenomenon, and does not require the dispatch of art from one culture to another.

The movement to restore Nazi art plunder turn did not discourage Sotheby's and Christies from selling the zodiac heads in Hong Kong. After that sale, China announced the formation of a special team to work on retrieving plundered art. Xie Zhenzhen of the Bureau of Cultural Relics declared that over a million high-quality Chinese cultural artifacts lie in the collections of 200 museums in 47 nations. The U.S. Metropolitan Museum of Art has the most paintings but the British Museum has the finest. Japan has the most oracle bones, and France has the best ceramics.[76] China knows where to go to find the art, but it must have a realistic notion of how difficult it would be to obtain even a small part.

China persuaded the United States in the final days of the Bush administration to agree to new restrictions to limit the trade in arts plunder. Over the objections of many American dealers and museum officials, the United States will ban imports of artifacts from Paleolithic times through the Tang dynasty.[77] In the wake of the 2009 failed auction of the rabbit and rat zodiac heads, many dealers anticipated reduced demand for Asian antiquities, especially in a climate of global economic decline.[78] Chinese are also expressing greater interest in making a common front with other nations which hope to repatriate looted artefacts, such as Egypt or Greece.[79] These factors, along with China's growing wealth, should facilitate future repatriation of plundered art.

The restoration of national glory must ultimately rest upon more solid accomplishments: economic prosperity, military might, and the encouragement of vibrant new cultural works are all likely to contribute more importantly to political legitimacy than the recovery of plundered art works. Episodes such as that of the zodiac heads can only be a small current in a much broader national effort. The particular circumstances of their partial recovery are unlikely to reappear, resting upon the coincidence of Hong Kong's return to China and the stubborn arrogance of Western auction houses. Yet the zodiac heads episode also reminds us that the Chinese state needs evidence that it is overturning China's past shame. In an era in which nationalist protest can easily move faster than the state desires, art recovery presents itself as a virtuous and controllable nationalist project that appeals to Chinese patriotism in the broadest manner.

The zodiac statues temporarily cloud the pride that many Chinese feel at finding their nation's art to be admired, coveted, and displayed abroad. The long campaign to repatriate these statues may boost the Party's domestic legitimacy, but it also complicates China's relations with art-collecting nations. Just as many in the West regard China as a difficult rising power in economic and military affairs, the politics of art repatriation may be used by some as a high art example of Chinese truculence in the existing international aesthetic order.

Notes

1 This chapter is an update of "When Legitimacy Resides in Beautiful Objects: Repatriating Beijing's Looted Zodiac Animal Heads," in Peter Hays Gries and Stanley Rosen, eds., *State and Society in 21st Century China: Crisis, Contention, and Legitimation* (New York and London: RoutledgeCurzon, 2004), pp. 195–215.
2 See Tania Branigan, "Chinese Fury at Sale of Plundered Treasures," *Guardian*, November 3, 2008, accessed at http://www.guardian.co.uk/world/2008/nov/03/china-fashion-yves-saint-laurent; Charles Bremner and Jane Macartney, "China Tries to Halt Yves Saint Laurent Art Sale," *The Times*, January 21, 2009; David Barboza, "China Seeks to Stop Paris Sale of Bronzes, *New York Times*, February 17, 2009; Lucien Libert, "YSL Partner Offers China Art for Human Rights," *Reuters*, February 21, 2009.
3 Le-Min Lim, "China Slaps Controls on Christie's after Bronzes Sale," *Bloomberg*, February 26, 2007.
4 Wu Zhong, "China's Renegade Patriot Faces Backlash," *Asia Times*, March 11, 2009, accessed at http://www.atimes.com/atimes/China/KC11Ad01.html.
5 Le-Min Lim, "Chinese Art Dealer in Unpaid YSL Bronzes Furor Weeps," *Bloomberg*, March 10, 2009; Kelley Crow, "Bidder Refuses to Pay, Stating Protest of Looting," *Wall Street Journal*, March 3, 2009.
6 "The Yves Saint Laurent Sale," March 5, 2009, accessed at www.economist.com.
7 I thank Ellen J. Laing for helpful comments on this piece.
8 A recent study of the *Yuanming Yuan* is Young-tsu Wong, *Paradise Lost: The Imperial Garden Yuanming Yuan* (Honolulu: University of Hawaii Press, 2001).
9 See Cécile and Michel Beurdeley, *Giuseppe Castiglione: A Jesuit Painter at the Court of the Chinese Emperors* (Rutland, VT: Charles E. Tuttle Company, 1971).
10 Quoted in Young-tsu Wong, *Paradise Lost*, p. 149.
11 See Christopher Hitchens, *The Elgin Marbles: Should They Be Returned to Greece?* (New York: Verso. 1998); Russell Chamberlin, *Loot! The Heritage of Plunder* (New York: Facts on File, 1983).
12 See James L. Hevia, *Cherishing Men from Afar: Qing Guest Ritual and the Macartney Embassy of 1793* (Durham: Duke University Press, 1995); Alain Peyrefitte, *The Immobile Empire* (New York: Alfred A. Knopf, 1992), pp. 135–51.
13 James L. Hevia, "Loot's Fate: The Economy of Plunder and the Moral Life of Objects 'From the Summer Palace of the Emperor of China'," *History and Anthropology* 6(4) (1994), p. 319.
14 The engravings were returned to Asia when put up for sale in a Singapore auction in 1997. Associated Press, "Rare Imperial Engravings on Sale," *South China Morning Post*, October 2, 1997.
15 See James Hevia, "Loot's Fate," pp. 319–45. Hevia reminds us that the bulk of the "British" troops were in fact Indian, which adds a piquant complexity to the event.
16 James Hevia, "Loot's Fate," p. 336.
17 William A. Callahan, "The Cartography of National Humiliation and the Emergence of China's Geobody," *Public Culture* 21(1) (2009), pp. 141–73.
18 J. David Murphy, *Plunder and Preservation: Cultural Property Law and Practice in the People's Republic of China* (Hong Kong: Oxford University Press, 1995), p. 183.
19 Personal communication from William A. Callahan (April 6, 2009).
20 See *Zhongguo wenhua changshi* [General Knowledge of Chinese Culture] (Hong Kong: Shijie jiechu huaren jijinhui, 2000), p. 52.

21 Eric Eckholm, "A Glorious Ruin and a Face-Life Furor," *New York Times*, August 10, 1999. Geremie Barmé reviews the physical and political status of the garden in "Yuanming Yuan, the Garden of Perfect Brightness," *China Heritage Quarterly*, no. 8 (December 2006), accessed at http://www.chinaheritagequarterly. org/editorial.php?issue=008.
22 A scaled down replica of the pre-looted *Yuanming Yuan* has been built as tourist attraction in Zhuhai, Guangdong, complete with fountain.
23 James Hevia, "Looting Beijing: 1860, 1900," in Lydia H. Liu, ed., *Tokens of Exchange: The Problem of Translation in Global Circulations* (Durham: Duke University Press, 1999), pp. 192–213.
24 The Christie's auction was on April 31, Sotheby's on May 2, 2000.
25 The Beijing Cultural Relics Company, owned by the Beijing Municipal Government, bought the vase from Sotheby's. General manager Qin Gong collapsed and died shortly thereafter, apparently from the stress of the deal. "Buyer of Looted Vase 'Killed by Stress of Sale'," *South China Morning Post*, May 12, 2000.
26 Mark Landler, "China Asks Auction Houses to Withdraw 4 Relics," *South China Morning Post*, April 29, 2000.
27 Mark Landler, "Christie's Auctions Relics Despite China's Objection," *South China Morning Post*, May 1, 2000.
28 Stella Lee and Niall Fraser, "Beijing Threatens Auction Houses," *South China Morning Post*, April 29, 2000.
29 The Poly Museum tells this story on a set of commemorative postcards: "Guobao huigui tezhan" [special exhibition of repatriated national treasures].
30 On Yi, see Wu Huan, "'Duo guobao' shijian di shenmi ren" [The mystery man of the "seizing national treasures" incident], *Mingbao Yuekan*, no. 414 (June 2000), pp. 36–9.
31 When I visited the Poly Art Museum on a Saturday afternoon in April, 2001, the absence of other visitors assured close, yet polite surveillance by guards and a staff member. The museum has prepared many volumes illustrating its collection, including *Baoli yishu bowuguan cang shike fojiao zaoxiang jingpin* [Selected works of sculpture in the Poly Art Museum] (Beijing: Baoli yishu bowuguan, 2000).
32 Ni Sha *et al.*, eds., *Shi shiren pipan shu* [The denunciations of ten poets] (Changchun: Mingdai chubanshe, 2001). The poets include two victims of Guomindang criticism (Guo Moruo and Xu Zhimo), but the others have all done battle with the communist state (such as Shu Ting, Bei Dao, and the chief editor, Ni Sha).
33 Oliver Chou, "Sold (to the Soldier at the Back)," *South China Morning Post*, November 22, 2000.
34 Josephine Ma, "Bronze Heads are Priceless: Buyer," *South China Morning Post*, October 19, 2000.
35 839 of these were pieces of fine and applied arts, 209 were architectural works. See the website of the Japanese Ministry of Education, Science, Sports, and Culture at http://www.monbu.go.jp/aramashi/1998eng/e602.html.
36 The Chinese National Artifacts Bureau classifies art objects into "valuable" and "ordinary" categories. There are three grades of valuable art objects. See Wang Hongjun, ed., *Zhongguo bowuguanxue jichu* [The Basis of Chinese Museology] (Shanghai: Shanghai guji chubanshe, 2001), pp. 148–57.
37 "Guobao huigui tezhan" [special exhibition of repatriated national treasures].
38 I am indebted to Professor Puay-peng Ho of the Chinese University of Hong Kong for his informative lecture, "Heads or Tails? The Flip Side of Chinese National Treasures," Hong Kong Anthropological Society, March 20, 2001.
39 Tong Dahuan, "Yuanming Yuan shoushou shijian" [The Yuanming Yuan animal heads incident], zhongguo qinguian bao, March 4, 2009.

40 *Huoshao Yuanming Yuan*, directed by Li Hanxian. Bai Hua was one of the script-writers for this patriotic epic. The scene with the fountain ignores the fact that it has not worked since 1786.

41 See Yang Renkai, *Guobao Chenfu Lu* [The rise and fall of national treasures] (Shanghai: Shanghai renmin chuban she, 1991); and Liu Jinku, *Guobao Liushi Lu* [The drain of national treasures] (Shenyang: Liaohai chuban she, 1999).

42 See Jeannette Shambaugh Elliott and David Shambaugh, *The Odyssey of China's Imperial Art Treasures* (Seattle: University of Washington Press, 2005); Dou Yingtai, *Wenwu da qianxi* [The great migration of the artifacts] (Zhengzhou: Henan wenyi chubanshe, 2001).

43 See "Hundreds Protest at Art Tour," *South China Morning Post*, January 8, 1996; "Imperial Treasures on Move Again," *South China Morning Post*, January 16, 1996.

44 Zhang Yang, "Gugong bowuyuan yingfou nanshe fenyuan" [Should the National Palace Museum establish a branch in the south?], *Mingbao yuekan*, no. 425 (May 2001), 114.

45 Sandy Huang, "Stop Mixing Culture with Politics, KMT Warns," *Taipei Times*, 16 January 2003, available online at www.taipeitimes.com/News/taiwan/archives/2003/01/16/191185.

46 Fong Tak-ho, "Approval Sought to Exhibit Art in Taipei," *South China Morning Post*, July 11, 2001; "National Treasures to Be Displayed in Taiwan," *People's Daily online*, November 28, 2001.

47 Other issues by which the meanings of Chinese sovereignty and Hong Kong auton-omy have been tested are immigration rights for Chinese relatives of Hong Kong residents, the importance of English language instruction in schools, and the visa status of a Chinese-American convicted of espionage in a mainland trial.

48 The same phrase, *huigui*, was used to refer both to the return or repatriation of Hong Kong and of the zodiac statues.

49 In 1864, one of the many Christie's sales of *Yuanming Yuan* plunder included the "skull of Confucius" made into a drinking cup. Hevia, "Loot's Fate," p. 330.

50 Kari Huus, "Do I Hear Three?" *Far Eastern Economic Review*, May 12, 1994, pp. 69–70.

51 Pamela Yatsko, "Seducing China's Rich," *Far Eastern Economic Review*, March 27, 1997;" Liu Widow to Sell Rare Antiques," *South China Morning Post*, November 2, 1996.

52 Gwyneth Roberts, "Sotheby's Bidding to Stimulate Interest in Future Generations," *South China Morning Post*, April 8, 2000.

53 "'Liangzhu' wenhua zao pohuai" [Liangzhu culture faces destruction], *Renmin ribao (Huadong xinwen)*, June 19, 2000.

54 Associated Press, "Chinese Tomb Robber Gets Death," June 12, 2001.

55 Sotheby's and its former executive, Diane ("Dede") Brooks confessed to collu-sion with Christie's; the chairmen of both firms were indicted, but the Christie's executive hid behind British law, which protected him against extradition to the United States. See Douglas Frantz, "Secret Partners: The Unraveling of a Conspiracy," *New York Times*, October 8, 2000; Carol Vogel, "Indictment Names Two Ex-Chairmen of Auction Houses," *New York Times*, May 3, 2001; and Ralph Blumenthal and Carol Vogel, "Ex-Chief of Sotheby's Is Convicted of Price Fixing," *New York Times*, December 6, 2001. See Christopher Mason, *The Art of the Steal: Inside the Sotheby's Christie's Auction House Scandal* (New York: G.P. Putnam's Sons, 2004).

56 Christie's recently attempted to auction a marble panel from the tenth century tomb of Wang Chuzhi in Hebei province, stolen in 1994, even characterizing it as similar to the Wang Chuzhi tomb. See Julian E. Barnes, "Alleging Theft, U.S. Demands Rare Sculpture Go Back to China," *New York Times*, March 30, 2000; Victoria Button and Cheung Chi-fai, "US to Return Panel Looted from Old Tomb,"

South China Morning Post, March 10, 2001; and Cheung Chi-fai, "Dealer Denies Knowing Marble Panel Looted Antique's Origins 'Unknown' before It Was Sent to US for Auction," *South China Morning Post*, March 10, 2001. Carelessness about origins is of course not limited to Chinese art. Robert D. McFadden, "Long after Napoleon's Conquests, a Tale of Intrigue Leads to Court, *New York Times*, April 6, 2001, describes a case in which Sotheby's offered for sale a copy of the 1814 Treaty of Fontainebleau which had been reported stolen from the French National Archives in 1988.

57 Pamela Yatsko, "Seducing China's Rich," *Far Eastern Economic Review*, March 27, 1997.

58 Cheung Chi-fai, "Disputed Bronzes Go for $16 m," *South China Morning Post*, May 1, 2000.

59 Chris Yeung, "Sale of Looted Relics 'Stupid'," *South China Morning Post*, May 3, 2000.

60 "International Help Sought to Recover Relics," *South China Morning Post*, July 25, 1997.

61 See Peter Simpson, "Things are lost in the fine," *South China Morning Post Magazine*, December 6, 2009.

62 "Aiji zhenbao di hu" [Egyptian treasures arrive in Shanghai], *Jiefang ribao*, August 6, 1999.

63 The following examples are all found in Lothar Ledderose, *Mi Fu and the Classical Tradition of Chinese Calligraphy* (Princeton: Princeton University Press, 1979), pp. 42, 24–5, 13.

64 On this point, see Rosemary J. Coombe, *The Cultural Life of Intellectual Properties: Authorship, Appropriation, and the Law* (Durham: Duke University Press, 1998), 222.

65 Among others, see Jeanette Greenfield, *The Return of Cultural Treasures*, 2nd edn. (Cambridge: Cambridge University Press, 1966); and Hitchens, *The Elgin Marbles*.

66 When Afghanistan's Taliban demolished the fourth-century Buddhist statues at Bamiyan in 2000, some in the West revived the care argument, yet it retains a nasty core that the poor and dusky cannot be trusted to maintain pretty things.

67 On plunder and illegal art sales, see Pernille Askerud and Etienne Clement, *Preventing the Illicit Traffic in Cultural Property: A Resource Handbook for the Implementation of the 1970 UNESCO Convention* (Paris: UNESCO, 1997); Harrie Leyten, ed., *Illicit Traffic in Cultural Property – Museums Against Pillage* (Amsterdam: Royal Tropical Institute in collaboration with Musée National du Mali, Bamako, 1995); Roderick J. McIntosh and Peter Schmidt, eds., *Plundering Africa's Past* (Bloomington: Indiana University Press, 1996); Kathryn W. Tub, ed., *Antiquities Trade or Betrayed: Legal, Ethical and Conservation Issues* (London: Archetype Publications, 1995); Neil Brodie, Jenny Dhole, and Peter Watson, *Stealing History: The Illicit Trade in Cultural Material* (Cambridge: McDonald Institute for Archaeological Research, 2000).

68 For example, Murphy, *Plunder and Preservation*; Paul M. Bator, *The International Trade in Art* (Chicago: University of Chicago Press, 1983); John H. Merryman, "The Retention of Cultural Property," 21 (1988), *University of California Davis Law Review* 477.

69 Murphy, *Plunder and Preservation*, p. 4.

70 Murphy, *Plunder and Preservation*, p. 157.

71 Murphy, *Plunder and Preservation*, p. 155.

71 For recent anthropological work on the art–money link, see George E. Marcus and Fred R. Myers, eds., *The Traffic in Art and Culture* (Berkeley: University of California Press, 1995).

72 "Canada returns stolen art to China," *Ottawa Citizen*, April 12, 2001. I cannot resist pointing out that the Canadian museum in question was, in 1970, located on yet another Elgin Street.
73 Eric Prideaux, "Japanese Museum to Return Stolen Statue," *Cleveland Plain Dealer*, April 19, 2001.
74 Recent books examining the issue of restoring art plundered during World War II include Lynn H. Nicholas, *The Rape of Europa: The Fate of Europe's Treasures in the Third Reich and the Second World War* (New York: Knopf, 1994); Caroline Moorhead, *Lost and Found: The 9,000 Treasures of Troy* (New York: Penguin Books, 1994); Hector Felciciano, *The Lost Museum: The Nazi Conspiracy to Steal the World's Greatest Works of Art* (New York: Basic Books. 1997); and Richard Z. Chesnoff, *Pack of Thieves: How Hitler and Europe Plundered the Jews and Committed the Greatest Theft in History* (London: Weidenfeld and Nicolson, 2000).
76 "Woguo jiang she haiwai 'zhuibao' jigou" [Our country is to set up an organ for "recovering national treasures" from abroad], *Gongren ribao*, May 21, 2000.
77 Benjamin Genocchio, "Deal to Curb Looting in China Worries Museums," *New York Times*, March 17, 2009.
78 Scott Reyburn and Dune Lawrence, "China-Art Sales May Drop as Bidder Refuses to Pay," *Bloomberg*, March 3, 2009.
79 See Zhang Wanchen, "Yuanming Yuan wenwa huijia zhi lu [The road home for the Yuanming Yuan artefacts], *Zhongguo qinguian bao*, March 3, 2009.

10 Tibetans, Uyghurs, and multinational "China"

Han–minority relations and state legitimation[1]

Colin Mackerras

I am Yi (彝) first and Chinese second. Lolo is the traditional name of my people. The meaning of the name was originally good until the Han turned it into a pejorative. I want to show people that to be a Lolo is respectable, and that we too have a culture.[2]

The speaker is a musician who calls himself "Lolo," after a traditional name for his Southwest China ethnic group that the Chinese state had renamed "Yi." Lolo and many other Lolo/Yi do not regard the changing of their name as legitimate. With a 2000 population of 7,762,272,[3] the Lolo/Yi have a strong and probably growing sense of ethnic identity that appears strongly resistant to any attempts to assimilate them.

The Lolo musician nonetheless still calls himself Chinese, though for him that is secondary to being Lolo/Yi, implying greater loyalty to his own ethnic group than to the Chinese state. Unlike several other ethnic groups, the Lolo/Yi have never shown any sign of wanting to secede from China. They are not especially near a national border. Yet they are unusual among China's ethnic minorities in the combination of the strength of their ethnic identity but weakness of separatist tendencies among them. The musician who calls himself Lolo shows one side of a very complex problem in China: what does Chineseness mean for the ethnic minorities, how do they relate to the majority Han, and how is state legitimacy implicated in Han–minority relations?

In China, every person belongs to a *minzu* (民族), which means a nationality or nation.[4] In the Preamble to its Constitution, the People's Republic of China (PRC) defines itself as "a unitary multinational state (*yige tongyide duominzu guojia* 一个统一的多民族国家) built up jointly by the people of all its nationalities".[5] It follows Stalin in defining a "nation" (*minzu* 民族) as "a historically constituted, stable community of people, having a common language, a common territory, a common economic life and a common psychological makeup, which expresses itself in a common culture." Ethnicity is rubbery at the best of times, but one significant point of silence in this definition is the idea of consciousness, which most scholars nowadays regard as a necessary attribute of an ethnic group.[6]

The census of November 2000 put the majority *minzu* in China, called the Han (汉族), at 91.59 percent of the total population of 1,265,830,000. The remaining 8.41 percent of China's total, or just over 106 million people, belong to fifty-five state-recognized "minority nationalities" (*shaoshu minzu* 少数民族). By far the most populous of the minorities is the Zhuang (壮族), with 16,178,811 people. The next most populous nationality after the Han is thus miniscule in comparison.[7]

Although the minorities are tiny in terms of population, they take up about five-eighths of China's total land mass, including almost the whole of the western half and many of the southwestern regions that include provinces like Yunnan (云南) and Guizhou (贵州). This lends them an importance politically, socially, and strategically out of proportion to their population. Over the centuries and especially under the PRC, Han migration to minority areas has been ongoing and extensive. But what is the basis for the claim that these minority areas should belong to Chinese territory? What is "China," and which territories should it include? Are the minorities really "Chinese," or are only the Han "Chinese"?

What is China?

Both the Republic of China (ROC) and the PRC inherited their territorial claims from the extent of China as it had become under the Qing Dynasty (1644–1911). There are two points of great interest about this empire.

- China was very much larger than under the preceding Ming Dynasty (1368–1644), having taken varying degrees of control over the Tibetan, Mongolian, Turkic Muslim, and Manchurian territories to the southwest, west, northwest, and northeast.
- The ruling family of the Qing Dynasty belonged to the Manchus (*Manzu* 满族), an ethnic group that was to integrate itself into the Han Chinese majority to the extent that most of the markers of its ethnicity like language declined greatly during its reign.

James Millward suggests that "Qing imperialism" led to the enlargement of China under the Manchus.[8] Yet Western and Japanese imperialism exonerated the Manchu Dynasty from the taint of imperialism from the early 1840s on by their own onslaughts on the decaying empire that was China. It is hardly surprising that the ROC was not interested in giving up over half its territory. What it did was to take over the same territory as its predecessor, adding claims over unfairly lost regions, such as Hong Kong to Britain in the case of Qing China.

Yet it is extremely ironic that the *Manchus*, who were not part of the Han Chinese majority, took over this foreign country, doubled its territorial size, and then were removed from power in favour of a *Han Chinese* regime, which chose to hold on to the enlarged territories as far as it could. It is also ironic that the overthrow of the Manchu (Chinese) Empire corresponded roughly in time with the disintegration of several other large empires in various parts of the world, examples being the Habsburg Austro-Hungarian Empire and the Ottoman Turkish Empire. Turkey and Austria are still very much smaller than in the days of those great empires, whereas since 1949 China has restored its previous territory, with the major exception of Mongolia, and has even resumed sovereignty over Hong Kong and Macau.

The western areas of the Qing Empire did not necessarily share the enthusiasm of successor regimes that they should be part of the ROC. No sooner had the Qing Dynasty fallen than both Tibet and Mongolia declared independence from China. The Republic of China refused to recognize the independence of either territory. As it turned out, half of one of the territories did achieve lasting independence, while the other did not, the single overwhelmingly important reason having to do with external military power.

In the case of what the Chinese called "Outer Mongolia" (*Waimenggu* 外蒙古), the northern part of Mongolia more distant from the Chinese heartland, Soviet troops intervened to eliminate the White Russian troops they believed threatened the Soviet Union. It was not Mongolia that interested the Soviets but the protection of the Soviet Union.

It was only in 1945 that the ROC came to terms with Mongolian independence. The ROC signed a friendship treaty with the Soviet Union on August 14, 1945, at the end of World War II. At the same time, the ROC government exchanged notes with the Soviet Union recognizing the Mongolian People's Republic (MPR) "should a plebiscite of the Outer Mongolian people confirm this desire." The referendum took place, with the voters overwhelmingly in support of independence, so on January 5, 1946, the ROC government issued a statement formally recognizing the independence of "Outer" Mongolia.

The Chinese Communist Party (CCP), however, had never been in any doubt about recognition of the MPR. Because it had been Soviet troops that had intervened to bring about Mongolian independence, the CCP accepted this reality from the start. On October 16, 1949, fifteen days after the PRC was established, the new Chinese government cabled recognition of the MPR and that has remained its formal position ever since.[9]

In the case of Tibet, the ROC never recognized independence, even though Chinese control over most Tibetan areas was very weak or even non-existent.[10] The British, who were in control of India, had interests in Tibet, but nothing remotely corresponding to the Soviet occupation of Mongolia occurred. Tibet continued to consider itself independent, or at least the western part further from the Chinese heartland, while Chinese governments continued to regard Tibet as part of China. In any case, the ROC had overwhelming concerns closer to home, including invasion by Japan, which relegated Tibet to a very low place on its list of priorities.

In Xinjiang, a succession of Han regimes followed the collapse of the Manchu Dynasty.[11] There were numerous rebellions against Han Chinese rule from the Turkic Islamic minorities, who could not see why they should be part of China. The neighboring Soviet Union was heavily involved in Xinjiang affairs. In 1944, local Uyghurs and other minorities declared an independent East Turkestan Republic, but it proved impermanent.[12] There was no repetition of the situation in Mongolia, where Soviet occupation had led to independence.

Finally, we may note that the heartland of the former Manchu rulers became firmly sinicized after restrictions against Han migration there were totally lifted at the end of the nineteenth century. There was a spectacular rise in the population from about 10 million at the turn of the twentieth century to just over 30 million in 1932, the year Japan set up its puppet state of Manchukoku, most of the increase owing to Chinese immigration.[13] The irony here is that the expanding sinicization coincided with the Japanese takeover, and their establishment of an independent Manchu state under the protection of Japanese bayonets. With Japan's defeat in 1945 there was no doubt that the territory would return to China.

So what does this history tell us about the meaning of "China"? The answer depends on how strongly the past weighs upon the present. PRC governments have always insisted that the minority areas are legitimately part of China, because the PRC state inherited these territories from earlier governments, making them "integral parts of China" (*Zhongguo bukefenge de bufen* 中国不可分割的部分). For all Chinese governments, the unity of China has ranked at or near the top of their priorities and that includes the ethnic territories. However, even the cursory glance offered above suggests that the inheritance of the ethnic territories is uneven in terms of legitimacy. During the Republican period, Chinese control over its territories was uneven at the best of times, but weaker over Xinjiang than Inner Mongolia and weak to negligible over Tibet. Over Manchuria it was non-existent from 1931 to 1945, but the sections of the international community that won World War II were more than happy to see the territory return to Chinese sovereignty after the war. All those territories Japan had taken over from China since the end of the nineteenth century, including Manchuria and Taiwan, reverted to China at the end of World War II and were claimed as "China" by the incoming PRC government in 1949.

Foreign governments have generally accepted Chinese claims over its minority areas, because it would be virtually impossible to redefine a country's territory every time it underwent a change of regime. Reality tells us that redefining territory leads to instability and even warfare. The special case of Israel, which was re-established in 1948 after a hiatus of more than two millennia, shows the trouble restorations of old states and boundaries can cause the international community. So it comes as no surprise that the international community continues to recognize the ethnic areas of China as part of the country.

History is an important criterion for the legitimacy of a state's intervention in ethnic areas. However, the major point of this section is that while the PRC does have some legitimacy in its territorial claims on the ethnic regions, this legitimacy is not at all obvious. History can be subject to differing points of view. Moreover, history is not the only criterion for establishing legitimacy. A regime may be legitimate in the eyes of the international community, but not in the eyes of its own ethnic minorities. It is also possible that ethnic relations may deteriorate to such an extent as to affect legitimacy. If relations with the majority deteriorate to the point where rebellions break out, or dissatisfaction becomes extreme, then the legitimacy of Han rule is again called into question.

Who is Chinese? Ethnic identity and Han–minority relations

"What is China?" raises another question: Who is Chinese? Are all those people who live within the borders of "China" equally "Chinese"? The second sentence of the 1982 PRC Constitution says that "The people of all nationalities in China have jointly created a splendid culture and have a glorious revolutionary tradition."[14] Article 4 states that all the nationalities are equal; it bans any action that might undermine "the unity of the nationalities" or instigate their secession.[15] This inclusiveness would seem to indicate that all people who live within the borders of the PRC, other than registered foreigners, are indeed equally Chinese. It also suggests very strongly that any attempt to secede from China's family of nationalities will be suppressed.

Part of this policy towards minority nationalities is a system of autonomy. In essence, this means that the government establishes "autonomous" (*zizhi* 自治) areas in places where there are concentrated communities of minority ethnic groups and allows them a limited degree of autonomy. This includes the need for the government head of the autonomous place to belong to the nationality exercising autonomy, although this privilege does not extend to the CCP, which holds the real power. It also includes the right to use their own language in the government and elsewhere, to follow their own customs and religion, provided there is no threat to the state, and to exercise some control over the local budget.[16] Also involved in "autonomy" is a system of "preferential policies" (*youhui zhengce* 优惠政策), such as exemption from the one-child-per-couple policy, preferential access to higher education and favorable treatment for entry into the job market.[17]

Many states around the world now strive to be multicultural, especially immigrant countries such as the United States, Canada, and Australia. There is no reason why people belonging to different ethnic groups should not be equally Chinese, any more than Italian or Chinese migrants to Australia cannot feel themselves Australian. There is a difference, of course. China is generally *not* a migrant country. The minorities have been there for centuries or millennia. An individual who migrates to another country may feel very differently towards the ethnic majority from an individual whose ancestors have always lived in a country but whose people have, over centuries, become more and more marginalized in society.

Dru Gladney has shown the ways in which the majority Han have represented the minorities as exotic, and in a sense inferior. He argues that such representation functions as a means of marking out Han identity and promoting Han nationalism. He describes this process as "essentializing the Han."[18] Many people have drawn attention to a haughty, even racist, streak in Chinese culture. One scholar, drawing attention to the concept of "Chinese nation" (*Zhonghua minzu* 中华民族), describes it as "deeply inflected by racism" because as an inclusive concept it presumes the Han as its core.[19] My own personal observations over many years in China lead me to think that many Chinese care little for minorities, let alone their cultures, and tend to look down on them. Racism is not a weakness exclusive to China but is certainly strong enough to cause serious resentments among those who suffer from it.

In the period of reform, there have been contrary tendencies concerning ethnic identity. In some cases, such as the Tujia (土家) of Hunan and Hubei, ethnic consciousness is extremely weak and probably getting weaker. In other cases ethnic consciousness has strengthened significantly as people try to avoid assimilation. It appears as though the relationship between the minorities on the one hand and the Han and Chinese state on the other has begun to change gradually in favor of the minorities as some successfully assert the autonomy the Constitution promises them. As Nimrod Baranovitch argues,

> Since the mid-1990s, a significant amount of control over the construction and representation of the public identity of China's different ethnic groups (both minorities and the Han majority) has shifted from the Chinese state and the Han majority to the minority people themselves. That some minority individuals can publicly present new alternative narratives about their ethnic identity, sometimes directly opposing the orthodox narratives, lends support to those who have observed that China became more liberal and pluralistic in the 1990s and that today the state is often forced into concessions by the pressures exerted by various groups.[20]

Many of China's ethnic minorities have indeed experienced an *increase* in ethnic identity. One example is the Yao (瑶族) people of Guangxi (广西) and other parts of southwest China (population 2,637,421 in 2000). Ralph Litzinger concluded from field research in the late 1980s and early 1990s that Yao identity was undergoing a strengthening process. Perhaps even more important, he found that "elite members of the Yao nationality" had been "active agents in the making of a modern socialist and, more recently, post-socialist Yao identity."[21]

Another nationality of interest is the Hui (回族), usually identified as Chinese Muslims. The 2000 census put their population at 9,816,805. Dru Gladney's intensive study of the Hui suggests a significant rise in their identity by the late 1980s. He concluded that this identity was ethnic, not merely religious, with Islam being only one of the markers of ethnic identity.[22] What is striking about this finding is that the Hui are among the very few ethnic minorities in China who lack their own language. They are culturally very similar indeed to the Han, except for their Islam. It is evident that the revival both of Hui identity and of Islam has gathered momentum strongly during the 1990s and beyond.[23]

One ethnic group in a rather special category is the Koreans (*Chaoxianzu* 朝鲜族), whose population the 2000 census put at 1,923,842. The Koreans have a very specific language and culture and, despite living in China, remain very close in terms of culture to their co-nationals in Korea. There is a strong sense of identity among the Koreans, and it appears to have grown stronger during the 1990s.[24] On the other hand, Korean identity poses no threat to the Chinese state or to the CCP, and relations between Han and Korean appear to be comparatively free of serious tensions. The reasons for this favorable situation are highly complex, but might include the following:

- The Koreans on the other side of the border (in North Korea) do not in any sense constitute a model that could inspire co-nationals in China to wish to separate from China and join up with the neighboring state.
- The Koreans in China have done remarkably well economically and socially, with standards of living (both urban and rural) just as high or higher than Han counterparts.
- Historically, Chinese influence over Korea was heavy, including sharing Confucianism-based culture. More recently, Koreans in China were far better disposed to the CCP than almost any other major ethnic minority in China, partly because they shared a strong hostility and resistance to Japanese imperialism in the first half of the twentieth century.
- Religion is not a factor in Han–Korean relations.[25]

China is diverse. And so are China's minorities. Even within minority communities there is a great deal of difference, just as there is among the Han and indeed other communities worldwide. At the same time, there are quite a few commonalities as well. All the minorities have been affected by the broad outlines of CCP policy. The thrust towards modernization that began in the late 1970s has had a major impact just about everywhere in China, although the *extent* of influence has varied greatly. In general, the cities have modernized much more quickly than the countryside and the Han areas more quickly than the minority.

Yet it appears that many minority members are quite keen to participate in the economic benefits that go together with modernization. Many perceive more tangible and stronger advantages in the integration of their people into the Chinese economy, even if it means a decline in those special features that set their nationality apart. They may remain proud of belonging to their own ethnic group, but that does not mean they have to disavow being Chinese or isolate themselves from China's economic rise. A very good example of this process is China's most populous nationality, the Zhuang. One major writer on these people claims that many Zhuang villagers, who might never have even heard the name Zhuang in 1949, "today boast of their membership in China's largest minority nationality." At the same time she states that these same people, whose villages were once remote and isolated, "have now begun to participate in a modernizing integrated market economy."[26]

Modernization presents minorities with a challenge. As Stevan Harrell notes of the Nuosu, the name applied in Sichuan to the state-recognized ethnic group called Yi with which the chapter began:

> The challenge now for Nuosu who have some knowledge of the wider world (and they are still a minority) is to manage wisely the tension between cultural survival and economic development. It would be a great loss for the Nuosu if development passed them by, for Nimu [a Nuosu area in Sichuan] is still a poor, unhealthy, and often brutal environment, despite its natural and cultural beauty. It would be an equally great loss for the Nuosu and for the world if development and consumer culture finally smeared out the exquisite mountain patterns that have survived the efforts of so many regimes to tame them and have regenerated themselves so spectacularly after the dark years of the Cultural Revolution.[27]

Harrell's argument applies equally well to many minority communities.

What follows from this material is that most members of minority ethnic groups are reasonably well integrated with the Han majority and enjoy relations with them that are not necessarily any more rancorous than the Han have with one another. They are keener to take advantage of economic progress and a rise in the standard of living than to assert their national status by breaking free of China. Some care nothing for their ethnic identity, even when it is offered. That suggests that there is no crisis of legitimacy on the grounds of ethnicity in most of the ethnic areas. It is likely that most members of ethnic minorities are quite happy to consider themselves Chinese, even if they do have a sense of ethnic consciousness that has strengthened over the years.

The Tibetans

In terms of legitimacy, by far the most problematic of the minority areas is the Tibetan heartland. China's claim to sovereignty over Tibet is less well grounded historically than for the other ethnic areas currently part of China. During the Republican era, the central Chinese government exercised very little influence in Tibet itself, though it had more control in other Tibetan areas and considered them all part of China. What this indicates is that the "inheritance" argument I have used elsewhere works less well for Tibet than for almost any other part of China.

China sent troops into Tibet in 1950 and the following year its representatives signed an agreement with the Tibetan authorities under which Tibet would return to the PRC but remain autonomous within it, including enjoying freedom of religion. However, in March 1959 a rebellion broke out, which the Chinese suppressed quickly but brutally. The head of the Tibetan government, the Fourteenth Dalai Lama (达赖喇嘛), fled to India and set up a government-in-exile there, while in Tibet itself both sides went back on the 1951 agreement. During the Cultural Revolution of 1966–76, radical Han and Tibetan Red Guards (*hongweibing* 红卫兵) made active attempts to stamp out traditional Tibetan culture and religion. However, the early 1980s saw a drastic change in policy, with a consequent revival of Tibetan culture. Great improvements in conditions did not prevent large-scale demonstrations for independence from 1987 to 1989. The Chinese authorities suppressed these firmly, and imposed martial law from March 1989 to May 1990. They also implemented policies promoting rapid economic development, coupled with some degree of freedom of religion, but zero tolerance for separatism or any religious activities with the potential to promote it.[28]

Countries that establish diplomatic relations with the PRC all recognize Tibet as part of China. In the sense that international recognition of territory is one criterion of legitimacy, then China's claim may actually have strengthened under the PRC. On the other hand, China has come under enormous international criticism for human rights abuses in Tibet, a factor that probably reduces at least the perception of legitimacy. In the United States and elsewhere there are movements that advocate Tibetan independence, some of them enjoying support in the high echelons of power. In 1989, the Dalai Lama won the Nobel Peace Prize, which greatly raised his already high prestige. Since that time his trips abroad have multiplied in frequency and he has become an icon of the new spirituality that is so widespread in Western countries. However, although governments have mostly welcomed him, none has moved towards granting him diplomatic recognition. Criticism of Chinese policy and actions in Tibet has mainly stayed at the level of condemning human rights abuses, few challenging that Tibet is part of China.[29]

Following the disturbances of the late 1980s, Tibet appeared for a time to be reasonably stable. State-organized celebrations commemorating the fiftieth anniversary of the 1951 agreement passed without incident. There were no serious disturbances in March 1999 marking the fortieth anniversary of the 1959 uprising and the tenth anniversary of the 1989 demonstrations that led to the imposition of martial law.

However, in March and April 2008, especially on March 14 and the few days thereafter, major disturbances took place in Lhasa (拉萨) and other Tibetan areas. In terms of their extent, these were much more serious than those of the late 1980s, for some four-fifths of them took place in the Tibetan areas of Sichuan and eastern Gansu (甘肃) and Qinghai (青海) Provinces. There were certainly casualties, though how many is unclear, figures by the Chinese authorities and the Tibetan government-in-exile varying wildly.

Although it was monks who led the initial non-violent disturbances, beginning on March 10, what was most striking about the riots was the large number of laity among the participants, both in Lhasa and elsewhere. These included students, farmers, and nomads. The riots of March 14 featured the "ordinary inhabitants of Lhasa," who indulged in what James Miles, the only accredited foreign journalist then in Lhasa, and Michael Sheridan in Hong Kong described as an "undoubtedly racial" and disorganized "orgy of wrecking and looting" directed mainly against Han Chinese but also Hui businesses.[30] Robert Barnett says of the later disturbances that "at least fifteen included major violence against state property, such as burning down rural police stations." Many other protests were peaceful.[31]

The causes of the riots were a matter of intense dispute. Western sources tended to blame Chinese repression, seeing the disturbances as owing to frustration over the failure of the Chinese authorities to hold meaningful dialogue with the Dalai Lama over the future of Tibet, suppression of culture and religious persecution, economic and educational inequality, marginalization of the Tibetans socially, and similar factors. However, the Chinese authorities blamed the "Dalai clique" (*Dalai jituan* 达赖集团), arguing that it was the Dalai Lama who had stirred up the riots, but then tried to blame the Chinese. They mounted an intense media campaign against this clique, portraying the Dalai Lama himself in the worst possible terms.

The signs pointing toward or against outside influence on or involvement in the disturbances were anything but straightforward. In October 2007, the United States had awarded the Dalai Lama the high honor of the Congressional Gold Medal of Honor and it appears to have been the March 10 demands by monks for the release of fellow monks detained for celebrating this event that sparked the whole tragic series of events.[32] In January 2008, the Tibetan Youth Congress and several other bodies began a Tibetan People's Uprising Movement. This included a march from Dharamsala beginning on March 10 that aimed to cross the border into Tibet, but the Indian government stopped it. Tibetan Youth Congress President Tsewang Rigzin denied the March 14 riots received any direct backing from the Tibetan People's Uprising Movement, claiming instead that they were spontaneous, but supported a boycott against the Olympic Games to fan domestic and international opposition against China over Tibet. Meanwhile, the Dalai Lama denied any role in the March 14 riots, which he opposed because of their violence, and attacked any move to boycott the Olympics.[33]

Outside fanning would to some extent absolve the Chinese from the charge of repression in Tibet. However, there appears no doubt that the disturbances both evidenced and caused a serious deterioration of ethnic relations in the Tibetan areas and pinpointed severe social and political tensions there. Moreover, it will likely take a long time to erase the legacy of bitterness from the disturbances, and they could be the seed for further trouble later on.

One of the most important ramifications of the repression of Tibetan protests lay in China's international relations. Western leaders tended to blame the Chinese and side with the Dalai Lama. French President Nicolas Sarkozy was among several other European leaders who announced their intention to protest by boycotting the August 8 Opening Ceremony of the Olympic Games. Although Sarkozy attended in the end, his threats caused considerable rancor in China. There was also a wave of resentment among ordinary Chinese against perceived bias in the Western media's reportage of the events, both at home and abroad. In particular, in April many Chinese living in major Western cities rushed to the defense of the Olympic Torch then in progress towards Beijing, especially after a Tibet activist wrestled the Olympic Torch from Chinese Paralympic athlete Jin Jing in Paris.

Following the 2008 disturbances, the Chinese leadership resumed talks with the Dalai Lama. These had begun again after a long break in 2002, but several rounds had gotten nowhere. In 1996 in London, the Dalai Lama repeated an earlier demand for "genuine autonomy" replacing full independence. World leaders, especially those of the West, supported the Dalai Lama's proposals, and were active in pressing the Chinese to talks after the 2008 disturbances, especially in the context of the disputes over the Olympic Torch and attendance at the Opening Ceremony of the Olympic Games. In July 2008 the Chinese requested that the Tibetans outline the details of their demands, and the Dalai Lama's representatives complied. However, in November talks broke down when China's representatives poured scorn on the demands, repeating an oft-made charge that they were simply full independence in disguise and that the Dalai Lama was a "splittist" (*fenlie fenzi* 分裂分子). In my opinion, what really riles the Chinese leadership is that genuine autonomy will apply to areas much greater than the Tibet Autonomous Region and give the Dalai Lama effective domestic control over areas covering about one-fifth of Chinese territory. They fear that the Dalai Lama or his successors will first demand genuine autonomy, but then demand full independence.

There is a very widespread feeling among Han Chinese that the Tibetans should be grateful because of the tremendous improvement of the economy and the standard of living in the Tibetan regions. Indeed, economic development has been very rapid. GDP has leapt ahead. The state has invested enormously in infrastructure projects, of which the Xining–Lhasa Railroad, opened in July 2006, is only one. It is of course important: apart from receiving a great deal of national and international attention, it has allowed an enormous expansion in tourism and economic and other contacts with the rest of China.

I first visited Tibet in 1985, and on subsequent visits in 1990, 1997, and 2002 I found economic conditions improving dramatically each time. People were better dressed, better educated, and apparently in better health. It is true that this rise in living standards is uneven. A study of development at the end of the twentieth century in Tibet came to the conclusion that an "extreme form of 'urban bias' skews development in Tibet, stratifying society across the ethnic divide and disparately benefiting the Han population mainly because it is urban."[34] The main site of disparities is urban/rural, not ethnic. And a 2008 study found that "there is no systematic discrimination of Tibetans by employers. The labor market operates according to market principles and the most skilled people are getting the jobs regardless of ethnicity."[35]

However, the same 2008 study found vast inequities in standards of living and employment opportunities, the result being that Tibetans have become marginalized in the economy. In the Tibet Autonomous Region, urban incomes are up to five times greater than rural ones. In the cities, Han immigrants tend to be more aggressive in opening and maintaining businesses, and the hope that Tibetans will admire and copy the Han mode of business has not been realized.[36] A further study by a Tibetan scholar has found that "Tibetans are poorly equipped to respond to and take advantage" of the business opportunities which China's policy of developing the west has provided.[37] Despite the preferential policies noted above, even Tibetan employers often prefer Han over Tibetan workers, simply because they find the former have more appropriate qualifications and better education. According to Ben Hillman, "local employers (Tibetan and non-Tibetan alike) would happily hire Tibetans if they could do the job."[38]

The reasons for the disparities are complex. However, one scholar has argued that "poor education is among the crucial factors explaining the inability of Tibetans to compete economically with non-Tibetan migrants."[39] There is a vast gap in literacy between rural and urban areas and thus between Tibetans and Han. The standard of schooling varies from place to place but is sometimes extremely low. Instruction in Tibetan, which is general at the primary level but declines the higher up one goes in the system, is very helpful for maintaining Tibetan culture. However, it is not so useful for preparing students for the job market or for competing with Han people in business, because it means that their knowledge of Chinese is likely to be less than Han immigrant rivals.

According to the 1990 and 2000 Chinese censuses, the Han population in the Tibet Autonomous Region rose from 81,217 or 3.68 percent of the total in 1990 to 155,300 or 5.9 percent of the total in 2000.[40] The army is not included in the census figures, but otherwise the 1990 census included all those who had been living in Tibet for at least a year at the time the census was taken, the 2000 census reducing the minimum time of residence to six months. So the rise in Han numbers may not actually be as high as shown, since the 2000 figure is likely to include more short-term Han stayers than that of 1990. The figures do not point to any mass influx of Han, but there appears to have been an increase in the last decade of the twentieth century, especially to the major cities. Andrew M. Fischer is probably right to suggest that the Han "have dominated urbanization" in the Tibet Autonomous Region.[41]

Table 10.1 shows selected years for annual population surveys. Unlike the census, these are based on *hukou* registration figures, which do not include short-term residents or migrants, let alone the army. These also show a rise in the Han proportion, but it still far from overwhelming.

Table 10.1 Annual population survey of the Tibet Autonomous Region, based on *hukou* (户口) registration figures[42]

Year	Total population	Han population	Han %
2001	2,537,001	77,003	3.0
2004	2,592,113	93,306	3.6
2007	2,735,867	110,429	4.0

Tibetan culture appears to me to be very much alive in the first decade of the twenty-first century, and in absolutely no danger of dying out. Tibetans are still overwhelmingly dedicated to the traditional Tibetan Buddhism, and there is no shortage of young men keen to enter the monastic life. One writer's reference to "dozens of robed novices, many no older than 12" amid 300 monks in a Tibetan monastery in Sichuan province early in 2003[43] accords with my own findings both in Tibet itself and in other Tibetan areas of China. In mid-2002, the Tibetan government actually issued regulations promoting the study, use, and development of the Tibetan language.[44]

At the same time, modernization is exercising a weakening effect on Tibetan traditions, as it tends to do everywhere, and the Xining (西宁)–Lhasa (拉萨) Railroad can only speed up the trend. According to a Tibetan college student, "The more money we Tibetans have, the higher our living standard is, the more we forget our own culture. And with or without the Chinese, I think that would be happening."[45] Tibetan language is tending to decline in favor of Chinese, simply because it is much more useful and opens more doors toward a good career and prosperity.[46]

Religious persecution persists. At the end of 2002, two Tibetan monks were tried for allegedly being accomplices in bombings and separatist activities. The younger monk was executed in January 2003.[47] Although the Chinese government no longer suppresses Tibetan culture unless it perceives it as a threat to CCP rule, the Chinese authorities keep an eagle eye out for "dangerous" activities, and may be quite happy to see Tibetan traditions weakening among the people.

What does all this tell us about Han–Tibetan relations? A 1996 survey concluded that relations may not have been as bad in the mid- to late 1990s as most in the West believed. It covered 586 families, 200 in Tibet itself, mainly in Lhasa, 170 in the Tibetan regions of Sichuan, and 216 in Gansu. The survey was carried out by a team of eighteen people led by Herbert Yee (Yu Zhen) of Hong Kong's Baptist College.[48] Responding to the statement that the Han were honest and reliable, 12.5 percent strongly agreed, 62.5 percent agreed, 9.7 percent disagreed, and 1.3 percent disagreed strongly (the remaining 14.1 percent had no opinion).[49] Surprisingly, the survey also found strong support for intermarriage between Han and Tibetans: among 547 respondents, 70.9 percent either agreed or strongly agreed with the comment that "as long as two people love each other sincerely, it doesn't matter whether they are the same nationality or not."[50]

On the other hand, there is a range of evidence suggesting that Tibetan–Han relations are bad or very bad. One scholar has claimed that the rise in the Tibetan economy never succeeded in "buying love."[51] Persistent religious tensions and cavalier Han attitudes toward Tibetan culture undermine ethnic harmony. Most importantly, the spring 2008 disturbances, which appear to have taken the Chinese authorities by surprise, suggest that even in times of economic prosperity Tibetans harbor more resentment toward Han people than they normally show.

The Uyghurs

The Uyghurs (*Weiwuerzu* 维吾尔族) are a Turkic people and the great majority believe in Islam. Their language, culture, and lifestyle are closer to those of the Turkic peoples of central Asia than to those of the Han Chinese. According to the November 2000 census, the total Uyghur population at that time was 8,399,393, all but a small minority living in Xinjiang.[52]

By the first decade of the twenty-first century, Han relations with the Uyghurs were worse than with any other ethnic minority in China, with the possible exception of the Tibetans.

In April 1990, a small-scale rebellion erupted in Baren Township, Akto County, in the southwest of Xinjiang. Inspired by the Islamic doctrine of the "holy war" (*shengzhan* 圣战), it gained some support but was quickly suppressed by the Chinese state. Despite its failure, it led to a series of violent incidents directed against Chinese rule. Among these, the largest in scale in the 1990s took place in February 1997 in Yining (伊宁 known to the Uyghurs as Gulja) near the border with Kazakhstan. As with previous riots, these were brutally suppressed by the authorities.[53] Executions of Uyghur separatists following the 1997 disturbances continued over several years. Several studies have suggested that Han–Uyghur relations in Xinjiang deteriorated over the 1990s.[54] A major reason for this deterioration is increasing Han immigration into Xinjiang. This is not a new phenomenon, but appears to have gathered momentum in the 1990s.[55] One study found a distinction in Uyghur attitudes towards the original Han settlers who came in the early decades after 1949 and the new Han immigrants. Uyghurs are not so badly disposed towards the old settlers, but hate the new ones intensely. The reason is that many of the "original settlers" were prepared to learn Uyghur and adopt Uyghur customs such as giving up pork, while the new ones behave like colonial masters, adopting "great Han chauvinist attitudes" (*dahanzu shawenzhuyi de taidu* 大汉族沙文主义的态度).[56]

Despite "preferential policies" and rising living standards among virtually all people, including ethnic minorities, Uyghurs feel a growing marginalization in education and work. Han immigrants tend to get the better jobs, while Uyghurs "end up doing blue-collar jobs or remain in traditional agricultural roles." In the cities the presence of more prosperous Han gives the Uyghurs something to compare themselves with, adding to resentments.[57]

The war against terrorism that followed the September 11, 2001, terrorist attacks also affected Han–Uyghur relations in Xinjiang. This is because the war has increased mutual fear and mistrust among the Han and Muslim populations. The Chinese government has been fearful of terrorism and Muslim fundamentalism in Xinjiang for some time. Since the early 1990s, Muslim extremists have indeed targeted civilians. For instance, on the same day as the funeral service for Deng Xiaoping, February 25, 1997, terrorists planted four bombs in buses in the Xinjiang capital of Ürümqi, killing at least nine people and wounding numerous others, mostly children on their way home from school.

With the war against terrorism, the Chinese authorities were quick to claim connections between the al-Qaeda network on the one hand and Uyghur separatists and Muslim extremists on the other. At first the United States was cautious in accepting the link, continuing to condemn PRC crackdowns as human rights abuses. However, in May 2002 the United States Department of State issued a report about worldwide terrorism the year before and was actually quite complimentary about China's actions in Xinjiang.[58] In August 2002, both the United States and the United Nations formally listed the most important of the Uyghur separatist organizations, usually known as the East Turkestan Islamic Movement, as "terrorist" (*kongbu fenzi* 恐怖分子). Uyghur diasporic groups reacted furiously, denouncing the move as treacherous, but in the atmosphere of the war against terrorism they did not win much international support.[59]

The next few years saw very little overt and publicized terrorist activity. According to an official claim, however, January 2007 saw a gun battle in the Pamirs near the border with Pakistan, in which police killed some East Turkestan Islamic Movement terrorists, and seized some armaments. In 2008 there was a range of incidents in Xinjiang from early in the year, probably seeking to embarrass China in the context of the Olympic Games. They reached a climax with three attacks in the first half of August, just before and during the Olympic Games. The Xinjiang CCP Secretary Wang Lequan was convinced that all three incidents were terrorist and responded by claiming that China was in a life-and-death struggle with the three evil forces of terrorism, separatism, and religious extremism.[60]

On July 5, 2009 China's most serious ethnic rioting for decades broke out in Ürümqi. On the initial day, the casualties were mostly Han, resulting from attacks by Uyghurs, but later the Han counterattacked. The Chinese authorities suppressed the rioting, with many arrests. The result of the rioting and heavy-handed suppression was further worsening of relations between Han and Uyghurs. However, unlike in the Tibetan areas in 2008, the Chinese authorities did succeed in preventing serious disturbances from spreading outside Ürümqi. The initial trigger was a violent incident in Guangdong Province, but, as in Tibet, the Chinese official media and those outside offered very different analyses of the deeper causes. The Western press tended to point to ethnic inequalities and discrimination exacerbated by severe government restrictions on Islam and other aspects of Uyghur culture. On the other hand, the Chinese authorities blamed outside forces, this time the Uyghur businesswoman Rebiya Kadeer, resident in the United States, and the World Uyghur Congress, of which she is president.

The deterioration of relations between Uyghurs and Han, combined with the greater hatred the Uyghurs direct towards the newly arrived Han in comparison to those of longer residence, suggests strongly that the legitimacy of Chinese rule in Xinjiang has suffered as far as the Uyghurs are concerned. However, for its part, the Chinese state seems more determined than ever to maintain social stability in Xinjiang, no matter what the cost in terms of Uyghur resentment. The international community has generally been quite condemnatory of China's heavy-handed suppression of disturbances in Xinjiang, but has not challenged the legitimacy of Chinese rule there.

Separatism and state legitimation

The Tibetans and Uyghurs are the minorities history has shown to have the greatest potential for separatism from China. There are members of both ethnic groups who would like to secede from China. However, early in the twenty-first century the likelihood seems slight in both cases. The Chinese have won over enough members of the economic and political elite, and the power of the Chinese army is such that successful secession under present conditions is more or less out of the question.

Separation of any territory from China would require:

- the collapse of the Chinese state, and/or
- armed foreign intervention.

By the collapse of the Chinese state, I mean not just the overthrow of the CCP, but a disintegration involving social, political, and economic turmoil, and probably civil war. The imminent collapse of China has indeed been predicted, but seems unlikely without something on the scale of a long-lasting recession.[61] A long-term economic downturn could trigger social instability and political fragmentation, but need not necessarily lead to national disintegration.

At present, the likelihood of foreign intervention to assist any separatist movement in China seems remote. Both the war against terrorism and the global financial crisis have made such an eventuality in China less likely than ever, because the most likely candidate for intervention – the United States – has a substantial interest in cooperating with China.

Tibetan independence enjoys a great deal of support in the West, including the United States, but supporters of an independent East Turkestan are still comparatively few and, although they have become much better organized in the twenty-first century, such supporters are still lacking in influence. The Free Tibet lobby may wish for American diplomatic recognition of the government-in-exile and later an independent Tibet, but would hardly favor armed intervention. American recognition of Tibetan independence would most certainly arouse fury in Beijing and in the foreseeable future is most unlikely to be a cause worth the trouble that would undoubtedly result in Washington and elsewhere.

A farmer begins a fascinating autobiography by observing: "I am, of course, Chinese; however, I should like to add one more word: I am Bai Chinese. I belong not to the great Hans of Central China but to the Bai National Minority."[62] For him, being Chinese comes *before* being Bai. At the beginning of the chapter we discussed the case of a Lolo/Yi musician who said, in contrast to the Bai farmer, that he was Lolo/Yi first and Chinese only second.

What this shows is that members of different ethnic groups frequently have different attitudes toward being Chinese. There are most certainly quite a few Tibetans and Uyghurs, and doubtless members of other minorities in China, who would deny being Chinese altogether. And among the same ethnic group not all people hold the same view of their identity.

During the reform period, the Chinese state has responded to the minorities in large part according to their loyalty to the Chinese state. It has reserved coercive responses for those ethnic groups with separatist tendencies, and violence has been sharpest at times when separatism flared into open rioting or rebellion. Such cases have included the Tibetans in the late 1980s and in 2008 and the Uyghurs throughout most of the 1990s and again in 2008 and 2009. Methods used toward other ethnic minorities have generally been more in line with what most would regard as legitimate. One thinks of ethnic groups like the Yi or Koreans, both with very strong ethnic consciousness but no separatist movements. Although these two peoples vary enormously in their histories, cultures, and economic levels, the Chinese state has been able to handle them without provoking excessive hostility. Indeed, the Koreans are a "model" (*mofan* 模范) ethnic minority in terms of economic development, literacy, and lack of opposition to the Chinese state, despite their strong culture and language, including their own script.

I have argued that the Chinese state has some legitimacy in its territorial claims, with Tibet being much more doubtful than any of the other ethnic territories. But the question remains: to what extent are the members of the ethnic minorities challenging the legitimacy of the CCP and the current Chinese state? This chapter has suggested that the situation varies greatly from ethnic group to ethnic group and within ethnic groups themselves.

For members of ethnic minorities, ethnicity *may* be the most important issue in determining CCP legitimacy but is not *necessarily* so. Among ethnic groups that have experienced separatist movements, notably the Uyghurs and Tibetans, ethnicity is bound to weigh more heavily than among those better integrated into the Chinese state, such as the Zhuang or Tujia. Ethnicity counts far more in determining how Tibetans or Uyghurs feel about the legitimacy of the CCP than it does among the Koreans or Zhuang, because their sense of identity is stronger and based more solidly on resentments against injustice.

Following China's accession to the World Trade Organization at the end of 2001, China began to become more and more integrated within the globalized world, as has been amply demonstrated since the global financial crisis struck toward the end of 2008. This does not necessarily mean the end of ethnic cultures. Indeed, there are cases where globalization provokes local-ization as a form of resistance. I do not see the imminent demise of Yao or Miao (苗族) culture in China, let alone Tibetan or Uyghur. But the overall impact of the globalization of markets, consumer practices, communications and tourism is to reduce the differences between cultures. Among the ten-sions operating in China and intensified by globalization is that between the CCP's Marxist–Leninist ideology and the non- or anti-Marxist tendencies in society. This cannot fail to weaken the legitimacy of the CCP overall, both among the Han and the ethnic minorities.

Notes

1 This chapter is a revision of "What Is China? Who Is Chinese? Han–Minority Relations, Legitimacy, and the State," in Peter Hays Gries and Stanley Rosen, eds., *State and Society in 21st Century China: Crisis, Contention, and Legitimation* (London and New York: RoutledgeCurzon, 2004).

2 Nimrod Baranovitch, "Between Alterity and Identity, New Voices of Minority People in China," *Modern China* 27(3) (July 2001), p. 378.

3 National Bureau of Statistics of China (comp.), *Zhongguo tongji nianjian, China Statistical Yearbook 2002* (Beijing: Zhongguo tongji chubanshe, 2002), p. 97.

4 The terms *min*, people, and *zu*, tribe or race, have existed in the Chinese language for millennia. However, the combination *minzu* in the modern sense of nation was first used by Liang Qichao in 1899. See Wu Shimin and Wang Ping, and others, *Minzu wenti gailun* (Chengdu: Sichuan Renmin chubanshe, 1999), p. 6.

5 "The Constitution of PRC," in *People's Republic of China Yearbook 2000* (Beijing: PRC Yearbook, 2000), p. 2.

6 In his definition of an "ethnic group," Richard Schermerhorn includes the fol-lowing sentence: "A necessary accompaniment is some consciousness of kind among members of the group." See his "Ethnicity and Minority Groups," in John Hutchinson and Anthony D. Smith, eds., *Ethnicity* (Oxford and New York: Oxford University Press, 1996), p. 17. Cited from *Comparative Ethnic Relations* (New York: Random House, 1970).

7 The figures given here do not include Taiwan, Hong Kong, or Macau. They come from *Zhongguo tongji nianjian 2002*, pp. 95, 97.

8 See, for instance, James A. Millward, *Beyond the Pass, Economy, Ethnicity, and Empire in Qing Central Asia, 1759–1864* (Stanford: Stanford University Press, 1998), pp. 15–18.

9 For an excellent coverage of the period and especially of Mongolia's role between China and the Soviet Union, see Xiaoyuan Liu, *Reins of Liberation: An Entangled History of Mongolian Independence, Chinese Territoriality and Great Power Hegemony, 1911–1950* (Stanford: Stanford University Press, 2006). For a treat-ment with a view sympathetic to the independence of Mongolia, see C.R. Bawden, *The Modern History of Mongolia* (London: Weidenfeld & Nicolson, 1968).

10 For an excellent history of Tibet in this period, see Melvyn C. Goldstein, *A History of Modern Tibet 1913–1951: The Demise of the Lamaist State* (Berkeley: University of California Press, 1989).

11 The best general history of Xinjiang is James A. Millward, *Eurasian Crossroads, A History of Xinjiang* (New York: Columbia University Press, 2007). An excellent book-length study of the Republican period in Xinjiang comes from Andrew D.W. Forbes, *Warlords and Muslims in Chinese Central Asia: A Political History of Republican Sinkiang, 1911–1949* (Cambridge: Cambridge University Press, 1986).

12 On the East Turkestan Republic, see David D. Wang, *Under the Soviet Shadow: The Yining Incident, Ethnic Conflicts and International Rivalry in Xinjiang 1944–1949* (Hong Kong: The Chinese University Press, 1999); and Linda Benson, *The Ili Rebellion: The Moslem Challenge to Chinese Authority in Xinjiang 1944–1949* (Armonk, NY: M.E. Sharpe, 1990). Wang's account claims much more Soviet involvement than Benson's.

13 See Colin Mackerras, *China's Minorities, Integration and Modernization in the Twentieth Century* (Hong Kong: Oxford University Press, 1994), pp. 120–1.

14 "The Constitution of PRC," p. 1.

15 "The Constitution of PRC," p. 3.

16 For a detailed treatment of policy from 1949 to the early 1990s, see Colin Mackerras, *China's Minorities*, pp. 139–66, and for the period from 1989 to 2002, see Colin Mackerras, *China's Ethnic Minorities and Globalisation* (London and New York: RoutledgeCurzon, 2003), pp. 37–55.

17 See Barry Sautman, "Expanding Access to Higher Education for China's National Minorities, Policies of Preferential Admissions," in Gerard A. Postiglione, ed., *China's National Minority Education, Culture, Schooling, and Development* (New York and London: Falmer Press, 1999), pp. 173–210.

18 Dru C. Gladney, "Representing Nationality in China: Refiguring Majority/ Minority Identities," *Journal of Asian Studies* 53(1) (1994), p. 98.

19 Uradyn E. Bulag, *The Mongols at China's Edge, History and the Politics of National Unity* (Lanham, MD: Rowman and Littlefield, 2002), pp. 17–18.

20 Baranovitch, "Between Alterity and Identity," p. 393.

21 Ralph A. Litzinger, *Other Chinas, the Yao and the Politics of National Belonging* (Durham and London: Duke University Press, 2000), p. xx.

22 Dru C. Gladney, *Muslim Chinese, Ethnic Nationalism in the People's Republic* (Cambridge, MA: Council on East Asian Studies, Harvard University, distributed by Harvard University Press, 1991), especially p. 323.

23 See Dru C. Gladney, *Ethnic Identity in China: The Making of a Muslim Minority Nationality* (Stanford: Harcourt Brace and Co., 1998); and Raphael Israeli, *Islam in China: Religion, Ethnicity, Culture and Politics* (Oxford: Lexington Books, 2002).

24 See also Bernard Vincent Olivier, *The Implementation of China's Nationality Policy in the Northeastern Provinces* (San Francisco: Mellen Research University Press, 1993), especially p. 262.

25 On this last point see Colin Mackerras, *China's Minority Cultures: Identities and Integration Since 1912* (New York: St. Martin's Press, 1995), pp. 117–18.

26 Katherine Palmer Kaup, *Creating the Zhuang, Ethnic Politics in China* (Boulder and London: Lynne Rienner Publishers, 2000), p. 171.

27 Stevan Harrell, "The Survival of Nuosu Culture," in Stevan Harrell, Bamo Qubumo, and Ma Erzi, *Mountain Patterns, the Survival of Nuosu Culture in China* (Seattle and London: University of Washington Press, 2000), p. 9.

28 The best history of Tibet under the PRC is Tsering Shakya, *The Dragon in the Land of Snows: A History of Modern Tibet Since 1947* (London: Pimlico, 1999). Another excellent study is A. Tom Grunfeld, *The Making of Modern Tibet*, revised edition (Armonk, NY: M.E. Sharpe, 1996).

29 For an interesting discussion of American government attitudes towards Tibet in the 1990s, see Melvyn Goldstein, *The Snow Lion and the Dragon, China, Tibet, and the Dalai Lama* (Berkeley, Los Angeles, and London: University of California Press, 1997), pp. 117–25.

30 James Miles and Michael Sheridan, "Fears of Another Tiananmen as Tibet Explodes in Hatred," *Sunday Times*, March 16, 2008, http://www.timesonline.co.uk/tol/news/world/asia/article3559355.ece (accessed January 23, 2009).

31 Robert Barnett, "Thunder from Tibet," *New York Review of Books* 55(9) (May 29, 2008), http://www.nybooks.com/articles/21391 (accessed January 23, 2009).

32 Barnett, "Thunder from Tibet."

33 Peter Wonacott, "Tibetan Youth Challenge Beijing – and Dalai Lama," *Wall Street Journal*, March 20, 2008, web version http://online.wsj.com/article/SB120596094739349681.html (accessed January 23, 2009).

34 Barry Sautman and Irene Eng, "Tibet: Development for Whom?," *China Information: A Journal on Contemporary China Studies* 15(2) (2001), p. 21.

35 Ben Hillman, "Money Can't Buy Tibetans' Love," *Far Eastern Economic Review* 171(3) (April 4, 2008), p. 10.

36 Hillman, "Money Can't Buy Tibetans' Love," pp. 11–12

37 Wang Shiyong, "The Failure of Education in Preparing Tibetans for Market Participation," *Asian Ethnicity* 8(2) (June 2007), p. 131.

38 Hillman, "Money Can't Buy Tibetans' Love," p. 10.

39 Wang, "The Failure of Education in Preparing Tibetans for Market Participation," p. 131.

40 The 1990 figure, from the census of that year, is given in Population Census Office of Xizang Autonomous Region (comp.), *Xizang zizhiqu 1990 nian renkou pucha ziliao, dianzi jisuanji huizong* (*Tabulation on the 1990 Population Census of Xizang Autonomous Region, Computer Tabulation*) (Lhasa: Xizang Publishing House, 1992), p. 38. The 2000 figure is from *Renmin ribao* (*People's Daily*), 3 April 2001, p. 1.

41 Andrew M. Fischer, in Anne-Marie Blondeau and Katia Buffetrille, eds., *Authenticating Tibet, Answers to China's 100 Questions* (Berkeley, Los Angeles: University of California Press, 2008), p. 150.

42 Tibet Autonomous Region Bureau of Statistics and Tibet General Team of Investigation under the National Bureau of Statistics (comp.), *Xizang tongji nianjian (Tibet Statistical Yearbook) 2008* (Beijing: China Statistics Press, 2008), item 3–4.

43 Erik Eckholm, "From a Chinese Cell, a Lama's Influence Remains Undimmed," *New York Times*, February 23, 2003, web version http://query.nytimes.com/gst/fullpage.html?res=9C03EEDC113DF930A15751C0A9659C8B63 (accessed January 26, 2009).

44 See Nicolas Tournadre, "The Dynamics of Tibetan–Chinese Bilingualism: The Current Situation and Future Prospects," *China Perspectives*, no. 45 (January–February 2003), p. 30.

45 Quoted in Sautman and Eng, "Tibet: Development for Whom?," p. 74.

46 Tournadre, "The Dynamics of Tibetan–Chinese Bilingualism," p. 35.

47 Eckholm, "From a Chinese Cell."

48 Yu Zhen and Guo Zhenglin, "Xizang, Sichuan Gansu Zangqu shehui fazhan diaocha baogao" ("Report of a social survey in the Tibetan areas of Tibet, Sichuan and Gansu"), in Yu Zhen and Guo Zhenglin, eds., *Zhongguo Zangqu xiandaihua, lilun, shijian, zhengce* (*The Modernization of China's Tibetan Regions, Theory, Practice, Policy*) (Beijing: Zhongyang minzu daxue chubanshe, 1999), pp. 35–6.

49 Yu and Guo, "Xizang," p. 81.

50 Yu and Guo, "Xizang," p. 82.

51 Ben Hillman, "Money Can't Buy Tibetans' Love," pp. 8–16.

52 *Zhongguo tongji nianjian 2002*, p. 97.

53 These are discussed in Mackerras, *China's Ethnic Minorities and Globalisation*, pp. 49–54.

54 There are quite a few studies of the situation in Xinjiang during the 1990s with some reference to or a focus on Han–Uyghur relations. The main ones include Nicolas Becquelin, "Xinjiang in the Nineties," *The China Journal*, no. 44 (July 2000), pp. 65–90; and Gardner Bovingdon, "The Not-So-Silent Majority, Uyghur Resistance to Han Rule in Xinjiang," *Modern China: An International Quarterly of History and Social Science* 28(1) (January 2002), pp. 39–78.

55 For some discussion of Han immigration into Xinjiang since 1949, and in particular during the 1990s, see Colin Mackerras, "Xinjiang at the Turn of the Century, and the Causes of Separatism," in Craig Benjamin and Samuel N.C. Lieu, eds., *Walls and Frontiers in Inner-Asian History*, Silk Road Studies VI (Turnhout, Belgium: Brepols, 2002), pp. 27–31. See also Bruce Gilley, "'Uighurs Need Not Apply'," *Far Eastern Economic Review* 164(33) (August 23, 2001), pp. 26–7.

56 See Joanne N. Smith, "'Making Culture Matter': Symbolic, Spatial and Social Boundaries between Uyghurs and Han Chinese," *Asian Ethnicity* 3(2) (September 2002), especially the conclusion, pp. 172–4.

57 Smith, "'Making Culture Matter'," p. 173. The point about job discrimination looms large in other accounts, such as Amnesty International, *Gross Human Rights Violations.*

58 U.S. Department of State, Counterterrorism Office, *Patterns of Global Terrorism 2001* (Washington, D.C.: U.S. Department of State, 2002), p. 17.

59 At counter-terrorism talks in Beijing early in 2003 the United States refused a Chinese request to designate a second body, the East Turkestan Liberation Organization, as a terrorist group.

60 Wang Lequan's statement was carried in the *Xinjiang Daily* of August 14, 2008 and reported by Reuters, among other places in "Xinjiang: China Admits 'Life and Death' Battle," *Indian Express*, web version posted 15 August 2008, http://www.indianexpress.com/news/xinjiang-china-admits-life-and-death-battle/349004/ (accessed 24 January 2009).

61 See especially Gordon G. Chang, *The Coming Collapse of China* (New York: Random House, 2001).

62 He Liyi, with Claire Anne Chik, *Mr China's Son, A Villager's Life* (Boulder: Westview Press, 1993), p. 3.

11 A question of confidence

State legitimacy and the new urban poor

Dorothy J. Solinger

If state benevolence is to serve as a critical condition for Chinese citizens' acceptance of their government as legitimate, as Vivienne Shue suggests in Chapter 2, then the concept and practice of official "benevolence" (*ren* 仁) demands some interrogation in today's China. Does benevolence obtain, and do those who would depend deeply upon it believe in its presence? And, as evidence of such belief, do they entertain an expectation that the state, in its guise as giver, can be counted upon for what for them are vital extensions of its current offerings in the days to come?

In this chapter I target the Minimum Livelihood Guarantee program (*Zuidi shenghuo baozhang* 最低生活保障) and its subjects/objects (*dibao duixiang* 低保对象) or households (*dibaohu* 低保户) to address this question. I claim that a major issue is the extent to which a bond of trust entwines beneficiary and benefactor in their interchange in this welfare sector, the degree to which, that is, the one has faith in the other. I will argue that, paradoxically, the recipients of this hand-out place far more confidence in the powers-that-be than the leaders are willing to lend to them. Thus, in querying the existence of any sense of legitimacy in the realm inhabited by the impoverished, it would seem that it is the state that raises questions of its partner, rather than the other way around.

In what follows, I first give a brief account of the context in which new poverty arose in Chinese cities in and after the mid-1990s and then of the social welfare program under consideration that was meant to address that penury. I next move on to substantiate my claim that the state is much more suspicious of the indigent than the latter is of the state. The upshot is that while the destitute treat their governors as legitimate, that honor is not requited.

Background

The cities, for the most part, appeared up until the middle of the 1990s to be islands within a larger Chinese political economy in which job-secured workers could be certain that their livelihood, health, education, and living abodes would evermore undergird their and their children's sustenance. At least until the late 1980s (and in most cases through to the mid-1990s), urbanites who stuck with the state sector considered good treatment on the job a kind of birthright, an entitlement that was sure to be enforced. Herein lies the root of the seemingly still unshakable expectation that the government is meant to, and will be able and inclined to, provide for its people, or for its urban people, at any rate.

In the cities after 1949, true, there had always been the disadvantaged – those without offspring or spouses, the disabled, and people unable to support themselves. But this relatively tiny batch of individuals generally survived in the shadows and out of sight, subsisting – but just barely – as members of the "three withouts" (*sanwu* 三无), if on a mere pittance, in the form of meager "social relief" (*shehui jiuji* 社会救济) disbursed by civil affairs departments.[1]

Not only did cities seem immune from the perils of hardship up until just over a decade ago, but there was even reason to hope that the rise in living standards that followed China's opening up after 1980 would continue for everyone in them. For the dawn of the switch to the market economy in the early 1980s was accompanied by the credo that the wealth being generated – first by the fertilization infused by the inrush of foreign capital along the coast and later by rapidly shooting sprouts of the private sector – would in time shed seeds that fostered prosperity much more widely.

But the drama of the displacement of those who are now destitute unfolded precisely in the midst of their state's hell-bent drive to "develop" (*fazhan* 发展). At first the effects were slow to appear. Throughout the late 1980s, there had been scattered reports of job losses among "redundant workers" (*xiagang gongren* 下岗工人).[2] In the main, however, managers were still constrained at that point from dismissing employees openly.[3] In the early 1990s, though, the state-owned firms began to succumb to competition from imports, as well as from the non-state and foreign-invested sectors.[4] The rivalry could be fierce as enterprises in these other portions of the economy lacked the responsibility that the state had long bestowed on the work units it owned and ran to provide welfare and other benefits for their staff and labor forces, a responsibility, again, that is at the root of the inclination of the presently poor to rely on the state. Clearly, the discrepancy in behavior among the various ownership forms of firms enhanced the non-state enterprises' profitability and competitiveness at the expense of their state-owned rivals.

There were other direct causes behind the plight of the official enterprises that came to visit adversity upon the old workforce. These included the obsolescence of much of these firms' equipment in the wake of burgeoning technological imports from the developed world. Added to this was the growing and serious mismatch between, on the one hand, the largely unschooled nature of a huge segment of the workforce (owing to its coming of age during the Cultural Revolution years, when schools were shut and the only education on offer entailed "learning from the workers, peasants and soldiers") and the type of demand issuing from the labor market as the economy underwent its marketization, on the other.

But it was finally at the end of the several-year-long austerity program introduced by then Vice Premier Zhu Rongji in mid-1993 that a sudden outbreak of unemployment began. This austerity program produced significantly heightened market pressures, with its temporary but stiff curtailment of the lavish and guaranteed credit that state firms (and their workers) had regularly counted on leading to massive firm losses.[5] Already in 1994, when a new Labor Law was written granting firm management freedom to fire workers if near bankruptcy or in serious difficulty,[6] the phenomenon called *xiagang* (下岗) – according to which employees in name retained their tie to their work unit (*danwei* 单位) but were in fact without any work to do – began to gather speed.[7] By spring 1996, urban unemployment, once strictly anathema to the Communist Party, was being termed "inevitable in a market economy," which in China by that time unquestionably obtained.[8]

Subsequently, a surge in job losses gathered new and ever-escalating momentum after the Communist Party's Fifteenth Party Congress in September 1997. At that meeting, then Party General Secretary Jiang Zemin put forward two critical chores: first, to "adjust and improve the ownership structure" (*tiaozheng he wanshan suoyouzhi jiegou* 调整和完善所有制结构); and, second, to "accelerate the reform of state-owned enterprises" (*jiakuai guoyouqiye gaige* 加快国有企业改革).[9] Neither of these objectives can be divorced from the subsequent flood of layoffs that followed the Congress. At the end of the year, the Ministry of Labor's National Work Conference announced, apparently with much chagrin in light of its customary munificence, that "Dismissing and laying off workers is a move against our will taken when we have no way to turn for help, but also the only way to extricate ourselves from [this] predicament."[10]

The upshot was that, for a significant section of the old proletariat in the factories of China's metropolises, mounting losses among state companies came to spell involuntary unemployment.[11] According to China's own State Statistical Bureau, "the number of workers employed in the state-owned sector fell from 113 million to 67 million, a decline of 40 percent over the five years from 1996 to 2001."[12] And so for the first time in the cities of the People's Republic,[13] there were widespread instances of people with work ability and a desire to work who were unable to land "jobs" or find employment of any sort.[14] These moves, executed with reluctance as they may have been, nonetheless generated a whole new unemployed sub-sector of city society, a segment apparently set to stay.[15]

The poverty-stricken (a prominent segment of the newly named *ruoshi qunti* (弱势群体), or weak masses, or the *tekunhu* (特困户), households in difficulty) then emerged as a most pitiable subset of those who had been discharged from their firms. These were the people most disadvantaged – whether by their age, their poor health or disability, or their total lack of any skills or credentials – those most unable to find a way to sustain their existence on their own.[16] A report by the Party's Organization Department that came out in 2001 disclosed that an investigation done by the State

Statistical Bureau, the State Council Research Office, and other units, discovered that, nationwide, 20–30 million staff and workers had fallen into poverty in recent years. With their family members it was judged that altogether these people amounted to 40–50 million,[17] or almost 13 percent of the urban population.[18] The presence of this part of the population, stranded amidst much plenty, is also the result of the as yet far from fulfilled need for the Chinese polity to undergird the livelihood of the unemployed masses in the cities with a workable and comprehensive social welfare system.[19]

The Minimum Livelihood Guarantee Program

During the socialist era, workers in municipal enterprises were given work-unit-grounded, relatively universal, automatic security packages. But the economic reform program saw this system gradually slip away. After a half-dozen years of grass-roots experimentation, the state inaugurated a discretionary, means-tested cash transfer program,[20] the Minimum Livelihood Guarantee, popularly called the "*dibao*," to take the place of the welfare these pre-reform units had provided. In practice, the *dibao* is much akin to what Tony Judt has written of "modern welfare reform" in Western settings, in that both introduce "conditionality" into "social citizenship" by forcing beneficiaries to "pass certain tests and demonstrate appropriate behavior."[21]

The openly announced charge of the *dibao* was to provide for urban residents whose household income failed to reach a municipality-determined minimal threshold; the method was to supplement that income to the extent necessary to bring the family's monthly wherewithal up to the level deemed requisite for basic survival in that city.[22] The project was proudly labeled by its publicists as a "standardized, legalized, social guarantee system" (*guifanhua he fazhihua de shehuibaozhang xitong* 规范化，系统化的社会保障系统),[23] a characterization more aspirational than actual, especially at the time of the plan's national promulgation in September 1999.[24] Much like "reformed" Western welfare programs, it reeks of distrust of its objects. Unlike similar schemes in democracies, however, its administrators' qualms are to be quieted by the watchful attention of the recipients' co-residents in their community (*shequ* 社区) courtyards.

Indeed, a central justification for the creation of the scheme was to ensure control over, and, ideally, the quietude of, the poverty-stricken. One writer went so far as to refer to the *dibao* as a "tranquilizer" (*zhendingyao* 镇定药), a kind of pill that would permit state factory reform in Shenyang's Tiexi district (a site of massive layoffs) to proceed without obstruction. Without it, the essayist unabashedly wrote, "these people must become a burden that the enterprises would find it hard to throw off . . . even to possibly arousing even larger social contradictions."[25] In essence, the policy amounted to supplying indigent individuals with funds that were "just enough to keep body and soul together," in the words of its leading scholar within China, Tang Jun.[26] That thrust of the mission is hard to miss when one learns that the average poverty line – a line set by individual cities – across China in 2003

was just 149 *yuan* (less than U.S.$20) per month; the average per person sub-
sidy, the sum meant to lift the insolvent up to the "poor" (*pinkun* 贫困) line,
was a piddling 58 *yuan* (about U.S.$7). Four years later these averages had
risen, but just to 179 and 95 *yuan*, respectively.[27]

But, oddly enough, a people whose plunge in fortune was more or less
purposively manufactured by state-sponsored market reforms still seems to
look to this same state to alleviate its pitiful position. Unfortunately, what guilt,
if any, the governors might experience for their prior choices is mixed with
a heavy dose of suspicion that significantly limits their largesse. These two
conflicting mindsets – one of hope and apparent faith among the recipients,
the other of doubt among the rulers – accord the relationship a strange tinge
of imbalance.

The state's suspicious stance towards the poor

That the authors of the *dibao* program shaped it primarily in the interest
of pacifying the payees is evidence enough of the leadership's misgivings
about the newly poor's dependability and their honor.[28] Indeed, the authorities' skepticism has slanted the execution of the project from the start. In
part this doubtfulness is displayed in official prohibitions that dictate the
type of people eligible for the funds and the activities of indigent people that
should bar them from getting any allocation; in part it crops up in the course
of determining whether or not specific households are in truth entitled to
receive the money. The extreme hesitancy with which applicants are vetted
bespeaks less of stinginess (since the necessary cash is not really so scarce),
than of a wariness in the face of what many donors judge very likely to be
immorality and laziness on the part of the impoverished, or at least on the
part of people felt by administrators to be fraudulently pretending to be poor
enough to qualify.

Representative regulations outlining every detail of how possible beneficiaries should be designated, along with all the procedures involved in ensuring that they are deserving, were issued in a typical ruling by the Hubei
Provincial Civil Affairs Bureau in mid-2003.[29] Within the province, city districts, and sometimes even street offices, are permitted to fine-tune and adapt
these rulings. But they clearly demand that residents should be excluded from
becoming recipients if their homes exhibit any of the following phenomena:
savings whose amount cannot be clarified, or "hidden income"(*yinxing
shouru* 隐性收入) that cannot be verified; if in the past three years the household has bought a home or undertaken high-quality renovation of its present dwelling; if it has purchased a refrigerator, an air conditioner, a digital
camera, a computer, or a camcorder; if it is discovered that there is some
type of power-driven vehicle in the family's possession that is not required
for someone's work; if the family has installed a telephone and/or has a phone
bill higher than 30 percent of the local *dibao* allowance; or if any family member owns any kind of mobile communication device and makes use of it in
the period when the *dibao* is being sought or enjoyed.

Pleasure, too, is also out of the question: if the home contains "high-class pets" (*gaoji chongwu* 高级宠物) or if family members are often encountered in restaurants or in places of entertainment, they are not to be funded. And as if to guarantee that the family persists in poverty over time, the regulations also mandate that if there are children enrolled in schools of their own choice or who are studying in private schools the household will not be certified as eligible for aid. Refusing to allow investigators to enter one's home is another way to lose the privilege of entering the program.[30]

The most rigorous regulation is about people of working age who are in good health but without employment; these individuals are sometimes treated as if they were in fact holding jobs. This behavior is justified by the same suspicion that pervades the program, a practice justified thus: "Since household income is very difficult to determine, hidden employment is pervasive, and hidden income and resources (are known to exist), flexible standards are adopted everywhere."[31] According to this logic, families may be rejected from receiving the *dibao* simply because they are perceived as having the ability to work, thereby considering them as having been given the wages they would have earned had they been on a job. Such reckoning "regards as income" salary or even benefits that properly speaking ought to have been – but were not – paid to a person, using their city's minimum wage or its unemployment insurance subsidy to assess the amount of the supposedly received income or benefit, and then taking that sum to be the person's actual income.[32] In short, those dispensing the funding are meant to determine that no one whose standard of living goes beyond the barest form of subsistence becomes a client.

Not only do community program workers probe into supplicants' style of life, occupation, and assets, but their neighbors are invited to join in the assessment. Each case must earn the approval of community members, who get an opportunity to protest when the details of the case are posted in a centrally located courtyard on a public bulletin board. Fellow citizens living nearby can be keen to raise objections when they believe that funds are being wrongly disbursed. When asked why a person's neighbors would report on him/her, the assistant chief of the *dibao* office in the Gansu Provincial Bureau of Civil Affairs replied with an idiom, "*bu huan gua er huan bujun*" (不患寡而患不均), whose meaning is something to the effect that "if you don't worry about the few, then your worry is unfair." "If you go to work, there are a lot of people in the courtyard who will see you; it's not just a matter of only one neighbor informing on you," he continued.[33]

Experimenters in Dalian pioneering a project that would compel *dibao* recipients to engage in community service learned in the course of their work that, indeed, many complaints had been leveled against beneficiaries with undeclared incomes who were nonetheless collecting allowances.[34] In the interest of preventing such dissatisfaction, a committee charged with "democratic assessment" (*minzhu pingyi* 民主评议) must certify that a family meets the criteria for aid before it can become a grantee. One further check is deemed necessary as well: if someone in the household happens to be employed, the unit for whom that person works must submit a document showing his/her salary.[35]

Permission to enroll in the program is only extended once the file has been fully reviewed at three levels, has successfully navigated three rounds of bulletin board examinations, and has achieved the endorsement of not just the community's residents' committee (*juweihui* 居委会) or community, but also of the corresponding committee at the street and then district levels.[36] Thus, only after successfully satisfying reiterations of surveys and surveillance will an applicant obtain a bank book enabling the household head to draw a measly sum of money every month. Besides, while restrictions from the start preclude the participation of persons found to be maintaining a "level of livelihood obviously higher than the norm pegged as [that city's] allowance," the scrutiny does not stop with the initial search. Instead, program personnel continue to inspect households at regular intervals to ensure that their style of life remains one of destitution if they are to continue on the rolls. And so it is only after invasive, extensive, and repetitive inquiries that a household can attain the lowly, and forever suspect, status of *dibaohu.*

Believing beneficiaries

Have these suspiciously handled poor lost their faith in their state? It would be no surprise if they angered, argued, and prepared to rebel. But that set of attitudes and actions has, by and large, not come to be, at least not among the members of the 65 households I and some Chinese graduate students were able to interview in the central China metropolis of Wuhan (武汉) and in the neighboring smaller city of Jingzhou (荆州) in the summers of 2007 and 2008. Based on my admittedly limited sample, it would seem that instead, and far more frequently, this pauperized populace in China's cities sits weakly at home, waiting, wishing, and hoping for greater beneficence from their official provider sometime later, in the future. Their passivity could in part be related to the fact that, like upwards of 60 percent of *dibao* recipients nationwide, a large majority of the families we talked with included one or more people with a chronic or hereditary disease.[37]

Setting aside the issue of whether these people are poised to act on their disappointments, our interviews uncovered what became for the researchers an all-too-familiar inventory of grievances. What the informants want amounts to three aspirations: more hard cash in hand; security of the essentials of livelihood – health care, housing, education, and work; and fairness in the allocations, all of which they see as dependent upon the generosity of the ruling elite and their current system. A number of these subjects expressed negative appraisals of the program in the form of desires for amelioration of their circumstances; this openness suggests that they did not shy away from criticizing their government.

In fact, whether their concerns were for more money for their own or their relations' health care, for financial help with their children's education, for more commodious dwellings, for vocational training or a place of employment, or whether they simply wanted more generous hand-outs, they almost to a person couched their yearnings in dreams of the present regime's turning more bounteous and charitable, instead of disparaging the churlish and grudging dispensations of the state they know. I would argue that this perspective comes from their training over decades of state socialism to expect provisioning from their government.[38] Perhaps the poorest among them, still subsisting in a state of denial, have not yet fully perceived the stiff limits to the now-neoliberal state's largesse. Or perhaps, from a different perspective, their situations have just been so undermined by the collapse of the scaffolding that once buttressed their existence that – no matter what they might believe – they have no capacity left to fend for themselves.

Many of the indigent spoke frankly of the necessity of even the piddling amounts of cash the *dibao* affords them. In the words of one: "Thanks to the government's giving us the *dibao* we can eat enough (*chi baofan* 吃饱饭). You can see that society is so chaotic, [but] because of having the *dibao* our child needn't go out to steal." Another vows her gratitude in even more desperate language: "If my health were better, I would think up a way to be self-supporting, but now I haven't the ability and can only depend on the government's policy; if we didn't have the *dibao* policy, my family possibly would already be dead."

However, despite these words of appreciation from some, desires for a greater outlay of state funds were common. One female recipient told me: "I feel the *dibao* amount is rather low, I hope it can increase a little. I'm now wearing clothes that others gave to me, in the evenings I go out to collect bottles to sell and feel embarrassed." A Mr. Fang, similarly, simply "hopes his *dibao* portion can be raised, to improve my living conditions." A third man remarked that, "We are grateful for the government's *dibao* policy, but now prices are rising; we feel the money is too low. We think about raising its amount." Apparently these recipients have confidence that the state is in possession of the wherewithal for additional payouts, and they hope to become the beneficiaries.

In this same frame of mind, a couple in poor health, in need of medical attention, thought just of the state as the source for succor: "I and my husband both have no work unit and no medical insurance; now our health isn't as good as it was before. We hope the government can give us more help." Another ill person, named Ms. Chen, was also strapped and, like her neighbor, signaled that relief was to be expected from her rulers. She worried that, "Because we have no work, we haven't gotten any medical insurance. If we get sick we don't dare see a doctor, just let our granddaughter take a little medicine. We hope the government can give us a medical treatment card. My husband has suffered a stroke three times, but now if you see a doctor you only get compensated for 30 percent of the bill. It's really too little, we hope the government can help us."

Housing problems were pervasive, and those stuck in tiny, rundown flats were also disposed to turn to the state for upgrades. One family had "applied earlier for appropriate housing, but it's still not been approved. Now the community will be torn down, and the family hasn't the money to buy new housing; the compensation won't be adequate. We've got no assets to renovate a new apartment, and we hope the government can give us a housing subsidy." A Mr. Huang, following the same line of thinking, "understand[s] the government also has difficulties, we are very grateful that now it can help us this much. But we hope the government can improve our housing conditions." Mr. Xie, his neighbor, "feels the apartment [they're] living in is too small, and in summer it's too hot." He goes on to explain that "in the future this community might be torn down and we'll have to move. Since our space is too small the compensation will be too little, and in the future we won't be able to afford a room." He is "very concerned that hereafter there won't be any place to live," and only "hopes the government can help solve this." More of the same comes from a Mr. Hu, a nearly blind head of a household of three. His desire is that "the government can improve my family's living conditions. Now our housing space is eighteen square meters. Each month the government's housing subsidy is very small.[39] We hope it can raise its housing subsidy." Lastly, Mrs. Hong, whose previous home of 80 square meters was demolished, bemoans the fact that "as far as housing goes, I hope the government can give us a cheap place to live; this is my greatest wish." She finds it "very unfair" (*hen bupingdeng* 很不平等) that a home whose market price was 1,700 *yuan* per square meter yielded a compensation of just 650 *yuan* per square meter, with the result that its market price was knocked down by two-thirds. True enough, the state sponsored the construction and allocation of low-cost housing in recent years, but without having been given any promises, these people appear automatically to assume that their leaders will eventually alleviate the living difficulties with which they struggle.

Anxiety over the fate of the next generation similarly simply aroused a craving for the state to provide more care. Turning her thoughts toward the time to come, Ms. Chen pointed out, "I'm not concerned about my son and his wife. They can do whatever they want (*ganma, jiu ganma* 干嘛就干嘛). But I'm very worried about our granddaughter's future. She's our whole family's hope. This year she's going to senior high. Her grades are very good, especially her English grades. She's received Wuhan City's first-level foreign language prize twice already. Because we're *dibaohu*, her school reduced her tuition by over 600 *yuan* per year. But we still have to pay her allowance and the fees for her classes outside school.[40] We hope the government can further reduce her school fees." Ms. Liu viewed her situation in precisely the same way. Her view of the *dibao* was this: "Speaking just of myself, I'm rather satisfied with it; each month it at least meets our most pressing needs. Like last week our son got sick and we used the money to send him to see a doctor. I just hope the government can reduce his tuition some."

Another parent, a Ms. Hong, similarly tormented about her child's education, fretted, "My son is studying art as a specialty, tuition is very high, and his school hasn't got a policy to reduce it. He's already examined into

Shashi district's best middle school, but the tuition is too high. We can't afford it, so he only can go to some other school." One woman lamented that her son was "now in senior high and each year the tuition is more than 1,600 *yuan*. This burden is very heavy and the government hasn't given us any subsidy, so I hope after entering college he can get a government stipend. I heard some colleges give school loans and some don't," she continued. "I'm rather worried that in the future we won't be able to afford college for him." The clear option for all these hard-up households was to look to the government, even without its announcing any aid of this sort for them.

Apprehensive about the issue of employment, another Mr. Hu (the elder brother of the Mr. Hu mentioned above) and his wife, both fully blind, "hope that after our daughter graduates the government can take care of finding her some work." Ms. Lei, once from the countryside, has no work unit, nor does her husband, a former labor-reform criminal. She also expressed unease about their inability to find work. "I haven't any work unit, [so I'm] very worried about the future when I'm old. I'll have no livelihood security, no pension; I hope the government can give us more help." Again, it is striking how people pushed from their work posts by government commands continue to seek sustenance from the very state that only recently had acted against their interests.

These varied forms of dependency, vulnerability, and incompetence uniformly incline these subjects – at a loss as to where else to look – toward the state as, they trust, the ultimate provider. Certainly the most disgruntled among them may rail bitterly against unfairness but do not seem enraged, just sorrowful about the scarcity and uncertainty that are their portion. But it is still under an understanding that the state stands for a certain decency to which they can appeal. This becomes evident in the information offered by a Wuhan social policy researcher characterizing the mood of the discontented. He pointed out that there have been occasions when *dibaohu* who are antagonistic attack community officials with violence and severity. But this is apt to occur, he commented, only when they compare themselves with others.[41] Such assaults, thus, are appeals to the state for justice, I would argue, in the expectation that this should be forthcoming from officialdom.

Another instance of this faith in the fairness of the authorities comes from another of my subjects, a Ms. Li, who referred longingly, if inaccurately, to Shanghai, where, she reported, "each person who gets the *dibao* is given 240 *yuan*,[42] while our whole family of three people gets only 355 *yuan*. I feel it's unfair." And several informants emphasized that the government ought to distribute funds on the basis of individual families' actual situations, especially when their plight is particularly difficult, instead of making the allocations simply in terms of the number of people residing in the household, as is the official rule. One who offered this opinion was a 51-year-old man with liquor on his breath, raising two children and caring for a wife whom illness had rendered deaf and dumb. He expressed this viewpoint after first claiming, "The *dibao* is okay (*shi keyide* 是可以的), without it our lives would be even worse (*geng nan* 更难)."

Most notable in this regard was one pugnacious 67-year-old widow, who went so far as to wrangle with the administrators in her community. Judging that her family was not being treated fairly, she charged that,

> In 2003, when we got into the system, the subsidy was very transparent, the public bulletin board told how much income each household had every month, what their subsidy was, and how much was deducted. But these past two years, it's changed. Among us *dibaohu* we don't know how much other people are getting.

Questioned whether she was being given a larger subsidy after inflation set in, "It's not like that," she inveighed. Going on, she charged:

> Since my daughter-in-law went out to work, and the residents' committee found out, my son's *dibao* was cut back. Getting 100-plus *yuan* each month is not as good as when it first began. We're a family with an old person (meaning herself), my son can't see and cannot work, my daughter-in-law's little money can take care of her son, but [because of this] the committee now deducts our family's allowance. Other people have two people going out to work and their money wasn't deducted. I argued passionately with the committee. They said I shouldn't compare myself with other people. But our family has no money, has no connections, so things can only be this way . . . I just hope to understand how this subsidy is granted, we ordinary people don't get to see the civil affairs department's documents . . . The committee ought to treat people equally, everyone should be equal before the regulations, and it shouldn't happen that because of a certain family's connections they can do whatever.

To judge from these interlocutors, the distress that grates most is the absence of justice, the lack of transparency, and the failure of officialdom to calibrate the charity to the case at hand. That the state and its servants should be held to these standards is something the new indigents assume they have a right to expect, along with their presumptions of material comfort.

Conclusion

Is the regime legitimate in the eyes of its most needy urban citizens? Do these people – many of whom once securely staffed the factories of a socialist society – continue to place their trust in the leaders who led them to their present impotent and impoverished position? My data – which, granted, comes from a set of especially downtrodden subjects – suggest that, despite their rulers' niggardly payouts – a stinginess born of suspicion that cheats are legion, that tricksters lurk everywhere in the threadbare and barren homes of the wretched – despite that state parsimony, still, these nearly abandoned wards continue to cling to what seems to an outsider to be best cast as an illusion: that they may yet find their relief in the beneficence of that state. For these beneficiaries, the state is legitimate; it is only themselves – in the eyes of their state – who are not.

Notes

1 The term "three withouts" refers to those unable to work, those without means of livelihood, and those without family support. See Nelson W.S. Chow, *The Administration and Financing of Social Security in China* (Hong Kong: Centre of Asian Studies, 1988); and Linda Wong, *Marginalization and Social Welfare in China* (London: Routledge, 1998).
2 U.S. Foreign Broadcast Information Service: China Daily Report (hereafter FBIS), September 14, 1988, p. 36, and September 28, 1988, pp. 52–3; Andrew G. Walder, "Workers, Managers and the State: The Reform Era and the Political Crisis of 1989," *China Quarterly* (hereafter *CQ*), no. 127 (1991), p. 477.
3 Walder, "Workers, Managers and the State," p. 473.
4 Barry Naughton, "Implications of the State Monopoly over Industry and Its Relaxation," *Modern China* 18(1) (1992), pp. 14–41.
5 Barry Naughton, *Growing Out of the Plan: Chinese Economic Reform 1978–1993* (New York: Cambridge University Press), pp. 274–300; *idem.*, "China's Emergence and Prospects as a Trading Nation," Brookings Papers on Economic Activity, 2 (1996), 294; Wing Thye Woo, "Crises and Institutional Evolution in China's Industrial Sector," in Joint Economic Committee, Congress of the United States, ed., *China's Economic Future: Challenges to U.S. Policy* (Armonk, NY: M.E. Sharpe, 1997), 164–65; and Xinhua [New China News Agency], October 14, 1998, in *Summary of World Broadcasts* (hereafter SWB) FE/3358 (October 15, 1998), G/3.
6 Translated in *FBIS*, July 19, 1994, pp. 18–26, from Xinhua, July 5, 1994.
7 Niu Renliang, "Xiagang zhigong chulu sikao" [Thoughts on the way out for the laid-off staff and workers], *Lingdao canyue* [Leadership consultations] 1 (1998), p. 8.
8 *FBIS,* June 14, 1996, p. 52, from *Jinrong shibao* (Beijing) [Financial Times], April 15, 1996, p. 1.
9 Jiang's report to the congress is in *SWB* FE/3023 (September 13, 1997), S1/1–S1/10.
10 *Ming Pao* [Bright Daily], December 19, 1997, in *SWB* FE/3107 (December 20, 1997), G/7.
11 Indeed, by 1996 a sharp increase had occurred in the number of state-owned firms throughout the country that were losing money, such that state industry for the first time experienced an overall loss (Thomas G. Rawski, "Reforming China's Economy: What Have We Learned?," *The China Journal,* 41 [January 1999], p. 144).
12 Cited in a recent paper by Albert Park and John Giles, "How Has Economic Restructuring Affected China's Urban Workers?" (*Ms.*, October 2003), p. 1. This paper, based on data from the China Urban Labor Survey conducted in five large Chinese cities at the end of 2001, found that unemployment reached double digits in all sample cities between the years 1996 and 2001. The Chinese source cited is State Statistical Bureau, *China Statistical Yearbook* (Beijing: China Statistical Press, 2002). Later, a revised version of this paper was published as John Giles, Albert F. Park, and J.W. Zhang, "How Has Economic Restructuring Affected China's Urban Workers?" *CQ*, no. 185 (2006), pp. 61–95. It should be pointed out, however, that one reason for the huge drop in numbers in the state-owned enterprises (SOEs) is the reclassification of many former SOEs as joint-stock companies and as entities with other similar new names. Athar Hussain (in "Social Security

in Transition," in Vivienne Shue and Christine Wong, eds., *Paying for Progress in China: Public Finance, Human Welfare and Changing Patterns of Inequality* [London and New York: Routledge, 2007], pp. 107–8) wrote that 68.9 million jobs were lost, of which 45 million came from the state sector.

13 Earlier periods of urban unemployment existed in the PRC, as in the early 1950s, the mid-1960s, and the late 1970s. But in each case the government was able to devise programs – sometimes distasteful ones, as in the 1960s rustication movement – that to a large extent disposed of the problem. Besides, in these earlier eras, it was for the most part the never-employed who searched for jobs; in the present era it is a case of massive dismissals of the labor-age, already employed, population.

14 Fulong Wu and Ningying Huang, "New Urban Poverty in China: Economic Restructuring and Transformation of Welfare Provision," *Asia Pacific Viewpoint* 48(2) (2007), p. 171, judges that, unlike the urban poor in the People's Republic under Mao, "a large percentage of the new urban poor are able and willing to work but cannot find stable jobs." On the same page, these authors quote the Ministry of Civil Affairs as having announced in 2003 that the "traditional" urban poor amount to a mere 6 percent of the *dibao* recipients, while 54 percent of these recipients came from state or collective enterprises. This statement must be read alongside John G. Taylor's report that officially disabled persons represent 40 percent of the urban poor (in John G. Taylor, "Poverty and Vulnerability," in Shahid Yusuf and Tony Saich, *China Urbanizes: Consequences, Strategies, and Policies* (Washington, D.C.: The World Bank, 2008) p. 93).

15 The size of this segment is the subject of many disparate estimates, in part because of the variable definitions of poverty in use (including subjective appraisals by the poor themselves of their own situations, expenditure criteria, and income criteria), and in part because the government has not specified a nationwide, official urban poverty line, leaving the determination up to individual cities, which are to set their own lines, in accord with the local cost of living, prices, the city's developmental level, and its financial capacity to assist its destitute. See Taylor, "Poverty and Vulnerability," p. 92.

16 According to an investigation reported in a 2006 piece ("Zhongguo chengshi jumin zuidi shenghuo baozhang biaojun de xiangguan fenxi, jingji qita xiangguan lunwen" [Chinese urban residents' dibao norm's relevant analysis; economic and other related treatises] (hereafter "Zhongguo chengshi"), http://www.ynexam.cn/html/jingjixue/jingjixiangguan/2006/1105/zhonggochengshijimin . . . (accessed August 18, 2007), it was found that, among adult targets, those with primary education and below represented 24.1 percent and 46.5 percent had been to junior high school, together amounting to 70.6 percent without any senior high school training. A mere 27.6 percent of these people boasted of having some sort of professional or handicraft skill, while just 2.9 percent claimed to have some work. As for their health, the Ministry of Civil Affairs announced that in a national study of 10,000 *dibao* households, 33.7 percent have disabled people, and 64.9 percent had one or more members with a chronic or serious illness.

17 Zhonggong zhongyang zuzhibu ketizu [Chinese central organization department research group], *2000–2001 Zhongguo diaocha baogao – xin xingshixia renmin neibu maodun yanjiu* [2000–2001 Chinese investigation report – research on internal contradictions within the people under the new situation], (Beijing: Zhongyang bianyi chubanshe [Central Compilation & Translation Press], 2001), pp. 170–1.

18 There are now a number of studies that characterize these people. Especially helpful are Ya Ping Wang, *Urban Poverty, Housing and Social Change in China* (London and New York: Routledge, 2004); Meiyan Wang, "Emerging Urban Poverty and Effects of the *Dibao* Program on Alleviating Poverty in China," *China & World Economy* 15(2) (2007), pp. 74–88; Jinjun Xue and Wei Zhong, "Unemployment,

Poverty and Income Disparity in Urban China," in Li Shi and Hiroshi Sato, eds., *Unemployment, Inequality and Poverty in Urban China* (London and New York: Routledge, 2006), pp. 43–64; Meng Xin, "Economic Restructuring and Income Inequality in Urban China," in Li and Sato, eds., *Unemployment, Inequality and Poverty in Urban China*, pp. 65–89; Li Shi, "Rising Poverty and Its Causes in Urban China," in Li and Sato, eds., *Unemployment, Inequality and Poverty in Urban China*, pp. 128–51; Bjorn Gustafsson, Li Shi, and Hiroshi Sato, "Can a Subjective Poverty Line Be Applied to China? Assessing Poverty among Urban Residents in 1999," in Li and Sato, eds., *Unemployment, Inequality and Poverty in Urban China*, pp. 152–72; Wu Fulong, "The Poverty of Transition: From Industrial District to Poor Neighbourhood in the City of Nanjing, China," *Urban Studies* 44(13) (2007), pp. 2673–94; Chen Shaohua, Martin Ravallion, and Youjuan Wang, "*Di bao:* A Guaranteed Minimum Income in China's Cities?," World Bank Policy Research Working Paper 3805, January 2006; John G. Taylor, "Poverty and Vulnerability," pp. 91–104; Zhang Shifei and Tang Jun, "Chengxiang zuidi shenghuo baozhang zhidu jiben xingcheng" [Urban and rural minimum livelihood guarantee system has basically taken form], in Ru Xin, Lu Xueyi, Li Peilin, zhubian [chief editors], *2008 nian: Zhongguo shehui xingshi fenxi yu yuce* [2008: Analysis and forecast of China's social situation] (Beijing: Social Sciences Academic Press, 2008), pp. 57–73; Li Chunyan and Ding Jianding, "Wuhanshi dibao guanlizhong cunzai de wenti yu gaijin duice fenxi – yi Wuchangqu weili" [Existing problems and an analysis of measures to make improvements in Wuhan City's management of the dibao-Using Wuchang district as an example], *Changjiang luntan* [Yangtze Forum] 1 (2006) (no. 76), pp. 25–29; and Arthar Hussain, "Social Security in Transition," pp. 96–116.

19 Jane Duckett, "China's Social Security Reforms and the Comparative Politics of Market Transition," *Journal of Transition Politics and Post-Communist Studies* (March 2003); and Dorothy J. Solinger, "Path Dependency Reexamined: Chinese Welfare Policy in the Transition to Unemployment," *Comparative Politics* 38(1) (October 2005), pp. 83–101. Though the situation is gradually improving, the remarks in these pieces still hold largely true, as of this writing.

20 This term comes from Sarah Cook, "The Challenge of Informality: Perspectives on China's Changing Labour Market," Paper for IDS Bulletin, 2008.

21 Tony Judt, "The Wrecking Ball of Innovation," Review of Robert B. Reich, *Supercapitalism: The Transformation of Business, Democracy and Everyday Life* (New York: Knopf, 2007), *New York Review of Books*, December 6, 2007, p. 24.

22 Athar Hussain *et al.*, "Urban Poverty in the PRC," Asian Development Bank Project No. TAR: PRC 33448, 2002. Wang Hui, "Chengshi zuidi shenghuo baozhang gongzuo zhi wo jian" [My opinion on the urban minimum livelihood guarantee work], *Zhongguo minzheng* [China Civil Affairs] (hereafter *ZGMZ*) 10 (1996), p. 34, explains that the concrete method for setting the line involves each locality adopting the "vegetable basket method," according to which it selects certain livelihood necessities, determines their minimum requisite consumption amount, and calculates the income necessary to purchase these goods based on the price index in the area.

23 Ding Langfu, "Cong danwei fuli dao shehui baozhang – ji zhongguo chengshi jumin zuidi shenghuo baozhang zhidu de dansheng" [From unit welfare to social security – recording the emergence of Chinese urban residents' minimum livelihood guarantee system], *ZGMZ* 11 (1999), p. 7.

24 For the 1999 Regulations officially announcing the program, see "Chengshi jumin zuidi shenghuo baozhang tiaoli" [Regulations on the urban residents' minimum livelihood guarantee] (hereafter "Chengshi jumin") *ZGMZ* 11 (1999), pp. 16–17.

25 Ding Langfu, "Cong danwei fuli dao shehui baozhang," p. 7.
26 Tang Jun, "The Report of Poverty and Anti-Poverty in Urban China – The Poverty Problems in Urban China and the Program of Minimum Living Standard" (hereafter "The Report"), ms., 2002, p. 4. Portions of the report were later translated and published as Dorothy J. Solinger, guest editor: Tang Jun, "Selections from Report on Poverty and Anti-Poverty in Urban China," *Chinese Sociology & Anthropology* (Winter 2003–4/Spring 2004).
27 Zhang and Tang, "Chengxiang zuidi shenghuo baozhang zhidu jiben xingcheng," p. 59.
28 It has been suggested to me that perhaps officials at the Ministry of Civil Affairs, the administrator for the program, understood that the *dibao* could only be acceptable to the central leadership if it were presented as a way to stave off instability. This possibility does not undermine my argument.
29 "Hubei Province Urban Residents' Minimum Livelihood Guarantee Work Plan," dated July 31, 2003, issued by Hubei Province Civil Affairs Bureau [in Chinese] (accessed at www.hbcz.gov.cn/arkcms/UploadFile/20060909051916234.doc).
30 *Ibid.*, Article 8.
31 "Zhongguo chengshi."
32 "Chengshi dibao: tashang xin zhengcheng" [The urban dibao: step onto a new journey], *ZGMZ* 1 (2000), pp. 24–5.
33 Interview, September 5, 2007.
34 Ge Daoshun and Yang Tuan, "Minimum Income Schemes for the Unemployed: A Case Study from Dalian, China," *International Social Science Journal* 5(179) (2004), pp. 47–56.
35 Interview at a community office, Jingzhou, Hubei, August 28, 2009.
36 Intricate procedures were laid out in interviews with community personnel in Hanyang, Qiaokou, and Qingshan districts of Wuhan in late August 2007.
37 Anthony Saich, *Providing Public Goods in Transitional China* (New York: Palgrave Macmillan, 2008), p. 163.
38 He Shenjing, Yuting Liu, Fulong Wu, and Chris Webster, "Poverty Incidence and Concentration in Different Social Groups in Urban China, a Case Study of Nanjing," *Cities* 25 (2008), pp. 121–32, makes this point, especially on pp. 125 and 131.
39 The district's housing subsidy is calculated by giving each needy household 6.2 *yuan* per person for each square meter less than 15 square meters per person in its current apartment.
40 In the fierce competition provoked by the constant and challenging tests to which Chinese teenagers are subjected, no high school student can hope to succeed educationally without these extra classes.
41 Interview in Wuhan, August 30, 2008.
42 In Shanghai in April 2008, the per person *dibao* norm was raised to 400 *yuan*. Information from http://www.jjwb.banzhu.net/article/jjwb-9-44340.html (accessed January 16, 2008).

12 Popular responses to China's emerging welfare state

Mark W. Frazier

In late 2008, the Standing Committee of the National People's Congress (NPC) posted the text of the draft Social Insurance Law (SIL) on its website for public comment. The draft SIL represented a major piece of social legislation aimed at erasing the highly fragmented and inequitable welfare practices in place since the early 1990s, in which rural residents and migrant workers were largely excluded from coverage under health care, pensions, and other programs that urban residents received. By the end of the 50-day comment period on February 15, 2009, the NPC had received a total of 70,501 responses (*yijian* 意见) from citizens from all 31 provinces and from social sectors including urbanites, workers, civil servants, students, soldiers, farmers, migrant workers, and retirees.[1]

While it is now common practice for the NPC to release draft legislation for public comment, the timing of and response to the SIL was highly significant for two reasons. First, the draft SIL had been held up within the NPC since 1994, in large part because it threatened the interests of multiple bureaucracies and local governments, who benefited from the status quo and stood to lose from provisions that weakened the authority of their agencies to administer health care, pensions, and other programs. Worse yet, the free health care and pensions that government officials had always enjoyed might well come to an end. And under the SIL, like ordinary urban workers they would be required to make payments to receive social insurance coverage. Second, while the SIL appeared to be headed toward passage even before the global economic crisis brought China's rapid growth to a standstill in late 2008, the comments from the public came during a tense environment of rising unemployment among migrant workers, collapsing exports, and dramatic declines in stock prices and real estate values.

After its eventual passage, the SIL will face the usual obstacles to enforcement that other laws in China encounter, from under-funded agencies to corrupt local officials, but the unlikely emergence of the draft SIL after 15 years marks an important milestone in the adaptability and responsiveness of the Chinese Communist Party (CCP) under Hu Jintao's leadership. The SIL represents a major step in the CCP's efforts to tackle problems of income inequality and inadequate welfare with legislation that reflects broad public support for erasing the complex array of welfare programs tied to employment status and place of residence. This chapter will discuss China's evolution toward equal rights to welfare based on citizenship by examining the most expensive, most fragmented, and most popular welfare program in China: old-age pensions. I first trace the evolution of China's new welfare regime from its origins in workplace-based provision of measures such as health care and pensions to the broader but still fragmented system in which urban governments administer these and other programs. This transition generated important political effects, including a deepening commitment on the part of the Chinese government to spend more on pensions, in spite of Beijing's professed objective of reducing the state's pension commitment. I then show how the draft SIL closely reflects public preferences for a national, unified pension system in which the state provides the majority of financing, and eligibility is based on citizenship rather than occupational or residential status, such as employment in state versus non-state enterprises, urban versus rural registration, civil servant versus civilian, and so forth.

The foundations of China's new welfare state

The CCP created new welfare policies based on social insurance in the late 1990s, primarily as a means to provide some cushion for the 30–40 million jobless state enterprise workers in cities. Such rudimentary social insurance programs (covering pensions, health care, workplace injury, unemployment, and maternity leave) have grown rapidly, although they remain far short of covering even the "employees of urban enterprises" who are technically eligible for them. The number of workers covered by social insurance has risen from 52 million workers covered by pensions in 1990 to 152 million in 2007.[2] For unemployment insurance the number of covered workers rose from 82.4 million in 1995 to 116 million in 2007; comparable figures for medical insurance rose from 7 million in 1995 to 180 million in 2007.[3] Proponents of the draft SIL claim that it would go far in ensuring the rights of all workers in urban and rural areas. Depending on implementation, the SIL could create as many as 770 million contributors to social insurance funds. The text of the draft law gives local governments considerable leeway to implement various provisions for coverage, and universal coverage for the Chinese workforce will take many years if not decades to achieve. Nonetheless, the institution of social insurance has generated an important political effect by conceiving of workers as "contributors" to various funds and therefore possessing rights to the money in them.

Before urban governments began running pensions and other social insurance benefits in the 1990s, welfare delivery was even more de-centralized than it is now. Work units distributed benefits such as pensions, health care, housing, and others to their employees, but enterprise management and supervisors enjoyed considerable latitude over which workers received preferred housing and could also approve or deny retirement applications. Moreover, the bureaucratic rank of an enterprise strongly influenced the scope and levels of welfare benefits for enterprise employees. With the discretion to turn down retirement applications, SOE managers could postpone or avoid making pension payments. By 1978, as many as two million workers and 600,000 officials who had applied to retire with pensions had been turned down by their work units.[4]

The transformation of enterprise-based pensions began in the mid-1980s, when urban governments in some regions began to levy payroll deductions from SOEs for use as local pension funds.[5] Most SOEs were willing to accept this arrangement because of the cost-sharing that came with the pooling of expenses for pensions, health care, and other programs. SOEs that would have had to pay pension costs from their operating budgets were now able to ask for pension benefit payments from the new "social pools" (*shehui tongchou* 社会统筹). Only full-time workers in SOEs and urban collectives enjoyed pension rights, even as the proportion of contract workers employed in these sectors grew rapidly in the 1980s. Regulations in 1986 brought SOE contract workers under pension coverage, but unlike most full-time SOE workers, they had 3 percent of their wages deducted and contributed to pension pools. Workers outside the state and collective sectors lacked social insurance coverage altogether.[6]

Pension regulations that the State Council issued in the 1990s contained specifics on basic issues such as eligibility standards, benefits calculations, and local administration of pension funds, but their broader significance was the manner in which successive regulations eroded the employment categories based on enterprise ownership and other traits. The most important pension regulations that came out in 1997 stipulated that all employees of "urban enterprises" (*chengzhenqiye* 城镇企业) would have pension rights. No distinctions were made as to whether enterprises were state owned, foreign invested, or whether workers were full or part time, with or without labor contracts.

The evolution of welfare policy and politics in China does not fit easily with existing explanations for how welfare states get their start. Most of the assumptions and theoretical perspectives on welfare regimes and the politics of welfare come from the experiences of today's advanced welfare states in North America, Western Europe, and Japan. To oversimplify, the scholarship on these regions and countries argues that welfare programs come into being as industrialization, urbanization, and related processes transform predominately rural societies, and that crucial political coalitions between political parties and trade unions must first form in order to create political pressures for the extensive welfare programs that exist in classic cases such as Northern Europe.[7] Such theorizing about welfare development took place with little regard for the narrow but substantial welfare provisions that were the trademark of communist regimes, as well as the even more exclusive but generous welfare provisions that many non-communist developing countries (such as those in East Asia) accorded to crucial constituencies such as the military, civil servants, and certain core sector employees.[8]

To understand the politics of welfare in China, it is best to conceive of twin pressures that at times work at cross-purposes. First, the dismantling of the socialist welfare state during the 1990s, a process that China shared with many of today's post-socialist economies such as Russia and Poland, led to demands to compensate those left jobless in the process. Second – and in sharp contrast to the East European and Russian cases – the ongoing process of urbanization and industrialization in China has created pressures to expand welfare provision. These twin pressures have led to demands on the Chinese government to compensate the victims of the dismantling of the micro welfare state found in state-owned enterprises and to generate new social policies for the workers who now participate in a highly uncertain labor market with tremendous heterogeneity in terms of jobs and employers, among much else.

China's experience demonstrates that welfare retrenchment and welfare expansion can take place at the same time, and in fact, arise from the same causes. As SOE reforms dismantled the enterprise-based welfare state, a new one grew in its place at local levels. China's new welfare state is designed with many of the programs and policies found in capitalist market economies, such as unemployment insurance and minimum income payments, yet these designs are also constrained by the legacies of the socialist welfare state. We can see this pattern most clearly in the example of pensions, which have rapidly escalated to become the most expensive function of the Chinese government.

China's new pension policies are often described as pension "reforms" because of the implicit reduction in the state's role of providing past levels of pension benefits. The term "pension reform" usually refers to cuts in public pensions, or to a reduced state role in paying for public pensions, or to outright privatization of pensions. By these standards, however, China has not really undergone pension reform. China's new pension policies have not led to cuts in pensions, but to rapid increases in pensions and their financing through new channels. The reforms have not made any changes to China's relatively young retirement ages, which were established in 1951 at age 60 for men and age 50 for women (age 55 for women in clerical occupations). While Beijing policymakers certainly invoked the reforms with the intention of reducing future pension burdens for the Chinese state by establishing mandatory personal retirement accounts, urban governments have undermined Beijing's objectives by "borrowing" from these personal accounts so that benefits could be paid to current retirees. Far from reducing its role in providing pensions, the Chinese government has taken on a much larger obligation with the shift in administrative responsibilities from SOEs to urban governments.

While China's central government spends between 50 and 100 billion *yuan* in annual subsidies to provincial governments for pension benefits, urban governments spend many times more than that on benefits for about 50 million retired factory workers and 12 million civil servants. In addition to the 404 billion *yuan* in pension benefits that local governments paid out in 2005, they also spent about 106 billion *yuan* for civil servant pensions that year. (The 404 billion *yuan* figure exceeded what urban governments spent on any other expenditure category, including education, urban construction, public security, and public health.) In 2006, urban government spending on social insurance pensions rose nearly 25 percent in one year alone, to 490 billion *yuan*. While these pension benefits are financed through payroll contributions of about 152 million urban workers with pension coverage, the remainder of China's workforce, or about 618 million workers, are largely without pension rights because they are not legally eligible, or their employers evade the law.[9] The draft SIL would narrow this gap with its proposals for rural pensions and stronger provisions for enforcing the welfare rights of migrant workers.

The expansion of pensions and other social insurance programs signals an important adaptive response by the CCP to create policies intended to cope with rising income inequalities. As I have shown elsewhere, it is not coincidental that pensions became the dominant form of welfare spending in China.[10] Pensions are as popular in China as they are elsewhere, and they are the least redistributive form of social spending, since they largely transfer wealth from the working-age population to the elderly, rather than from rich to poor. China's increased pension spending cannot be expected to reduce income inequalities, but pensions have had important political effects.

The rapid increase in pension spending and coverage can be explained in part as a response to protests by workers who had lost jobs during SOE restructuring in the 1990s. These well-documented and often dramatic urban protests posed multiple challenges to the CCP's legitimacy. Most directly, the protests challenged the CCP's right to rule based on its claims to uphold the interests of the working class. Labor protests in Liaoyang, Chongqing, Baotou, Daqing, and elsewhere in the early 2000s arose after laid-off workers and retirees received inadequate compensation in enterprise bankruptcy proceedings, which also gave by comparison generous benefits to retired enterprise cadres.[11] In response to the protests, the Chinese government took two crucial steps: it permitted local social insurance agencies (SIAs) to use funds from personal retirement accounts of current workers and meant for their eventual retirement. In addition, the central government began in the early 2000s to channel subsidies to provinces and cities that suffered from chronic shortfalls in what was collected in pension revenues and spent on pension benefits. In 2000, the central government began transferring subsidies to provinces that had failed to pay local pensioners on time. With this implicit backing of their pension deficits, urban governments have increased pension benefits. Average pensions reached 9,251 *yuan* in 2005.[12] By 2007, this figure stood at 11,100 *yuan*.[13] Subsidies and benefits increases appear to have reduced the size and frequency of pension protests, but they have also created long-term pension deficits and undermined the entire thrust of China's initial pension reforms, which had aimed to encourage less reliance on state support for pensions and greater reliance on individual and market-based sources of pensions.[14]

The aspirations of the CCP to reduce the role of the state in welfare provision have also foundered under accusations that the party has overseen a massive theft of state assets. Why should citizens be asked to save for retirement when, as is frequently noted on Internet forums, officials have squandered the accumulated resources of a generation of factory workers? One such popular view is that the CCP has mismanaged, if not outright stolen, the accumulated assets to which SOE workers had contributed under the pre-reform economy. As a blog posting from a retired steelworker on Tianya noted in 2006, his generation had worked for low wages under the rapid industrialization drive of the command economy, and after the state had accumulated trillions of *yuan* in "public property" (*quanmin zichan* 全民资产) over 40 years, where were public pensions? "To our great regret, the pensions we entrusted to the state have shockingly turned out to be an 'empty account!' . . . So we retired old workers ask: motherland, the mother who raised and educated us, how could you give us an empty account?" After citing a scholar's estimate of 8 trillion *yuan* in long-term pension debts that face the younger generation of workers, this commentator concluded, "How strange that the result of our generation having gone to such risks to make revolution is that, not only is there nothing to show for it, but there's a lifetime's debt to the next generation! What kind of absurdity is this? What kind of plight has the state's chaotic mismanagement put us in?"[15] Another blog post from a retired worker reflected a similar argument: "Where did the capital for reform and opening come from? It certainly wasn't dropped from heaven, nor was it given by foreigners, but it was accumulated from old workers' blood and sweat over several decades. Without the primitive accumulation of the elderly, who would the state have relied on to do the reforms?"[16]

Besides such general musings about where the forced savings of the command economy have gone, Chinese workers and pensioners can point to a more direct form of theft: the chronic misuse of pension funds by local governments. The most notorious case of pension fund abuse emerged in 2006 when CCP authorities revealed that Shanghai's SIA had illegally diverted as loans and other investments a total of 32.9 billion *yuan* (U.S.\$4.2 billion). Shanghai's pension fund had financed many of the city's landmark real estate developments and commercial plazas.[17] The Shanghai pension scandal also brought down Chen Liangyu (陈良于), who at the time was both the Party Secretary of Shanghai and a member of the Politburo. In addition, dozens of the city's leading politicians and executives of its leading SOEs and private businesses were implicated in the case. While the Shanghai pension scandal must also be explained in terms of factional politics – it represented Hu Jintao's move against the rival "Shanghai faction" (*Shanghaipai* 上海派) presided over by Hu's predecessor Jiang Zemin – the scandal also revealed a major problem in the decentralized administration of social insurance programs, whose funds had become a potential and inviting source of extra-budgetary revenue for local officials.

Shanghai was hardly an exceptional case in using its pension funds for questionable purposes. A subsequent investigation by the National Audit Office (NAO) found that in Guangzhou two officials diverted 600 million *yuan* in pension funds. In Hunan 71 million *yuan* was diverted, in Liaoning 11.5 million *yuan*, and in Zhejiang "hundreds of million *yuan*." The general pattern was similar to that found in Shanghai.[18] Local SIA officials turned pension funds over as loans to local firms, in exchange for the promise of better rates of return on pension funds than what could be achieved under investment restrictions for pension funds. A former SIA official in Guangzhou faced charges of losing 520 million *yuan* in pension funds when he loaned out 750 million *yuan* during the 1990s. According to a 2007 report, prosecutors had undertaken this and another 17 criminal cases related to the diversion of pension funds in Guangzhou.[19] The NAO estimated that local governments in China – excluding Shanghai – had made over 7.1 billion *yuan* (U.S.\$857 million) in loans using pension, medical, and unemployment insurance funds.[20]

The draft of the SIL thus emerged in a context in which the transition from enterprise-based welfare to urban government-centered welfare provision had created more problems than they had resolved: about half of the urban workforce lacked any social insurance coverage, pension debt was rising even as many pensioners failed to receive benefits on time, and local government corruption eroded both tangible assets in pension funds and the overall legitimacy of the CCP.

Social Insurance Law

For over a decade since its first draft in 1994, the SIL was held up by bureaucratic rivalries over regulatory control and over the right to manage sizeable pension, health care, and other social insurance funds. The Ministry of Labor and Social Security (MOLSS, renamed in 2008 the Ministry of Human Resources and Social Security, or MOHRSS), the Ministry of Personnel, and the Ministry of Civil Affairs (MCA) each sought to defend or expand pension programs for various sectors of the population. For example, the Ministry of Personnel was in charge of distributing relatively generous pensions to retired civil servants and employees of public sector units (*shiye danwei* 事业单位). The old (pre-1998) Ministry of Labor managed pensions for state enterprise employees. MCA provided pensions to eligible military veterans, and to peasants in counties that had voluntarily set up pension funds.[21] When the Ministry of Finance, with the strong support of Premier Zhu Rongji, tried to push through pension reforms in the late 1990s that would consolidate various pension programs, bureaucratic conflict naturally ensued. For example, as the State Council's 1997 regulations on pensions were being drafted, the MCA tried but failed to defend its control over rural pensions, which were transferred to MOLSS.[22] After being transferred to MOLSS, the rural pension program stagnated.[23] Although there were a reported 3.9 million rural residents receiving pensions in 2007, coverage had fallen drastically from 82.8 million in 1997 to 51.7 million that year.[24] In addition to pensions, the issue of health insurance engaged an even more complex set of bureaucratic interests. The Ministry of Health no doubt had a strong interest in wresting authority over health insurance funds from the SIAs belonging to the MOLSS and its successor, the MOHRSS.[25] As with pensions, MCA had legitimate claims to regulate rural health insurance, and it already had responsibility for administering rural and urban minimum income support, or *dibao* (低保, a separate program from social insurance discussed by Dorothy Solinger in Chapter 11). These bureaucratic rivalries over the draft SIL meant that even the text of the legislation was a tightly kept secret.

When it was finally issued in late 2008, the draft SIL ambitiously but vaguely proposed to address the problem of fragmentation by calling for the introduction of a national pension fund after first completing the steps toward provincial-level pooling. For other forms of social insurance, the State Council was to issue further regulations on pooling at provincial levels. The evasion of explicit measures to centralize pensions and other forms of social insurance reflects the ongoing rivalries both among bureaucracies and the various levels of sub-national governments that stand to benefit or lose from changes to the status quo of municipal and county pooling. The draft SIL also contained much more explicit provisions that delineated social insurance coverage for migrant workers and dealt with the problem of their losing pension rights when switching jobs by making pensions portable across regions. It also explicitly gave pension and health insurance rights to peasants whose land had been requisitioned, and gave subsidies for health insurance coverage to those receiving *dibao*, to those with disabilities, and to anyone over age 60 from a low-income family.

Regardless of how well such provisions can be implemented, the timing of the release of the draft SIL is significant. One explanation for its release is the rise in the number of labor disputes over social insurance questions, usually having to do with coverage (or lack thereof) provided by employers. In 2004, disputes with employers over rights to social insurance coverage became the leading cause of labor disputes, exceeding disputes over wages and labor contracts. In 2000, national labor dispute statistics classified 31,350 labor disputes in 2000 as arising over "social insurance and welfare" issues. This made up just over 25 percent of the total number of cases for that year.[26] By 2004, the number of labor disputes said to involve social insurance and welfare issues had risen to 88,119, amounting to 33.8 percent of total labor disputes.[27]

In addition, the draft SIL's release came as social security issues loomed large in the minds of the public, according to social surveys. In the run-up to the National People's Congress session in 2009, an online survey administered by the Sociology Institute of the Chinese Academy of Social Sciences and *Guangming Daily* (光明日报) received nearly 400,000 responses. When given the choice of 15 social problems and asked to rank the three to which they paid the most attention, social security (58.1 percent) was second behind corruption (66.8 percent) and ahead of income inequality (57.7 percent) and health care reform (56.9 percent), and even ahead of employment (43.9 percent). Among the most important problems with social security, 74.7 percent of respondents named health care, with pensions second at 61.8 percent. Unemployment, social security for migrants and for farmers, and minimum income payments were named by between 38 and 30 percent of the respondents as the most important social security issues.[28] The NPC did not make available the full record of public responses to the draft SIL, but the summaries published in NPC documents as well as in official and commercial media suggest that one of the most common views voiced was the pressing need to eliminate the employment- and residential-based distinctions by which social benefits were calculated and distributed. One summary of the public comments that had been received by January 12, 2009 listed first among nine categories of comments the demand for universal welfare coverage for all citizens. "The state should implement universal compulsory social insurance coverage, without distinctions among civil servants, public sector employees, enterprise employees, farmers, and self-employed workers. As long as a citizen is over age 18, regardless of occupation, he or she must contribute to all forms of social insurance."[29] One post on a popular bulletin board site said of the SIL:

> With 1.3 billion people, and putting aside about 400 million who are not yet adults and are taken care of by their families, 900 million urban and rural residents need social insurance coverage. However, at present there are only over 200 million people who are covered by social insurance (not including civil servants). Under the present social insurance pooling system, vast numbers of farmers and unemployed, and those without steady work have difficulty receiving social insurance. The promise of social insurance coverage for every citizen is a lie![30]

Public comments on the draft SIL also endorsed the centralization of the locally managed social insurance funds that urban governments now administer, and the provisions to give migrant workers some means to retain benefits eligibility (and accumulated personal retirement funds) wherever they moved to seek employment.

While it is difficult to determine the attitudes of migrant workers from social surveys (which are largely biased toward the urban registered population), coverage for migrant workers has increased. A Xinhua report in 2006 quoted surveys showing that over 90 percent of migrants did not have pension coverage, and nearly the same proportion, or about 83 percent, were unwilling to buy pension insurance. Their reluctance was for good reason.

With the average tenure in factories and restaurants estimated at between four and six years, and the average tenure in construction and other manual labor jobs even shorter at between two and three years, there was little chance that a migrant worker would fulfill the 15-year eligibility requirement for pensions within the same city.[31] When a migrant switched jobs, for all practical purposes she would lose her pension eligibility, along with whatever funds her employer would have deducted in pension and other social insurance contributions. The study's authors called for national pension pools for migrant workers, as well as social relief programs for migrants, who lacked access to support networks and resources in the cities where they worked.

By 2010, the avoidance and evasion of social insurance on the part of migrants and their employers appeared to be receding. A *Caijing* article from December 2008 noted that, since 2006, SIA offices in the Pearl River Delta had aggressively expanded their coverage of migrant workers. A Zhongshan University (中山大学) survey of migrant workers discovered that 32 percent of more than 2,500 workers in the sample were covered by pensions, 44 percent had medical insurance, and 51 percent had workplace injury insurance. The same research team in 2006 had found that only 8–9 percent of migrants had these forms of social insurance coverage.[32]

If ex-SOE workers in the 1990s demanded pensions from a state that had broken its promises and used the collective frame of subsistence rights to voice their grievances, migrant workers a decade later in the high-growth regions had a very different view of pension rights. For migrants, pensions were not an abstract promise by the state, but personal funds held as wage deductions by government agencies. When it was time to switch jobs, migrants lined up at SIAs to "cash out" (*tuibao* 退保) or withdraw their pension savings. In 2007, reports from China's southern boomtowns such as Shenzhen and Dongguan stated that thousands of migrant workers were standing in lines for hours, even days, at the offices of local social insurance agencies to remove themselves from pension coverage and to withdraw their accumulated savings from personal retirement accounts. Press reports explained that migrants were "cashing out" because they suspected that local SIAs would not transfer funds in their personal retirement accounts to their next place of work or residence. One report estimated that as many as 600,000 workers in Dongguan in 2007 had withdrawn from the local pension fund by "cashing out."[33]

The contrasts in how older and newer segments of the Chinese workforce view pension rights are in part a story of generational change. However, they also demonstrate how institutional change, in this case the introduction of social insurance, alters the nature of demands that workers make of the state. As ever larger segments of China's urban workforce receive social insurance coverage, the nature of state–labor relations will also change in important ways. Workers who a generation ago were expected to be loyal subjects who received welfare benefits from a benevolent state are becoming "contributors" or "taxpayers" (*nashuiren* 纳税人) who will demand social services and accountability for the operation of pension and other social insurance funds.

Public perceptions of China's new welfare state

More specific evidence on popular attitudes toward pension rights and the expectations on the Chinese state to provide them can be found in survey results drawn from the Beijing Area Study (BAS), which the Research Center for Contemporary China at Beijing University has conducted on an annual basis since 1995. The 2004 BAS (held in March 2005) included a special section on pensions, and the results presented here offer a look at attitudes toward pensions among a random sample of 617 Beijing residents in the middle of the current decade.[34] The discussion also includes results from a survey of 540 Shanghai residents, who were administered the same set of questions on pensions in March–April 2005, using different sampling procedures.[35] In neither case was the survey sampling method able to include migrant workers, and this fact is important to keep in mind in the results discussed below.

One of the items in the 2004 BAS included a statement regarding the role of the state in welfare provision: "Who do you think should be the main provider of pensions?" The three response choices were "Mainly the state"; "Mainly contributions by workers and their units"; and "Mainly by commercial insurance purchased by individuals." A total of 60.5 percent of the BAS respondents said the state should be the primary provider of pensions, while 34.2 percent indicated that employers and employee contributions should form the main source of pension provision. Only 1.5 percent favored commercial pensions as the primary source of old-age income. In the Shanghai sample, albeit with different sampling methods from those used in the BAS, only 49.8 percent of Shanghai respondents identified the state as the primary provider of pensions, and 49.1 percent favored employer-based pensions. Respondents in the BAS also elicited strong support for the state's role in social security (referring not just to pensions but to employment and other social protections). A majority of BAS respondents strongly agreed (26.9 percent) or agreed (42.3 percent) with the statement that "China is a socialist country; the state should have full responsibility for providing social security." A total of 28.3 percent of respondents disagreed or strongly disagreed with this statement. The Shanghai respondents offered a stronger endorsement of this view, with nearly four-fifths agreeing (24.6 percent) or strongly agreeing (54.6 percent) with the statement. Only 18.2 percent disagreed or strongly disagreed. This support for a strong state role in the provision of pensions is consistent with the support for and trust in state largesse found among urban recipients of minimum income payments in Chapter 11.

A second important point about urban attitudes as measured in these two surveys is that they elicited very strong support for pension rights. The 2004 BAS respondents strongly endorsed the statement that "Receiving pensions is a basic right of citizens" (*xiangshou yanglaojin shi gongmin de jiben quanli* 享受养老金是公民的基本权利). A majority of 58.5 percent of respondents strongly agreed with the statement, and 39.2 percent agreed, with only 1.6 percent disagreeing. A similar result was found in the Shanghai sample, in which 75.0 percent strongly agreed, 19.8 percent agreed, and 4.7 percent disagreed or strongly disagreed. When asked about specific groups and rights to pensions, the respondents in both surveys backed up their endorsement of pension rights.

The BAS respondents were asked what level of pension benefits migrant workers should receive in relation to urban workers. The five response categories were: more, the same, less, no benefits, or don't know. A total of 62.2 percent of the respondents said that migrants should receive the same benefits, and only 24.0 percent said that migrants should receive fewer pension benefits. (A very small portion of 1.3 percent said that migrants should not receive pensions at all.) About 8.3 percent of the BAS respondents claimed that migrants should receive higher pension benefits than those enjoyed by urban residents. The contrast with the results of the Shanghai survey sheds light on probable regional variation in attitudes toward migrants: A much greater share in Shanghai (9.3 percent) said that migrants had no pension rights, and only 41.7 percent said that migrants should receive the same level of pension benefits as urbanites. A total of 41.1 percent of the Shanghai respondents (compared with 24.0 percent in the Beijing sample) said that migrants should receive less in pension benefits.

When it came to farmers, Beijing respondents were nearly as supportive of pension rights as they were for migrants. In the 2004 BAS, 57.1 percent said farmers should receive the same level of pension benefits, and 26.6 percent said farmers should receive smaller levels of pension benefits. Only 0.5 percent said that farmers should not be eligible for pensions. In the Shanghai sample, the contrast was again evident as only 33.1 percent said that farmers should receive the same level of pension benefits as urban residents, and 43.0 percent said they should receive less. A total of 13.1 percent of the Shanghai sample said that farmers should not have pension benefits.

In both the Beijing and the Shanghai samples, respondents offered more sympathetic views of pension support for veterans and for retired military personnel (*tuixiu junren* 退休军人) and retired cadres (*lixiu ganbu* 离休干部). In the BAS, a majority of respondents said that retired military personnel (54.6 percent) and retired cadres (54.0 percent) should receive greater pension benefits than those enjoyed by urban residents. Those favoring the same level of pension benefits amounted to 37.4 percent for both retired military and retired cadres. A small share of respondents (5.8 percent for retired cadres, 3.4 percent for retired military) said these groups should receive less in pension benefits. In the Shanghai sample, a plurality of respondents favored the same level of pension benefits for retired cadres (53.5 percent) and military service personnel (49.3 percent). Less than half of those in the

Shanghai sample favored providing retired cadres (42.0 percent) and retired military service personnel (46.3 percent) with the same level of pension benefits as those received by urban residents.

One important issue that the drafters of the SIL completely avoided but which the CCP will eventually have to address is the question of increasing the retirement age. As noted above, the legal ages of retirement (separate for men and women) were set in 1951 and have remained unchanged despite the increase in life expectancy over the last 60 years. The reason that the draft SIL eschewed the issue of adjusting retirement ages is because they are so controversial. As is the case in countries with well-entrenched public pensions, raising retirement ages often results in public protests by those potentially affected by the changes (usually those near retirement). Chinese public attitudes toward retirement age increases are no different. In the 2004 BAS sample, 71.2 percent of respondents disagreed or strongly disagreed with the statement that the government should gradually increase the retirement age. In Shanghai, an even larger proportion of respondents (78.7 percent) disagreed with the idea of raising retirement ages. Moreover, a nearly two-thirds majority of 2004 BAS respondents (65.0 percent) disagreed or strongly disagreed with a statement proposing to equalize the retirement ages between men and women. In Shanghai, 64.2 percent of respondents disagreed or strongly disagreed. This opposition to equalizing retirement ages found the same levels of support among men and women.

The attitudes toward social welfare found among urban residents might be interpreted in part as a legacy of state socialism, but they also stem from workers' experience in a highly competitive and uncertain market environment. Not surprisingly, urban residents want their government to provide a greater assurance that the risks they now face in the labor market can be cushioned in some way by payments from the government and their employers. Marc Blecher has shown that urban workers seem to accept the principles of market allocation of labor.[36] If such "market hegemony" is met with little worker resistance, it is less likely that the unfettered operation of labor markets in the absence of social safety nets would be met with equal acceptance. Consistent with Karl Polanyi's central thesis from the first epoch of industrialization, the commodification of labor in China has created demands for state protection from the unfettered operations of the labor market.[37]

Conclusion

China's new welfare state, to be sure, reflects its Maoist legacies and the ruling strategies of an authoritarian regime. Just as capitalism and its varieties produced different configurations of welfare states, different post-socialist trajectories also generate different forms of welfare policies. Pensions have risen to a position of pre-eminence in China's welfare state not because of population aging – which will really begin to be felt first in 2015 – but because of localized but potent popular pressures to compensate the jobless. Pensions and other forms of social insurance have expanded rapidly since the 1990s in part because local governments have strong pecuniary incentives to collect the extra revenues for social insurance, and in part because of the obvious need to cushion the risks of the market that China's workforce now faces.

Rising inequalities, especially in the gaps between rural and urban living standards, have propelled social welfare to the top of the political agenda, as Hu Jintao has strived to create a "harmonious society" (*hexie shehui* 和谐社会) amidst a polity that at times seems to be growing more polarized than harmonized. The adaptive, illiberal responses that Bruce Dickson in Chapter 1 and other scholars elsewhere have written about entail the creation of new institutions, including welfare and social insurance programs as described above. Yet in fostering such institutions, analysts often suggest that the regime itself remains unchanged in its character – or at least that it retains the core of its non-democratic or authoritarian identity. While this is no doubt true, we should not overlook the fact that subtle policy changes such as those noted above for pensions in the 1990s can generate their own political momentum as new groups gain incorporation into existing welfare programs and policies. The political significance of this expansion in rights should not be underestimated.

In her description of welfare policy in the late 1990s, Elisabeth Croll identified a dilemma that the Chinese Communist Party faced as it attempted to deal with the highly fragmented, inconsistent set of policies for welfare that the CCP had overseen since the reforms. The dilemma, as Croll put it, was that "if [the state] attempts to impose and fund a new nation-wide system of social welfare it requires both resources and political authority which it now lacks; yet if it withdraws from welfare provisioning it negates the social contract and risks losing popular support and political authority."[38] Croll identified the basis of a "new and explicit social contract" between citizens and the CCP as an exchange of "support for its legitimacy or mandate to rule in return for social security, welfare, and services."[39] A decade later, the terms of this social contract remained intact, but the CCP had created the impression at least that it was prepared to expend greater resources and effort to establish a welfare state in which citizenship rather than status was the main criterion for eligibility. The passage of the SIL and the fate of its eventual implementation will say much about the Hu administration's legacy and the CCP's ability to lay the legislative foundations for a "harmonious society."

Notes

1 "Guanyu shehui baoxianfa caoan zhengqiu yijian de qingkuang" (On the Solicitation of Comments on the Draft Social Insurance Law). February 23, 2009, www.npc.gov.cn (accessed February 27, 2009).

2 State Statistics Bureau (SSB) and Ministry of Labor and Social Security (MOLSS), *Zhongguo laodong tongji nianjian 2005* (China Labor Statistics Yearbook, 2005) (Beijing: Zhongguo laodong shehui baozhang chubanshe, 2005), p. 574; Ministry

of Human Resources and Social Security (MOHRSS), "2007 nian laodong he shehui baozhang shiye fazhan tongji gongbao" (2007 Report on Labor and Social Security Developments), http://w1.mohrss.gov.cn/gb/zwxx/2008-06/05/content_240415.htm (accessed August 9, 2008).

3 SSB and MOLSS, *Zhongguo laodong tongji nianjian 2005*, p. 579; MOHRSS, "2007nian tongji gongbao."

4 Xie Jianhua and Ba Feng, *Shehui baoxian faxue* (Social Insurance Legal Studies) (Beijing: Beijing daxue chubanshe, 1999), p. 123.

5 Peter Whiteford, "From Enterprise Protection to Social Protection: Pension Reform in China," *Global Social Policy*, vol. 3, no. 1 (2003), p. 48.

6 Xie and Ba, *Shehui baoxian*, p. 126.

7 The most widely cited work remains Gosta Esping-Andersen, *The Three Worlds of Welfare Capitalism* (Princeton: Princeton University Press, 1990).

8 Stephan Haggard and Robert R. Kaufman, *Development, Democracy, and Welfare States: Latin America, East Asia, and Eastern Europe* (Princeton: Princeton University Press, 2008).

9 MOHRSS, "2007nian tongji gongbao."

10 Mark W. Frazier, *Socialist Insecurity: Pensions and the Politics of Uneven Development in China* (Athica, NY: Cornell University Press, 2010).

11 Ching Kwan Lee, *Against the Law: Labor Protest in China's Rustbelt and Sunbelt* (Berkeley: University of California, 2008), pp. 102–11; *China Labor Bulletin*, "Oil Workers in Sichuan Get Organized to Fight for Pensions and Employment," September 14, 2002, www.china-labour.org.hk/en/mode/2146 (accessed February 17, 2003); John Pomfret, "China Cracks Down on Worker Protests," *Washington Post*, March 21, 2002; James Kynge, "Chinese Miners Riot Over Severance Pay," *Financial Times*, April 3, 2000; Keith Bradsher, "Factory Dispute Tests China's Loyalty to Workers' Rights," *New York Times*, July 18, 2002.

12 Felix Salditt, Peter Whiteford, and Willem Adema, "Pension Reform in China: Progress and Prospects," Working Paper, OECD Social, Employment and Migration, No. 53, 2007, p. 28.

13 MOHRSS, "2007nian tongji gongbao."

14 The term "implicit pension debt" (IPD) refers to the present value of the money that a government owes to future generations of the expected eligible number of retirees in a given year. Measures of IPD vary based on the assumptions that are used for life expectancy, retirement age, average benefits, and several other variables. China's implicit pension debt has been estimated in a World Bank study to be at 141 percent of GDP for 2001, or 13.23 trillion *yuan* (U.S.$1.6 trillion) in future obligations to pensioners, and will stay above 100 percent of GDP for most of the twenty-first century (Yvonne Sin, "Pension Liabilities and Reform Options for Old Age Insurance," Working Paper Series on China [Washington, DC: World Bank, 2005], pp. 30–1). The World Bank study did not include pension costs for civil servants or for rural pensions. Under the SIL, expansion in coverage for migrant workers and peasants will make China's IPD rise rapidly.

15 Xinhuawang (Xinhuanet), bbs.city.tianya.cn/new/TianyCity/content (accessed October 2, 2007).

16 Xinhuaboke (Xinhua blog), http://blog.xinhuanet.com/blogIndex (accessed October 2, 2007).

17 Chen Fang, "Shenji: Shanghai shebao heimu" (The Audit: Behind the Scenes of the Shanghai Social Insurance Agency), *21st Century Business Herald*, March 26, 2008, www.21cbh.com/print.asp?NewsId=30916 (accessed March 28, 2008). Wang Heyan, Zhao Hejuan, and Ji Minhua, "End of the Line for the Shanghai Scandal," *Caijing*, April 1, 2008, www.caijing.com.cn/English/Cover/2008-04-01/54869.shtml (accessed April 2, 2008).

18 National Audit Office (NAO), "Qiye zhigong jiben yanglao baoxian jijin, chengzhen zhigong jiben yiliao baoxian jijin he shiye baoxian jijin shenji jieguo" (Audit Results for Enterprise Employees' Basic Pension Insurance Funds, Urban Employees' Basic Medical Insurance Funds, and Unemployment Insurance Funds), November 24, 2006, www.audit.gov.cn/cysite/docpage/c516/200611/1123_516_17913.htm (accessed January 2, 2008).
19 Xinhua, "Official on Trial Over Vanished Pension Funds," October 30, 2007, www.chinadaily.com.cn/china/2007–10/30/content_6217416.htm (accessed October 30, 2007).
20 NAO, "Qiye zhigong jiben yanglao baoxian."
21 Stuart Leckie and Yasue Pai, *Pension Funds in China: A New Look* (Hong Kong: ISI Publications, 2005), p. 35.
22 Lutz Leisering, Gong Sen, and Athar Hussain, *People's Republic of China: Old-Age Pensions for the Rural Areas: From Land Reform to Globalization* (Manila: Asian Development Bank, 2002), p. 18.
23 *Ibid.*, pp. 24–26.
24 *Ibid.*, p. 18; MOHRSS, "2007nian tongji gongbao."
25 Jane Duckett, "Bureaucratic Interests and Institutions in the Making of China's Social Policy," *Public Administration Quarterly*, vol. 27, no. 1, 2 (2003), pp. 210–37.
26 SSB and MOLSS, *Zhongguo laodong tongji nianjian* (China Labor Statistics Yearbook) (Beijing: Zhongguo tongji chubanshe, 2000), p. 429.
27 *Ibid.*, pp. 525–26.
28 "Sheke yuan lianghui redian diaocha baogao gongbu: Fanfu lieguanzhudu shouwei" (Academy of Social Sciences Releases On the Spot Survey Report at the Two Congresses: Anti-Corruption Ranks at the Top), *Guangming Ribao*, March 4, 2009, http://www.sina.com.cn/c/2009-03-04/162217335683.shtml (accessed March 4, 2009).
29 "Shebaofa caoan shoudao jin wuwan tiao yijian: zhuyao jizhong zai jiufangmian" (Draft Social Insurance Law Receives Nearly 50,000 Comments: Most Concentrated in 9 Areas), http://news.qq.com/a/20090112/001366.htm (accessed January 12, 2009).
30 "'Shehui baoxian fa' yingdang zhaokai lifa tingzhenghui" ("Social Insurance Law" Should Have a Legislative Hearing), Phoenix Forum, bbs.ifeng.com (accessed January 5, 2009).
31 "Laoyousuoyang: cong 'nongmingong tuibao' kan shehui baozhang zhidu de wanshan" (Elderly Support: Looking at Perfecting the Social Security System From "Migrants Cashing Out"), *Gongren Ribao* (Workers' Daily), January 9, 2006, Xinhuanet.com/fortune/2006–01/09/content_4028139.htm (accessed January 24, 2009).
32 "Dongguan shiye nongmin zhengxiang 'tuibao'" (Dongguan's Unemployed Migrant Workers Struggle to "Cash Out") *Caijing*, December 18, 2008, http://www.chinaelections.org/PrintNews.asp?NewsID=139942 (accessed on March 20, 2009).
33 China Labor News, "Migrant Workers Leaving Shenzhen Queue All Night to Cash in their Pensions," 2008, www.clntranslations.org/article. Translated from *Nanfang dushibao (Southern Metropolitan Daily)*, January 15, 2008, news.sina.com.cn/c/2008-01-15/030113258863s.shtml (accessed September 20, 2008).
34 The BAS target group is the registered urban population of residents 18–65 years old, randomly drawn from 50 communities (*shequ, juweihui*) in 8 urban districts. The BAS uses the "probabilities proportional to size" (PPS) sampling method. For the 2004 BAS, 1,099 individuals were contacted, and 618 surveys were completed – a response rate of 56.1 percent.

35 The Shanghai survey was administered by a local scholar from the Shanghai Academy of Social Sciences and was a stratified sample using 9 communities within 3 urban neighborhoods of 3 urban districts. The 3 urban neighborhoods were selected on the basis of their having low, medium, and high levels of income.
36 Marc Blecher, "Hegemony and Workers' Politics in China," *China Quarterly* 170 (2002), pp. 283–303.
37 Karl Polanyi, *The Great Transformation* (Boston: Beacon Hill, 2001 [1957]).
38 Elisabeth J. Croll, "Social Welfare Reform: Trends and Tensions," *China Quarterly* 159 (September 1999), p. 697.
39 Ibid., p. 685.

Index

al-Qaeda 236
art objects, repatriation of 11, 199–216

Baranovitch, Nimrod 227
Barmé, Geremie 180
Barnett, Robert 231
Becker, Jasper 181
Beijing Area Study (BAS) 268–70
Beijing Youth Daily 188
Bergé, Pierre 199
Berinsky, J. 74
Bernstein, Thomas 118
Blecher, Marc 270
Boxer Rebellion 43
British Museum 212, 214
Bu Wei 183
Bulag, Uradyn E. 227
Bush, George W. 216
Byron, Lord 214

Cai Mingchao 199
Carrefour 161
Carter, Jimmy 200
Castiglione, Giuseppe 201–2, 206
censorship 5, 41, 172, 180–3, 190, 194
Chang Ping 186
"Charter 08" 194
Chen Liangyu 263
Chen Sheng 100
Chen Shengluo 167, 170
Chen Shui-bian 208
Chiang, Faina 208
Chiang Kai-shek 207
China, definition of 225–6
China and the World 189
China Daily 180, 187–8
Chinese Academy of Science (CAS) 186
Chinese Academy of Social Sciences
  (CASS) 165, 186–7, 265–6

Chinese Communist Party (CCP):
  features of rule by 24–6; groups
  represented by 29–34; inclusion
  policies of 26–9; and income
  inequality 258–9, 262, 271;
  legitimacy of 9–12, 16–17, 25,
  30–1, 34, 206, 216, 262, 264;
  membership of 26–9, 32–3, 119,
  165, 173
Christie's auction house 199, 203–4,
  209–10, 215–16
cigarette lighter industry 75–9
civil society 4, 27, 34, 69, 183
Confucius 167
cooptation 27–9
corporatism 27, 29
corruption 2–8, 52–3, 264
Croll, Elisabeth 271
Cromwell, Oliver 207
Cui Luokun 93
Cultural Revolution 26–7, 61, 93, 162,
  200, 213, 230

Dahl, Robert 18
Dalai Lama 230–2
Dean, Kenneth 55–6
democratization 14–15, 22, 70
Deng Xiaoping 1, 15, 30, 33, 50,
  110–11, 167, 194
Deng Zisheng 95
dibao program 246–54, 265
Ding Xueliang 186
disadvantaged groups 147–9, 245
discrimination 233
Dong Feng 193
Dongnan Morning News (*Dongnan
  zaobao*) 187
Duara, Prasenjit 54–5
Dynamic Internet Technology 182